Form in Intellectual Property Law

To Moira, Josh and Richard

Form in Intellectual Property Law

David Booton

University of Manchester, UK

Edward Elgar
PUBLISHING

Cheltenham, UK • Northampton, MA, USA

Published by
Edward Elgar Publishing Limited
The Lypiatts
15 Lansdown Road
Cheltenham
Glos GL50 2JA
UK

Edward Elgar Publishing, Inc.
William Pratt House
9 Dewey Court
Northampton
Massachusetts 01060
USA

A catalogue record for this book
is available from the British Library

Library of Congress Control Number: 2016962561

This book is available electronically in the **Elgar**online
Law subject collection
DOI 10.4337/9781783470556

MIX
Paper from responsible sources
FSC® C013056

ISBN 978 1 78347 054 9 (cased)
ISBN 978 1 78347 055 6 (eBook)

Typeset by Columns Design XML Ltd, Reading
Printed and bound in Great Britain by TJ International Ltd, Padstow

Contents

Acknowledgements vi
Table of cases vii
Table of legislation xv

1 Introduction 1

2 Form and legal adjudication 25

3 Legislative power and harmonization 89
3.1 *Ex ante* versus *ex post* decision making 92
3.2 Avoiding perceptions of bias 105
3.3 European integration, harmonization and form 125

4 A conflict at the foundation 147

5 Form and the interpersonal/social dimension 178
5.1 Copyright law 192
5.2 Patent law 223
5.3 Trade mark law 232

6 Form and justifications 257

Index 293

Acknowledgements

Jonathan Griffiths and Hazel Carty took the time to read this book in draft and I am grateful to them for their insightful comments and suggestions for improvement. Not least of all I thank them for their encouragement.

Table of cases

Abbott Laboratories Ltd v *Evysio Medical Devices UCL* [2008] EWHC 800 (Ch) ... 225
Acorn Computers v *MCS Microcomputer Systems* (1985) 4 IPR 214 (Federal Court of Australia) ... 74
Actavis Ltd v *Eli Lilly and Co* [2015] EWHC 3294 (Pat) ... 225
Actavis Ltd v *Merck & Co Inc* [2008] EWCA Civ 444 ... 128
Actavis Ltd v *Novartis AG* [2010] EWCA Civ 82 ... 133
Adam Opel AG v *Autec AG* (C-48/05) [2007] ETMR 33 ... 234, 235, 238, 239, 240, 241, 247
Aerotel Ltd v *Telco Holdings Ltd and Macrossan's Application* [2006] EWCA Civ 1371 ... 70, 126, 129, 132, 134, 139, 140
Aerotel Ltd v *Wavecrest Group Enterprises Ltd* [2009] EWCA Civ 408 ... 226
A-G v *Guardian Newspapers* (No. 2) [1990] 1 AC 109 ... 113
Allmanna Svenska Elektriska A/B v *The Burntisland Shipbuilding Co Ltd* (1952) 69 RPC 63 ... 34
American Cyanamid Co (Dann's) Patent [1971] RPC 425 ... 135
American Cyanamid Co v *Ethicon Ltd* [1975] AC 396 ... 84, 87
Anheuser-Busch v *Budejovický Budvar, Národní Podnik* (C-245/02) [2005] ETMR 27 ... 240, 242
Antiquesportfolio.com Plc v *Rodney Fitch & Co Ltd* [2001] FSR 23 ... 201
Apimed Medical Honey Ltd v *Brightwake Ltd* [2012] EWCA Civ 5 ... 225
Apple Corps Ltd v *Apple Computer Inc* [2006] EWHC 996 (Ch) ... 237, 238
Arsenal Football Club Plc v *Reed* [2001] RPC 922 ... 237, 238
Arsenal Football Club Plc v *Reed* (C-206/01) [2003] RPC 144 ... 176, 234, 238, 240, 241, 251, 255
Arsenal Football Club Plc v *Reed* (No. 2) [2002] EWHC 2695 (Ch) ... 238
Arsenal Football Club Plc v *Reed* (No. 2) [2003] EWCA Civ 696 ... 238
Ashdown v *Telegraph Group Ltd* [2001] EWCA Civ 1142 ... 39, 44, 45, 113, 230
Association for Molecular Pathology v *Myriad Genetics* 569 US __ (2013) (US Supreme Court) ... 119
Attorney-General v *Guardian Newspapers* (No. 2) [1990] 1 AC 109 ... 113
Autospin (Oil Seals) Ltd v *Beehive Spinning* [1995] RPC 683 ... 216
Availability to the Public (G1/92) [1993] EPOR 241 ... 151
Baigent v *Random House Group* [2007] EWCA Civ 247 ... 206, 207, 216
Baschet v *London Illustrated Standard Co* [1900] 1 Ch 73 ... 112
Beloit Technologies v *Valmet Paper Machinery Inc* [1997] RPC 489 ... 225
Benmax v *Austin Motor Co Ltd* [1955] AC 370 ... 34, 42
Die BergSpechte Outdoor, Reisen und Alpinschule Edi Koblmüller GmbH v *Günter Guni, trekking.at Reisen GmbH* (C-278/08) [2010] ETMR 33 ... 243

Bezpečnostní softwarová asociace – Svaz softwarové ochrany v *Ministerstvo kultury* (C-393/09) [2011] ECDR 3 .... 161, 165, 212, 221
Billhöfer Maschinenfabrik v *Dixon* [1990] FSR 105 .... 216, 248
Biogen Inc v *Medeva Plc* [1993] RPC 475 81
Biogen Inc v *Medeva Plc* [1995] RPC 25 150
Biogen Inc v *Medeva Plc* [1997] RPC 1 .... 34, 42, 55, 94, 150
Bleistein v *Donaldson Lithographing Co* 188 US 239 (1903) (US Supreme Court) 203
Bristol Myers Squibb Co v *Baker Norton Pharmaceuticals Inc* [1999] RPC 253 129
Bristol Myers Squibb v *Paranova* (C-427/93) [1996] ETMR 1 264
Bristol-Myers Co (Johnson's) Application [1975] RPC 127 172
British Westinghouse v *Braulik* (1910) 27 RPC 209 225
Brugger v *Medic-Aid* [1996] RPC 635 157
Burke and Margot Burke Ltd v *Spicers Dress Designs* [1936] Ch 400 210
Cadbury-Schweppes Pty Ltd v *The Pub Squash Co Ltd* [1981] RPC 429 280
Cairnstores Ltd v *Aktiebolaget Hassle* [2002] FSR 35 170
Campina Melkunie BV v *Benelux-Merkenbureau* (C-265/00) [2004] ETMR 821 250
Canon Kabushiki Kaisha v *Metro-Goldwyn-Mayer Inc* (C-39/97) [1999] RPC 117 .... 100, 236
Cantor Fitzgerald International v *Tradition (UK) Ltd* [2000] RPC 95 .... 205, 213
Carl Zeiss Stiftung v *Herbert Smith* (No. 2) [1969] 2 Ch 276 72
Catnic Components Ltd v *Hill and Smith Ltd* [1982] RPC 183 .... 15, 209
CBS Songs v *Amstrad* [1988] AC 1013 216
Céline SARL v *Céline* (C-17/06) [2007] ETMR 1320 .... 234, 240
CFPH LLC's Application [2005] EWHC 1589 .... 68, 69, 131, 133, 135
Chappell & Co Ltd v *Colombia Graphophone Co* [1914] 2 Ch 745 78
Chiron Corporation v *Organon Teknika Ltd* (No. 3) [1994] FSR 202 225
Chiron Corporation v *Organon Teknika Ltd* (No. 10) and *Chiron Corporation* v *Murex Diagnostics Ltd* (No. 10) [1995] FSR 325 .... 79, 80, 81
Cnl-Sucal v *Hag* (C-10/89) [1990] 3 CMLR 571 264
Commissioners of Inland Revenue v *Muller and Co's Margarine Ltd* (1901) AC 217 66
ConAgra Inc v *McCain Foods (Aust) Pty Ltd* [1992] FCA 176 (Federal Court of Australia) 66
Conor Medsystems Inc v *Angiotech Pharmaceuticals Inc* [2006] EWHC 260 (Pat) 156
Conor Medsystems Inc v *Angiotech Pharmaceuticals Inc* [2007] EWCA Civ 5 .... 32, 61, 94
Conor Medsystems Inc v *Angiotech Pharmaceuticals Inc* [2008] UKHL 49 .... 38, 62, 63, 152
Cooper v *Baedeker* (1900) 17 RPC 209 154
Couture Tech Ltd's Application (R 1509/2008-2) [2010] ETMR 774 .... 115, 116
Cramp & Sons Ltd v *Smythson Ltd* [1944] AC 329 195
Crane v *Price* (1842) 4 MAN & G 580 .... 154, 156
Crossley v *The Derby Gas Light Co* (1834) 4 LT 25 76
Davis (J&S) Holdings v *Wright Health Group* [1988] RPC 403 216

Designer Guild Ltd v *Russell Williams (Textiles) Ltd* [2001] FSR 113 .... 37, 43, 167, 205, 206, 207, 211
Dow Corning Corporation's Application [1969] FSR 338 64
Dun's Licensing/Estimating Sales Activity (T154/04) [2007] EPOR 38 132
Dyson Appliances Ltd v *Hoover Ltd* [2001] RPC 473 56
Dyson Appliances Ltd v *Hoover Ltd* (No. 2, 'Springboard' Relief) [2001] RPC 544 .... 4, 77, 78
Dyson Appliances Ltd v *Hoover Ltd* [2001] EWCA Civ 1440 .... 56, 57
eBay v *MercExchange LLC* 547 US 388 (2006) (US Supreme Court) 79
Elanco Products v *Mandops* [1979] FSR 46 .... 85, 209, 220
Enterprise Holdings v *Europcar Group UK Ltd* [2014] EWHC 2498 (Ch) 101
Erven Warnink Besloten Vennootschap v *Townend & Sons (Hull) Ltd* [1979] AC 731 .... 49, 50, 52
Esure Insurance v *Direct Line Insurance* [2008] RPC 34 .... 101, 175
Fenty v *Arcadia Group Brands Ltd* [2015] EWCA Civ 3 54
Fisher v *Brooker* [2006] EWHC 3239 162
Fisher v *Brooker* [2009] UKHL 41 79
Flour Oxidising v *Carr* (1908) 25 RPC 428 35
Foley v *Ellot* [1982] RPC 433 208
Football Association Premier League v *QC Leisure* (C-403/08) and *Murphy* v *Media Protection Services* (C-429/08) [2012] FSR 5 .... 166, 218
Football Dataco Ltd v *Brittens Pools Ltd* [2010] EWCA Civ 1380 164
Football Dataco Ltd v *Yahoo! UK Ltd* (C-604/10) [2013] FSR 1 164
Forensic Telecommunications Services Ltd v *Chief Constable of West Yorkshire* [2011] EWHC 2892 (Ch) 164
Francis Day & Hunter v *Bron* [1963] Ch 587 20
French v *Mason* [1999] FSR 597 74
Fujitsu's Application [1996] RPC 511 .... 129, 135, 140
Fujitsu's Application [1997] RPC 608 .... 129, 135, 140
Gale's Application [1991] RPC 305 129
General Electric Company/Method for determining nuclear core loading arrangement (T914/02) [2006] EPOR 143 132
General Electric Company's Applications [1964] RPC 413 .... 223, 224, 226
General Tyre and Rubber Co v *Firestone Tyre and Rubber Co Ltd* [1972] RPC 457 159
Generics (UK) Ltd v *Daiichi Pharmaceutical* [2009] EWCA Civ 646 152
Generics (UK) Ltd v *Lundbeck A/S* [2007] RPC 32 .... 38, 63, 152
Generics (UK) Ltd v *Lundbeck A/S* [2009] UKHL 12 90
Generics BV v *Smith Kline & French Laboratories Ltd* (C-316/95) [1997] RPC 801 75
Gerber Garment Technology Inc v *Lectra Systems Ltd* [1997] RPC 443 75
Gillette Safety Razor Co Ltd v *Anglo-American Trading Co Ltd* (1913) 30 RPC 465 .... 157, 171, 172
Glyn v *Weston Feature Films Co* [1916] 1 Ch 261 .... 111, 112
Google France and Google Inc v *Louis Vuitton Malletier* (C-236/08); *Google France* v *Viaticum Luteciel* (C-237/08); and *Google France* v *CNRRH* (C-238/08) [2010] ETMR 30 .... 235, 242, 243, 245, 251
Graham v *John Deere Co* 383 US 1 (1966) (US Supreme Court) 269

Graver Tank & Mfg Co v *Linde Air Products Co* 339 US 605 (1950) (US Supreme Court) 86
Haberman v *Jackel International Ltd* [1999] FSR 683 226
Halliburton Energy Services Inc v *Smith International (North Sea) Ltd* [2005] EWHC 1623 (Pat) 70
Harries v *Air King* 183 F2d 158 (1950) (US Federal Circuit) 153
Harrods Ltd v *Harrodian School Ltd* [1996] RPC 697 49
Harvard/Onco-Mouse (T19/90) (OJ EPO, 1990, 476) 117
Harvard/Onco-Mouse (V6/92) (OJ EPO, 1992, 589) 117
Harvard/Onco-Mouse, Decision of the Opposition Division 7 November 2001 (OJ EPO, 2003, 419) 118, 122
Harwood v *The Great Northern Railway Company* (1865) XI House of Lords Cases (Clark's) 654 157
Hawkes v *Paramount* [1934] 1 ChD 593 206
Hitachi/Auction Method (T258/03) (OJ EPO, 2004, 575) 131, 132
Hi-Tech Autoparts Ltd v *Towergate Two Ltd* (No. 2) [2002] FSR 270 3
Hölterhoff v *Freiesleben* (C-2/00) [2002] ETMR 79 240
Hotchkiss v *Greenwood* 52 US 248 (1850) (US Supreme Court) 156
Howard Florey Institute/Relaxin, Decision of the Opposition Division 8 December 1994 (OJ EPO, 1995, 388) 119, 120, 202
HRH Prince of Wales v *Associated Newspapers Ltd* [2006] EWCA 1776 ... 230, 231
Hubbard v *Vosper* [1972] QB 84 .... 45, 230
Human Genome Sciences Inc v *Eli Lilly & Co* [2010] EWCA Civ 33 129
Human Genome Sciences Inc v *Eli Lilly & Co* [2011] UKSC 51 ... 28, 107, 130, 151, 265, 276
Hyde Park Residence Ltd v *Yelland* [1999] RPC 655 113
Hyde Park Residence Ltd v *Yelland* [2000] RPC 604 .... 113, 230
Hymac Ltd v *Priestman Brothers Ltd* [1978] RPC 495 85
Hyperion Records Ltd v *Sawkins* [2005] EWCA Civ 565 ... 162, 193, 199, 200, 201, 202, 204
Ibcos Computers Ltd v *Barclays Mercantile Highland Finance Ltd* [1994] FSR 275 .... 195, 212, 213
IBM/Document abstracting and retrieving (T22/85) (OJ EPO, 1990, 12) 68, 139
Improver v *Remmington* [1990] FSR 181 15
Infopaq International v *Danske Dagblades Forening* (C-5/08) [2010] FSR 495 .... 165, 217, 218
Interflora Inc, Interflora British Unit v *Marks & Spencer plc, Flowers Direct Online Ltd* (C-323/09) [2012] ETMR 1 .... 243, 245, 246, 247, 251
Interflora Inc v *Marks & Spencer plc* [2014] EWCA Civ 1403 .... 241, 244, 264
Interlego v *Tyco Industries* [1988] RPC 343 .... 163, 198, 199
IPC Media v *Highbury Leisure* [2004] EWHC 2985 .... 211, 212
Irvine v *Talksport* [2002] EWHC 367 52
Jian Tools for Sales Inc v *Roderick Manhattan Group* [1995] FSR 924 .... 85, 86
Johns-Manville Corp's Patent [1967] FSR 327 .... 59, 94
Johnstone Safety Ltd v *Peter Cook (Int) plc* [1990] FSR 161 210
Jones (by Caldwell) v *First Tier Tribunal, Criminal Injuries Compensation Authority* [2013] UKSC 19 42
Jones v *London Borough of Tower Hamlets* [2001] RPC 407 213

Kastner v *Rizla* [1995] RPC 585 15
Killen v *MacMillan* (1932) 49 RPC 258 170
Kirin-Amgen Inc v *Hoechst Marion Roussel Ltd* [2004] UKHL 46 15
Kirin-Amgen Inc v *Transkaryotic Therapies Inc* (No. 3) [2005] FSR 875 ...... 78, 79, 80
Klinger v *Conan Doyle Est Ltd* No. 14-1128 (7th Cir 2014) (US Federal Circuit) 169
Koninklijke KPN Nederland NV v *Benelux-Merkenbureau* (C-363/99) [2004] ETMR 771 250
Koninklijke Philips Electronics NV v *Nintendo of Europe GmbH* [2014] EWHC 1959 (Pat) 172
Krisarts SA v *Briarfine Ltd* [1977] FSR 557 205
Ladbroke (Football) Ltd v *William Hill (Football) Ltd* [1964] 1 WLR 273 ... 93, 162, 168, 195
Lawrence v *Smith* 7 ER 928 112
Lawson v *Serco* [2006] ICR 250 42
LB (Plastics) Ltd v *Swish Products Ltd* [1977] FSR 87 .... 194, 195
Leslie v *Young & Sons* [1894] AC 335 .... 196, 198
Liardet v *Johnson, Morning Post* 23 February 1778 (No. 1667, p. 2, col.4) 228, 229
Libertel Groep BV v *Benelux-Merkenbureau* (C-104/01) [2003] ETMR 63 ... 27, 28
Linde AG (C-53/01); *Winward Industries Inc* (C 54/01); and *Rado Uhren AG Applications* (C-55/01) [2003] ETMR 963 250
Lloyd Schuhfabrik Meyer & Co. GmbH v *Klijsen Handel BV* (C-342/97) [2000] FSR 77 .... 101, 175
Loendersloot v *George Ballantine* (C-349/95) [1998] ETMR 10 264
The London Taxi Corporation Ltd v *Frazer-Nash Research Ltd* [2016] EWHC 52 (Ch) 250
Longbottom v *Shaw* (1891) 8 RPC 333 154
L'Oréal SA v *Bellure NV* [2007] EWCA Civ 968 .... 110, 223
L'Oréal SA v *Bellure NV* (C-487/07) [2010] RPC 1 244
L'Oréal SA v *Bellure NV* [2010] EWCA Civ 535 246
L'Oréal SA v *eBay International AG* (C-324/09) [2011] ETMR 52 .... 234, 243
Lucas v *Gaedor* [1978] RPC 297 225
Lux Traffic Controls Ltd v *Pike Signals Ltd* [1993] RPC 107 151
Lloyd Schuhfabrik Meyer & Co GmbH v *Klijsen Handel BV* (C-342/97) [2000] FSR 77 .... 101, 175
MacMillan Publishers v *Reed* [1993] FSR 455 162
MacMillan v *Cooper* (1924) 40 TLR 186 .... 162, 193, 195, 200, 216
MacMillan v *Suresh Chunder Deb* ILR 17 C 951 (Calcutta High Court) 193
Macrossan's Application [2006] EWHC 705 134
Marks & Spencer plc v *Interflora Inc* [2012] EWCA Civ 1501 101
Mentor v *Hollister* [1993] RPC 7 228
Merck & Co Inc v *Generics (UK) Ltd* [2003] EWHC 2842 (Pat) 187
Merck Canada Inc, Merck Sharp & Dohme Ltd v *Sigma Pharmaceuticals plc* [2012] EWPCC 21 78
Merck Canada Inc, Merck Sharp & Dohme Ltd v *Sigma Pharmaceuticals plc* [2013] EWCA Civ 326 78

Merck's Patents [2003] EWCA Civ 1545 42
Merrell Dow Pharmaceuticals Inc v *Norton* [1996] RPC 76 .... 128, 172, 227
Microsoft/Data transfer with expanded clipboard formats (T424/03) [2006] EPOR 414 .... 131, 134
Milliken Denmark v *Walk Off Mat* [1996] FSR 292 151
Miss World Ltd v *Channel Four Television Corp* [2007] EWHC 982 (Pat) 175, 240
Mobil/Friction reducing additive (G02/88) [1990] EPOR 73 173
Mölnlycke AB v *Procter & Gamble* [1994] RPC 49 .... 152, 153, 156
Navitaire Inc v *Easy Jet Airline* [2005] EWHC 0282 (Ch) 79, 211
Nestec SA v *Dualit Ltd* [2013] EWHC 923 (Pat) 96
News Group v *Rocket* [1981] FSR 89 85
Newspaper Licensing Agency v *Marks & Spencer* [2001] UKHL 38 ... 168, 205, 213
Newspaper Licensing Agency v *Meltwater Holding BV* [2010] EWHC 3099 (Ch) 220
Newspaper Licensing Agency v *Meltwater Holding BV* [2011] EWCA Civ 890 220
Nokia Oyj (Nokia Corp) v *IPCom GmbH & Co KG* [2012] EWCA Civ 567 225
Norowzian v *Arks Ltd* (No. 2) [2000] FSR 363 42
North-Eastern Marine Engineering Co v *Leeds Forge Co* (1906) 23 RPC 529 ... 170
Nova Productions Ltd v *Mazooma Games Ltd* [2006] EWHC 24 (Ch) 211
Nova Productions Ltd v *Mazooma Games Ltd* [2007] EWCA Civ 219 .... 161, 211, 219
Novartis v *Johnson & Johnson* [2010] EWCA Civ 1039 228
O2 Holdings Ltd v *Hutchison 3G Ltd* [2006] EWHC 534 (Ch) 102
O2 Holdings Ltd v *Hutchison 3G Ltd* [2006] EWCA Civ 1656 .... 102, 103
O2 Holdings Ltd v *Hutchison 3G Ltd* (C-533/06) [2008] RPC 33 .... 102, 103
OCH-ZIFF Management Europe Ltd v *OCH Capital LLP* [2010] EWHC 2599 (Ch) 176, 235
OHIM v *Wrigley* [2004] ETMR 121 249
Okotoks Ltd (Formerly Spicerhaart Ltd) v *Fine & Country Ltd* [2013] EWCA Civ 672 .... 42, 43
Omnipharm v *Merial* [2011] EWHC 3393 (Pat) 38
Oystertec's Patent [2003] RPC 29 170
Painer v *Standard Verlags GmbH* (C-145/10) [2012] ECDR 6 .... 165, 201
Paragon Finance plc v *Thakerar & Co* [1999] 1 All ER 400 72
Parfums Christian Dior SA v *Evora BV* (C-337/95) [1997] ECR I-6013 244
PBS Partnership/Controlling Pension Benefits System (T931/95) (OJ EPO, 2001, 441) 131, 133, 135
Petra Fisher's Application [1997] RPC 899 223
Philips v *Remington* (C-299/99) [2001] ETMR 509 115
Place v *Blackburn* (1912) 29 RPC 656 154
Plant Genetic Systems/Plant cells resistant to glutamine synthetase inhibitors (T356/93) (OJ EPO, 1995, 545) 117, 120
PLG Research Ltd v *Ardon International Ltd* [1993] FSR 197 173
Point Solutions Ltd v *Focus Business Solutions Ltd* [2005] EWHC 3096 169
Pope Appliance Corporation v *Spanish River Pulp and Paper Mills* [1929] AC 269 228

Portakabin Ltd v *Primakabin BV* (C-558/08) [2010] ETMR 52 .... 243, 245
Pozzoli SpA v *BDMO SA* [2007] EWCA Civ 588 55
President's Reference/Computer program exclusion (G3/08) [2009] EPOR 9 .... 141, 142, 144
Purefoy Engineering v *Sykes Boxall* (1955) 72 RPC 89 216
Qualcast (Wolverhampton) v *Haynes* [1959] AC 743 63
R. v *X/Same Invention* [2002] EPOR 167 96
Raleigh International TM [2001] RPC 11 100
Ravenscroft v *Herbert* [1980] RPC 193 209
Reckitt & Colman Products Ltd v *Borden Inc* [1990] RPC 341 .... 49, 65, 280
Reed Executive Plc v *Reed Business Information Ltd* [2004] EWCA Civ 159 176
Regan v *Paul Properties Ltd* [2006] EWCA Civ 1391 79
Research in Motion UK Ltd v *Inpro Licensing SARL* [2006] EWHC 70 .... 68, 130
Resolution Chemicals Ltd v *Lundbeck A/S* [2013] EWCA Civ 1515 109
Rose Plastics GmbH v *William Beckett & Co (Plastics) Ltd* [1989] FSR 113 210
Roussel-Uclaf v *Searle & Co Ltd* [1977] FSR 125 80
Rovi Solutions Corp v *Virgin Media Ltd* [2015] EWCA Civ 781 225
Russian Commercial and Industrial Bank v *British Bank of Foreign Trade Ltd* [1921] 2 AC 438 169
SA Société LTJ Diffusion v *SA Sadas* (C-291/00) [2003] ETMR 83 .... 100, 175, 176, 240
Saint-Gobain PAM SA v *Fusion Provida Ltd* [2005] EWCA Civ 177 60
Sandman v *Panasonic* [1998] FSR 651 .... 209, 212
SAS Institute Inc v *World Programming Ltd* [2010] EWHC 1829 (Ch) 218
SAS Institute Inc v *World Programming Ltd* [2013] EWCA civ 1482 ..... 14, 93, 218, 220, 222
Schlumberger Holdings Ltd v *Electromagnetic Geoservices AS* [2010] EWCA Civ 819 .... 57, 225, 226
SEB SA v *De'Longhi SpA* [2003] EWCA Civ 952 42
Sheldon v *Metro-Goldwyn Pictures Corp* 81 F2d 49 (2d Cir. 1936) (US Federal Circuit) 202
Shopalotto.COM Ltd's Application [2005] EWHC 2416 (Pat) 68, 70, 130
Smith & Nephew plc v *Convatec Technologies* [2013] EWHC 3955 (Pat) ... 4, 76, 78
SmithKline Beecham v *Apotex* [2003] EWCA Civ 137 .... 84, 86
Société des Produits Nestlé SA v *Cadbury UK Ltd* (C-215/14) [2015] ETMR 50 250
Société des Produits Nestlé SA v *Cadbury UK Ltd* [2016] EWHC 50 (Ch) 250
Société Technique de Pulverisation Step v *Emson Europe Ltd* [1993] RPC 513 .... 156, 172
Southey v *Sherwood* 35 ER 1006 112
Southwark LBC v *Williams* [1971] Ch 734 179
Spalding Brothers v *Gamage Ltd* [1914-15] All ER Rep 147 50
Specsavers International Healthcare Ltd v *Asda Stores Ltd* (No. 2) [2012] EWCA Civ 24 .... 87, 104
Specsavers International Healthcare Ltd v *Asda Stores Ltd* (C-252/12) [2013] ETMR 46 104
Starbucks (HK) Ltd v *British Sky Broadcasting Group plc* [2015] UKSC 31 .... 64, 65, 67

Stockdale v *Onwhyn* 108 ER 65 ... 112
Supreme Petfoods Ltd v *Henry Bell & Co (Grantham) Ltd* [2015] EWHC 256 (Ch) ... 241
Swift & Co's Application [1962] RPC 37 ... 223
Synthon BV v *Smithkline Beecham plc* [2005] UKHL 59 ... 159
Technograph Printed Circuits Ltd v *Mills & Rockley (Electronics) Ltd* [1972] RPC 346 ... 55, 225
Thomson v *American Braided Wire* (1889) 6 RPC 518 ... 154
TNS Group Holdings Ltd v *Nielsen Media Research Inc* [2009] FSR 23 ... 170
Traction Corp v *Bennett* (1908) 25 RPC 819 ... 170
Twentieth Century Fox Film Corp v *Harris* [2013] EWHC 159 (Ch) ... 74
Unilever plc v *Griffin* [2010] EWHC 899 (Ch) ... 234
Union Carbide Corporation v *BP Chemicals Limited* [1998] FSR 1 ... 77
United Biscuits Ltd v *Asda Stores Ltd* [1997] RPC 513 ... 51, 52
University of London Press Ltd v *University Tutorial Press Ltd* [1916] 2 Ch 601 ... 162, 212
Valensi v *British Radio Corporation* [1973] RPC 337 ... 228
Vestergaard Frandsen A/S v *Bestnet Europe Ltd* [2009] EWHC 1456 (Ch) ... 4, 76, 77
Vicom Systems Inc/Computer-related invention (T208/84) (OJ EPO, 1987, 14) ... 68, 130, 131
Viking Gas A/S v *Kosan Gas A/S* (C-46/10) [2011] ETMR 58 ... 243, 245
Virgin Atlantic v *Premium Aircraft* [2009] EWCA Civ 1513 ... 78, 79
Walcot v *Walker* (1802) 32 ER 1 ... 112
Walter v *Lane* [1900] AC 539 ... 163, 200
Warner-Lambert Company LLC v *Sandoz GMBH* [2015] EWHC 3153 (Pat) ... 85
Warwick Film v *Eisenger* [1969] 1 Ch 508 ... 168
Watson v *Croft Promo-Sport Ltd* [2009] EWCA Civ 15 ... 79
Western Front v *Vestron* [1987] FSR 66 ... 74
Wilson v *Wilson Bros* (1911) 28 RPC 733 ... 154
Windsurfing Chiemsee Produktions- und Vertriebs GmbH v *Boots- und Segelzubehör Walter Huber and Franz Attenberge* (C-109/97) [1999] ETMR 585 ... 249, 250
Windsurfing International Inc v *Tabur Marine (Great Britain) Ltd* [1985] RPC 59 ... 36, 55, 157, 159
Wyko Group Plc v *Cooper Roller Bearings Co Ltd* [1996] FSR 126 ... 169
Young v *Bristol Aeroplane Company* [1944] KB 718 ... 128

Table of legislation

UNITED KINGDOM

Sculpture Copyright Act 1798 200
Sculpture Copyright Act 1814 ...... 200, 203
Stamp Act 1891 66
Copyright Act 1911 161
Patents and Designs Act 1932 .... 153, 154
Trade Marks Act 1938 102
Patents Act 1949 .... 7, 135, 172, 223
  s.14 224
  s.32 .... 154, 224
Patents Act 1977 .... 4, 55, 77, 156
  s.1 .... 68, 135, 151
  s.2 .... 33, 94, 173, 229
  s.3 .... 34, 55
  s.4 151
  s.5 95
  s.14 .... 227, 228
  s.15 227
  s.16 229
  s.24 229
  s.39 74
  s.40 .... 38, 71
  s.41 .... 38, 39, 40, 71, 111
  s.48A 71
  s.60 77
  s.61 .... 74, 77
  s.62 74
  s.63 74
  s.64 173
  s.72 .... 170, 228
  s.74 170
  s.130 .... 125, 128
Supreme Court Act 1981
  s.37 77
  s.50 79
Copyright, Designs and Patents Act 1988 40
  s.1 160
  s.5A 160
  s.5B 160
  s.6 160
  s.8 160
  s.9 73
  s.11 73
  s.16 .... 71, 93, 168, 204, 219
  s.17 93
  s.18 93
  s.19 93
  s.20 93
  s.21 93
  s.29 71
  s.30 71
  s.30A 71
  s.32 71
  s.90 73
  s.96 .... 73, 74
  s.97 .... 71, 74
  s.98 74
  s.99 74
  s.100 74
Trade Marks Act 1994
  s.3 .... 115, 174
  s.4 174
  s.5 .... 10, 71, 100, 174, 175, 176
  s.10 .... 71, 234
  s.14 74
  s.15 74
  s.16 74
  s.17 74
  s.18 74
  s.19 74

s.47 176
The Trade Mark (Relative Grounds) Order 2007 (SI 2007, No.1976)
Art.5 176
The Patents Rules 2007 (SI 2007, No.3291)
r.26 229

EUROPEAN AND INTERNATIONAL

Paris Convention for the Protection of Industrial Property 1883 96
Convention for the Protection of Human Rights and Fundamental Freedoms 1953 (ECHR)
Art.8 230–31
Convention on the Grant of European Patents 1973 (EPC) 7, 29, 70, 127, 172
Preamble 127
Art.52 .... 67, 68, 69, 130, 131, 135, 136, 139, 141, 142, 151
Art.53 .... 117, 118, 120, 122, 123
Art.54 139
Art.56 139
Art.69 15
Art.83 228
Art.87 96
Art.112 137
First Council Directive of 21 December 1988 to approximate the laws of the Member States relating to trade marks (Directive 89/104/EEC), OJ L 040, 11/02/1989, p. 1 (REPEALED under Art.17 Directive 2008/95)
Rec.(10) 239
Council Directive of 14 May 1991 on the legal protection of computer programs (Directive 91/250/EEC), OJ L 122, 17/05/1991, p. 42
Art.4 219
Agreement on Trade-Related Aspects of Intellectual Property Rights: Annex 1C of the Marrakesh Agreement Establishing the World Trade Organization, 1994 (TRIPs Agreement) 96
Art.16 176
Directive 96/9/EC of the European Parliament and of the Council of 11 March 1996 on the legal protection of databases, OJ L77, 27/3/1996, p. 20.
Art.3 164
Directive 98/44/EC of the European Parliament and of the Council of 6 July 1998 on the legal protection of biotechnological inventions, OJ L 213, 30/7/1998, p. 13 127
Art.6 123
Directive 2001/29/EC of the European Parliament and of the Council of 22 May 2001 on the harmonisation of certain aspects of copyright and related rights in the information society, OJ L 167, 22/6/2001, p. 10 .... 165, 220, 221, 222
Art.2 .... 165, 168, 217
Directive 2004/48/EC of the European Parliament and of the Council of 29 April 2004 on the enforcement of intellectual property rights, OJ L 157, 30/4/2004, p. 16 75
Rec.(22) 84
Directive 2006/116/EC of the European Parliament and of the Council of 12 December 2006 on the term of protection of copyright and certain related rights (codified version), OJ L 372, 27/12/2006, p. 12.
Art.6 164
Directive 2006/114/EC of the European Parliament and of the Council of 12 December 2006 concerning misleading and comparative advertising (codified version), OJ L376, 27/12/2006, p. 21
Art.3 233

Directive 2008/95/EC of the European Parliament and of the Council of 22 October 2008 to approximate the laws of the Member States relating to trade marks (codified version), OJ L299, 8/11/2008, p. 25 (REPEALED with effect from 15 January 2019 under Art.55 Directive (EU) 2015/2436).
Rec.(11) 239
Art.3 .... 114, 249
Art.5 .... 239, 240, 241, 244, 245
Art.6 239
Council Regulation (EC) No. 207/2009 of 26 February 2009 on the Community trade mark, OJ L78, 24/3/2009, p. 1 246
Art.7 115
Directive 2009/24/EC of the European Parliament and of the Council of 23 April 2009 on the legal protection of computer programs (codified version), OJ L 111, 5/5/2009, p. 16
Art.1 164
Directive (EU) 2015/2436 of the European Parliament and of the Council of 16 December 2015 to approximate the laws of the Member States relating to trade marks, OJ L 336, 23/12/2015, p. 1 246
Regulation (EU) 2015/2424 of the European Parliament and of the Council of 16 December 2015 amending Council Regulation (EC) No 207/2009 on the Community trade mark and Commission Regulation (EC) No 2868/95 implementing Council Regulation (EC) No 40/94 on the Community trade mark, and repealing Commission Regulation (EC) No 2869/95 on the fees payable to the Office for Harmonization in the Internal Market (Trade Marks and Designs), OJ L 341, 24/12/2015, p. 21 246

OVERSEAS

US Patents Act 1952 (Title 35 USC) 126
s.102 98
s.112 228
US Copyright Act 1976 (Title 17 USC)
s.408 150
s.411 150
US Leahy-Smith America Invents Act 2011 (AIA) 97

1. Introduction

This book sets out to expose, analyse and evaluate conflicting conceptions of legal judgement that operate in intellectual property law. It is concerned with the opposition between law-making by way of the creation of generally applicable rules and law-making done at the point of application through case-by-case decisions tailored to the particulars of individual circumstances.[1] Within the field it is no challenge to find instances of central and important interests being determined by reference to relatively vague standards which permit courts to take ad hoc and situation-sensitive decisions. Saying that throughout intellectual property law important issues are decided by the application of standards is not to deny that the field has a fair share of rules that, on the face of it and within the scope of their application, provide clear and predictable outcomes and constrain decision makers to judge particular cases mechanically by applying these rules to readily ascertainable facts. The relative strength of arguments that favour one form of directive over another are as finely balanced in the field of intellectual property as they are in any other area of law. This book starts with the fundamental premise that the choice of form of legal directives is significant and that there is something interesting and useful to say about form and about the relationship between form and substance in intellectual property law.[2]

Demonstrating that a number of important contemporary controversies in intellectual property law reflect the rules–standards conflict and that the tension between differing conceptions of legal judgement is a feature

[1] On these as 'stylized conceptions of legal judgement' see: Sunstein, C, 'Problems with Rules' (1995) 83 California L Rev 953, 956–7. The working title for this book throughout most of the time it took to write was *Form and Substance in Intellectual Property Law*, in open acknowledgement of the inspiration drawn from the work of Duncan Kennedy, and in particular from Kennedy, D, 'Form and Substance in Private Law Adjudication' (1976) 89 Harvard L Rev 1685. The shortened current title, however, gives a better indication of what actually is to follow.

[2] It thus rejects the claim that an explanation of form in terms of substance does not just reveal more and the same form, on which see: Schlag, P, 'Rules and Standards' (1985) 33 UCLA L Rev 379, 427.

of innumerable disputes about who has the right to appropriate, access and exploit the fruits of the human intellect is a primary object of the chapter which follows. Here and elsewhere in the book I make no claim to be comprehensive in the sense of trying to identify all instances of tension across the whole field. Indeed the first part of the work tends to focus on patent law for no other reason than it is in this field where the most illuminating examples are to be found. But they are examples and the analysis can do no more than hint at the ubiquity of the conflict and the equally ubiquitous and deeper conflict between the need for the law to provide certainty and the desire for it to be flexible enough to do justice in individual cases and to adapt and respond to technological, economic and social changes.

A rule is a provision which provides a before-the-fact specification of legal outcome. If a rule applies, then decision making is concerned with establishing, on a balance of probabilities, what the relevant facts are. That done it is a simple matter of stating the 'inevitable' outcome dictated by rule. Thus, decision making according to rules is understood to be desirable when certainty, uniformity, stability or security are particularly valued. It is almost routinely argued that in matters of property and of commercial law, the social interest in security of transactions favours rules because of the exceptional need of certainty in order to uphold the economic order.

Standards differ from rules in the degree of discretion they allow the decision maker. Discretion is never entirely free from restriction and in Chapter 2, in getting to grips with the notion of a standard, I explore in some detail what it means to say that a judge has discretion. Commonly, decision making under standards involves the identification and weighing of a number of relevant factors with discretion lying in the identification of factors, how these factors are to be interpreted and applied to the circumstances in issue, and the relative weight to attach to each of the factors deemed relevant. In this way decisions can be tailored, within limits, to the circumstances of individual disputes but at the cost of introducing a degree of uncertainty in the decision making process.

This cost needs to be set against the difficulties and costs of promulgating detailed rules, which can be significant where the law aims at responding to, or regulating, widely varying or otherwise unpredictable conduct. In such circumstances it will be difficult if not impossible to draft a rule that embraces all the circumstances that it is intended to govern without it also touching upon other areas. At the same time, the very unpredictability of the circumstances it is intended to regulate means that some targeted circumstances are likely to be missed. One solution is to forego any attempt at precision and instead adopt a more 'open-textured' legal direction. Thus standards, which allow some discretion, are thought useful when flexibility and dynamism in the law are understood to be important and intellectual property law, as much as any other area, is home to many such legal directions of this form.

There is a value in flexibility in two senses. A rule that is pertinent today may become increasingly anachronistic as social, technological or economic conditions change. Chapter 2 also then provides me with an opportunity to show how the common law is particularly well suited to addressing the problem of anachronism. Although judges are constrained in their decision making by dicta in earlier cases, the law is always understood and applied by contemporary judges faced with contemporary disputes and judges have some power to formulate, review and reformulate the guides and constraints on their own decision making in ways that allow the law to maintain a contemporary relevance whilst remaining principled.

Flexibility is also of value when the law aims at regulating widely varying conduct. For instance it would be difficult if not impossible to draft a rule that enumerated all the conceivable relationships between the intellectual objects protected by law and the various forms of imitation, copying, adaptation and other borrowings in a way that might provide a precise bright-line indication of what, in any instance, is within the scope of protection and what without. The solution typically lies in the incorporation into the law of touchstones such as 'fairness' or 'reasonableness' and others with similar effect. Such touchstones have in common that they set out to create an open texture to the law by demanding evaluative judgements to be made by decision makers.

Nevertheless, especially in matters of property and of commercial law, the belief that the law needs to be certain exerts a powerful and sometimes overriding influence and with this comes a commitment to the precision and clarity provided by rules. Such commitment does not solve the problems associated with the over- and under-inclusiveness of rules but rather manifests an acceptance that the rule will produce an undesirable outcome in a proportion of the cases in which it is applied. For instance, denying 'artistic quality' as a relevant consideration in deciding whether copyright subsists in artistic works no doubt avoids subjectivity in decision making but has led to the consequence that the full panoply of economic and moral rights accorded to artistic works under copyright law can be claimed in the embossed patterns on rubber car mats as a species of engraving.[3] Such a finding might surprise a layman who would

---

3 *Hi-Tech Autoparts Ltd* v *Towergate Two Ltd* (No. 2) [2002] FSR 270.

struggle to see it as rational or in accord with his rudimentary understanding of the purpose of copyright, but it would likely provoke little more than a shrug of the shoulders from a lawyer used to the operation of 'bright line' rules as instruments directed to achieving certainty in the law.

If a large number of applications of the rule produce an undesirable outcome there is a strong case for changing the rule to better fit its desired aim. More challenging is the circumstance where, in the great majority of cases the rule provides a good outcome but in a small proportion it does not. Here a solution lies in the individualization of decisions in circumstances notionally embraced by the rule. For centuries apparently inflexible rules have been subject to the supplementary code of equity which is intended to mitigate some of the harshness of the common law. Courts have, for instance, on occasion used the tool of the constructive trust to bypass the formalities normally required to effect transfers of copyright in circumstances where they judge it unconscionable to hold the parties to the clear but inflexible statutory scheme for the allocation of rights. Important though such mechanisms are, they can hardly be described as commonplace. But that description is apt in relation to remedies, in relation to which equity makes the most significant contribution to the field of intellectual property law.

The injunction is a ubiquitous and flexible equitable remedy. It is flexible in the sense that the form of the order has sometimes been adapted by courts to meet specific factual circumstances. Springboard injunctions, for instance, can be ordered where a defendant has, by way of their infringing activities, gained an advantage by building up a bridgehead into the claimant's market. No one can doubt the usefulness of this remedy and the inequities which might result if it were not available. But those benefits are bought at the cost of certainty in that the acts restrained by the injunction would, but for the injunction, otherwise be lawful (for instance because the right in issue has expired or the restrained activity otherwise falls outside the scope of the claimed right).[4] Thus, an examination only of the scheme provided in the Patents Act 1977 which lays out with apparent clarity the term of protection and what constitutes infringement gives a misleading picture of the scope of protection available to patentees.

---

[4] See e.g. *Smith & Nephew plc* v *Convatec Technologies* [2013] EWHC 3955 (Pat); *Dyson Appliances Ltd* v *Hoover Ltd* (No. 2, 'Springboard' Relief) [2001] RPC 544; and as a remedy for breaches of a duty to keep information confidential *Vestergaard Frandsen A/S* v *Bestnet Europe Ltd* [2009] EWHC 1456 (Ch).

The injunction is also flexible in that courts have frequently described it as a discretionary remedy which must be fair and equitable and proportionate. Outside intellectual property law, individual circumstances will dictate its availability on a case-by-case basis. However, within intellectual property law that discretionary character is recognized only in statements of principle and courts have been extremely reluctant to refuse such an order once infringement has been established. Here then is an instance where an understanding that the law needs to be certain exerts an overriding influence. Remedies give value to rights and uncertainty as to remedies is uncertainty as to the right itself.

That is true so far as the remedy of the final injunction is concerned and Chapter 2 concludes with a consideration of the way in which courts approach interim injunctions. The way courts approach such orders differs from the approach taken to final injunctions and the tension between rules and standards is much clearer. So far as it aims to balance the guarantees provided to the owner by her property right against the justice of providing her an interim remedy pending resolution of the dispute, the so-called 'balance of convenience' test manifests this tension.

The recourse to equity in order to do justice in an individual case notwithstanding a rule that would provide for a different outcome, often prompts the response that in this the courts have in some way overstepped the mark. The complaint is not always that such interventions compromise efforts to provide certainty of expectation but rather that this usurps the legislature's power to make law. For reasons expanded upon in the narrative which follows, rule making is the province of the legislature. The more open textured a legislative provision is, the more interpretive scope is given to courts. The choice between rules and 'rulelessness' can thus be seen as presenting a principal/agent problem, where the legislature, as principal, by the adoption of a certain form of legal direction exercises control over the decisions of the courts. In Chapter 3, I move away from an evaluation of form based only on the desirability or otherwise of certainty and consider other factors that have in common that they raise the question of who is best positioned to make the law: the legislature or courts. In setting out to answer this question I adopt three evaluative points of focus: the merits and demerits of *ex ante* versus *ex post* decision making; the avoidance of the perception of bias in decision making; and the demands and attendant costs of harmonizing the national intellectual property laws of European countries.

As to the first of these, rules, it is said, require of their draftsmen some degree of foresight. The draftsmen must be able to anticipate the range of circumstances over which the rule is to operate and decide upon the appropriate legal response. By contrast, the legal response under a standard is decided only once a precise set of factual circumstances have occurred. For this reason standards can be useful when foresight is clouded. Trade mark law provides an opportunity to explore the differences between *ex ante* and *ex post* decision making so far as the test of whether there exists 'a likelihood of confusion' serves both as a relative ground for refusing registration to a sign which is similar to an existing mark and as a ground for establishing whether use of a sign infringes a similar registered mark. The two grounds are supposedly conceptually indistinguishable and the scheme makes sense so far as it aims to exclude from registration, marks whose use would constitute infringement of a mark already on the register. Except this is not how the scheme works in practice. At the infringement stage, whether there is a likelihood of confusion is decided in a situation-sensitive way and assessments are limited to the circumstances and context of the complained of use. But at the application stage, the same test becomes coarsened and the assessment of similarity is based on an entirely acontextual comparison between the sign complained of and the registered mark. At the application stage the test thus becomes more rule-like. The conclusion is that a provision, even if drafted as a standard, will take on the characteristics of a rule if applied in an *ex ante* context.

The second theme developed in Chapter 3 explores the commonly heard assertion that decisions made under standards risk accusations of bias. The risk is undoubtedly there, but typically the concern is overstated. Certainly, without rules judges must identify and apply principles and values as reasons for any decision. But decisions must comply with the requirement of coherence. This demands that decisions be seen to be rational in the sense of evidencing the pursuit of intelligible principles or policies. In Chapter 2 I make the point that intellectual property law is partly autonomous by which I mean that it has an established set of values, principles and policies that characterize it. It is these values, principles and policies that provide the belt of restriction surrounding judicial discretion. This matters in avoiding accusations of bias because, even if called upon to decide under a condition as open as, for instance, 'fairness', a judge is not free to give effect to their personal convictions. Rather, if their decision is to be coherent, the judge must adopt a particular conception of fairness and give reasons for adopting that view. Only rarely does the requirement of coherence not work in this way so as to restrict judicial discretion. In the field of intellectual property law, one such rare instance occurs where judges are required to decide whether a sign, invention or work is in some way or another immoral. The problem facing judges in such instances is that the autonomous values, principles and policies that characterize intellectual property law do not intersect with, and so cannot limit or qualify, the condition of morality. Judges are thus forced to make their judgements seem intelligible according to values, principles and policies that lie outside intellectual property law. The problem is particularly acute in patent law. Whereas in trade mark law and copyright law, in deciding whether a particular mark or work offends against morality, tribunals have been able to rely on values, principles and policies manifested in other areas of law; in patent law the morality condition is framed in a way that appears to prohibit this strategy. For all the challenges facing decision makers and the risks that their decisions will be seen as biased or arbitrary, the peculiar features of decisions as to whether an object is immoral or otherwise means that such criticisms cannot be levelled against determinations made under standards more generally.

Of the three evaluative points of focus adopted in Chapter 3, the demands and attendant costs of harmonizing the national intellectual property laws of European countries most clearly manifests the tension between rules and standards as a principal/agent issue and introduces a theme that recurs at various other points in this book. Rules are essential tools in the efforts to harmonize laws. A binding supra-national rule constrains decision making at the national level so avoiding the risk of the emergence of divergent national norms. There is a tension, however, if there are factors which otherwise favour a standard over a rule, for instance because the area of governance is subject to rapid and unpredictable change making the flexibility of a standard more attractive. Nowhere is this tension more apparent than in respect of the attempts to arrive at a common understanding of what is patentable subject matter and in particular the law determining the patentability of computer software-implemented inventions. The inability to predict the direction and scope of technical advances creates a strong functional preference for a standards-dominated definition of what should be patentable. Indeed this was the position under the Patents Act of 1949 which was characterized by a flexible and versatile policy-driven approach to patentability facilitated by a very open-textured statutory framework allowing considerable discretion in decision making.

When the Convention on the Grant of European Patents (EPC) was drafted it was not intended that the European Patent Office (EPO) have a wide-ranging discretion in respect of the identification of patentable subject matter. The open texture of the old UK Act was not replicated in the EPC which then, as now, sets out what is patentable by way of a list of things not to be regarded as inventions. Thereby excluded from patentability are 'programs for computers', though, in common with the other categories of excluded subject matter (various other abstract, intellectual and mental objects), only to the extent that an application or patent relates to the specified subject matter 'as such'. What is patentable is one of those areas where the EPC sets out to create a uniformity of understanding amongst its member states, and the contemporary UK Patents Act, in common with those of other EPC member states, contains provisions which correspond to those contained in the EPC. That being so UK courts set out to construe those provisions so as to give them the same effect as the corresponding articles of the EPC and, in this, treat as persuasive the decisions of the EPO on the construction of the EPC. Thus, the objective of harmonization is seen as imposing a duty on national tribunals to look to decisions of the EPO. Much of Chapter 3 is given over to consideration of the nature and extent of any corresponding obligation on the EPO's Boards of Appeal to provide authoritative guidance. What is presented is a long and complex story throughout which the law, as to what is patentable in Europe, has remained stubbornly uncertain notwithstanding the numerous efforts, both judicial and legislative, to 'correct' this state of affairs and to inject certainty. The EPO are the shameless architects of this uncertainty but that is hardly surprising. If the EPO Boards have an obligation to further harmonization of patent law in Europe, this is secondary to their primary obligations relating to search, examination and grant. The EPO's primary responsibility is to decide individual cases and it is in this context that it interprets the provisions of the EPC. In this, its primary role, the EPO has an interest (perhaps even a duty) to maintain the flexibility in what constitutes patentable subject matter.

Up to this point the text, one way or another, is aimed at evaluating the likely consequences of adopting rules or standards in particular situations judged against the different objectives that policy makers aim to achieve in those situations. The remainder of the book attempts the more challenging task of relating broad 'pro-rules' and 'pro-standards' positions in intellectual property law to ideas concerning the use and sharing of ideas and the role of law in this aspect of the ordering of society. Put simply, it attempts to relate the values in intellectual property law that can be said to be intrinsic to form to extrinsic values that are, in whole or in part, achieved through the implementation and exercise of the law. At this point in the narrative it is perhaps natural for the reader to assume that there is nothing much more interesting to say other than sometimes circumstances dictate that rules are appropriate, and sometimes not. Often, though not invariably, the choice comes down to a decision as to whether certainty of expectation should be given priority over flexibility in the particular context subject to regulation. There are many areas of intellectual property law which conform to this pattern. But there is a more complex story to tell in respect of the fundamental context of marking the boundaries of protectable subject matter: a story that I set out to tell in Chapter 4. In patent, copyright and trade mark law, there are certain rules that contribute to the marking of these boundaries. But in every case, the context over which any rule operates is simultaneously subject to a standard that entirely subsumes the rule within its scope such that, so far as that context is concerned, the rule is instrumentally superfluous. So for instance, a patent will be granted for an invention which is new, which involves an inventive step and which is capable of industrial application. In the great majority of cases, the significant hurdles which an applicant must surmount are the requirements to show that what is claimed is new and involves an inventive step. The question of whether a claimed invention is new is a rule, or as close to a rule as is possible to get, requiring only that a decision maker decide whether, seen through the eyes of the skilled addressee, what is claimed is already available to the public. Whether the claimed invention involves an inventive step, in requiring the decision maker to decide whether what is claimed would have been obvious to the skilled addressee, involves evaluation: it is more standard-like. The uncertainty that this evaluation introduces has been a feature of patent law for hundreds of years and one can find instances as far back as the sixteenth century of courts rejecting claims because the quantity or degree of invention was insufficient to support a patent. In their modern form, there are no significant qualitative differences between the tests for whether what is claimed is new and whether it involves an inventive step. Both tests involve the decision maker taking on the mantle of the skilled addressee and then comparing what is claimed with what is known. Which test is immediately relevant turns on the degree of difference between what is claimed and what is known. That being so, the novelty rule seems superfluous given that something which is not new is a fortiori obvious.

Copyright law is similar. For copyright to subsist in a work, it must be original. A commitment to European harmonization is prompting change and I should perhaps note at this point that I do not plan to disregard the attempts to formulate harmonized conditions for the subsistence of copyright throughout Europe. A consideration of originality as meaning the product of the author's intellectual creativity is only postponed to the point at which I feel I can approach this novel conception of originality critically. But my initial focus is on the 'traditional' UK conception of originality and, until relatively recently and in the great majority of cases, 'originality' meant no more than that the work originated from the claimed author: that is to say it had not been copied. Deciding whether a work is original in this sense requires no evaluation. Either the work has been copied or it has not. In the great majority of cases then, the test as to whether a work is original is understood and applied as a rule. In some circumstances, courts have tested originality according to a standard using a test which looks to the degree of skill and labour involved in producing the work. But this has not been seen as a universal test and has typically been applied only where copyright is claimed in some form of compilation. Why a standard is appropriate in these circumstances but not others I shall attempt to explain at little later but for the moment it is enough to note only that it is atypical.

For the long history of copyright law and in the great majority of cases, the requirement that a work be original has required of the decision maker only that they establish whether the work has been copied or not. To what end is something of a mystery given that there can be no infringement of a work which is itself copied nor can an infringement claim be made out where the alleged infringement is in copying a part of a work which part is itself copied. One factor that contributes to the standard-like test employed in deciding whether a partial taking is 'substantial' looks to the originality of that part of the claimant's work that has been taken. Bearing in mind that the question of whether a work is original is almost invariably considered where there is some dispute, dispensing with originality as a condition for copyright to be claimed[5] would be apparently without consequence given that its effects are entirely embraced by the test for whether a partial taking is substantial enough to count as an infringement.

Trade mark law provides the clearest example of a rule, the scope of which is entirely embraced by a standard. Section 5(1) Trade Marks Act 1994 prohibits the registration of a sign that is identical to an existing registered mark. In requiring only a comparison between what is claimed and what exists and the question, 'are these the same?', it is a rule-like test that has much in common with that used to assess the novelty of a patent application. To be registered, a sign must also display a sufficient degree of difference from marks already on the register. So for instance, under section 5(2) Trade Marks Act 1994, a decision maker must form a judgement as to whether the use of the sign would likely confuse average consumers as to the 'trade origin' of the goods and services associated with the sign. In cases where there is precise identity as between sign and registered mark, the conclusion that consumers would be so confused is, I think, inevitable. Both tests are directed to establishing whether a sign

5 'Claimed' in the sense of a being a necessary condition to support a right of action against an alleged infringer.

is relatively distinctive, differing only in the degree of similarity as between sign and mark that must be shown for a sign's distinctiveness to be challenged. Why then have a separate ground, effected by way of a rule that looks only to identity?

Intuitively it seems reasonable to suppose that, in the context over which they exercise control, the rules in patent, copyright and trade mark law must contribute to a desirable certainty of expectation and stability. That a standard simultaneously exercises control over the same context suggests with equal force that flexibility and dynamism are desirable features of the law. A provisional explanation lies in the observation that legal provisions have a hortatory function. Intellectual property, like all private property, is a form of both private and public power. The private nature of this power is manifested in the relation between the right holder and a specific duty bearer. If the parties disagree as to their respective rights and duties then the law provides the means by which these competing interests can be brought to an accord. The public power of intellectual property derives from it creating rights 'good against the whole world', and is manifested in the ways in which rights influence the behaviour of an indefinite class (the public if you will). The law here provides right holders with the means of signalling to the world the boundaries of the territory over which they claim dominium. To understand the function of form then requires a consideration of the interpersonal dimension of intellectual property law and this is the subject matter of the penultimate chapter of this book.

Generally speaking, owners of private property can exercise their property rights absolutely as they choose and in this need have no regard for the interests of others. In modern Western societies, outside the tax system, there is generally no compulsion for individual wealth to be shared.[6] One reason for this reticence is that for most private property any redistribution scheme requires us to justify not only why someone should receive but also why another should donate. Thus, that there is a rivalry in consumption of private goods ceases to be a merely abstract notion and becomes a concrete reality. But intellectual property is different because there is no rivalry in the consumption of information and ideas. The owner of an intellectual property right who is forced to share the protected information with another is not themselves deprived of that information. In this sense, nothing is taken from them. Arguments

[6] I say generally because there are rare exceptions such as the restrictions on testation and the concept of 'forced heirs' that apply under certain civil law rules of succession: Pelletier, G and Sonnenreich, M, 'A Comparative Analysis of Civil Law Succession' [1966] Villanova L Rev 323, 349–53.

as to whether information should be shared are not then necessarily complicated by a challenge to the claimed ownership rights. Unlike other forms of private property, the forced sharing of intellectual property is far from unusual. For example, a user can take advantage of one of the fair dealing defences in copyright law without mounting any kind of attack on the owner's claim to enjoy copyright in the work in issue. Trade rivals can engage in comparative advertising without forcing the removal of marks from the register. Furthermore, not only are uses of marks outside the course of trade permitted, but so too are uses that do not affect the function of a protected mark. There are numerous other examples. In Chapter 5 I set out to test whether there is a demonstrable relationship between choice of form and substantive debates about the values inherent in a commitment to the political paradigms of, on the one hand individualism, and on the other altruism. In this I borrow extensively from the arguments advanced several decades ago by Duncan Kennedy in his exploration of form and adjudication in private law.[7] Kennedy sought to show that advocating rules over standards or vice versa could be seen as an invitation to choose between these competing sets of values. He saw parallels between the moral, economic and political arguments typically advanced in defence of the stricture of rules and the values linked to individualism. On the other hand the values of sharing and sacrifice that characterized 'altruism' were, he said, paralleled in the legal arguments favouring a relaxation in the rigour of a regime of rules. The analysis in Chapter 5 proceeds on the basis that there is some insight to be gained by testing the hypothesis that, in intellectual property law, the rule form is associated with securing claims and strengthening the position of right holders whereas the standard form is associated with limiting scope and facilitating public access.

So far as copyright is concerned, that association on the face of it seems to hold good. Throughout most of its history and in the great majority of cases the condition of originality has operated as a rule requiring only an assessment of whether the work has been copied or not. The more standard-like test of originality that requires a judgement as to whether sufficient skill, labour and judgement has been expended is applied only in instances where copyright has been claimed in works which are to some extent copies of existing productions and, more often than not, productions which are in the public domain. As I shall show, copyright claims are supportable only to the extent that the demonstrable effort enhances access to the publicly available material or improves its

7 Kennedy, above n.1.

utility and to claim copyright in such circumstances it is not enough to say merely, 'I have laboured'. Thus it is possible to say that the test, 'not copied', is a rule and is clearly associated with securing the claims of right holders; the test that looks to the degree of skill, labour and judgement exercised is much more clearly associated with facilitating public access and encouraging individuals to labour for the benefit of others. That in practice the latter test has proved very easy to satisfy perhaps suggests that courts tend to favour right holders in balancing the interests at stake.

That the standard-form manifests a commitment to altruism is also manifested in the way in which courts approach the issue of infringement by way of substantial taking. That copyright can be infringed by an unlicensed taking of only a substantial part of a work can be seen as enhancing right owners' interests by giving them the means to restrain the activities of unscrupulous copyists who set out to avoid liability by introducing only minor variations into an otherwise copied work. Whilst this may be the original motivation underlying the provisions on infringement, the test of what counts as a substantial part for the purposes of infringement has been more effective in restricting rather than extending rights. Whether a substantial part of a claimant's work has been copied is a test that is standard-like in form, being a matter of impression based on the quality of what has been taken rather than the quantity. Thus, showing only that a defendant has copied part of a work is not sufficient to establish infringement. What is required is to show that the defendant has taken a substantial part of the author's skill and labour. But even showing that the defendant has appropriated some of the author's skill and labour is insufficient. If what has been taken is characterized as 'an idea', then notwithstanding that it might have involved considerable skill and effort on the author's part to arrive at that idea, it will not be protected. The test thus operates in a way that ensures that at least some of what the author has done is available to others. As I set out to show in Chapter 5, this is particularly clear when one examines those instances where courts have refused protection for the 'ideas' expressed in literary works that are not works of fiction, and technical ideas and information expressed in technical drawings and similar works.

It is in the context of deciding whether a work has been infringed, rather than whether it is original, that UK law has drawn lines between that which is protectable and that which is not, using the dichotomy between ideas and expression as means and justification. In this way, the scope of a claimed right is determined in a process that pitches an individual claim against an individual correlative duty. One huge advantage of this scheme is that it avoids the problem of attempting to balance competing interests *ex ante*. This is difficult in the case of copyright law because even identifying the interests that are at stake *ex ante* is hugely problematic given the social diversity of copyright law's reach.

In this respect, UK copyright law is in the process of changing to be in line with the demands of harmonization of European copyright law. In light of a series of decisions of the European Court of Justice (ECJ), the UK Court of Appeal now understands that the test for determining whether a restricted act has been done in relation to a substantial part of a work is that the parts in question must contain elements which are the expression of the intellectual creation of the author of the work.[8] Prior to this change, courts had the option of declaring that whilst a defendant had taken something of the skill and labour of the claimant, what was taken was not substantial because the skill and labour taken was of the 'wrong kind' and directed to the production of ideas or other subject matter in which copyright could not be claimed. Whether that option has now gone remains to be seen in light of the specific legal arrangements that will govern the future relationship between the UK and the institutions and member states of the European Union (EU). If European jurisprudence continues to exert an influence on UK courts then the test for infringement by partial taking is much more 'rule-like' than was previously the case. But at the same time, UK courts have embraced the European standard of originality. Of course whether they continue to do so is also open to question but, for the moment, what is required for a work to count as original is that the work must be the intellectual creation of the author. This is far more standard-like than the typical traditional UK test which required only that the work not be copied for it to count as original. The difference in the new, European-influenced, approach is that the realm of individual duties will no longer be the testing ground for claims of right. Rather the new test is desert-based and if the duties imposed by the recognition of a right are taken account of at all then at best it will be as a speculative concern over duties understood in abstract rather than concrete terms.

Patent law does not on the face of it comfortably fit with the idea that the rule form is associated with securing claims whereas the standard form is associated with limiting scope. Patent law is unusual in there being a legislative direction that makes explicit that the interests of third parties should figure in courts' interpretation of the scope of a claimed

---

8 *SAS Institute Inc* v *World Programming Ltd* [2013] EWCA civ 1482.

invention.[9] In the UK this demand is met through the adoption of a so-called 'purposive approach' under which the scope of protection is set according to what a person skilled in the art would understand the patentee to have intended to claim.[10] In effect then, the realm of duties is made the testing ground for claims of right. Unsurprisingly, the House of Lords has criticized attempts to make the test rule bound.[11] But in patent law it is much less easy to say that the rule form is associated with securing rights. To secure a patent for an invention, the claimed invention must be both new (a condition assessed by way of a rule) but also must involve an inventive step: a condition assessed by way of a standard. That said, a patent will be refused only where it is clear that it is not inventive. The question of whether a claimed invention is obvious is approached with rather less subtlety at the examination stage than it is post grant. At the examination stage the test is coarsened and is more rule-like than when it is applied in a revocation action. The reason advanced for this is that examiners have a limited range of evidence on which to base their assessment of inventiveness. In these circumstances, any doubt is resolved in favour of the applicant on the assumption that a more thorough analysis will follow in a post-grant revocation action brought by an alleged infringer. To this extent the adoption of the rule form favours right owners but, even so, although the test for whether a claimed invention is obvious when applied at the examination stage is coarser and

---

[9] Thus Article 69 EPC provides that the extent of the protection conferred by a European patent or a European patent application shall be determined by the claims. As a guide for national courts, there is a Protocol on the interpretation of Article 69 EPC, Article 1 which provides inter alia that Article 69 should be interpreted in a way that combines a fair protection for the patentee with a reasonable degree of certainty for third parties.

[10] As is well known to patent lawyers this approach has its origins in the speech of Lord Diplock in House of Lords decision *Catnic Components Ltd* v *Hill and Smith Ltd* [1982] RPC 183, 243 and was stated to be the correct approach under the 1977 Act in *Improver* v *Remmington* [1990] FSR 181 and by the Court of Appeal in *Kastner* v *Rizla* [1995] RPC 585. This was confirmed by the House of Lords in *Kirin-Amgen Inc* v *Hoechst Marion Roussel Ltd* [2004] UKHL 46, though in a form that rejected the overly rigid 'Protocol Questions' that had by then become routinely adopted by courts and counsel.

[11] Lord Hoffmann in *Kirin-Amgen Inc* v *Hoechst Marion Roussel Ltd* distinguished between the principle of purposive construction and the guidelines for applying that principle to equivalents encapsulated in the Protocol questions. He observed that 'the cases show a tendency for counsel to treat the Protocol questions as legal rules rather than guides which will in appropriate cases help to decide what the skilled man would have understood the patentee to mean': [2004] UKHL 46 [52].

more rule-like than the test applied by courts in a revocation action, it nevertheless differs from the test for whether a claimed invention is new. The test for obviousness, at whatever stage it is applied, is not a rule.

One reason why the pattern is less than clear in the case of patent law is that securing a patent is not entirely an individualistic act. It clearly is in that it is a claim made by an individual to exclusive rights in an invention but importantly this comes at the cost to the patentee of being forced to share information as to how to arrive at her claimed invention. Demanding of patentees that they disclose what they claim to have invented as a condition for the grant of a patent has long been a feature of patent law. And in this respect patent law differs from copyright in that the copyright owner enjoys exclusive rights in their work whether or not that work ever sees the light of day. Indeed the exclusive rights to copy and publish a work are sometimes relied on by copyright owners precisely to prevent publication. Patent law's forced disclosure does a number of things. The most overt 'good' is that it teaches the public something that they did not previously know (assuming that the claimed invention is novel). By openly specifying what is claimed to be protected it also prevents rivals in the same technical field from wasteful investments directed to achieving the same end. If the claim is good, this deterrent effect in this way benefits the patentee's rivals. But if the claim is bad, the benefits of the monopoly grant are only the patentees: they are shielded from competition that without the patent would be lawful. Extracting the maximum social value from the patent system requires a robust examination of applications. Applying for a patent is an individualistic act but not entirely so and the examination of applications is concerned in large part with limiting scope and so facilitating public access. It is no surprise that both rules and standards play a part in the assessment of patentability.

The tension between individualism and altruism can be seen chiefly in that aspect of trade mark law that is concerned with governing how far a right owner can restrain the use of a protected mark by other traders who are not competing directly with the mark owner. Precisely because trade marks are such a common feature of the modern trading environment such uses and the tensions they create are increasingly common. For instance, appropriately scaled or rendered reproductions of 'real-world' objects in toys or games must necessarily reproduce the trade marks attached to these objects if the reproduction is to be accurate. Sports clubs, broadcasters, performers and the like have turned badges of allegiance into marks that support their merchandising efforts, creating a tension between those that attach the original meaning to the sign and those who see it as a trade mark. Trading on an established reputation also underpins the trend of brand extension, which in turn can create conflicts between new entrant trade mark owners and established undertakings in the newly entered market.

The exclusive rights provided to trade mark owners under European trade mark legislation are, however, subject to an entirely judge-made limitation which requires that use of a sign by a third party must affect or be liable to affect one of the functions of the mark if it is to infringe. The effect is to make what rules there are under the legislation subject to a standard that looks to the impression made in the minds of consumers by the complained of use, and whether this would be liable to affect the essential function of guaranteeing to consumers the origin of the goods. By this means the scope of trade mark rights is limited in a way that ensures that at least some free use can be made of the protected mark. To be sure, the European Court has more recently held that uses that affect other functions of trade marks (related to advertising, communication and investment) can also be restrained but it is important not to lose sight of the fact that this 'enhancement' of mark owners' rights is in lessening (in a rather uncertain way) a limitation on the exercise of the rights apparently guaranteed under the legislation.

Notwithstanding this, the relationship between form, the claims of right owners versus the claims of others, and with this an apparent commitment to a particular political paradigm is far from clear in trade mark law. If there is a relationship it is at best hinted at. A key reason for this is that trade mark rights are often referred to in a way that indicate that these rights are aligned with the interests of consumers and it is these interests that justify the right and determine its scope. That the interest of consumers features so significantly in arguments concerning the recognition and scope of trade mark rights matters because consumers have an ambivalence between individualism and altruism that does not align precisely with the perspective of trade mark owners vis-à-vis other traders, nor necessarily with the perspective of the public and the use of marks in free public discourse. Modern patterns of production and consumption anticipate an individual's pattern of consumption to be a central element in how that individual constructs their identity. Somewhat paradoxically then, it is anticipated that consumers will set out (through acts of purchase) to emulate others so as to differentiate themselves from the mass. In this, trade marks play a central role not least of all because the social significance of any individual's pattern of consumption is, in whole or in part, shaped by the associations and meanings which trade marks are understood to stand for. To declare, in a social situation, that 'I wear a Rolex watch, drive a Porsche and wear Armani suits', is to make a statement as to how you wish to be regarded within that social space: either as a 'legitimate' member of the social group addressed; or as importantly, someone who sits outside it. The social significance of any act of purchase turns on the informational content of that act which is influenced by the trade mark owner's advertising and other efforts at communication; actual patterns of consumption; and public discourse. Sometimes these will all act to reinforce one another to produce a single coherent message. At other times they may run counter to one another.

To say that trade mark law is justified so far as it serves the interest of consumers but that the ambivalence inherent in those interests confuses the relationship between form and substance is to acknowledge that there must be some engagement with the theoretical underpinnings of intellectual property law to make sense of the relationship. The final chapter of this book takes aspects of contemporary theories and attempts to relate form to key economic and other justifications commonly advanced in support of intellectual property law.

The most commonly voiced economic justification for both copyright and patent law is that these rights are necessary to address a market failure. Without this form of intervention, so the argument goes, the creative individual risks being unable to recoup the resources invested in arriving at their invention, film, sound recording or whatever because competitors could otherwise be able to free-ride on this investment, by copying the invention and so on, and without the burden of the costs in arriving at it. Under such a view, patents and copyright work by increasing security of expectation. The expectations secured by clear and ascertainable rules provide the degree of security necessary to make what would otherwise be unattractive investments seem worth pursuing.

Certainty of expectation is no less a requirement under 'proprietary' economic justifications, whether based on the social benefits that derive from the efficient management of valuable, scarce and exhaustible resources or on transaction cost economics.

The most frequently advanced economic justification for according rights in trade marks is that they reduce consumer search costs by providing coded but reliable information regarding the source and quality of the goods to which any mark is attached. Like copyright and patents, trade mark rights can be thought of as having a role in managing uncertainty and reducing transaction costs, though the uncertainty here is that facing the consumer who has a choice to make between competing products.

Starting with these economic justifications and the understanding that one way or another intellectual property rights function by reducing some of the uncertainties associated with free and competitive markets, it is easy to get to the assertion that the law must be clear and the scope of rights predictable if that function is not to be compromised. But the law is frequently not certain and the scope of rights not predictable. The understanding that the law must be capable of adapting to varied and changing circumstances exerts a powerful influence and standard-based determinations are commonplace in intellectual property law.

Although one frequently encounters the criticism that some aspect of the law is uncertain, I do not think anyone would seriously argue that an economic justification requires that every component of the intellectual property system must operate so as to reduce uncertainty. To so argue would require us to accept that the overall goal of reducing uncertainty cannot sometimes give way to other principles or policies the demands of which run counter to this overall goal. It is enough that that goal is the product of the sum of the parts.

What is nevertheless quite surprising is just how infrequently rules are encountered in intellectual property law. If the overall goal of patent, copyright and trade mark law is to reduce uncertainty, then what component rules there are must be doing some heavy lifting. The final chapter of this book looks at those rather rare instances where there are rules within the system and the particular contexts over which they exercise control with a view to testing the credibility of the assertion that intellectual property laws enhance security of expectation and thereby change patterns of behaviour.

The efficiency gains of adopting a rule over a standard increase the more frequently a legal command is applied. This is because generally rules are more costly to promulgate as compared to standards but are less costly to administer. Given that all patent applications are subject to formal examination there are considerable efficiency gains in the conditions of grant being rule based. That is certainly true of the requirement that to be patentable a claimed invention must be new. But this is partnered by the requirement that the claimed invention involve an inventive step: a condition that involves a much less rule-like test of compliance. However, as I noted above, the question of whether a claimed invention is obvious is approached with rather less subtlety at the examination stage than it is post grant. At the examination stage the test is coarsened and is more rule-like than when it is applied in a revocation action. This reduction in complexity brings with it savings in the time and cost of examination. These reduced costs mean that applicants are more likely to make use of the patent system over alternative ways of protecting their invention.

No formalities attach to the claiming of copyright in a work. On the face of it the rule-like test that traditionally has been applied in deciding whether a work is original cannot be explained as a means of promoting efficiency in examination. But care must be taken here and thought given not only to what is done but by whom it is done. Asking, 'who decides whether a claimed invention is patentable?', produces the confident answer, 'a patent examiner in the Intellectual Property Office'. And having answered in that way, in answer to the question, 'and who decides whether a copyright work is original?', the temptation is to answer 'no one'. That would be wrong. Although there is no formal examination, this does not mean that the question of originality is not asked and answered. In the first instance it is the author rather than some official who must judge whether his work meets the criteria for legal protection. The question of whether a work is 'original' in the sense of being not copied is one which the author can answer with some confidence both because they know the history of production of a work and because the test is a simple rule which does not require the exercise of any judgement. An author can be as confident of the exclusive rights that they enjoy in their work as the patentee can be of the exclusive rights they enjoy in their invention notwithstanding that the former does not have some official endorsement.

One problem with the way in which copyright works is that it is open to abuse by the dishonest, who may claim to have authored an original work when in fact they have not.[12] Precisely because applications are subject to formal examination, the opportunities for the patent system to be so abused are limited. But making legal rights subject to formal examination brings its own problems. A substantive examination of claimed invention is only possible because inventions can be described concisely and with precision in text.[13] And it is also relatively easy to arrive at a coherent taxonomy of inventions which makes it practical to search for relevant prior art. It is these characteristics that make examination possible but they also make possible the adoption of objective measures of novelty and inventiveness as conditions for legal rights to be claimed. The adoption of these objective measures provides something of a guarantee of public benefit so far as only inventions which advance the

---

[12] More rarely an author may be under a delusion believing that they have produced something original when in fact it was copied, such as where there has been subconscious copying on which see e.g. *Francis Day & Hunter* v *Bron* [1963] Ch 587.

[13] For a fuller account of the development of the patent specification as a means of representing a claimed invention see Chapter 7 in Pottage, A, and Sherman, B, *Figures of Invention. A History of Modern Patent Law* (Oxford University Press, 2010), 127 *et seq.* Indeed, central to Pottage and Sherman's study is the premise that 'representation brings the invention into existence': ibid., 129.

state of the art are given legal protection. For individual inventors, this carries the risk of losing much of the investment made in arriving at something they believe to be a patentable invention but which a formal search and examination reveals to be otherwise. A wise inventor will set out to lessen that risk by undertaking their own search of the relevant prior art before starting out on a costly programme of research and development (R&D).[14] Because the novelty and (pre-grant) obviousness tests are rule-like, the inventor can have confidence that they are working towards something patentable. Form here matters because it encourages investment in inventive activities. Of course, the well-informed inventor will know that securing a patent is no guarantee that it will not be subsequently challenged and revoked for want of novelty or inventiveness. But it is unlikely that the fear of revocation has much of an effect on decisions to invest in R&D given that so few issued patents are ever challenged post-grant.[15]

One consequence of the difference between the pre- and post-grant tests for inventiveness (the pre-grant test being coarser and more rule-like) is that issued patents remain of questionable validity and may if scrutinized by a court be shown to be bad. There are some social costs associated with this. First, and most obviously, because there is publication of a notice of the grant of a patent, granted patents will deter potential competitors from entering a field of endeavour. If the patent is good then this brings the social benefit of discouraging wasteful replication. But if the patent is bad legitimate competition is stifled. However, it will be a rare instance where a competing firm alters its business plan without even entering into a licence negotiation with the patent owner.[16]

Another social cost associated with the uncertain status of issued patents is that this uncertainty has the potential to discourage patent owners from making necessary investment in the commercialization of an invention. But again the net effect of this is likely to be small. Patent

---

[14] Empirical studies suggest that companies indeed search and read patent-relevant literature before undertaking R&D: Graham, S, Merges, R, Samuelson, P and Sichelman, T, 'High Technology Entrepreneurs and the Patent System: Results of the 2008 Berkeley Patent Survey' (2008) 24 Berkeley Technology LJ 1255.

[15] Certainly the ones that are challenged are likely to be the most valuable. But the fact that a particular invention will be a commercial success is something that cannot be reliably predicted at the stage when decisions whether to invest in R&D are made.

[16] Lemley, M, 'Rational Ignorance at the Patent Office' (2001) 95 North Western University L Rev 1495, 1516–17.

applicants do not make decisions in complete ignorance of the prior art and can act to manage the uncertainty associated with this form of legal protection.[17] An applicant can decrease the possibility of a granted patent subsequently being revoked by drafting claims of narrow scope: claims that are less likely to intersect with the prior art. But such claims are also less likely to capture the activities of competitors who set out to work around the legal protection. Claims of wider scope may embrace such activities but at the risk that the claims will be found obvious in light of the prior art. Uncertainty then, as to validity, is positively correlated to the impact that a granted patent has on the activities of third parties. The key point then is that the uncertainty arises because, in patent law as much as in copyright, the realm of duties is the testing ground for claims of right.

In trade mark law the test for assessing whether a sign which is the subject matter of a trade mark application is confusingly similar to an already registered trade mark is more rule-like than the corresponding test for whether a sign used in the course of trade is confusingly similar to a registered trade mark. The rule-like character of the test applied at the examination stage contributes to a lower cost of examination so increasing the likelihood that individuals will make use of the trade mark system rather than alternatives such as the tort of passing off. To the extent that the system of registered trade marks is a more effective means of reducing consumer search costs than these alternatives, it can be said that encouraging businesses to make use of the trade mark system brings a net social benefit.

Whether talking of copyright, patents or trade marks then, the rule-like character of those conditions that must be satisfied if a right is to be claimed is directed at influencing the behaviour of authors, investors and businesses, so encouraging investment in the various species of creativity recognized and at the same time encouraging participation in a system of legal protection designed to channel the benefits of that investment in a way that serves the public interest. In very simple terms, rights are easy to secure but once obtained are uncertain in scope and precarious and are tested by reference to the impact the rights have on third parties.

There are many who are not convinced by the economic arguments used to support intellectual property law and Chapter 6 concludes with a reflection on the relationship between form and certain non-economic justifications that have been advanced in support of intellectual property

---

[17] Applicants will know of the relevant prior art from their own research efforts and from the results of an official search by a patent examiner.

rights. In this I use as a springboard the ideas recently advanced by Robert Merges in his 2011 book *Justifying Intellectual Property*.[18] For me, Merges' argument is chiefly interesting because it relies on seeing a correspondence between form and substance and for this reason provides a useful jumping off point to consider the non-economic justifications more generally. Merges relies heavily on an idiosyncratic reading of the philosophy of Immanuel Kant. In particular, he understands Kant to argue that individuals must have secure rights over things if they are to use things to set and pursue their personal ends. A major criticism that has been levelled at Merges' work is that in this he misrepresents Kant as an originator of liberal individualism.

His argument is founded on the understanding that autonomy in the Kantian sense follows from conceiving of intellectual property as 'a right'. By 'a right' he means a legal guarantee which cannot be overridden by conflicting interests such as those directed to the maximization of social utility. Substituting the word 'right' for 'rule' shows that Merges' argument points to a perceived correspondence between the structures of arguments in the formal dimension in favour of rules and those in the moral dimension in favour of individualism.

Merges' argument is unsupported because intellectual property rights are not 'rights' as he defines these. What guarantees there are provide a false security and the scope of an owner's interest is made concrete and secure only once tested against the conflicting interests of duty bearers. That no amount of effort or investment of personality guarantees exclusive rights over that created presents a considerable difficulty for those who seek to justify intellectual property law as necessary to give effect to certain ethical obligations that society owes to those of its members who have created something, whether as reward for their efforts or because they have invested something of their personality in their creation. Those who see evidence of that are as much duped by the subtleties of the system as authors and inventors.

It should be clear by now that the arguments I advance and analysis I offer will be illustrated by examples almost entirely drawn from the law of the United Kingdom: laws that nowadays are significantly shaped by European and international influences. Until very recently I could have argued that as a common law country at the heart of Europe the UK is particularly suited to provide illuminating examples. But characterizing the UK as being at the heart of Europe seems no longer appropriate in

---

[18] Merges, R, *Justifying Intellectual Property* (Harvard University Press, 2011).

light of its citizens' decision to leave the EU. Nevertheless, the laws of the UK have been significantly influenced by its membership of the Union and, until now, the UK has played a significant part in shaping the directives and regulations that comprise European intellectual property law. That said I have to accept that the narrow jurisdictional focus is a weakness of the analysis presented and without considerable further research, analysis and thought, I would be very reluctant to claim that the arguments I advance apply to other legal systems. Furthermore, although the analysis purports to say something about how intellectual property works, I say very little of the law outside the specific fields of patent, copyright and trade marks.[19] Rather than attempt to be comprehensive in my coverage of the field I have naturally selected materials that I think best support the arguments that I advance. I have also, especially in the second half of the book, focussed on what I see as the core of the subject. A consequence is that I don't doubt that some effort would reveal counter-examples and exceptions. That is hardly surprising given that the common law is a complex patchwork and it is not uncommon to find an outlying decision that does not fit with any particular rationalization of the law.

The book is not specifically directed only to those who already have a considerable knowledge and understanding of intellectual property law and I make no assumptions about the prior knowledge of readers. However, for those readers who count themselves as experts my hope is that this book will cause you to look at familiar material in a new way.

---

[19] The common law has what could be described as an intellectual property effect through the actions of passing off and breach of confidence. I spend some time looking at the tort of passing off below starting at p. 48 and then later at p. 64.

2. Form and legal adjudication

This chapter begins with the most traditional of primary objects: the definition of terms. This is not the main aim of the chapter and serves as an excuse to explore in some detail the ways and means of judicial decision making. Somewhat indirectly then, this chapter also charts instances of the conflict between rules and standards, whether overt or obscure, as that plays out in intellectual property law. There is no attempt to be comprehensive in the sense of trying to identify all instances of tension across the whole field. That would be a mammoth task beyond my capabilities and patience. The chapter thus does no more than hint at the ubiquity of the conflict and the equally ubiquitous and deeper balance struck between certainty and flexibility. I aim to demonstrate that the tension between differing conceptions of legal judgement is central in innumerable disputes about who has the right to appropriate, access and exploit the fruits of the human intellect.[1] Following on then from defining what I mean by the terms 'rule' and 'standard', I set out by way of an analysis of the tort of passing off to show how the common law is well adapted to balance certainty with flexibility. I show how the tort, though grounded in clear principles, nevertheless has been adapted in ways that have allowed it to maintain a contemporary relevance and to accommodate contemporary marketing practices. I go on to explore the mechanisms that allows the law to remain open to change even within a principled framework. Discretion, I observe, typically lies in the weight attached to various factors deemed relevant in a particular determination. Judges faced with a novel development can respond by modifying or adding to the factors that they take into account so ensuring that the law continues to have contemporary relevance. To illustrate the process, I show how the 'prejudices' of the person skilled in the relevant art came to be considered relevant in deciding whether a claimed invention is obvious. How courts approach the question of whether a claimed invention is obvious where that invention is the product of experimentation allows me then to explore the restrictions and flexibilities attached to

[1] Disputes that pit a rule against a standard are extremely common in legal discourse: Schlag, P, 'Rules and Standards' (1985) 33 UCLA L Rev 379, 380.

earlier binding precedents. The evaluative nature of the inductive reasoning employed by courts is illustrated by showing how courts in different jurisdictions with common starting points and common points of reference nevertheless can arrive at different understandings of the law. The chapter then concludes with a consideration of the role that equity plays in allowing decisions to be tailored to match specific circumstances. In the field of intellectual property, equity's influence is most keenly felt in the area of remedies. Through an exploration of injunctive relief, I attempt to show how the need to provide certainty set against a desire to do justice in individual cases compete for influence in judicial decision making.

Throughout intellectual property law important issues are decided by the application of standards. But, the field also has a fair share of rules that, within the scope of their application, provide clear and predictable outcomes. Often disputes over central issues, such as who can claim rights over precisely what, whether a claimed right is infringed, and what defences are available to the alleged infringer, involve adjudicators applying both rules and standards. The conclusion is that intellectual property, as much as any other area of the law, shows evidence of a simultaneous commitment on the part of legislators, administrators and courts both to constrain decision makers to judge particular cases mechanically, by applying rules to readily ascertainable facts, and at the same time to allow decision making by way of informal standards which permit ad hoc situation-sensitive decisions to be taken. The key observation made in this chapter then is not that rules or standards dominate decision making in the field of intellectual property, but that in many if not most disputes, rule-like solutions and standard-based solutions coexist.

The contradictory impulse to resolve particular disputes with a rule or with a standard can be, and indeed often is, accompanied by equally contradictory and finely balanced consequential arguments.[2] There are certain characteristics of rules and standards that can make them seem well- or ill-suited to resolve particular disputes in particular circumstances.[3] Probably the most frequently made assertion is that decision making according to rules is appropriate when certainty, uniformity,

---

[2] Pierre Schlag has argued that this is because the ways of understanding the rules versus standards dispute are located within the bounds of that dispute and thus there is no explanation of the dispute that allows form to be tied to substance: Schlag, above n.1, 381.

[3] The arguments tend to be pretty much the same regardless of the specific issue involved or the area of law involved: ibid., 380.

stability or security are particularly valued. Standards, by contrast, are seen as more appropriate guides where flexibility and dynamism are important.[4] There are other functional characteristics of rules and standards that can be used to add weight to any justification for choosing one over the other in any particular dispute and I shall consider these in a later chapter.[5]

A significant challenge faces any attempt to categorize instances of the rules versus standards conflict across a field as wide as that normally embraced by the term 'intellectual property'. The natural inclination is to approach the mapping exercise by setting boundaries around sub-sets of the whole. For instance, I could aim to chart instances of the conflict in defining the subject matter that can be protected; and then in defining the scope of rights; and in the application of defences and exceptions; and so on and so forth. Whilst convenient for the purpose of explanation this would be a hopelessly artificial division. In the first place, such boundaries are more or less leaky in ways that vary according to the rights being discussed. So for instance, whilst such a classification might work well enough for patents, as I shall show in Chapter 4, it is impossible independently to discuss subsistence and infringement in considering a claim to copyright whilst the grounds on which a registered trade mark can be infringed correspond to the relative grounds for refusing the registration of a sign.

But the greater and more significant difficulty is in avoiding the artefact in the analysis that is inherent in any such categorization. The problem arises because the certainty of a rule depends on the context over which it is said to exercise control.[6] For instance, since the *Libertel* decision,[7] applicants seeking to register a colour as a trade mark have been required to describe the colour by reference to a standard international code.[8] As is often the case, this rule is justified as a means of promoting certainty. Thus, in arriving at this rule, the European Court observed that merely reproducing on paper the colour in question is not a

---

[4] Kennedy, D, 'Form and Substance in Private Law Adjudication' (1976) 89 Harvard L Rev 1685, 1687–9; and Schlag, above n.1, 400.

[5] For instances see Kelman, M, *A Guide to Critical Legal Studies* (Harvard University Press, 1987), 43–5.

[6] Schlag, above n.1, 407. Of course this observation applies not only to certainty but the other consequential characteristics of rules.

[7] C-104/01 *Libertel Groep BV* v *Benelux-Merkenbureau* [2003] ETMR 63.

[8] Bently, L and Sherman, B, *Intellectual Property Law*, 4th edition (Oxford University Press, 2014), 894.

form of graphic representation that is sufficiently 'clear, precise, self-contained, easily accessible, intelligible, durable and objective'.[9] But how far this demand actually contributes to certainty by allowing other traders to know where the boundary of the protected territory lies may be questioned given that infringement of registered marks turns on whether the alleged infringing sign is confusingly similar to that which is registered. From a consumer's perspective, an indeterminable range of colours are likely to be considered confusingly similar to the registered mark no matter that this is represented objectively and with precision on the register.[10] This is one manifestation of a common feature of intellectual property law: that the tests surrounding infringement claims tend to be more fact and situation sensitive than the tests that determine claims to rights.

Where necessary then I shall cross borders and explore multiple territories so as to avoid the artefacts created by any particular classificatory scheme. At the same time, adopting too broad a perspective risks oversight of an important dimension of the conflict between rules and standards. Courts are called upon to decide questions relating to the specific facts and laws applicable to the dispute before them. As is relevant to a consideration of form,[11] the context of actual adjudication is

---

[9] C-104/01 *Libertel Groep BV* v *Benelux-Merkenbureau* [2003] ETMR 63 [68].

[10] As observed by Burrell and Handler, although it is partly true that the requirement of graphic representation performs a definitional function, the 'assertion that it is the representation of the sign on the register that determines the scope of the property is deeply problematic' because 'infringement of a registered trade mark is not confined to use of a mark identical to that which is registered, nor even to a mark which has been colourably altered. Rather, infringement extends to the use of a "similar" mark': Burrell, R and Handler, M, 'Making Sense of Trade Mark Law' (2003) IPQ 388, 398 and 405. See also Davis, J, 'Between a Sign and a Brand: Mapping the Boundaries of a Registered Trade Mark in European Union Trade Mark Law' in Bently, L, Davis, J and Ginsburg, J (eds) *Trade Marks and Brands: An Interdisciplinary Critique* (Cambridge University Press, 2008), 90.

[11] Of course courts, especially appellate courts, will often widen their field of view so as to compare the social and/or economic consequences of the alternative interpretations of the law that they are being invited to consider, for instance the decision of the Supreme Court in *Human Genome Sciences Inc* v *Eli Lilly & Co* [2011] UKSC 51 considered below at p. 107. Lord Neuberger has admitted extra judicially to a discomfort about making that decision precisely because there 'was a great deal of commercial and public interest policy, as opposed to legal principle, in the issue of when a chemical should be patentable on the ground that it has therapeutic potential': Lord Neuberger, 'Intellectual

relatively narrow and largely framed by the arguments advanced by the disputants in court. In the field of intellectual property the importance of context is all the greater because decision making is often undertaken by different adjudicative bodies, each with its own defined set of competencies and policy concerns. In the case of registered rights such as patents, trade marks and designs, the initial determination as to whether what is claimed is eligible for protection is typically made by an administrative agency though subject to *ex post* review by courts. Once secured by registration, the scope of the rights and of any defences to claims of infringement, as well as matters such as ownership and transfer fall to be decided by courts. The pattern of distribution of decision making competence has an added facet in the European patent system where it is the European Patent Office that decides whether a claimed invention is patentable under the terms of the EPC but it is national courts which decide whether granted European patents are infringed.[12]

In this preliminary review of the significance of form in intellectual property law then, I shall adopt, as the primary restraint on context, the context of adjudication. One great advantage of so doing is that this context lends itself to Wesley Hohfeld's scheme of analysing rights in terms of the correlative proposition about duty that they entail.[13] Hohfeld's mode of analysis is particularly seductive so far as intellectual property rights are concerned.[14] Most students of the subject learn early on that intellectual property rights are negative in character – the exercise of control over the defined territory is effected by way only of a legal right to exclude others. Given its negative character, intellectual property law can perhaps best be seen as creating a scheme of duties rather than a scheme of rights. Hohfeld understood that a property owner's right to

---

Property in the United Kingdom and Europe' (2014) 36 EIPR 693, 696. E W Thomas, a former judge of the New Zealand Court of Appeal, has asserted that in the process of making law judges frequently formulate public policy: Thomas, E, *The Judicial Process. Realism, Pragmatism, Practical Reasoning and Principles* (Cambridge University Press, 2005), 4–6.

[12] Under the unitary patent, post-grant matters, such as infringement and revocation will be dealt with by a Unified Patent Court which will have both first instance and appellate divisions. The future of the unitary patent is in doubt in light of the UK's probable exit from the European Union.

[13] Hohfeld, W, 'Fundamental Legal Conceptions as Applied in Judicial Reasoning' (1913) 23 Yale LJ 16. As suggested by the full title of Hohfeld's work, he derived this thesis from an analysis of case law.

[14] For instance see Waldron, J, 'From Authors to Copiers: Individual Rights and Social Values in Intellectual Property' (1992–93) 68 Chicago-Kent L Rev 841; and Drahos, P, *A Philosophy of Intellectual Property* (Ashgate, 1996).

exclude others from a particular territory entails that these others have a duty not to use or occupy that territory without the owner's permission. The owner has a legal right to initiate proceedings aimed at having trespassers removed from or prevented from using the protected territory and officials have a duty to respond to these proceedings. Like all property, intellectual property can be seen as primarily facilitative. It provides a legal framework that supports the achievement of personal goals. But this primary theme of facilitation is frequently accompanied by a counter theme of inhibition. Inevitable conflicts arise between interested parties and, as has been observed in relation to land, these conflicts create a tension between facilitation and inhibition. It is in that tension that most of the difficulties of property law arise.[15]

Furthermore, because of their position and function within the common law, courts are uniquely positioned to exploit form in their decision making. Judges must do justice according to law. This is how judges in a developed legal system are expected to operate.[16] To say that courts sometimes create law rather than merely interpret it is nowadays a trite observation.[17] More interesting from my perspective is to consider the controlling mechanisms that on the one hand restrain and on the other liberate judicial decision making. This in turn invites a more detailed reflection on what is meant by 'a rule' and what by 'a standard'.

As between rules and standards, rules are the easier to comprehend. Cass Sunstein defines an ideal rule as a provision which provides a complete, or nearly complete, before-the-fact specification of legal outcome.[18] To similar effect, Ronald Dworkin observes that if the facts a rule stipulates are given and the rule is valid then the answer it supplies

---

[15] Birks, P, 'Before We Begin: Five Keys to Land Law' in Bright, S and Dewar, J (eds) *Land Law: Themes and Perspectives* (Oxford University Press, 1998), 461.

[16] See e.g. MacCormick, N, *Legal Reasoning and Legal Theory* (Clarendon Press, 1978), 17.

[17] As E W Thomas, a former judge in the New Zealand Court of Appeal puts it,

> [n]one, other than the uninitiated who seemingly lack an understanding of the dynamic of the common law, seriously question the fact that judges make law. The belief that judges do not make law is hopelessly out of date. As Lord Reid famously said as long ago as 1972: 'We do not believe in fairy-tales anymore'.

Thomas, above n.11, 3.

[18] Sunstein, C, *Legal Reasoning and Political Conflict* (Oxford University Press, 1996), 22.

must be accepted.[19] In application, this requires that courts reach decisions (conclusions) by way of a deductive argument in which the major premise is the rule and the minor premise findings of fact:

> The law says that in circumstances X there must be the consequence Y;
>
> The evidence proves that circumstances X have [have not] occurred;
>
> Therefore I must order that Y is [is not] to happen.

At its simplest, the court process is concerned with establishing, on a balance of probabilities, what the relevant facts are. That done it is a simple matter of stating the 'inevitable' outcome dictated by deductive logic. The judge is compelled by her duty to do justice according to law to reason in this way.[20] Thus, however desirable a judge believes a given ruling might be, it cannot be adopted where to do so would contradict a valid and binding rule of the system. For instance, if a statutory provision clearly covers the situation before a judge and demands a particular outcome based on certain facts being proved then, if the evidence shows that on the balance of probabilities those facts must be taken to be true, the judge has no choice but to follow the statute no matter that she may feel that the consequences of so doing are not desirable either because such a decision will frustrate the pursuit of some general policy which she believes worthwhile or because the compelled decision offends against her perception of what justice demands given the particular

---

[19] Dworkin, R, *Taking Rights Seriously* (Harvard University Press, 1977), 24. How effective a rule is in achieving these ends will turn on the words used to express the intention. As observed by Colin Diver, a rational rulemaker will first,

> want to use words with well-defined and universally accepted meanings within the relevant community … Second, the rulemaker will want his rule to be 'accessible' to its intended audience – that is, applicable to concrete situations without excessive difficulty or effort. Finally, of course, a policy-maker will care about whether the substantive content of the message communicated in his words produces the desired behaviour.

Diver, C, 'The Optimal Precision of Administrative Rules' (1983) 93 Yale LJ 65, 67.

[20] MacCormick refers to this as the requirement of consistency: MacCormick, above n.16, 106. An emphasis on deductive syllogistic reasoning is arguably a key feature of the view of law as 'legal science' and with this the belief that law enjoys an existence which is separate and apart from the political process out of which it arose: Lundmark, T, 'Legal Science and European Harmonisation' (2014) 130 LQR 68, 73.

circumstances of the case in issue.[21] In *Conor Medsystems Inc* v *Angiotech Pharmaceuticals Inc*, Jacob LJ gave the following example of this principle in operation:

> There are old or obvious ideas which take a lot of work, expense and time to develop and turn into something practical and successful. Without the incentive of a monopoly, people may not do that work or spend the time and money. The Fosamax case … is an example of an obvious invention which cost lots to bring to market. But patent law provided no protection for all that investment because the basic invention was obvious. The courts' job is not, however, to uphold any claim to a monopoly for an idea which requires investment and risk to bring to market, only those for ideas which are new, non-obvious and enabled.[22]

What then is the source of valid binding rules? Neil MacCormick identifies legislation as par excellence the process whereby valid rules of law are made,[23] justifying this assertion by observing that legislation is unique in yielding rules in fixed verbal form which have a single and uniquely authoritative formulation and because, in the case of legislation, there are precise criteria of validity which make it possible to distinguish reasonably clearly what is, from what is not, duly enacted law.[24] The great value in MacCormick's observation is that it identifies two distinct elements of a rule: a rule must be both formulated as a rule; and it must be recognized as binding by the court applying it. Flexibility in decision making is possible not only through the more obvious mechanism of wording legal directions in ways that admit discretion, but also in the ways in which courts understand themselves to be bound to follow a particular legal direction.

Legislative provisions must be formulated as rules if they are to operate as such.[25] Deliberately or otherwise, many statutory provisions are drafted using imprecise language such that, without more, they

---

21 Schauer, F, *Thinking Like a Lawyer. A New Introduction to Legal Reasoning* (Harvard University Press, 2009), 18. Later Schauer observes that 'conflicts between the outcome that the words of a rule indicate and the outcome indicated by the rationale behind the rule are ubiquitous': ibid., 24.

22 [2007] EWCA Civ 5 [50].

23 MacCormick, above n.16, 57. Whether the legislation is the only source of rules is another matter. Cass Sunstein for instance clearly thought that courts (certainly higher courts) could create binding rules: Sunstein, C, 'Problems with Rules' (1995) 83 California L Rev 953, 973.

24 MacCormick, above n.16, 58.

25 'The principle feature of rules – and the feature that makes them rules – is that what the rule *says* really matters': Schauer, above n.21, 17–18.

cannot function as rules because they lack the necessary precision to provide a complete before-the-fact specification of outcome.[26] Indeed it has been argued that absolute precision in the drafting of rules is never possible.[27] Certainly it is true that all words require some interpretation to be justiciable. To say that a claimed invention must be 'new' if it is to be patentable requires a judge to have some conception of novelty before that condition can be applied. Legislation may be so drafted with the intention of reducing the scope of possible constructions. In the case of the requirement that a claimed invention is new for instance, the Patents Act provides that 'an invention shall be taken to be new if it does not form part of the state of the art'.[28] Of itself, that legislative provision does little more than direct judges to compare what is claimed (the invention) with what is known (the state of the art). But the legislation then goes on to specify in considerable detail what must and what must not be included in the state of the art.[29] The precision with which the legislation embodying the requirement that a claimed invention be new is drafted makes this, I would argue, as 'rule-like' as it is possible for any legal direction to be.

Legislative provisions do not always provide such precise direction. In the following chapter I will explore in some detail the power relationship between the judiciary and the legislature and how this is mediated through the language of legislation. For the moment it is enough to make the superficial observation that the more detailed a legislative provision, the less flexibility judges have in applying it and, by the same token, imprecision of statutory language creates opportunities for varied interpretation.[30]

---

26 Schauer gives some examples: ibid., 188–9.

27 Sunstein, above n.23, 984–5.

28 Section 2(1) Patents Act 1977.

29 Sections 2(2)–(4) Patents Act 1977.

30 Thus calls to simplify copyright legislation in response to rapid technological change are in effect calls to increase the opportunities for judges to be flexible in deciding what should fall to be protected by copyright. For instance, Andrew Christie has argued that the development in and the convergence of the information technologies has reached a stage that it is no longer helpful to treat every copyright subject matter as being one of the various classes of work identified within the copyright legislation and has called for abolition of the classification of works altogether: Christie, A, 'Reconceptualising Copyright in the Digital Era' (1995) 17 EIPR 522, 525; and Christie, A, 'A Proposal for Simplifying United Kingdom Copyright Law' (2001) 23 EIPR 26, 28–30. There is some evidence that the Court of Justice of the European Union (CJEU) believes that a harmonized European copyright law demands the abandonment of

Comparing and contrasting the statutory demand that a claimed invention be new with the requirement that, to be patentable, a claimed invention must also involve an inventive step provides an illustration. The statute provides that a claimed invention shall be taken to involve an inventive step if it is not obvious to a person skilled in the art having regard to any matter which forms part of the state of the art.[31] Although the Act says something more about what is to be included in 'the state of the art' it says nothing more on the content of the test of obviousness. Whether a claimed invention is obvious has been said to be a question of fact: 'a kind of jury question',[32] a feature it shares with the test for whether a claimed invention is new. But to describe both tests as involving findings of fact disguises an important difference. As observed by Viscount Simonds in *Benmax* v *Austin Motor Co Ltd*, a so-called finding of fact involves two distinct stages:

> some confusion may have arisen from failure to distinguish between the finding of a specific fact and a finding of fact which is really an inference from facts specifically found, or, as it has sometimes been said, between the perception and evaluation of facts. An example of this distinction may be seen in any case in which a plaintiff alleges negligence on the part of the defendant. Here it must first be determined what the defendant in fact did and, secondly, whether what he did amounted in the circumstances (which must also so far as relevant be found as specific facts) to negligence … A judge sitting without a jury would fall short of his duty if he did not first find the facts and then draw from them the inference of fact whether or not the defendant had been negligent. This is a simple illustration of a process in which it may often be difficult to say what is simple fact and what is inference from fact, or, to repeat what I have said, what is perception, what evaluation.[33]

Adopting this language, then what is contained in the prior art and what an inventor claims are 'simple facts' are each only a matter of perception. But whether a claimed invention is new and whether it involves an inventive step requires an inference from fact. The language adopted by courts in describing the assessment of novelty indicates that the inference necessary is one requiring little evaluation. In one common formulation,

---

the classic copyright categories in 1988 Act in favour of a more fluid conception of protectable work on which see below at p. 161.

[31] Section 3 Patents Act 1977.

[32] Lord Hoffmann in *Biogen Inc* v *Medeva Plc* [1997] RPC 1, 45 citing Jenkins LJ in *Allmanna Svenska Elektriska A/B* v *The Burntisland Shipbuilding Co Ltd* (1952) 69 RPC 63, 70.

[33] *Benmax* v *Austin Motor Co Ltd* [1955] AC 370, 373–4.

an attack on the claimed novelty of an invention will succeed if the prior art contains, 'clear and unmistakeable', directions to do what the patentee claims.[34] By contrast, a judge faced with deciding whether a claimed invention involves an inventive step cannot apply the mandated test mechanically. Rather the judge has discretion in the sense that the vagueness of the statutory direction (that, seen through the eyes of the skilled technician, what is claimed must not be an obvious step to take given what is publicly known) means she must exercise judgement in arriving at the decision. Saying that she has discretion does not mean that the judge is entirely free to decide as she pleases. Discretion, as observed by Ronald Dworkin, is 'like the hole in a doughnut' in that it does not exist except as an area left open by a surrounding belt of restriction.[35] But some doughnut holes are bigger than others.[36]

A tentative preliminary conclusion then is that whilst the definitional line between rules and standards is not pristine, 'a standard' can be said to differ from 'a rule' in the degree of discretion required of the decision maker in making inferences from fact. Other commentators have suggested that standards have a more distinct character. Duncan Kennedy, for instance, sees rules and standards as at opposite poles and defines a standard as referring directly to, 'one of the substantive objectives of the legal order … The application of a standard requires the judge both to

---

[34] Parker J in *Flour Oxidising* v *Carr* (1908) 25 RPC 428, 457. To similar effect, the *Guidelines for Examination in the European Patent Office* provide that, '[a] document takes away the novelty of any claimed subject matter derivable directly and unambiguously from that document including any features implicit to a person skilled in the art in what is expressly mentioned in the document': *Guidelines for Examination in the EPO*, Part G, Chapter VI, para.2, accessed 20 January 2017 at http://www.epo.org/law-practice/legal-texts/guidelines.html.

[35] Dworkin, above n.19, 31 but c.f. Cass Sunstein who is prepared to accept the notion of 'untrammelled discretion' though he accepts this is rare: Sunstein, above n.23, 960.

[36] Dworkin notes that there is an ambiguity in the concept of discretion and distinguishes between discretion in a 'weak sense' to describe the situation where the standards an official must apply cannot be applied mechanically and in a 'strong sense' to describe a situation where an official is not bound by standards set by the authority: Dworkin, above n.19, 31–4 and 69. I am not entirely convinced that there is such a sharp distinction at least not in the way courts operate under the common law, but in any event for the purposes of my immediate argument the distinction does not matter.

discover the facts of a particular situation and to assess them in terms of the purposes or social values embodied in the standard'.[37]

Though using different terms, Kennedy in talking of the 'discovery' and 'assessment' of facts clearly has in mind the difference between the finding of a specific fact and an inference from facts specifically found. As I have already noted, those two steps are common to any application of a legal direction (whether rules or standard). What Kennedy seems to be suggesting, however, is that standards differ from rules in that the former invite an evaluation in light of the purposes (or social values) embodied in the standard. This is another way of saying that a standard is a legal direction that is binding as to its purpose.

That is a problematic definition chiefly because it does not help to explain how it is that a standard demands that a decision maker exercise discretion in a way that is not demanded under a rule. If a legal provision's purpose is clear and the provision is read in light of that purpose, then the provision will be read as a rule. If, however, that purpose can only be expressed in vague terms, then courts must necessarily exercise discretion in deciding on its application. Consider in this regard the comments of Oliver LJ in *Windsurfing International Inc* v *Tabur Marine (Great Britain) Ltd*:

> the notion behind anticipation is, as we understand it, that it would be wrong to enable the patentee to prevent a man from doing what he has lawfully done before the patent was granted. No doubt, the philosophy behind [the requirement of inventiveness] is different to this extent, that a patent is granted only for an invention and that which is obvious is not inventive, but it also must, we think, take into account the same concept as anticipation, namely that it would be wrong to prevent a man from doing something which is merely an obvious extension of what he has been doing or of what was known in the art before the priority date of the patent granted ...[38]

Imagine a patent law where the only condition of grant was such as this: 'a patent will be granted for an invention where it is right to do so'. A tribunal called upon to apply this provision might well arrive at similar conclusions to those of the Court of Appeal in *Windsurfing* as to the rights and wrongs of allowing a patent to be granted. And if they did so they would arrive at a test for inventiveness that required discretion (in deciding what is or is not obvious) but a test of novelty that was much more rule-like. To say that it would be wrong to enable the patentee to

---

[37] Kennedy, above n.4, 1688.

[38] Per Oliver LJ in *Windsurfing International Inc* v *Tabur Marine (Great Britain) Ltd* [1985] RPC 59, 75.

prevent a man from doing what he has lawfully done before the patent was granted would inevitably lead the court to a test of novelty as rule-like as that which exists under the actual law. Although it might differ in detail, it would be impossible to escape the conclusion that if the prior art contained a disclosure that enabled someone skilled in the art to perform what was claimed, then a patent should be refused because the claimed invention was anticipated.

To understand the difference between rules and standards in terms of allowable discretion in decision making, there is I think more profit in the classification of legal directions adopted by Cass Sunstein. Sunstein contrasts rule-bound procedures with approaches that allow particular judgements to emerge through the decision maker's assessment and weighing of a number of relevant factors.[39] Where this is the case, he observes, the decision maker cannot simply apply the law to the perceived facts. There might be discretion in deciding which factors to take into account, in how to interpret each factor and most of all in the relative weight to attach to each factor in arriving at the decision.

Certainly this understanding of the basis of discretion finds support in certain dicta of our most senior judges. Lord Hoffmann for instance, in *Designer Guild Ltd* v *Russell Williams (Textiles) Ltd*, reflected on the nature of the test determining whether copyright has been infringed by a partial taking of a work. Noting that the question of whether a defendant has copied a *substantial* part of a claimant's work was one of impression, Lord Hoffmann went on:

> When judges say that a question is one of impression, they generally mean that it involves taking into account a number of factors of varying degrees of importance and deciding whether they are sufficient to bring the whole within some legal description. It is often difficult to give precise reasons for arriving at a conclusion one way or the other (apart from an enumeration of the relevant factors) and there are borderline cases over which reasonable minds may differ.[40]

---

[39] Sunstein, above n.23, 963–4. For a similar approach see also Ehrlich, I and Posner, R, 'An Economic Analysis of Legal Rulemaking' (1974) 3 J Legal Stud 257, 258.

[40] *Designer Guild Ltd* v *Russell Williams (Textiles) Ltd* [2001] FSR 113, 119. See also Caddick, N, Davies, G and Harbottle, G, *Copinger and Skone James on Copyright*, 17th edition (Sweet & Maxwell, 2016), at section 7-52 (the test, 'is often a matter of impression, in the sense that it generally involves taking into account a number of factors of varying degrees of importance and deciding whether they are sufficient to bring the whole within the legal description of "substantial part"').

And to similar effect, in *Conor Medsystems Inc* v *Angiotech Pharmaceuticals Inc*[41] Lord Hoffmann approved the following statement by Kitchin J in *Generics (UK) Ltd* v *Lundbeck A/S*:

> The question of obviousness must be considered on the facts of each case. The court must consider the weight to be attached to any particular factor in the light of all the relevant circumstances. These may include such matters as the motive to find a solution to the problem the patent addresses, the number and extent of the possible avenues of research, the effort involved in pursuing them and the expectation of success.[42]

Sunstein argues that 'standards' are a separate category again, which share with factors a refusal to specify outcomes in advance, but which depart from factors in refusing to enumerate considerations that are relevant in particular applications.[43] How far that distinction stands up in a common law system is questionable. By way of illustration, compare two uses of the condition that something be 'fair' as it applies in two different intellectual property statutes. Sunstein's distinction between 'factors' and 'standards' looks credible on a superficial reading of the legislative provisions. Under section 40 Patents Act 1977, employee inventors are entitled to 'compensation' for certain inventions. The amount of the award is determined under section 41 which provides that compensation will be such as to secure for the employee *a fair share* of the benefit which the employer has derived. The section goes on to specify a list of relevant factors that must go into the determination of what amounts to a 'fair share', directing that the court or the comptroller shall, among other things, take the following matters into account:

> (a) the nature of the employee's duties, his remuneration and the other advantages he derives or has derived from his employment or has derived in relation to the invention under this Act;
> (b) the effort and skill which the employee has devoted to making the invention;
> (c) the effort and skill which any other person has devoted to making the invention jointly with the employee concerned, and the advice and other

---

41 [2008] UKHL 49 [42].

42 [2007] RPC 32 [72] and followed by Floyd J in *Omnipharm* v *Merial* who stated that the question as to whether a claimed invention was obvious was to be answered by reference to the non-exhaustive list of factors identified by Kitchin J: [2011] EWHC 3393 (Pat) [92].

43 Sunstein, above n.23, 965. Dworkin seems to point to a similar distinction in pointing out the difference between the concept of 'fair' and conceptions of 'fair': Dworkin, above n.19, 135–6.

assistance contributed by any other employee who is not a joint inventor of the invention; and

(d) the contribution made by the employer to the making, developing and working of the invention by the provision of advice, facilities and other assistance, by the provision of opportunities and by his managerial and commercial skill and activities.[44]

Although this list is not exhaustive, section 41 Patent Act is a clear instance of the decision maker being directed to assess and weigh a number of relevant factors in arriving at a judgement as to what, in the circumstances, is 'fair'. In this respect it can be contrasted with the statutory defences to copyright based on the 'fair dealing' with a work. Under UK copyright law, the 'fair dealing' with a work is permitted so far as it relates to certain specified purposes. What amounts to 'fair dealing' is not defined by the legislation and courts accordingly would seem to have a considerable discretion in arriving at a decision as to what is or is not fair. This then, in Sunstein's terminology, is an instance of a 'standard'. However, this would be to overlook how appellate courts have sought to guide lower courts in the application of the test. In what is the most recent and comprehensive consideration of the defence, the Court of Appeal in *Ashdown* v *Telegraph Group* enumerated the following relevant considerations themselves drawn from earlier cases:

> It is impossible to lay down any hard-and-fast definition of what is fair dealing, for it is a matter of fact, degree and impression. However, by far the most important factor is whether the alleged fair dealing is in fact commercially competing with the proprietor's exploitation of the copyright work, a substitute for the probable purchase of authorised copies, and the like. If it is, the fair dealing defence will almost certainly fail ... The second most important factor is whether the work has already been published or otherwise exposed to the public. If it has not, and especially if the material has been obtained by a breach of confidence or other mean or underhand dealing, the courts will be reluctant to say this is fair ... The third most important factor is the amount and importance of the work that has been taken ... in some circumstances the taking of an excessive amount, or the taking of even a small amount if on a regular basis, would negative fair dealing.[45]

---

44 Section 41(4) Patents Act 1977 which applies only to determining the fair share of the benefit to be secured for an employee in respect of an invention which has always belonged to an employer. Section 41(5) lists a different set of factors that are to be used in determining the fair share of the benefit to be secured for an employee in respect of an invention which originally belonged to her.

45 *Ashdown* v *Telegraph Group* [2001] EWCA Civ 1142.

In operation then, both section 41 Patents Act 1977 and the fair dealing provisions of the Copyright, Designs and Patents Act 1988 allow judgements to emerge through the decision maker's assessment and weighing of a number of relevant factors. It seems to me that it creates a false impression of the difference between the two provisions to adopt Sunstein's terminology and label only the latter as a 'standard'.[46] In the case of section 41 and the fair dealing provisions, courts have discretion both in weighing of factors and, since in neither case is it provided that the list is exhaustive, in the recognition of factors.

Ronald Dworkin suggests a further way of categorizing legal directions. Dworkin draws an essential distinction between rules on the one hand, and principles and policies on the other. A principle, he says, is observed because, 'it is a requirement of justice, fairness or some other dimension of morality'.[47] He distinguishes these from 'policies' which, he says, set out a goal to be reached and which are thus observed because they advance or secure an economic, political or social situation deemed desirable.[48] What Dworkin labels as policies would seem to be what Duncan Kennedy had in mind when he said that a characteristic of a standard referred, 'directly to one of the substantive objectives of the legal order'. Indeed Kennedy might also have intended to embrace within his conception of standards 'principles' since, as Dworkin observes, the distinction between policies and principles can be collapsed by construing a principle as stating a social goal or by construing a policy as stating a principle.[49] However, Dworkin does that which Kennedy does not and goes on to explain how they differ from rules in the restrictions they place on decision making.[50] Principles and policies, as defined and unlike

---

[46] Sunstein seems, however, to have thought that the standard-like character of a legal provision (as he defined that) would be 'transient' and interpretive practices would lead to the provision being understood as a rule or may instead be interpreted as requiring the enumeration of a set of factors: Sunstein, above n.23, 965.

[47] Dworkin, above n.19, 22.

[48] Ibid. He notes that the distinction can be collapsed by construing a principle as stating a social goal or by construing a policy as stating a principle but that the distinction has uses which are lost if so collapsed: ibid., 23. For a further classification and commentary see Lamond, G, 'Analogical Reasoning in the Common Law' (2014) 34(3) OJLS 567–584 and for a criticism of the distinction, Thomas, above n.11, 195–201.

[49] Dworkin, above n.19, 22–3. Later he says: 'principles are propositions that describe rights; policies are propositions that describe goals': ibid., 90.

[50] The contrast between Dworkin's ideas in this respect, and those of the scholars allied to the critical legal studies movement (including of course Duncan

rules, he observes, have the dimension of weight. Thus, where conflicting principles intersect, a decision must take into account the relative weight of each.[51]

To this extent Dworkin's analysis is similar to Sunstein's in that both understand the discretion exercisable by decision makers is in according differing weights to relevant but competing considerations. The examples drawn from the field of intellectual property given above suggest a way of understanding the relationships at play here. I would suggest that a principle, such as 'fairness', is contextualized through the adoption of relevant factors. So whilst in a sense both of the examples given are instances where the principle of fairness is applied, the content of that principle is different and matched to the specific context (e.g. whether it is 'fair' that a defendant should escape liability for copyright infringement or what is a 'fair' amount of compensation that should be paid by an employer to an employee who has devised an outstanding invention) by the identification of differing contextually relevant factors. The dimension of weight is a consequence of principles being given effect by taking into account a number of factors which themselves will vary in importance according to the circumstances in issue. Within each principle then, different factors compete for influence in deciding if and then how that principle is to be applied in the circumstances. When different principles come into conflict, the constituent factors of each compete for influence in deciding which of those principles carries more weight in the circumstances. The upshot of all this is that I think for the purposes of my analysis no great harm is done if, as a matter of convenience, I now refer only to 'standards', accepting that in other contexts the same thing might be better described as a 'principle', 'policy' or 'multi-factorial issue'.

Remaining is the question of how a judge, called upon to apply a particular standard, is to decide upon the relevant factors where these have not been comprehensively spelt out. Insight here requires us to consider the paradoxical feature of standards: that they allow discretion whilst still binding decision makers. As noted above, discretion does not exist except as an area left open by a surrounding belt of restriction.[52] Thus it is that one sense in which the term 'discretion' is used is to describe the situation where some official in a hierarchy has final authority to make a decision which cannot be reviewed and reversed by

---

Kennedy) is explored more fully in: Hunt, A, 'The Theory of Critical Legal Studies' (1986) 6 OJLS 1, 21–2.

[51] Dworkin, above n.19, 26.

[52] See above at p 35

another official positioned higher up in the line of authority.[53] This matters to us because it has long been the case that a judge's findings of primary fact, particularly if founded upon an assessment of the credibility of witnesses, have been treated as 'unassailable' on appeal. Appellate courts have been slightly more willing to differ from the judge's *evaluation* of those facts by reference to some legal standard such as obviousness but this is approached extremely conservatively.[54] Lord Hoffmann, for instance, has expressed the view that, 'where the application of a legal standard such as negligence or obviousness involves no question of principle but is simply a matter of degree, an appellate court should be very cautious in differing from the judge's evaluation'.[55]

The current position then is that appellate courts will be reticent to hear an appeal from a decision based on an evaluation of facts unless it can be shown that the lower court's decision was founded on an error of principle. So for instance, an assertion that in the assessment of obviousness a judge was simply wrong or had wrongly evaluated the evidence cannot then form the basis of a successful appeal.[56] In copyright law, appellate courts are reticent to reverse the finding of a trial judge as to whether a defendant has copied a substantial part of a claimant's work[57] and an appeal cannot succeed if it is grounded merely in the hope that the

---

53 Dworkin, above n.19, 32. See also Davis, K, *Discretionary Justice. A Preliminary Inquiry* (Louisiana State University Press, 1969), 54–5.

54 *Benmax* v *Austin Motor Co Ltd* [1955] AC 370, 373–4. See also *Okotoks Ltd (Formerly Spicerhaart Ltd)* v *Fine & Country Ltd* [2013] EWCA Civ 672 [51]–[52].

55 Per Lord Hoffmann in *Biogen Inc* v *Medeva Plc* [1997] RPC 1, 45. Outside the area of intellectual property law Lord Hoffmann has expressed the view that whether one characterizes an evaluation as a question of fact depends, 'upon whether as a matter of policy one thinks that it is a decision which an appellate body with jurisdiction limited to errors of law should be able to review': *Lawson* v *Serco* [2006] ICR 250 [34], discussed and applied by the Supreme Court in *Jones (by Caldwell)* v *First Tier Tribunal, Criminal Injuries Compensation Authority* [2013] UKSC 19.

56 This is so even if the judges in the Court of Appeal felt that they might themselves have reached the opposite conclusion: *SEB SA* v *De'Longhi SpA* [2003] EWCA Civ 952; and *Merck's Patents* [2003] EWCA Civ 1545. In the latter case Buxton LJ held that seeking to challenge a trial judge's conclusions on obviousness, the grounds of appeal should contain a statement of the principle that the judge is said to have infringed and that, 'it should further be demonstrated, unless the matter is self-evident, what is the authority for that principle': [2003] EWCA Civ 1545 [70].

57 This being understood to be a question of fact and degree: *Norowzian* v *Arks Ltd* (No. 2) [2000] FSR 363, 368. See also the observations of Lord

impression formed by appeal court judges will be different from that of the trial judge. Again, for an appeal to succeed there must have been a demonstrable error of principle.[58]

What then is an error of principle? I suppose that such an error must include adopting completely the wrong principle. But statements such as, 'a patent will only be granted when it is fair to do so'; or, 'copyright is only infringed by the negligent copying of a work', are likely to feature only in the exam scripts of the hopelessly confused student. Such errors will be incredibly rare in judgements since the offending judge would have to be both a dolt and deaf to the arguments of counsel to err in this way.[59] It might be thought that a judge has gone wrong in attaching too little or too much weight to a particular factor in her evaluation but, as noted above, typically the weight to be attached to a factor, as a matter of degree, is one that falls within the scope of acceptable judicial discretion and cannot then count as an error of principle.

What then is left? A great part of the difficulty in pinning down what an error of principle is when it comes to decisions made under standards is that the reasoning put forward by a judge for a particular outcome will typically lack the clarity and precision of deductive argument. As Lord Hoffmann observed in *Designer Guild Ltd* v *Russell Williams (Textiles) Ltd*, in matters of impression, a judge will be able to do little more than enumerate the factors that she took to be relevant by way of reasons for her decision. The enumeration of factors then is the hunting grounds for errors of principle: has the judge erred by taking account of factors that she should not have included in her reasoning; or has she entirely disregarded a relevant factor?[60]

What a word like 'fair' does is make the application of the legal provision containing it depend to some extent upon principles lying

---

Hoffmann and Lord Scott in *Designer Guild Ltd* v *Russell Williams (Textiles) Ltd* [2001] FSR 113 [29] and [77]–[78] respectively.

[58] *Norowzian* v *Arks Ltd* (No. 2) [2000] FSR 363, 370. See also Caddick et al., above n.40, at section 7-52.

[59] As observed by the Court of Appeal regarding its role, 'our function is to review the judgement and order of the trial judge to see if it is wrong. If the judge has applied the wrong legal test, then it is our duty to say so. But in many cases the appellant's complaint is not that the judge has misdirected himself in law, but that he has incorrectly applied the right test': *Okotoks Ltd (Formerly Spicerhaart Ltd)* v *Fine & Country Ltd* [2013] EWCA Civ 672 [50].

[60] I shall provide some illustrations shortly and only postpone doing so because the examples usefully demonstrate how standards can adapt to new and unforeseen circumstances in ways that rules cannot, which is a topic for later in this chapter.

beyond the provision. So too do words like 'reasonable', 'negligent', 'unjust', 'obvious' and 'substantial'. But although the effect of such words is to liberate decision making as compared to the situation under a rule such terms nevertheless restrict the principles that a judge can draw on in arriving at a decision.[61]

There is arguably a difference between words like 'fair' and 'obvious' in the degree to which they confine decision making. The direction that a decision must be 'fair' is a common feature of many laws. On the other hand, so far as I am aware, the 'obviousness' standard is unique to patent law. Words like 'fair' where these appear in legal directions, thus seem to allow judges to fish in deeper and wider seas for relevant factors in deciding whether the direction applies, than do words like 'obvious' and 'substantial'. Yet the factors identified by the Court of Appeal in *Ashdown* v *Telegraph Group* as relevant to a determination as to whether a particular course of dealing with a copyright work is fair are clearly tailored to that particular context. Notwithstanding the ubiquity of the term 'fair' in English law, I doubt that the same factors have influenced decisions outside copyright law. The reason, I would argue, is that intellectual property law is in this respect at least partly autonomous.[62] What I mean by this is that judges, called upon to apply a direction containing a word like 'fair', cannot give effect to their background convictions. Decisions under standards, like all judicial decisions, must be coherent.[63] That is to say they must be seen to be rational and to pursue intelligible principles or policies.[64] Copyright, patent and trade

---

[61] Dworkin, above n.19, 28.

[62] I don't think intellectual property law is particularly special in this respect and many other specialist areas of the law are also partly autonomous in the same way. And I doubt that any area of the law is totally autonomous in the sense operating without any extrinsic influence. For instance and notably in *Ashdown* v *Telegraph Group*, the enactment of the Human Rights Act 1998 required the court to introduce 'rights thinking' into the sphere of copyright: [2001] EWCA Civ 1142.

[63] Note MacCormick, above n.16, 107; and Dworkin, above n.19, 37; 101–2; and 116.

[64] J D Heydon (formerly a judge of the High Court of Australia) has argued that '[j]ustice is not delivered and the law is not satisfactorily developed by judges who simply propound propositions attractive to their minds' and that principles must be 'closely related to the crucial detail of the particular facts': Heydon, J, 'Threats to Judicial Independence: The Enemy Within' (2013) 129 LQR 205, 219. And to similar effect, that judge-made laws should be, 'substantially consistent … [and] harmonious, without anomaly or internal conflict. They should hang together in a connected fashion': Heydon, J, 'Limits to the Powers

mark law have established characters (by which I mean a collection of values, policies and principles) that a judge's decision must respect. This requirement of coherence explains why the factors that are deemed relevant to a determination as to whether some circumstance or other is 'fair' differ in different legal contexts. Where a judge, in applying a particular standard, ignores an established consideration or introduces a novel one, she must justify that decision by reference to the principles and policies that characterize the law in issue. It is this element of her reasoning which is subject to review by an appellate court and this is what it means to say that an appeal from a decision based on an evaluation of facts must demonstrate that the decision was founded on an error of principle. This does not mean that the same parameters will invariably feature in all judgements concerned with the same legal issue – at least not explicitly. The particular facts in issue will inevitably shape the choice and weight attached to the factors put in the balance in arriving at a particular decision. But the factors that are drawn on must comply with the condition of coherence.[65]

Having defined terms and outlined in part the mechanisms involved, I am now in a position to start exploring the functional arguments advanced in support of rules on the one hand and standards on the other as a further step in understanding the ways and means of decision making. Because rules provide a complete before-the-fact specification of legal outcomes they promote certainty but at the cost of being inflexible. Standards are preferable to rules in circumstances where flexibility in the law is desirable. Rules are preferable where clarity and predictability are recognized as of greater value than flexibility and it is often asserted that in matters of property and of commercial law, the social interest in security of transactions favours rules because of the exceptional need of certainty in order to uphold the economic order.[66]

---

of Ultimate Appellate Courts' (2006) 122 LQR 399, 414. C.f. Thomas, above n.11, 186–8 (though note that Thomas distinguishes between coherence as a feature of legal decision making and coherence as intrinsic to the law itself).

65 So for instance, in considering whether the publication of private memoranda amounted to 'fair dealing', Phillips MR in *Ashdown* v *Telegraph Group* tested fairness according to the impact that publication would have on the commercial interests the claimant had in the work: [2001] EWCA Civ 1142 [72]. That concern did not figure in Lord Denning MR's judgement in *Hubbard* v *Vosper* [1972] QB 84, 94–5.

66 Pound, R, *An Introduction to the Philosophy of Law* (Yale University Press, 1922), 139.

Furthermore, standards, because they require more of decision makers, also increase the costs of administration since decision makers must not only ascertain the facts but must also ascertain the law as it applies to those facts. This is not to say that law done according to standards is per se less efficient than rules. A fuller consideration of the economic justifications underpinning intellectual property law is for the final chapter in this book. For the moment it is sufficient to note that even if the goal of maximizing utility is set up as the primary objective of the law this does not resolve the conflict between rules and standards because there are circumstances where efficiency demands the flexibility and openness of standards rather than the certainty and predictability of rules.[67] In particular the costs of uncertainty associated with standards need to be set against the difficulties and costs of promulgating detailed rules.[68] Such difficulties can be significant where the law aims at responding to, or regulating, widely varying or otherwise unpredictable conduct within a particular legal context.[69] If this is so then the costs of promulgating a rule will only be worthwhile if the rule is to be frequently applied.

There are two ways in which the inflexibility of rules can be problematic. To criticize a rule as inflexible may be to criticize its over or under-inclusiveness as to purpose.[70] This is a static problem and can be contrasted with the criticism that rules are dynamically inflexible so creating the problem that they can become anachronistic in light of advances in technology or in light of changes in social or economic

[67] Kaplow, L, 'Rules versus Standards: An Economic Analysis' (1992) 42 Duke LJ 557; and Booton, D, 'The Informal Acquisition of Copyright' (2011) IPQ 28.

[68] Long before the law and economics movement, Roscoe Pound anticipated this conclusion when he said that, 'the judiciary inevitably will be obliged to exercise a certain lawmaking function where the statutory rules are not adequate to cover the case on which they have to decide and that attempts to foreclose this process by minute detailed legislation are likely to fail': Pound, above n.66, 104–5.

[69] Spence, M and Endicott, T, 'Vagueness in the Scope of Copyright' (2005) 121 LQR 657, 662–3; and in relation to patents for inventions, Nard, C, 'Legal Forms and the Common Law of Patents' (2010) 90 Boston University L Rev 51, 92; and more generally Diver, above n.19, 73.

[70] At least if read literally: Kennedy, above n.4, 1689; Kelman, above n.5, 40; and Sunstein, above n.23, 990. Couched in economic terms the problem is that, '[g]reater specificity of legal obligation generates allocative inefficiency as a result of the necessarily imperfect fit between the coverage of a rule and the conduct sought to be regulated': Ehrlich and Posner, above n.39, 268.

conditions.[71] These problems require different solutions. In the case of the former, in the great majority of instances, an application of the rule will provide a good outcome. That is to say, the rule's purpose is given effect in the great majority of instances where it is found applicable. But in a proportion of cases, the application of the rule produces an undesirable outcome: an outcome that is not consistent with the rule's purpose or which manifestly conflicts with some other rule or principle. If the certainty provided by a rule is not an overriding concern, then the obvious solution would be to adopt a standard that would allow judges to avoid undesirable outcomes by giving weight to competing principles. But if having a rule is thought desirable because the certainty it provides is consistent with its purpose, then the solution is to create individual qualifications of, or exceptions to, the rule. In the case of the latter, with the passage of time so the rule becomes increasingly unfit for the purpose for which it was enacted. The solution here is to change the content of the rule so that its purpose is not frustrated by the changed circumstances.

I spent some time earlier in this chapter considering how it is that standards can allow flexibility in decision making whilst also being 'binding' and it is now time to say a little bit more about the doctrine of binding precedent and how this operates to meet this problem of anachronism. The key observation in this respect is that the content and scope of legal directions embedded in court decisions is the product of collaboration between judges separated in time. The content of a legal direction emerges not at the time a case is decided but later in light of what is made of the decision by later tribunals. The process by which a guiding legal direction is extracted from an earlier decision requires later tribunals to identify the material facts of the earlier case and then settle on the degree to which those facts are to be abstracted in arriving at a statement of the proposition of law for which the earlier case is authority.[72] The earlier judge influences this process in advancing reasons for her decision. But the earlier judge's influence is limited. If she attempts to specify the precise details of a legal direction she believes should apply to future cases, then to the extent that the detail differs from the facts in the case before her, what she says will be labelled as *obiter dicta* and treated as persuasive at best by those that follow her. The judge

---

71 Sunstein, above n.23, 993.

72 Llewellyn, K, *The Bramble Bush. On Our Law and its Study* (Oceana Publications, 1951), 48–52; Goodrich, P, *Reading the Law. A Critical Introduction to Legal Method and Techniques* (Basil Blackwell, 1986), 73–4; Lamond, above n.48, 579.

thus cannot adopt the legislature's tactic of using detail to limit the discretion of future decision makers. Rather, if she intends her decision to guide future decisions, she must advance reasons for her instant decision that articulate an abstract statement of the relevant law that is wide enough to embrace not only the circumstances of the case before her but a range of 'similar' circumstances: that is to say reasons that are not framed to be particular but generic.[73] The doctrine of precedent requires courts not only to decide cases but to do so in a principled way: 'that I must treat like cases alike implies that I must decide today's case on grounds which I am willing to adopt for the decision of future similar cases'.[74] But even where on the face of it a clear general proposition of law is given in a case, subsequent courts typically have significant 'explanative discretion' and at most it is the proposition, not the particular words in which it was couched, that binds later courts which in turn are free to re-express the proposition together with further conditions or qualifications which may be deemed appropriate to novel types of circumstance.[75] The key point is that the way in which the law is understood and applied is always done through the eyes of contemporary judges faced with contemporary disputes.

Given that explanative discretion as a tool to guard against anachronism is a feature of the common law, it is unsurprising that some of the better illustrative examples are in the development of the action of passing off, the common law nature of which gives it a flexibility that has

[73] MacCormick, above n.16, 70; and Schauer, above n.21, 53–4.

[74] MacCormick, above n.16, 75. A justified decision on a particular point requires a decision of the generic point: ibid., 79. See also Dworkin, above n.19, 113. Notable also are the comments of Lord Diplock who suggested extra-judicially that, 'by the very nature of their functions [courts] are compelled to act as legislators' and that every judgement implicitly speaks both to the future and generally such that a judgement 'says not only to the particular party … but to all to whom [it] becomes known: "If anyone does this kind of thing in the future this kind of consequence will follow"': Diplock, K, 'The Courts as Legislators' (Holdsworth Club of the University of Birmingham, 1965), 2. See also Schauer, above n.21, 36; and Nard, above n.69, 56.

[75] MacCormick, above n.16, 85. See also Dworkin, above n.19, 110–11; and Thomas, above n.11, 131–5. As observed by Grant Lamond,

> the common law is more provisional and partial than statutory rules. It is more open to being developed in cases, due to the processes of distinguishing and analogy, and it often provides only a general sketch of the structure of an area. In addition, the common law regards the rationale for a doctrine as integral to its content.

Lamond, above n.48, 571 and 581.

proved particularly important where there have been changes in business practices to which the legislature has been slow to respond.[76] In the 'Jif Lemon' case, Lord Oliver observed that the principles of law were in no doubt and that the law of passing off could be summarized in the short general proposition that no man may pass off his goods as those of another. More specifically, he said the law could be expressed in terms of the three elements which a claimant had to prove in order to succeed:

> First, he must establish a goodwill or reputation attached to the goods or services which he supplies in the mind of the purchasing public by association with the identifying 'get-up' ... Secondly, he must demonstrate a misrepresentation by the defendant to the public (whether or not intentional) leading or likely to lead the public to believe that goods or services offered by him are the goods or services of the plaintiff. Whether the public is aware of the plaintiff's identity as the manufacturer or supplier of the goods or services is immaterial, as long as they are identified with a particular source which is in fact the plaintiff. For example, if the public is accustomed to rely upon a particular brand name in purchasing goods of a particular description, it matters not at all that there is little or no public awareness of the identity of the proprietor of the brand name. Thirdly, he must demonstrate that he suffers or, in a quia timet action that he is likely to suffer, damage by reason of the erroneous belief engendered by the defendant's misrepresentation that the source of the defendant's goods or services is the same as the source of those offered by the plaintiff.[77]

This so-called classical trinity is an articulation of the principles of law which bind present and future courts. It is notable that Lord Oliver's speech contains an interesting change in declarative mode when describing the condition of misrepresentation. He starts by describing this condition in very abstract terms: the claimant, he says, must, 'demonstrate a misrepresentation by the defendant to the public (whether or not

---

[76] Famously Lord Diplock observed in *Erven Warnink Besloten Vennootschap* v *Townend & Sons (Hull) Ltd* that: 'unfair trading as a wrong actionable at the suit of other traders who thereby suffer loss of business or goodwill may take a variety of forms ... but most protean is that which is generally and nowadays, perhaps misleadingly, described as "passing off"': [1979] AC 731, 740.

[77] *Reckitt & Colman Products Ltd* v *Borden Inc* [1990] RPC 341, 406. For an alternative formulation see Lord Diplock's Speech in *Erven Warnink Besloten Vennootschap* v *Townend & Sons (Hull) Ltd* [1979] AC 731, 742. In *Harrods Ltd* v *Harrodian School Ltd*, whilst acknowledging Lord Diplock's formulation as authoritative, Millett LJ said that he thought Lord Oliver's analysis more helpful: [1996] RPC 697, 711. Lord Diplock's formulation seems to be relied upon more often in 'extended' passing off cases like *Erven Warnink Besloten Vennootschap* v *Townend & Sons (Hull) Ltd* itself.

intentional) leading or likely to lead the public to believe that goods or services offered by him are the goods or services of the plaintiff'. He continues in the same mode by adding the qualification that, 'whether the public is aware of the plaintiff's identity as the manufacturer or supplier of the goods or services is immaterial'. But in then using the phrase 'for example' in adding that, 'if the public is accustomed to rely upon a particular brand name in purchasing goods of a particular description, it matters not at all that there is little or no public awareness of the identity of the proprietor of the brand name', Lord Oliver ceases to declare a binding principle and in so doing sets the degree of abstraction at which to understand the operation of the principle. What is offered is merely an example: a particular factual circumstance that falls within a broader but largely undefined class of circumstance.

Some form of misrepresentation is thus, as a matter of principle, a necessary condition. The conceptual foundations governing precisely what misrepresentations are material were laid by Lord Parker in *Spalding Brothers* v *Gamage Ltd*[78] whose clarifications of the nature of the tort set the agenda for its modern development. Lord Parker identified the right, the invasion of which is the subject of passing off actions, as being the 'property' in the business or goodwill likely to be injured by the misrepresentation.[79] Crucially he observed that it was impossible to enumerate or classify all the possible ways in which a trader may make the representation relied upon.[80] It is easy to read Lord Parker's statement simply as one of fact, but it is more important to appreciate its normative significance for later courts. This was expressly recognized by Lord Diplock when he said that, '[t]he significance of this decision [*Spalding* v *Gamage*] in the law of passing off lies in its recognition that misrepresenting one's own goods as the goods of someone else was not a separate genus of actionable wrong but a particular species of wrong included in a wider genus ...'[81] *Spalding* v *Gamage*, he said, 'led the way to recognition by judges of other species of the same genus'.[82] The point is

---

[78] [1914–15] All ER Rep 147.

[79] Ibid., 150. See also Lord Diplock's account of Lord Parker's speech in *Erven Warnink Besloten Vennootschap* v *Townend & Sons (Hull) Ltd* [1979] AC 731, 741.

[80] So long as the representation confuses the public in a relevant way, the means by which this comes about is irrelevant: *Spalding Brothers* v *Gamage Ltd* [1914–15] All ER 147.

[81] *Erven Warnink Besloten Vennootschap* v *Townend & Sons (Hull) Ltd* [1979] AC 731, 741.

[82] Ibid., 741–2.

that the necessary condition of a deceptive misrepresentation has been allowed to change and adapt so preventing either the condition or the tort as a whole to become anachronistic in light of changes in business practices and the relevant public's familiarity with such contemporary practices.

Illustrative is the decision in *United Biscuits Ltd* v *Asda Stores Ltd.*[83] During the 1970s, the major supermarket chains became an increasingly important retail outlet for many groceries in the UK and by the 1990s most sales of the 'Penguin' branded biscuit (manufactured by United Biscuits) were made in supermarkets.[84] All of the major supermarkets also sold their own brand biscuits in competition and in 1996 the defendant supermarket Asda began to sell its own-brand 'Puffin' biscuit. The defendant openly acknowledged that the choice of name and elements of the packaging were intended to signal to consumers that theirs was a market substitute for the claimant's product.[85]

Though similar, there were sufficient differences between the names and the overall packaging for the judge to conclude that it was unlikely that a significant proportion of supermarket shoppers would fail to distinguish between the two products if both were on sale next to each other.[86] Nevertheless, the judge concluded that there had been a misrepresentation because the similarities in the packaging led consumers to believe that Puffin biscuits were made by the same manufacturer as made Penguin biscuits.[87] There was a line of authority, the judge observed, that led to the conclusion that inducing the belief in the minds of consumers (by deceptive suggestion) that the claimant was in some way responsible for the defendant's goods or services could amount to actionable passing

---

[83] [1997] RPC 513.

[84] [1997] RPC 513, 518 and 521. Indeed the supermarkets were by this time by far the most important retail outlet for this product.

[85] As observed by the judge the,

> public perception, which seems to be more or less correct, is that the big supermarket chains originally introduced their own-brand groceries to compete on price, rather than on quality. In order to emphasize that point some supermarkets used to put their own-brand goods into simple or even austere packaging. That has however been changing. Although own-brand goods still compete (very effectively) on price, price differentials and quality differentials have (as a broad generalisation) both tended to narrow, and own-brand packaging is designed to compete with brand leaders. The Puffin was intended to be a 'brand beater' competing directly with the Penguin.

[1997] RPC 513, 536.

[86] Ibid., 530.

[87] Ibid., 529–30.

off. Plainly, he said, that included the manufacturer of a supermarket's own-brand product.[88]

That consumers could reasonably assume that Puffin and Penguin biscuits had a common manufacturer was because of certain collaborative practices between manufacturers and retailers that were intended to hide from consumers who in fact made supermarkets' own brand goods. As noted by the judge, the actual manufacturer of own-brand products tended not to be identified by name on the packaging. Although some manufacturers had a policy of never producing own-brand goods for supermarkets, many others (including United Biscuits) did, although they did not publicize the fact. Furthermore, where the manufacturer of well-known branded goods did make goods for supermarkets, the precise specification for the own-brand product (and in particular, whether or not it was identical in quality with the brand leader) was not generally known to the public.

By the time of the action then, an element of deceit had become a routine part of contemporary retailing which practice changed the implicit messages that consumers take from the marketing and packaging of goods and this in turn invited a reappraisal of the notion of misrepresentation.[89] That reappraisal could be accommodated but only within a principled framework. Thus, as concluded by the judge:

> The importance of brands and the emergence of competing own-brands means that the law's tests of what is fair and what is unfair competition have to be applied in new and changing conditions. But the basic tests are the same. I have to apply the non-statutory principles of the law of passing off as they have developed over the years ...[90]

Another now routinely adopted feature of contemporary retailing which has also changed the implicit messages that consumers take from the way goods and services are marketed is that of celebrity endorsement and which too has led to changes to the tort of passing off. As noted by Laddie J in *Irvine* v *Talksport*,[91] a false endorsement was not actionable

---

[88] Ibid., 532.

[89] Although early cases of passing off action involved cases involving the deceptive use of trade names and the like, in its modern form, passing off does not require deceit: *Erven Warnink Besloten Vennootschap* v *Townend & Sons (Hull) Ltd* [1979] AC 731, 740.

[90] [1997] RPC 513, 537.

[91] [2002] EWHC 367.

during the nineteenth century because during this period, goods-for-goods substitution was an essential ingredient of the tort.[92] This was also a time when celebrity endorsement, false or otherwise, was understandably rare, the perception being that, 'gentlemen ... would not soil their hands or their reputation by being involved "in trade"'.[93] That is no longer the case. As observed by Laddie J in *Irvine*:

> [I]t is [nowadays] common for famous people to exploit their names and images by way of endorsement. They do it not only in their own field of expertise but, depending on the extent of their fame or notoriety, wider afield also. It is common knowledge that for many sportsmen, for example, income received from endorsing a variety of products and services represent a very substantial part of their total income. The reason large sums are paid for endorsement is because, no matter how irrational it may seem to a lawyer, those in business have reason to believe that the lustre of a famous personality, if attached to their goods or services, will enhance the attractiveness of those goods or services to their target market. In this respect, the endorsee is taking the benefit of the attractive force which is the reputation or goodwill of the famous person.[94]

What is interesting here is how Laddie J describes the intention behind celebrity endorsement: the endorsee, he says, takes the benefit 'which is the reputation or goodwill' of the celebrity. The language used is a clear attempt to position celebrity endorsement within the principles of the tort: it is the language of the 'classic trinity' articulated by Lord Oliver in the 'Jif Lemon' case. A false endorsement thus becomes an appropriation of goodwill as much as is done if a person represents his goods as the goods of somebody else. Laddie J in effect created a new form of goodwill – promotional goodwill rather than source or product goodwill. That accepted, Laddie J's conclusion that the law of passing off in its modern form and in modern trade circumstances should apply to cases of false endorsement[95] was inevitable. But if anything he was more vehement in pointing out that, in reaching this conclusion, he was not creating some new right in response to the growth of character merchandising.[96]

---

92 Ibid. [18].

93 Ibid.

94 Ibid. [39].

95 Ibid. [43].

96 Ibid. [44]–[45]. The distinction between celebrity endorsement and celebrity merchandising featured in the arguments advanced in *Fenty* v *Arcadia Group Brands Ltd*. Here the Court of Appeal in upholding the finding at first instance that the defendants' marketing of a shirt bearing the image of the claimant was a false endorsement amounting to passing off, again referred to the Lord Oliver's

As has already been noted, the use of words like 'fair', 'unjust', 'obvious' and 'substantial' by requiring judges to make evaluative choices within a principled framework indirectly also confers a limited power to formulate, review and reformulate abstract principles that operate to constrain decision making within the relatively open textured statutory framework. Guarding against the possibility that the law will become anachronistic may not be the primary motive behind the legislature's resort to imprecision in drafting. It is generally the case that precision is undesirable (perhaps even impossible) when the law aims at regulating widely varying conduct.[97] Allowing judges' discretion in deciding whether copyright is infringed by a partial taking makes sense but not because of fears that any precise test will rapidly become anachronistic but rather because all the possible relationships between works and borrowings are impossible to enumerate.[98] One reason for this arises because the intangible abstract objects of intellectual property rights can be used to unite otherwise very different physical objects.[99] Much the same could be said of the test aimed at establishing whether a claimed invention involves an inventive step except that here the difficulties are in defining with precision all the possible ways in which the exercise of inventive faculties intersect with what is known.[100] These are questions

---

identification of the three elements which a claimant must establish in order to succeed in a claim for passing off: [2015] EWCA Civ 3 [30]. The Court also endorsed the approach taken by Laddie J in *Irvine* v *Talksport* as to how those elements were to be understood and applied in cases of celebrity endorsement: ibid. [35]–[40].

[97] Spence and Endicott, above n.69, 662–3. Put another way, the 'problems of overinclusion and underinclusion are more serious the greater the heterogeneity (or ambiguity, or uncertainty) of the conduct intended to be affected': Ehrlich and Posner, above n.39, 270.

[98] Spence and Endicott, above n.69, 662. Graham Dinwoodie and Dev Gangjee make the same point in respect of trade marks: Dinwoodie, G and Gangjee, D, 'The Image of the Consumer in EU Trade Mark Law' in Leczykiewicz, D and Weatherill, S (eds) *The Images of the Consumer in EU Law. Legislation, Free Movement and Competition Law* (Hart Publishing, 2016), 369.

[99] So for instance under copyright law, a film might 'reproduce' a literary work and a three-dimensional work artistic work reproduce a two-dimensional work; and see also Drahos, above n.14, 155; and Griffiths, J, 'Dematerialization, Pragmatism and the European Copyright Revolution' (2013) 33 OJLS 767, 769–70.

[100] As observed by Lord Hoffmann,

> whenever anything inventive is done for the first time it is the result of the addition of a new idea to the existing stock of knowledge. Sometimes, it is the idea of using established techniques to do something which no one had

which require of judges that they form an impression by taking into account a number of factors of varying degrees of importance and deciding whether they are sufficient to bring the whole within some legal description.[101] As I have already said, decisions are nevertheless principled and it is in the enumeration of the relevant factors where principle lies. By modifying, adding or removing a factor, so judges are able to ensure that the law continues to have contemporary relevance. And appellate courts have a crucial role here in concretizing changes. By way of example, I want to consider an aspect of how courts approach the question of whether a claimed invention involves a step not obvious to a person skilled in the art.[102]

The Patents Act 1977 itself provides no guidance as to how this question is to be approached leaving courts to determine relevant factors. A fundamental element in the process is the adoption of the mantle of the person skilled in the relevant art. It is through the eyes of such a person that the inventive concept, the prior art and the differences between the two are judged.[103] Adopting the mantle of the relevant skilled person involves two prior steps: the identification of the attributes of the notional 'person skilled in the art' and secondly identification of the common general knowledge of such a person.[104] For over forty years, courts have accepted that this person is a skilled technician who is well acquainted with workshop technique but is 'incapable of a scintilla of invention'.[105] It was something of a novelty for the judge in *Dyson Appliances Ltd* v

---

> previously thought of doing. In that case, the inventive idea will be doing the new thing. Sometimes, it is finding a way of doing something which people had wanted to do but could not think how. The inventive idea would be the way of achieving the goal. In yet other cases, many people may have a general idea of how they might achieve a goal but not know how to solve a particular problem which stands in their way. If someone devises a way of solving the problem, his inventive step will be that solution, but not the goal itself or the general method of achieving it.

Biogen Inc v *Medeva Plc* [1997] RPC 1, 34.

[101] See above at p. 37.

[102] '[H]aving regard to any matter which forms part of the state of the art': section 3 Patents Act 1977.

[103] *Pozzoli SpA* v *BDMO SA* [2007] EWCA Civ 588 [14]–[16] reviewing and restating the approach advocated in *Windsurfing International Inc* v *Tabur Marine (Great Britain) Ltd* [1985] RPC 59, 73–4

[104] *Pozzoli SpA* v *BDMO SA* [2007] EWCA Civ 588 [16].

[105] *Technograph Printed Circuits Ltd* v *Mills & Rockley (Electronics) Ltd* [1972] RPC 346, 355.

Hoover Ltd to add 'prejudices' to the list of characteristics possessed by the person skilled in the relevant art:

> Common general knowledge has both positive and negative aspects … in certain cases (and I believe this to be one of them), negative aspects of knowledge must in approximation to reality, play their part. At the priority date of the Patent, I believe that such was the 'mindset' within the vacuum cleaner industry, no notional, right-thinking addressee would ever have considered the viability of purifying dirt-laden air from a vacuum cleaning operation, other than by means of using a bag or bag and final filter. For present purposes, the addressee is nonetheless deemed to have been presented with (in effect) three items of prior art wherein it is proposed to clean dirt-laden air by means not of bags but by cyclonic action alone. He is also assumed to take some interest in them however inimical the proposals may be to his likely way of thinking at the time. In terms of its impact on the issue of obviousness, I believe that this negative thinking which … amounted to prejudice, would at least have caused the addressee to regard modification to any of these prior art proposals with considerable reserve if not overt scepticism.[106]

What is particularly notable is how far the judge here seeks to avoid generalisation. The existence of prejudice in the minds of those skilled in the relevant art is presented as a specific finding of fact. Perhaps the clearest indication of this is in his description of this prejudice as an aspect of the common general knowledge that is imputed to those skilled in the art.[107] The conservatism of the first instance judgement in this

---

[106] *Dyson Appliances Ltd* v *Hoover Ltd* [2001] RPC 473 [156]. However, this did not mean that the person skilled in the art would instantaneously reject the prior art without thought. But the extent of the engagement was limited and the period of tinkering with the cited prior art was, in that case, assumed to be abbreviated (prejudice being held likely to gain the better of patience rather more swiftly than in some other obviousness cases): [2001] RPC 473 [162]. The Court of Appeal subsequently held that the trial judge did not err in taking into account the prejudices of the person skilled in the relevant art, Aldous LJ observing that,

> the mantle of the skilled person is that of an actual skilled person. The purpose of assuming the mantle of the skilled person is to enable the decision as to what is obvious to be a decision based on actual facts. They include all the attitudes and perceptions of such a person.

[2001] EWCA Civ 1440 [57].

[107] A prejudice is manifestly not 'knowledge' (though it may be grounded in limited knowledge) but rather a way of approaching information. In a later case, Jacob LJ in commenting on the decision in *Dyson Appliances Ltd* v *Hoover Ltd* characterized the mindset as part of the 'skills' attributed to the notional person skilled in the art saying,

respect stands in contrast to the general terms adopted by Aldous LJ in the Court of Appeal:

> The mantle of the skilled person is that of an actual skilled person. The purpose of assuming the mantle of the skilled person is to enable the decision as to what is obvious to be a decision based on actual facts. They include all the attitudes and perceptions of such a person.[108]

Here then is a clear instance of a decision based on grounds which serve not only to justify the decision in the immediate case, but which also provides a basis for deciding future cases. And Sedley LJ, in articulating a justification for the adoption of the new principle does so in equally abstract terms:

> [T]he intellectual horizon of practical research and innovation is in part set by the economic milieu, commercial realities cannot necessarily be divorced from the kinds of practical outcome which might occur to the law's skilled addressee as potentially worthwhile. It is one thing to accept that this technologically skilled but wholly unimaginative person is a lawyer's construct – a ventriloquist's dummy ... – who thinks only of how things work or could be made to work. It is another to expel him altogether from the real world, where ideas do not occur to people in (so to speak) a vacuum.[109]

Consciously or otherwise, in this UK courts have adapted one aspect of the law to take account of a typical feature of modern industrial production in a way that serves the patent system's overall goal of stimulating innovative activity. The point about technical prejudices is that they can act to paralyse investment in innovation. So much of industrial research is nowadays carried out in a structured corporate environment where competencies play a key role in limiting innovation. Over time, firms operating within an industry acquire and develop capabilities comprising broadly the body of skills, experience and knowledge necessary for a firm to carry out the various activities involved in

---

> I think one can draw from this case that the Court, in considering the skills of the notional 'person skilled in the art' for the purposes of obviousness will have regard to the reality of the position at the time. What the combined skills (and mind-sets) of real research teams in the art is what matters when one is constructing the notional research team to whom the invention must be obvious if the Patent is to be found invalid on this ground.

Schlumberger Holdings Ltd v *Electromagnetic Geoservices AS* [2010] EWCA Civ 819 [42].

[108] *Dyson Appliances Ltd* v *Hoover Ltd* [2001] EWCA Civ 1440 [57].

[109] [2001] EWCA Civ 1440 [88].

producing its output.[110] And the products of a particular firm are thus likely to have qualities attributable to the specific organizational capabilities that have produced them. Such capabilities are important determinants of any particular firm's competitiveness. Acting positively, they serve to define that firms output in a competitive market. But they can also hinder a firm's capacity to respond to the dynamics of the market and, in particular, can act as barriers to adopting and mastering unfamiliar technologies.[111] This effect is enhanced in large firms. Empirical studies have shown that most large firm executives are risk adverse.[112] Professional managers tend to aim for stability of profit levels and share prices rather than pursuing unfamiliar but potentially highly profitable novel strategies.[113] Thus, '[o]nce caution has become habit, new products are designed to fit the existing setup – instead of the setup being refitted to suit the new product; and advances in the technology are limited to small refinements of existing procedures.'[114]

It is useful at this point to reiterate what I think it going on. Legislation, through the use of words such as 'substantial' and 'obvious',

---

[110] Richardson, G, 'The Organisation of Industry' (1972) 82 Economic Journal 883, 888; Teece, D, 'Capturing Value from Knowledge Assets: The New Economy, Markets for Know-How, and Intangible Assets' (1998) 40 California Management Review 55, 75; and Langlois, R, *The Dynamics of Industrial Capitalism: Schumpeter, Chandler and the New Economy* (Routledge, 2007), 14–15. These capabilities can affect the way a firm in a particular industry uses patents: Cohen, W, Nelson, R and Walsh, J, *Protecting Their Intellectual Assets: Appropriability Conditions and Why US Manufacturing Firms Patent (or Not)*, NBER Working Paper 7552 (National Bureau for Economic Research, 2002), 21.

[111] Piore, M and Sabel, C, *The Second Industrial Divide: Possibilities for Prosperity* (Basic Books, 1984), 264; Kamien, M and Schwartz, N, 'Market Structure and Innovation: A Survey' (1975) 13(1) Journal of Economic Literature 1, 12–13; and, in relation to the pharmaceutical industry, Comanor, W, 'Research and Competitive Product Differentiation in the Pharmaceutical Industry in the United States' (1964) 31(124) Economica NS 372, 380.

[112] See e.g. MacCrimmon, K and Wehrung, D, with Stanbury, W, *Taking Risks: The Management of Uncertainty* (The Free Press, 1986), 260.

[113] McEachern, W and Romeo, A, 'Stockholder Control, Uncertainty and the Allocation of Resources to Research' (1978) 26(4) Journal of Industrial Economics 349, 350. See also Gordon, R, *Business Leadership in the Large Corporation* (The Brookings Institution, 1949), 322; Baumol, W, *Business Behaviour, Value and Growth* (The MacMillan Company, 1959), 90–91; and Monsen, R Jr and Downs, A, 'A Theory of Large Managerial Firms' (1965) 73(3) Journal of Political Economy 221, 226, 232, 234 and 235.

[114] Piore and Sabel, above n.111, 264.

requires judges to make evaluative choices within a principled framework. No doubt, the way the legislation is drafted reflects the understanding that it would be undesirable, if not impossible, to be more precise given the range of factors to take into account in deciding whether a partial taking should infringe copyright or the multiple ways in which people can be inventive. The legislation then is drafted to avoid the static problem of inflexibility in the sense of over or under inclusiveness as to purpose. But the relatively open-texture of the legislation also confers on judges a limited power to formulate, review and reformulate the abstract principles that operate to guide and constrain their own decision making in ways that allows the law to maintain a contemporary relevance. The great strength of this mechanism is that this is done in the context of deciding actual cases. This is also its greatest weakness. Its strength is in the fact that this kind of law-making is based on evidence rather than theory or speculation. It is a weakness because the evidence from which the principle is derived is likely to be very narrowly drawn and intimately linked to the circumstances of the particular case in issue. The risk then is that any principle that emerges from a particular case may prove to be founded on circumstances that are not representative of the class of circumstance to which the principle is taken to apply.

Whilst this is certainly a risk, it should not be overstated given that, as already noted, courts faced with decision making in light of a binding precedent have considerable explanative discretion regarding their understanding of how the binding element of earlier judgements is to be understood and applied. Consider for instance the development of the approach to claimed inventions which are the product of experimentation. The original and unrefined modern position was articulated by Diplock LJ in *Johns-Manville Corporation's Patent.*[115] Diplock LJ held that a claimed invention should be deemed to be obvious if the experiment leading to the discovery of that invention would be considered by a person skilled in the art 'worth trying out', or more specifically, if a person skilled in the art would assess the likelihood of success as sufficient to warrant actual trial.[116] In arriving at this test, Diplock LJ specifically rejected a test where only 'certainty of success' would point to an experimental outcome that was obvious.

The choice of alternatives and the principle arrived at made sense given the circumstances of the case. The claimed inventive step was in the idea of using a recently developed flocculating agent in an existing

---

[115] *Johns-Manville Corp's Patent* [1967] FSR 327.
[116] [1967] FSR 327, 332.

filtration process in which it had not been used before. The prior art documents disclosing the flocculating agent were addressed primarily to the mining and paper industries. However, Diplock LJ observed that filtration processes were common to many industries, including that of the patentee (the manufacture of asbestos cement), and that persons skilled in the relevant art would have read the prior art documents and realized that here was a newly introduced flocculating agent which it was well worth trying out in their own filtration process. The experiments undertaken in *Johns-Manville Corp's Patent* thus were grounded in theory in the sense that there were good reasons to undertake the experiment based on the levels of existing knowledge and understanding. To be sure, the outcome of the experiments could not be predicted with absolute certainty but there was evidence enough to suggest that the flocculating agents tested would work in any number of filtration processes.

Unlike the circumstances applicable in *Johns-Manville Corp's Patent*, much modern commercial research is undertaken in circumstances where the theoretical grounding of experiments is at best poor and sometimes completely absent[117] and commercial experimentation may be largely a process of trial and error. This was certainly the position in the later case of *Saint-Gobain PAM SA* v *Fusion Provida Ltd.*[118] Here, the patent in issue related to a means of reducing corrosion in underground pipes by way of a specified external coating which included a layer of zinc/aluminium alloy. The invention differed from what was known only in the use of this alloy rather than in using zinc alone as a coating. In seeking to challenge the patent, the defendants argued that this substitution was a simple one that was 'obvious to try'. All the expert evidence suggested that prediction in the field of underground pipe corrosion was

[117] This has been particularly well documented in the pharmaceutical industry and throughout most of its history, pharmaceutical research has often involved doing little more than screening a vast range of compounds in the hope of finding something useful. For instance, see Gambardella, A, *Science and Innovation: the US Pharmaceutical Industry during the 1980s* (Cambridge University Press, 1995), 1, 23 and 42–3; National Research Council, *Intellectual Property Rights and Research Tools in Molecular Biology: Summary of a Workshop Held at the National Academy of Sciences, February 15–16, 1996* (National Academy Press, 1997), 50; and Henderson, R, Orsenigo, L and Pisano, G P, 'The Pharmaceutical Industry and the Revolution in Molecular Biology: Interactions among Scientific, Institutional and Organizational Change' in Mowery, D and Nelson, R (eds) *Sources of Industrial Leadership* (Cambridge University Press, 1999), 267–311, 267–8, 283 and 294.

[118] [2005] EWCA Civ 177.

impossible and there were no simple rules governing how corrosion of pipes was affected by soils. From our perspective, what is interesting is how Jacob LJ treated the earlier authority:

> The oft-cited case on this is *Johns-Manville's Patent* [1967] RPC 479. The alleged invention was for producing shaped asbestos cement articles by the use of a particular class of flocculating agent. This class had recently come on the market and found use in other applications. Diplock LJ put the possible inventive step this way:
>
> 'If there is any inventive step involved in the appellants' claim, it is in the idea of using a known, but recently developed, flocculating agent in a known filtration process.'
>
> … That is miles away from the present case. It was in that context that Diplock LJ said, when discussing the judgement below:
>
> 'The learned judge preferred the expression "see without difficulty that these newly-introduced polymers would be of advantage in his filtration step." I think that "would be" puts it too high if it postulates prior certainty of success before actually testing the polymers in the filtration process; it is enough that the person versed in the art would assess the likelihood of success as sufficient to warrant actual trial'.[119]

Diplock LJ's dicta in *Johns-Manville Corp's Patent* was thus re-contextualized by being positioned within the specific factual circumstances in which it was first given and with this, the articulated principle narrowed in its application. The 'obvious to try' test, Jacob LJ said, really only works where it is more-or-less self-evident that what is being tested ought to work.[120] The justification for so restating and narrowing the existing authority was based on Jacob LJ's understanding of the decision making processes in commercial research:

> Mere possible inclusion of something within a research programme on the basis you will find out more and something might turn up is not enough [to show obviousness]. If it were otherwise there would be few inventions that were patentable. The only research which would be worthwhile (because of the prospect of protection) would be into areas totally devoid of prospect.[121]

Later in *Conor Medsystems Inc* v *Angiotech Pharmaceuticals Inc*,[122] Jacob LJ made the same point about how he thought Diplock LJ's

---

119 Ibid. [26]–[27]
120 Ibid. [35].
121 Ibid. [35].
122 [2007] EWCA Civ 5.

judgement in *Johns-Manville Corp's Patent* should be understood, again linking what was said to the particular facts of that case; again repeating the justification he put forward in *Saint-Gobain* but adding to the justification the observation that this reading corresponded to the approach taken by courts in Australia, Canada and the United States.[123]

It is important to note that, neither in *Saint-Gobain* nor in *Conor* v *Angiotech* did Jacob LJ attempt to reformulate a test of obviousness applicable to inventions that were the product of experimentation. Indeed in *Conor* v *Angiotech* he expressly eschewed so doing:

> In the end the question is simply 'was the invention obvious?' This involves taking into account a number of factors ... Some factors are more important than others. Sometimes commercial success can demonstrate that an idea was a good one. In others 'obvious to try' may come into the assessment. But such a formula cannot itself necessarily provide the answer. Of particular importance is of course the nature of the invention itself.[124]

The subsequent appeal gave the House of Lords the opportunity to nail the coffin lid down on the 'obvious to try' test.[125] Noting that *Johns-Manville Corp's Patent* was decided over 40 years ago, and was concerned with a fairly low-tech process, Lord Walker grounded his justification for laying aside the test on it having become anachronistic in light of the highly competitive environment in which modern high-tech research was conducted. Citing comments made by Sir Hugh Laddie out of court, Lord Walker observed that in such an environment the test was unworkable or irrational:

> If the reward for finding a solution to a problem and securing a monopoly for that solution is very high, then it may well be worthwhile for large players to examine all potential avenues to see if one gives the right result, even though the prospects of any one of them succeeding are much less than 50/50. What makes something worth trying is the outcome of a simple risk to reward calculation. Yet, if the reward is very large, the avenues worth trying will be expanded accordingly. So, the more commercially attractive the solution and the more pressing the public clamour for it, the harder it will be to avoid an obviousness attack.[126]

---

[123] Ibid. [39]–[42].

[124] Ibid. [45].

[125] *Conor Medsystems Inc* v *Angiotech Pharmaceuticals Inc* [2008] UKHL 49.

[126] Per Lord Walker citing Sir Hugh Laddie writing extra-judicially: [2008] UKHL 49 [48].

Lord Hoffmann on the other hand made no such claim, but rather endorsed a multi-factored, formula-free approach to inventiveness of the kind advocated by Jacob LJ in the Court of Appeal. The question of obviousness, Lord Hoffmann said, had to be considered on the facts of each case. Relevant factors included the motive to find a solution to the problem the patent addresses, the number and extent of the possible avenues of research, the effort involved in pursuing them and the expectation of success. The weight to be attached to any particular factor had to be considered in light of all the relevant circumstances.[127]

Lord Hoffmann's direction that the question of obviousness has to be considered on the facts of each case approach provides a convenient introduction to a further tool used by courts to preserve flexibility notwithstanding the doctrine of binding precedent. As observed by Neil MacCormick, judges have on occasion drawn a distinction between earlier decisions which contain rulings in points of law, and those which contain nothing more than 'propositions of good sense'.[128] MacCormick suggests that this distinction turns on a judge's perception of the problem in issue as either one of interpretation or of classification. MacCormick's distinction, adapted to apply to readings of the decision in *Johns-Manville Corp's Patent*, can be illustrated thus:

1. Should the rule that a claimed invention shall be taken to involve an inventive step if it is not obvious to a person skilled in the art be interpreted as meaning that something obvious to try does not involve an inventive step (which includes the idea of using a known, but recently developed, flocculating agent in a known filtration process); or
2. For the purpose of applying the rule that a claimed invention shall be taken to involve an inventive step if it is not obvious to a person skilled in the art, does the idea of using a known, but recently developed, flocculating agent in a known filtration process count as an instance of something that is obvious?[129]

---

[127] [2008] UKHL 49 [42] citing with approval *Generics (UK) Ltd* v *Lundbeck A/S* [2007] RPC 32 [72].

[128] MacCormick, above n.16, 96 citing the judgement of Lord Denning in *Qualcast (Wolverhampton)* v *Haynes* [1959] AC 743, 762. In essence the distinction is the same as that drawn by Grant Lamond in his account of the use of 'classificatory analogies' versus 'close analogies' in legal reasoning: above n.48, 568.

[129] Adapted from MacCormick, above n.16, 94.

And as noted by MacCormick, for the purposes of the doctrine of precedent it may be convenient to treat classification decisions as purely factual just so binding precedents should not be established.[130] The saga surrounding the *Johns-Manville Corp's Patent* decision and the 'obvious to try' test demonstrates two further points. The first is that the identification of the type of problem addressed in a particular case (i.e. whether it is one of classification or interpretation) is done by later tribunals in their reading of the earlier decision and the constraints that they then understand that decision places on their decision making. Secondly, the identification of the type of problem addressed can alter with the passage of time and a contemporary court may read an earlier decision as one of classification notwithstanding that it has previously been read as one of interpretation.[131]

In MacCormick's scheme, problems of interpretation and classification are seen as conceptually distinct. However, they can also be seen as outcomes of an inductive process by which a court, in deciding a contemporary case, attempts to rationalize earlier decisions as specific instances of an overriding general principle.[132] The breadth of that principle decides its contemporary relevance and its application to the circumstances in issue. A finding that an earlier decision is one of classification confines the legal relevance of that decision to future cases which share identical material facts.

The evaluative nature of such inductive reasoning can be neatly illustrated by comparing how courts in different jurisdictions have arrived at different understandings of the scope of a particular cause of action notwithstanding common starting points and common points of reference. In *Starbucks (HK) Ltd* v *British Sky Broadcasting Group plc*[133] the

---

[130] Ibid., 96.

[131] So far as the 'obvious to try' test is concerned, the distinction is particularly apparent in the different treatment afforded to Lord Diplock's dicta in *Johns-Manville Corp's Patent* by the superintending examiner at first instance and by Graham J on appeal in *Dow Corning Corporation's Application* [1969] FSR 338.

[132] The decision thus both rationalized the existing law, revealing within the specific exclusions an underlying common purpose, whilst at the same time providing a justification for the decision to refuse the specific application in issue. For a fuller account of this 'basic pattern of legal reasoning': Levi, E, *An Introduction to Legal Reasoning* (The University of Chicago Press, 1948), 1–27; MacCormick, above n.16, 125–6; and Lamond, above n.48, 578.

[133] *Starbucks (HK) Ltd* v *British Sky Broadcasting Group plc* [2015] UKSC 31. For commentary see: Brophy, D, 'The Supreme Court Decision in *Starbucks (HK)* v *British Sky Broadcasting*: Is That Crazy Horse Still Running?' (2015) 37

UK Supreme Court was invited to consider whether the claimant broadcaster, which was based in Hong Kong, could succeed in a claim of passing off against a competitor over the use of the name 'NOW TV'. The particular challenge facing the claimant was that although it had a demonstrable reputation in the UK, it did not conduct any business there. In terms of the classic trinity articulated by Lord Oliver in *Reckitt & Colman Products Ltd* v *Borden Inc*[134] the claimant thus had to overcome the hurdle of establishing that it had goodwill or a reputation attached to its services in the mind of the purchasing public by association with the name NOW TV. The judge and the Court of Appeal thought that it was not enough for the claimant to establish that it had a reputation among a significant number of people in the UK, if it had no goodwill in the UK.

The Supreme Court was not short of judgements on which to rely. Both the parties to the dispute had referred to numerous earlier decisions in support of their respective cases. Lord Neuberger's conclusion (with which the other members of the court concurred) was formed on the basis of a review of English authorities and of case law from other common law countries. What is particularly interesting is the claimants' attempt to have the earlier decisions seen as addressing problems of classification rather than interpretation. In particular, the claimants contended that the notion that goodwill should be limited to jurisdictions where the claimant had business was wrong in principle: the question of where the claimant had goodwill was a matter of fact and evidence, not a matter of law.[135] Lord Neuberger disagreed:

> It seems to have been the consistent view of the House of Lords and Privy Council from 1915 to 1990 that a plaintiff who seeks passing off relief in an English court must show that he has goodwill, in the form of customers, in the jurisdiction of the court. While it can be said that, in none of the cases discussed ... above was that point the main focus of attention, it nonetheless seems clear that that is what a succession of respected judges, many of whom had substantial experience in this area, considered to be the law.[136]

EIPR 661; Hiu Fai Kwok, K, 'Protection of a Reputable Foreign Trader's Legitimate Interests under the Law of Passing-off' (2016) LQR 186; and Davis, J, 'The Continuing Importance of Local Goodwill in Passing Off' (2015) CLJ 419.

134 [1990] RPC 341, 406.

135 [2015] UKSC 31 [28].

136 Ibid. [48]

The decision can be contrasted with that of the Federal Court of Australia in *ConAgra Inc* v *McCain Foods (Aust) Pty Ltd.*[137] Here an American food company, with no customers in Australia, sought to prevent a rival firm from marketing frozen foods under the name 'Healthy Choice'.[138] Apart from being concerned with trading goodwill in respect of goods rather than services,[139] the legal issue was thus the same as in *Starbucks (HK) Ltd* v *British Sky Broadcasting Group plc* and centred on whether the tort of passing off required proof of relevant commercial activity within the jurisdiction by the party claiming relief. Unsurprisingly then, there was considerable overlap in the authorities reviewed by the Australian and English courts. The Federal Court, however, arrived at a different conclusion from the Supreme Court. 'Reputation', Lockhart J said, was the key business facet that passing off protected and the requirement of 'goodwill' was never meant to have a different meaning to reputation.[140] Central to Lockhart's reasoning was the observation that the definition of goodwill, that which linked goodwill to local customers, derived from the House of Lords' decision in *Commissioners of Inland Revenue* v *Muller and Co's Margarine Ltd.*[141] As Lockhart J observed, that case involved the question whether the goodwill of the relevant business was property 'locally situate out of the United Kingdom' within the meaning of the United Kingdom Stamp Act 1891. Their Lordship's speeches, he observed, were therefore directed to the question of whether goodwill can have a separate locality from the business to which it is attached. In this, Lockhart J thus re-contextualized the definition of goodwill provided in *Muller*, positioning this within the specific factual circumstances in which it was given, and narrowed that application of that definition in a way that meant that the Australian law of passing off ceased to be 'trammelled by definitions of goodwill developed in the field of revenue law'.[142] Lockhart J was then free to develop a conception of protected subject matter that was in accordance with what he understood to be the needs of contemporary business and international commerce:

---

137 [1992] FCA 176.

138 There was evidence that the US firm intended to enter the Australian market sometime in the future.

139 The Supreme Court's decision in *Starbucks* has been criticized for not making a distinction between goodwill relating to sales of goods and goodwill relating to the provision of services: Brophy, above n.133.

140 [1992] FCA 176 [106].

141 (1901) AC 217.

142 [1992] FCA 176 [106].

> It is no longer valid, if it ever was, to speak of a business having goodwill or reputation only where the business is carried on. Modern mass advertising through television (which reaches by satellite every corner of the globe instantaneously), radio, newspapers and magazines, reaches people in many countries of the world. The international mobility of the world population increasingly brings human beings, and therefore potential consumers of goods and services, closer together and engenders an increasing and more instantaneous awareness of international commodities ... Goods and services are often preceded by their reputation abroad. They may not be physically present in the market of a particular country, but are well known there because of the sophistication of communications which are increasingly less limited by national boundaries, and the frequent travel of residents of many countries for reasons of business, pleasure or study.[143]

Lord Neuberger in *Starbucks (HK) Ltd* v *British Sky Broadcasting Group plc* whilst not blind to current patterns of business and commerce, attached more weight to the benefits of maintaining legal certainty through consistency:

> It is of course open to this court to develop or even to change the law in relation to a common law principle, when it has become archaic or unsuited to current practices or beliefs. Indeed it is one of the great virtues of the common law that it can adapt itself to practical and commercial realities, which is particularly important in a world which is fast changing in terms of electronic processes, travel and societal values. Nonetheless, we should bear in mind that changing the common law sometimes risks undermining legal certainty, both because a change in itself can sometimes generate uncertainty and because change can sometimes lead to other actual or suggested consequential changes.[144]

The evaluative nature of inductive reasoning is also evident in the divergent approaches to patentable subject matter under the EPC. This is an untypical example only so far as inductive patterns of reasoning are typically applied to the interpretation and application of case law rather than statutory provisions.[145] Amongst EPC member states, national legislative provisions on patentable subject matter correspond to Article 52 EPC, which provides that, amongst other things, programs for

---

143 Ibid. [115].

144 [2015] UKSC 31 [49].

145 The EPO's resort to this technique as a mode of statutory interpretation certainly changed, and arguably extended, the EPO's law-making power beyond that envisaged by the drafters of the EPC. This issue of legislative competence is dealt with more fully in the following chapter.

computers 'as such' are not to be regarded as inventions.[146] The inclusion of computer programs on the list of subject matter not regarded as inventions has proved controversial,[147] which in turn has led to some divergence in the way in which the exclusion has been read.

How this particular exclusion was to be understood and applied by the EPO was first tested in *Vicom Systems Inc/Computer-related invention*[148] which concerned a claim relating to a computer-implemented method of processing digitally encoded images.[149] The EPO's Technical Board of Appeal (TBA) held that decisive to patentability was the 'technical contribution' the claimed invention made to the known art.[150] Later, in *IBM/Document abstracting and retrieving*[151] the TBA refused a claim relating to a computer-implemented means of abstracting, storing and retrieving documents on the grounds that this lacked 'technical character'. The Board argued that, whatever their differences, the exclusions listed in Article 52(2) had in common that they referred to activities

---

146 Article 52(2) EPC. The corresponding UK provisions are contained in section 1(2) Patents Act 1977. On the influence of Article 52 on the interpretation of the UK Act see the comments of Pumfrey J in *Shopalotto.COM Ltd's Application* [2005] EWHC 2416 (Pat) [5]; and *Research in Motion UK Ltd* v *Inpro Licensing SARL* [2006] EWHC 70 [184].

147 In large part, the categories of subject matter expressly excluded under Article 52(2) EPC reflected a consensus of opinion of the majority of parties contracting to the EPC at the time of its drafting: see e.g. T22/85 *IBM/Document abstracting and retrieving* (OJ EPO, 1990, 12) at reason 3; and Paterson, G, *The European Patent System. The Law and Practice of the European Patent Convention*, 2nd edition (Sweet & Maxwell, 2001), 409. Computer programs were eventually added to the list of excluded subject matter contained in Article 52(2) EPC following the UK delegation's observation that a computer program 'was merely the mathematical application of a logical series of steps in a process which was no different from a mathematical method': Davies, S, 'Computer Program Claims: The Final Frontier For Software Inventions' (1998) 20 EIPR 429, 432; Pila, J, 'Article 52(2) of the Convention on the Grant of European Patents: What Did the Framers Intend? A Study of the Travaux Preparatoires' (2005) 36 IIC 755, 769; and note also the comments of Peter Prescott QC in *CFPH LLC's Application* [2005] EWHC 1589 [35]–[37].

148 T208/84 *Vicom Systems Inc/Computer-related invention* (OJ EPO, 1987, 14).

149 The EPO's Examining Division rejected the claim as being directed to a mathematical method on the basis that digital image processing was just a calculation carried out on two-dimensional arrays of numbers: T208/84 *Vicom Systems Inc/Computer-related invention* (OJ EPO, 1987, 14), at reason 2.

150 Ibid., at reason 16.

151 T22/85 *IBM/Document abstracting and retrieving* (OJ EPO, 1990, 12).

which did not aim at any direct technical result but were rather of an abstract and intellectual character[152] and added:

> The requirement that an invention must have a technical character or in other words, must provide a technical contribution to the art is at the basis of a long-standing legal practice in at least the majority of Contracting States of the EPO. Neither from the terms of Article 52 EPC, nor from the legislative history of that Article as appearing from the preparatory documents can it be deduced that these Contracting States would have intended to deviate from their national laws and jurisprudence in this respect. On the contrary, it seems to be borne out by the list of exceptions in Article 52(2)(a) to (d) EPC that they did not wish to do so.[153]

Thus, the exclusions listed in Article 52(2) EPC, were rationalized as specific instances of the overriding general principle that, to be patentable, a claimed invention must have technical character. The assumption made by the TBA seems to be that the legislature (the Munich Diplomatic Conference responsible for drafting the EPC), in arriving at a consensus view of the concept of invention, merely catalogued instances of non-patentable subject matter derived from decisions of national courts.[154]

The Technical Board of Appeal's view that an absence of technical character both explains the content of the list contained in Article 52(2) EPC and can (therefore) serve as a basis for deciding future cases is in stark contrast to that of Peter Prescott QC, sitting as a Deputy Judge, in *CFPH LLC's Application*:[155]

> When we come to look at the list of excluded items … , and if we pay careful attention, we can notice that they are like a miscellaneous rag-bag. Except superficially, they do not constitute what logicians call a genus, or logical class. Indeed I believe that they were not all excluded for the same reason. On the contrary, they were excluded for policy reasons; but the policy may not be

---

152 Ibid., at reason 2.

153 Ibid., at reason 3. The Board added that further support for its interpretation of Article 52 EPC was to be found in the wording of those EPC Rules governing the formalities of application which required applicants, inter alia, to identify certain 'technical' aspects of a claimed invention.

154 In fact the Munich Diplomatic Conference deliberately avoided using the term 'technical' in framing the concept of invention under the EPC, opting instead to list specific items that were regarded as outside the concept with the intention that the EPO should not have to deal with difficult questions: Kolle, G, 'The Patentable Invention in the European Patent Convention' (1974) 5 IIC 140, 144–5 and 151.

155 [2005] EWHC 1589 Pat.

> at all the same in each case … If that is right it would be dangerous to adopt reasoning that was applied to one excluded item and blindly carry it over to a different item.[156]

So for instance, he observed that the policies underlying the exclusion of discoveries from patentable subject matter were quite different from the reasons that computer programs are not allowed to be patented.[157] A test involving 'technical contribution' or 'technical features' he dismissed as too vague to be workable at the margin.[158]

Pumfrey J too, in the High Court, expressed the view that the excluded subject matters do not have anything in common but rather are a heterogeneous collection each excluded on different policy grounds.[159] Whilst a lack of technical effect may be common to many members of the list, this is not a necessary characteristic of the excluded items.[160] And in *Aerotel Ltd* v *Telco Holdings Ltd*[161] the UK Court of Appeal endorsed this perspective. Explaining why the provisions about what are not to be regarded as inventions are not easy, Jacob LJ observed that there was no underlying purpose behind the provisions as a group and that an overall approach cannot be adopted to what is a disparate group.[162] In contrast to the conclusion reached by the TBA of the EPO, which he labels as a mistaken assumption,[163] Jacob LJ said that an examination of the debates amongst the framers of the Convention which led to the excluded categories reveals that the various categories were the result of compromises and distinct discussions about each and that no overarching principle was intended.[164] That in different jurisdictions, the same starting point can lead to quite radically different developments in the law serves to illustrate that the process of inductive reasoning is one that involves evaluation: reasonable people can arrive at different, though reasoned, conclusions.

---

[156] Ibid. [21].

[157] Ibid. [34]–[35].

[158] Ibid. [37] and see also Prescott QC's comments at [78].

[159] *Halliburton Energy Services Inc* v *Smith International (North Sea) Ltd* [2005] EWHC 1623 (Pat) [212]; and *Shopalotto.COM Ltd's Application* [2005] EWHC 2416 (Pat) [8].

[160] *Shopalotto.COM Ltd's Application* [2005] EWHC 2416 (Pat).

[161] Joined cases *Aerotel Ltd* v *Telco Holdings Ltd and Macrossan's Application* [2006] EWCA Civ 1371.

[162] Ibid. [9].

[163] [2006] EWCA Civ 1371 [30].

[164] [2006] EWCA Civ 1371 [11].

So far, my emphasis has been on the problem of the inflexibility of rules in the dynamic sense. But as has already been noted, to criticize a rule as inflexible may be to criticize its over or under-inclusiveness as to purpose.[165] This is a static problem. It arises where applying the rule produces an undesirable outcome in a proportion of the cases to which it applies. By an undesirable outcome I mean one that is not consistent with the rule's purpose or one which manifestly conflicts with some other valid rule or overarching principle. If this happens in the majority of cases where the rule applies, then the solution lies in changing the rule. More challenging is the circumstance where, in the great majority of cases the rule provides a good outcome, but in a small proportion of cases it does not.

Of course this problem only arises where there is a rule creating it. The legislature frequently has insight enough to avoid the static problem of inflexibility and drafts legislation such that applicability turns on the interpretation of words such as 'substantial' and 'obvious' which allow judges to make evaluative choices. Sometimes the legislation may be explicit as to the values that must be taken into account. The legislation may for instance explicitly direct that judges apply values such as 'fairness' or 'justice'.[166] More commonly, the legislation is vaguer both as to the factors to be taken into account and the evaluative framework to be applied in balancing them. So for instance, the use of the word 'substantial' in section 16 Copyright Designs and Patents Act 1988

---

165 At least if read literally: Kennedy, above n.4, 1689; Kelman, above n.5, 40; and Sunstein, above n.23, 990.

166 See e.g., fairness is an explicit consideration in the various 'fair dealing' defences contained in sections 29, 30, 30A and 32 Copyright Designs and Patents Act 1988, whilst under section 97, the justice of the case is an explicit factor to take into account in determining damages for infringement. Justice features in the determination of whether an employee inventor is entitled to compensation for his invention under section 40 Patents Act 1977, whilst under section 41, in circumstances where an employee inventor is entitled to a compensatory award, the amount is that which would secure for the employee a fair share of the benefit which the employer has derived. Under section 48A, one of the grounds on which a compulsory licence of a patent can be ordered is where the establishment or development of commercial or industrial activities in the United Kingdom is unfairly prejudiced. Under section 5(3) Trade Marks Act 1994, a sign may be refused registration if identical or similar to an earlier mark, but is to be registered for goods or services that are not similar to those for which the earlier mark is registered, where, inter alia, this would take unfair advantage of the repute of the earlier mark (assuming the mark had a reputation). There is a corresponding ground of infringement contained in section 10(3) which again refers to 'unfair advantage'.

allows judges' discretion in deciding whether copyright is infringed by a partial taking. Whatever else might be at play, it is clear that judges are influenced in the impressions formed in individual cases by a sense of fairness.[167]

But legislation is not always open textured. The problem of inflexibility arises where the advantages of having a clear and inflexible rule come into conflict with the general and fundamental notion that harm should not be done except in case of pressing necessity.[168] A solution lies in the individualization of decisions in circumstances notionally embraced by the rule. A crucially important agency that operates to introduce standards into decision making is equity.[169]

The utility of equity in dealing with the static problem of inflexibility can be illustrated by a consideration of non-express trusts. The reasons why equity raises non-express trusts are diverse and cannot be systematically ordered[170] but generally it can be said that a constructive trust arises by operation of law whenever the circumstances are such that it would be unconscionable for the owner of property to assert his own beneficial interest in the property and deny the beneficial interest of another.[171] The touchstone of 'unconscionability' is given specific content *ex post* and not *ex ante* and in this way decisions are 'individualized'.

Consider for example the law relating to the ownership of rights. The UK Copyright Designs and Patents Act 1988 contains a simple scheme

---

[167] What amounts to a substantial taking is considered in more detail below at p. 204.

[168] See in respect of formalities for the transfer of land, Birks, above n.15, 484.

[169] 'Standards of conduct' are a feature of equity. Peter Millett, for instance, noting that although the common law insists on honesty, diligence, and the due performance of contractual obligations, has argued that there is still a need to impose on those who engage in commerce the nobler and subtler qualities demanded by equity of, 'loyalty, fidelity, integrity, respect for confidentiality, and the disinterested discharge of obligations of trust and confidence': Millett, P J, 'Equity's Place in the Law of Commerce' (1998) 114 LQR 214, 216. See also Mason, A, 'Equity's Role in the Twentieth Century' (1997–98) 8 KCLJ 1, 2. But such standards are not the exclusive province of equity and indeed it has been cogently argued that, in recent times, equitable notions such as 'unconscionable' and 'inequitable' have drawn closer to common law concepts such as 'fair', 'reasonable' and 'just': Mason, A, 'The Place of Equity and Equitable Remedies in the Contemporary Common Law World' (1994) 110 LQR 238, 242 and 258–9.

[170] Birks, above n.15, 477 and note also the comments of Davies LJ in *Carl Zeiss Stiftung* v *Herbert Smith* (No. 2) [1969] 2 Ch 276, 300.

[171] Per Millett LJ in *Paragon Finance plc* v *Thakerar & Co* [1999] 1 All ER 400, 409.

for the initial allocation of rights in a work. Rights in literary, dramatic, musical and artistic works will usually first belong to the person who created the work.[172] It is otherwise if such a work is made by an employee in the course of his employment. Here the employer will be the first owner of any copyright in the work subject to an agreement to the contrary.[173] Ostensibly then, ownership of copyright is determined under an inflexible but certain rule-based scheme. The first legal owner of copyright in a work is determined by statute and cannot be altered except by agreement and then only for future works and works made by employees. Rights of ownership can be transferred but only by written instruments.[174] 'Ostensibly' because there are instances where the courts have distributed rights other than according to the scheme laid down in the Act and have bypassed the formalities of writing and signature normally required to effect transfers of copyright. In this, the courts have used the tool of the constructive trust so that what is acquired is an equitable rather than a legal interest in the copyright work. Thus the rigidity of the rule-based statutory scheme of ownership and disposition is set in conflict with a standards-based equitable one.[175] In this way such decisions can go some way to dealing with the problem of over-and under-inclusiveness.

Such individualized decisions will not undermine a rule so as to render it entirely superfluous providing the particular circumstances giving rise to the decision are likely to recur so infrequently so as not to pose a significant threat to the policies pursued through the rule.[176] Thus, whilst courts have on occasion been prepared to bypass the statutory formalities regarding assignments of copyright, they have not accepted the assertion that a copyright owner has a proprietary claim to the proceeds of an infringement of copyright.[177] As observed by Newey J in *Twentieth Century Fox Film Corp* v *Harris and others*: 'given the potency of

---

[172] Section 9(1) read in conjunction with section 11(1) Copyright Designs and Patents Act 1988. The position is otherwise for sound recordings, broadcasts and typographical arrangements.

[173] Section 11(2) Copyright Designs and Patents Act 1988.

[174] Section 90(3) Copyright Designs and Patents Act 1988 provides that 'an assignment of copyright is not effective unless it is in writing signed by or on behalf of the assignor'.

[175] For a comprehensive account of the operation of equity in the ownership of copyright see Booton, above n.67.

[176] Birks, above n.15, 484.

[177] Section 96 Copyright Designs and Patents Act 1988 makes no mention of so-called 'proprietary injunctions' in the list of remedies available to copyright owners in an action for infringement.

proprietary claims, they could be expected to be asserted routinely in breach of copyright cases were they available'.[178]

The neatness of the constructive trust mechanism is that it allows the assertion that, although sometimes ownership rights are distributed other than according to the statutory scheme, nonetheless the principle of consistency is adhered to. Thus, in answer to the criticism that any finding of an equitable interest in copyright drives a coach and horses through the formal statutory demands regarding assignments of copyright, the equitable interest arises in such circumstances, not by way of transfer, but by activation in equity of the conscience of the owner of the legal interest. In such circumstances then, a trust is said to have been created rather than there being any transfer or assignment of an interest.[179] The persuasiveness of this argument is of course entirely dependent on recognizing the duality between law and equity.[180] Extremely useful though it is, recognizing this duality is no more than a common lawyer's sleight of hand.

For all this tinkering with the rules on ownership, the most significant contribution equity makes to the field of intellectual property law is in relation to remedies.[181] In the UK, procedures and remedies are matters traditionally understood to be the province of judges;[182] however, the rights and remedies of the owners of intellectual property have been put on a statutory footing[183] and indeed the enforcement of intellectual

---

[178] *Twentieth Century Fox Film Corp* v *Harris* [2013] EWHC 159 (Ch) [13]. In this respect it is also notable that courts have held that a patent for an invention can be held on constructive trust if it comes into the hands of the alleged trustee by way of unconscionable dealing or in breach of fiduciary obligations or in consequence of a breach of trust. However, in the far more routine case in which an employee makes an invention which is deemed by operation of section 39 Patents Act 1977 to belong to the inventor's employer, there is no question of the employee retaining beneficial ownership as against the employer: *French* v *Mason* [1999] FSR 597.

[179] *Western Front* v *Vestron* [1987] FSR 66, relying in large part on *Acorn Computers* v *MCS Microcomputer Systems* (1985) 4 IPR 214 (a decision of the Federal Court of Australia).

[180] For a discussion of this duality see Birks, above n.15, 476.

[181] For a brief review of the historical development of equitable remedies see Cornish, W, Llewelyn, D and Aplin, T, *Intellectual Property: Patents, Copyrights, Trademarks & Allied Rights*, 8th edition (Sweet & Maxwell, 2013), 71–2.

[182] Ibid., 54.

[183] See for instance, sections 61–3 Patents Act 1977; sections 96–100 Copyright Designs and Patents Act 1988; and sections 14–19 Trade Marks Act 1994.

property rights is the subject of a European harmonization initiative.[184] Generally, acts of infringement are treated at tortious invasions of property. The Copyright Designs and Patents Act 1988 for example, contains a typical scheme in providing that, 'in an action for infringement of copyright all such relief by way of damages, injunctions, accounts or otherwise is available to the plaintiff as is available in respect of the infringement of any other property right'.[185]

The owners of intellectual property rights are primarily entitled to claim damages from infringers to compensate for the harm they have suffered from infringing acts. The principles governing damages recoverable for infringement are the 'normal' ones applicable to many other torts. The overriding principle is that the victim should be restored to the position she would have been in if no wrong had been done and can recover loss which is foreseeably caused by the wrong.[186]

From very early in the history of intellectual property, owners of rights have also sought orders directed to restraining the actions of potential infringers and owners are entitled and will normally claim by way of remedy an injunction restraining the defendant from any apprehended future act of infringement.[187] It is thus common in intellectual property cases for a court to order a final injunction at trial to prevent a defendant from committing in future an act which the defendant was threatening and intending to commit but which the court has now decided would be unlawful. Because of the almost routine nature of such orders, it is easy to lose sight of their equitable character. But when one explores some of the more creative manifestations of this form of remedy that basis becomes clear as does its significance.

The so-called springboard injunction, for instance, is neatly illustrative of how equitable remedies are used by courts to individualize outcomes notwithstanding an apparently inflexible rule-bound framework for decision making. The word 'springboard' is used to refer to an injunction granted in circumstances where a defendant has, by way of their infringing activities, built up a bridgehead or springboard into a market.

---

184 Directive 2004/48/EC of the European Parliament and of the Council of 29 April 2004 on the enforcement of intellectual property rights.

185 Section 96(2) Copyright Designs and Patents Act. Similar provision is made in section 61(1) Patents Act 1977 and section 14(2) Trade Marks Act 1994.

186 *Gerber Garment Technology Inc* v *Lectra Systems Ltd* [1997] RPC 443, 452.

187 For a brief historical overview see García Pérez, R, 'Injunctions in Intellectual Property Cases: What is the Power of the Courts?' (2016) IPQ 87, 88–90.

The injunction then is designed to deprive the defendant of that benefit.[188] The conceptual difficulty with this species of remedy is that that acts restrained by the injunction would, but for the injunction, otherwise be lawful, for instance because the right in issue has expired or the restrained activity otherwise falls outside the scope of the claimed right.[189] This problem has greatly vexed the judiciary especially where such an injunction is requested as a remedy for a breach of confidential information in circumstances where the information is no longer secret.[190] The difficulties are compounded by the obvious tensions that such a remedy creates when set against a clear statutory scheme. As observed by Fysh QC (sitting as deputy Judge) *in Dyson Appliances Ltd* v *Hoover Ltd* (No. 2, 'Springboard' Relief):

> On its face, the notion of an injunction to restrain the use of an invention after the date of expiry of the patent to which it relates, seems anomalous, going against the very purpose of the patent system. The consideration which the patentee gives for his original grant is that once the period of monopoly has

---

[188] *Smith & Nephew plc* v *Convatec Technologies* [2013] EWHC 3955 (Pat) [116]. This form of relief is by no means newly recognized. Post-expiry relief was granted in *Crossley* v *The Derby Gas Light Co* (1834) 4 LT 25 in which the defendant manufactured gas meters in infringement of a patent. Shortly before the expiry of the patent, the patentee moved for an injunction to take effect after the expiry of the patent and to restrain the sale of meters which had been manufactured (and stocked) during the life of the patent. The Court granted the relief sought holding that an injunction after the expiration of a patent may be granted so as to prevent a defendant, 'reaping the reward of his improbous labour'.

[189] *Smith & Nephew plc* v *Convatec Technologies* [2013] EWHC 3955 (Pat) [117] and [121].

[190] On which, note the comprehensive analysis undertaken by Arnold J in *Vestergaard Frandsen A/S* v *Bestnet Europe Ltd* [*2009*] EWHC 1456 (Ch) [42]–[93]. I think it fair to say that there is a tone of scepticism running throughout Arnold J's judgement. Following a thorough review of the decided cases, Arnold J concluded that there was never any sound authority for the proposition that an injunction can be granted to restrain continued misuse of confidential information once that information has ceased to be confidential: ibid. [76]. However, he was prepared to accept that a limited degree of confidentiality can remain even once information can be ascertained by a process of reverse engineering and an injunction would be available to prevent a defendant from benefiting from not having to undertake the steps which persons without direct access to the information would have to take: ibid. [80]. He was rather more cautious in concluding that an injunction could also be granted to prevent a defendant from benefiting from a past misuse of confidential information noting that the authorities on this point were conflicting: ibid. [93].

> expired, anyone is free to work the patent. In addition, Parliament has spelled out what constitutes infringement in s.60 and the remedies for patent infringement in s.61 of the Act. Such statutory statements one might think, should be the end of the matter. Furthermore, from the procedural point of view, the proposition that an injunction can legitimately be granted in respect of past infringement and in the absence of a basis of threat, actual or implied, to infringe the patentee's rights in the future, makes the injunction prayed for, on its face, implausible. Injunctions in general protect existing rights and threats to infringe such rights ...[191]

In order to accommodate such novel tools as springboard injunctions, courts have been forced to declare that the Patents Act 1977, although going a long way to set out the remedies available to a patentee, is not a complete code as to remedies.[192] The jurisdiction to order a post-expiry (or other springboard) injunction derives from section 37 of the Supreme Court Act 1981 (and probably in addition from an inherent equitable jurisdiction).[193] Section 37 grants an unlimited discretion as to the terms and conditions of any injunction. The touchstone for making any such order is that it must be 'just and convenient to do so'.

As to whether such an injunction is 'just' or 'reasonable', courts sometimes find these conditions satisfied by reference to the circumstances of the claimant and sometimes by reference to the behaviour of the defendant. The distinction is really no more than one of emphasis since in most cases any detriment to the claimant corresponds to an advantage to the defendant. As to the former, it has been held that a post-expiry injunction is reasonable and proportionate so far as it aims to place the proprietor of the patent in the position it would have been have been had its rights been respected.[194] So for instance, in *Dyson Appliances Ltd* v *Hoover Ltd* (No. 2), a 12-month post-expiry injunction was granted to prevent the defendants taking advantage of design materials, tooling and stock used in the production of infringing products. The period of the injunction came from the fact that it took the defendant 12 months to develop and launch the infringing product. In respect of the

---

[191] [2001] RPC 544 [17]. The decision in *Dyson* v *Hoover* briefly mentioned in the comprehensive review undertaken by Arnold J in *Vestergaard Frandsen A/S* v *Bestnet Europe Ltd* [2009] EWHC 1456 (Ch) [92]. Whilst not expressly criticised, Fysh QC's judgement is equally not obviously approved.

[192] *Union Carbide Corporation* v *BP Chemicals Limited* [1998] FSR 1, 6–7.

[193] *Dyson Appliances Ltd* v *Hoover Ltd* (No. 2, 'Springboard' Relief) [2001] RPC 544 [36].

[194] Ibid. [44]–[46] citing C-316/95 *Generics BV* v *Smith Kline & French Laboratories Ltd* [1997] RPC 801.

latter, courts have ordered post-expiry injunctions so as, 'to deprive an infringer of an unwarranted advantage gained from their act of infringement'.[195] Thus obtaining regulatory approval for a new product is an unwarranted advantage where obtained as a result of infringing a patent and this notwithstanding that the final marketed product itself does not infringe.[196] Springboard relief is not necessarily confined to a (prohibitory) injunction. Courts have for instance ordered the delivery up of goods imported into the United Kingdom in infringement of a patent notwithstanding that the effect of the order was to prevent the sale of the products in the UK after the expiry of the rights in issue.[197] Nor is springboard relief of this kind confined to patent cases.[198] Fysh QC's observation in *Dyson Appliances Ltd* v *Hoover Ltd* that the notion of an injunction to restrain the use of an invention after the date of expiry of the patent to which it relates seems anomalous reflects the key point that the clear statutory scheme, that lays out clearly and with precision the term of protection, is subject to judicial variation by way of this remedy and in the name of doing justice in an individual case.

So far as final injunctions of more conventional form are concerned, courts certainly pay lip service to the equitable character of this form of order, declaring it as a discretionary remedy which must be fair and equitable and proportionate.[199] Neuberger J (as he then was), for instance, in *Kirin-Amgen Inc* v *Transkaryotic Therapies Inc* (No. 3) was of no doubt that courts have a discretion either to refuse such an order outright or else to grant it on a qualified basis or on terms, and cited in

---

[195] *Smith & Nephew plc* v *Convatec Technologies* [2013] EWHC 3955 (Pat) [129].

[196] *Smith & Nephew plc* v *Convatec Technologies* [2013] EWHC 3955 (Pat). See also *Kirin-Amgen Inc* v *Transkaryotic Therapies Inc* (No. 3) [2005] FSR 875.

[197] *Merck Canada Inc, Merck Sharp & Dohme Ltd* v *Sigma Pharmaceuticals plc* [2012] EWPCC 21; [2013] EWCA Civ 326.

[198] See for instance in relation to copyright: *Chappell & Co Ltd* v *Colombia Graphophone Co* [1914] 2 Ch 745. In *Dyson Appliances Ltd v Hoover Ltd* (No. 2, 'Springboard' Relief) the claimants sought a post-expiry injunction prohibiting both the sale of products and the use of the trade mark used by the defendant to market the infringing products. The court held that a good deal of the law in relation to the post-patent-expiry injunctions applied with equal force to the question of the propriety of granting the trade mark injunction: [2001] RPC 544 [52]. However, the Court refused to grant the order considering it as unjust and disproportionate on the facts: ibid. [59].

[199] *Virgin Atlantic* v *Premium Aircraft* [2009] EWCA Civ 1513 [23]. See also García Pérez, above n.187.

support of that proposition the statement made by Aldous J in *Chiron Corporation* v *Organon Teknika Ltd* (No. 10):

> as a general rule, a defendant, who interferes with a proprietary right of a plaintiff and threatens to continue to do so, will be injuncted. It follows that as the defendants have infringed the patent and intend to continue to do so, an injunction to restrain infringement would normally be granted. However the Court has power under section 50 Supreme Court Act 1981 to refuse to award an injunction and award damages instead. That I believe includes the power to award a restricted injunction and to award damages as compensation for the restriction.[200]

Despite recognizing their discretionary power, whenever invited to do so courts have been extremely reluctant to refuse such an order taking the view that this would amount to the court sanctioning the defendant's wrongdoing by in effect allowing the purchase of the claimant's rights.[201] So far as UK courts are concerned, it would thus have to be a very strong case for an injunction to be withheld.[202] As put by Neuberger J, '[w]hile each case inevitably turns on its facts, there has to be a good reason

---

200 *Chiron Corporation* v *Organon Teknika Ltd* (No. 10) and *Chiron Corporation* v *Murex Diagnostics Ltd* (No. 10) [1995] FSR 325, 328, and cited by Neuberger J in *Kirin-Amgen Inc* v *Transkaryotic Therapies Inc* (No. 3) [2005] FSR 875 [22].

201 *Navitaire Inc* v *Easy Jet Airline* [2005] EWHC 0282 (Ch) [104]. See also *Regan* v *Paul Properties Ltd* [2006] EWCA Civ 1391 [36] approved in *Watson* v *Croft Promo-Sport Ltd* [2009] EWCA Civ 15 at [46]. Until recently, courts in the United States adopted a similar standpoint with the Court of Appeals for the Federal Circuit (CAFC) consistently holding that a permanent injunction would only be denied in exceptional circumstances: see e.g. Mueller, J, 'The Evanescent Experimental Use Exemption from United States Patent Infringement Liability: Implications for University and Nonprofit Research and Development' (2004) 56 Baylor L Rev 917, 967. However, the US Supreme Court has recently softened the approach and has held that for a court to grant a permanent injunction, a plaintiff must demonstrate: (1) that it has suffered an irreparable injury; (2) that remedies available at law, such as monetary damages, are inadequate to compensate for that injury; (3) that, considering the balance of hardships between the plaintiff and defendant, a remedy in equity is warranted; and (4) that the public interest would not be disserved by a permanent injunction: *eBay* v *MercExchange* LLC 547 US 388 (2006). For critical commentary on the *eBay* decision and its aftermath see Epstein, R and Kieff, F, 'Questioning the Frequency and Wisdom of Compulsory Licensing for Pharmaceutical Patents' (2011) 78 U Chicago L Rev 71, 87–91.

202 *Virgin Atlantic* v *Premium Aircraft* [2009] EWCA Civ 1513 [23]–[25]. See also *Fisher* v *Brooker* [2009] UKHL 41 [18] (per Lord Walker) and [74] (per Lord Neuberger).

before the court departs from the normal form of order. After all, one is concerned with protecting a proprietary right'.[203]

It is hard to conceive of a case where a final injunction would be refused. In *Roussel-Uclaf* v *Searle & Co Ltd*, Graham J thought that a court would not grant an injunction the effect of which would be to deprive members of the public of the benefit of a unique life-saving drug.[204] But this was later doubted by Aldous J in *Chiron Corp* v *Organon Teknika* (No. 10).[205] The patent in issue in *Chiron* disclosed aspects of the nature of the Hepatitis C virus (HCV) and a family of cDNA sequences for portions of the HCV genome. Those sequences had been used by the claimants to prepare immunoassay kits for detection of blood samples infected with HCV. Aldous J refused the defendant company's request to limit an injunction so as to allow them lawfully to undertake R&D into HCV using the patented invention. Aldous J observed that it was in the public interest that patent monopolies be enforced with the resulting restrictions upon competition that are inherent in the patent system. It followed that the fact that an injunction to restrain infringement of a patent would have the effect of restricting competition did not of itself mean that the grant of an injunction would be contrary to the public interest.[206]

Professor David Vaver has criticized this conservatism as rooted in a set of principles developed in Victorian times mainly around cases of nuisances on land[207] and has contrasted the approach taken by UK courts with the position in the US where courts are prepared to consider the public interest as a relevant factor in deciding whether a request for injunctive relief should be refused.[208] This criticism is only partly warranted in that the US patent legislation does not contain provisions allowing for the grant of a compulsory licence where this would be in the

---

[203] *Kirin-Amgen Inc* v *Transkaryotic Therapies Inc* (No. 3) [2005] FSR 875 [26].

[204] *Roussel-Uclaf* v *Searle & Co Ltd* [1977] FSR 125, 131.

[205] *Chiron Corporation* v *Organon Teknika Ltd* (No. 10) and *Chiron Corporation* v *Murex Diagnostics Ltd* (No. 10) [1995] FSR 325, 334–5.

[206] Ibid., 333. Presumably, in order to establish that the grant of an injunction would be so contrary would require proof that the patent not only leads to static inefficiency (which is consistent with its economic rationale) but also dynamic inefficiency.

[207] Vaver, D, 'Sprucing Up Patent Law' (2010) A Report to the Strategic Board for Intellectual Property Policy (SABIP), 23.

[208] Ibid., 22–3.

public interest.[209] It is clear that Aldous J was of the view that the assessment of where the public interest lay was best done by the legislature rather than courts and the (UK) legislature envisaged that in certain situations the public interest required a refinement of patent rights and took appropriate steps to safeguard the interests of the public.[210] Thus the legislature, he observed, laid down the conditions required for a compulsory licence to be granted and the matters of public policy that should be taken into account in granting such a licence.[211] Earlier, in *Biogen Inc* v *Medeva Plc*[212] he made much the same points adding that if damages were granted in lieu of an injunction, that would amount to expropriation of the patent owner's property and that it was not the task of the court to legalise wrongful acts even if the defendant could be considered to be a public benefactor because it was producing a life-saving vaccine.[213] He continued by saying that, '[o]n general principles, it would seem that the legislature has contemplated that production of life-saving medicines may be affected by patent rights. The public is safeguarded by the right given to the minister to authorise use and the compulsory licence provisions'.[214]

So, whilst acknowledging that there are circumstances where the rights normally available to a patent owner can be restricted to give effect to the public interest, courts have adopted the stance that it is for the legislature to define those circumstances by way of a procedure allowing for the grant of a compulsory licence.

This reluctance to exercise their discretion tells us something about the value that courts attach to the normal form of the final injunction. It is a reflection of the view that intellectual property rights depend for their effectiveness on the speed and efficiency with which they can be enforced.[215] Put simply, the value of a right is measured in terms of the

---

209 In the US compulsory licences are available pursuant to section 1498, title 28 USC and antitrust consent decrees but are rarely granted: O'Connor, S, 'Intellectual Property Rights and Stem Cell Research: Who Owns the Medical Breakthroughs?' (2005) 39 New England L Rev 665 (characterizing section 1498 as a 'formalized takings provision'); and Lee, P, 'Contracting to Preserve Open Science: Consideration-Based Regulation in Patent Law' (2009) 58 Emory Law Journal, 889, 912.

210 [1995] FSR 325, 333–4.

211 Ibid., 33–3 and for criticism see Vaver, above n.207, 22.

212 [1993] RPC 475.

213 Ibid., 486–7.

214 Ibid., 487.

215 Harms, L, 'The Role of the Judiciary in the Enforcement of Intellectual Property Rights: Intellectual Property Litigation under the Common Law System

remedies available for its enforcement.[216] Above it was noted that the certainty of a rule depends on the context over which it is said to exercise control.[217] The reverse is also true: that is to say, the uncertainty generated by a standard depends on the context over which it is applied. Given the centrality of remedies in determining the value of any intellectual property right, uncertainty as to remedies, and in particular the availability of injunctive relief, is uncertainty as to the right itself. Because of the breadth of impact that the regular exercise of discretion would have, and the difficulty of foreseeing the consequences of the exercise of that discretion, the conservatism of judges in denying injunctive relief (notwithstanding their undoubted power to do so) is understandable.

Although post-expiry injunctions demonstrate a willingness to depart from the clear statutory scheme, and with this the introduction of uncertainty in the field of remedies, this is not a measure of the importance courts attach to that scheme and the certainty it promotes. Rather, consciously or otherwise, courts here are acknowledging that the circumstances in which a post-expiry order will be granted are likely to be so infrequent as not to pose a significant threat to the policies pursued through the legislative scheme.

There are also sound economic reasons that can be put up in defence of this reluctance to deny final injunctive relief. In economic terms, the availability of the remedy of the injunction forces would be users of the patented invention to negotiate with the owner. The potential user does not have the choice to go ahead and use the patented invention without permission and risk the consequence of paying court-assessed damages for that use.[218] The remedy of the injunction channels transactions to the market with decisional authority entirely in the hands of the patent owner.[219]

---

with Special Emphasis on the Experience in South Africa' (2004) 26 EIPR 483; and Cornish et al., above n.181, 54.

216 Cornish et al., above n.181, 71.

217 Schlag, above n.1, 407.

218 Rose, C, 'Crystals and Mud in Property Law' (1988) 40 Stanford L Rev 577, 594; and Landes, W and Posner, R, *The Economic Structure of Intellectual Property Law* (Belknap, 2003), 7–8 and 310 *et seq.*

219 Calabresi, G and Melamed, A, 'Property Rules, Liability Rules, and Inalienability: One View of the Cathedral' (1972) 85 Harvard L Rev 1089, 1092; and Burk, D, 'Muddy Rules for Cyberspace' (1999–2000) 21 Cardozo L Rev 121, 127.

Only where transaction costs are impossibly high is efficient resource allocation facilitated by denying owners of property an injunctive remedy against invasions of their rights and instead limiting them to a remedy in damages.[220] In such circumstances the entitlement is better protected by 'liability rule' under which anyone may destroy the initial entitlement if she is willing to pay an objectively determined value for it.[221] This is because, under liability rules, decisional authority vests not with the owner of the entitlement but with outside parties who can exercise the choice whether to take the entitlement or not.[222] However, the transfer or sharing of the entitlement is allowed on the basis of a value determined by some organ of the state (typically a court) rather than by the parties themselves.[223] Thus, where an actual market is infeasible, liability-type remedies permit state-mediated comparison of the value of conflicting activities and can thus simulate the result of voluntary transactions in the market but which for various reasons are impossible.[224] But for this to be justified, a market must be infeasible. Having a court or other authority determine a price in this way is a less efficient method of resource allocation than would be achieved through direct negotiation between the parties because the costs of court mediation adds very significantly to transaction costs. Such intervention is justified only because, even if the intervention operates imperfectly, the market alternative is worse.[225]

---

[220] See for instance: Rose, C, 'The Shadow of the Cathedral' (1996–97) 106 Yale LJ 2175, 2178; and Posner, R, *Economic Analysis of Law*, 7th edition (Wolters Kluwer Law & Business, 2007), 69. Thus it has been argued that because highly fragmented rights increase transaction costs, right owners should have only liability-type remedies: Parisi, F, Schulz, N and Depoorter, B, 'Duality in Property: Commons and Anticommons' (2005) 25 International Review of Law and Economics 578, 590. These arguments have been criticized on the grounds that problems in obtaining and processing information are as likely to impede efficient damage calculations by a judge as obstacles to bargaining are likely to impede efficient exchanges by private parties: Krier, J and Schwab, S, 'Property Rules and Liability Rules: The Cathedral in Another Light' (1995) 70 New York University L Rev 440, 453.

[221] Calabresi and Melamed, above n.219, 1092.

[222] Burk, above n.219, 127.

[223] Calabresi and Melamed, above n.219, 1092.

[224] Ibid., 1106; and Posner, above n.220, 69.

[225] Liability rules are typically preferable to property rules where the market valuation of the entitlement is deemed inefficient, that is, it is either unavailable or too expensive compared to a collective valuation: Calabresi and Melamed, above n.219, 1108–10.

The tension between rules and standards is, however, much more acutely felt in respect of interim injunctions. As much as final injunctions, interim orders are understood to be an essential element in the right holder's armoury of remedies. Underpinning this is the understanding that any delay in the termination of infringement can cause irreparable harm to the holder of an intellectual property right.[226] Courts then have acknowledged that the purpose of such injunctions is to protect right owners against violations of their property right. On the other hand, such interim orders are also understood to be discretionary remedies aimed at preventing injustice between the parties.[227] The balance of convenience test can be seen as a manifestation of the tension between rules and standards so far as it seeks to set the core guarantees provided to the owner by her property right against the justice of providing her an interim remedy pending resolution of the dispute being mediated by the court. As Lord Diplock said in *American Cyanamid Co* v *Ethicon Ltd*:

> The object of the interlocutory injunction is to protect the plaintiff against injury by violation of his right for which he could not be adequately compensated in damages recoverable in the action if the uncertainty were resolved in his favour at the trial; but the plaintiff's need for such protection must be weighed against the corresponding need of the defendant to be protected against injury resulting from his having been prevented from exercising his own legal rights for which he could not be adequately compensated under the plaintiff's undertaking in damages if the uncertainty were resolved in the defendant's favour at the trial. The court must weigh one need against another and determine where 'the balance of convenience' lies.[228]

There is a parallel here with the way in which courts wield the tool of the constructive trust in bypassing the formalities associated with the transfer of interests in copyright. In both cases, equity is being used as an instrument of justice[229] where 'justice' is understood as demanding a balance between rule and discretion. In both cases, general rules of law

---

[226] On which see e.g. Recital (22) of Directive 2004/48/EC on the enforcement of intellectual property rights.

[227] *SmithKline Beecham* v *Apotex* [2003] EWCA Civ 137 [18].

[228] *American Cyanamid Co* v *Ethicon Ltd* [1975] AC 396, 406.

[229] Courts have, for a very long time, been willing to qualify formalities in the interests of justice: Cornish et al., above n.181, 523.

become subject to refinements or qualifications aimed at making them more responsive to the merits of individual cases.[230]

Under the balance of convenience test, individualization primarily involves courts making an assessment of the impact of granting or refusing injunctive relief on the respective parties: the outcome being based on the course leading to the least net harm.[231] But achieving justice through individualization necessarily demands that courts are not blind to any factor. Thus, courts will sometimes decide upon the question of whether or not to grant interim injunctive relief based on factors other than the immediate impact that grant or refusal will have on the parties. Put another way, the conception of justice in this context includes considerations outside those which can be measured in economic terms.[232]

One such factor is whether the defendant deliberately took a risk.[233] In *News Group* v *Rocket*[234] the defendant record company planned to release a recording incorporating lyrics and under a title which, in the court's view, would have led them to anticipate that theirs was a project to which the claimant newspaper would object. In granting the injunction sought, the court took into account that the defendants had nevertheless embarked on the project and did so at their own risk and with their eyes open as to the possible consequences.[235] In *Elanco Products* v *Mandops*,[236] an interim injunction was also ordered not least of all because, in the court's view, the respondents had acted in a way that had 'brought

---

[230] This can be described as a 'modern' trend so far as a balance between rule and discretion is a feature of mature legal systems: Pound, above n.66, Chapter III 'The application of law', 100–143.

[231] For a relatively recent account see: Gibbons, G, 'Trade Mark Remedies in the United Kingdom and Ireland: Recent Developments' (2014) 36 EIPR 22, 26.

[232] *Jian Tools for Sales inc* v *Roderick Manhattan Group* [1995] FSR 924, citing *Hymac Ltd* v *Priestman Brothers Ltd* [1978] RPC 495.

[233] This is not the only factor and generally courts will exercise their power to grant or refuse interim relief 'to attempt to ensure that parties who try to steal a march on other parties … do not benefit from such conduct': *Warner-Lambert Company LLC* v *Sandoz GMBH* [2015] EWHC 3153 (Pat) [48].

[234] [1981] FSR 89.

[235] Ibid., 107.

[236] [1979] FSR 46.

their difficulties upon themselves'.[237] The same was true in *SmithKline Beecham* v *Apotex*[238] and *Jian Tools for Sales Inc* v *Roderick Manhattan Group*.[239]

That courts take into account whether a defendant has deliberately taken a risk shows both that they are aware of one of the problems with rules as well as illustrating how that problem can be overcome by individualization of decision making made possible by the recognized duality between law and equity. Rules, precisely because they set out to define clearly what is within and without their scope, allow the unscrupulous to 'walk the line' in ways that can undermine the purpose of the rule.[240] Indeed, rules can positively encourage this so far as, faced with a clear rule, people will arrange their affairs so that they are favoured by the rule. There is no reason to believe that the intellectual property system is devoid of this effect: in fact quite the opposite.[241] How

---

237 Ibid., 56.

238 [2003] EWCA Civ 137 [40] (the court noting that, '[the defendants] walked into the situation that they find themselves in with their eyes open to the risk that they were taking. They knew the risk and decided that it was best not to remove it').

239 [1995] FSR 924, 943–4 (the court noting that, 'the defendants took a calculated risk in adopting "BusinessPlan Builder" in the same typographical format as [the claimant's mark]').

240 Kennedy, above n.4, 1696; Kelman, above n.5, 41; and Sunstein, above n.23, 995. A variant of this applies where a rule fixes the magnitude of a penalty for breach of a particular legal directive. This can allow the unscrupulous to treat the penalty simply as a fixed cost of doing business: Schlag, above n.1, 385. In the area of intellectual property it was concerns over encouraging the unscrupulous to 'walk the line' that motivated US courts to reject a rule-based approach to patent claim construction. Famously the US Supreme Court in *Graver Tank & Mfg Co* v *Linde Air Products Co* 339 US 605 (1950) recognized that,

> to permit imitation of a patented invention which does not copy every literal detail would be to convert the protection of the patent grant into a hollow and useless thing. Such a limitation would leave room for – indeed encourage – the unscrupulous copyist to make unimportant and insubstantial changes and substitutions in the patent which, though adding nothing, would be enough to take the copied matter outside the claim and hence outside the reach of law.

241 That the defendants deliberately 'sailed close to the wind' is often observed in intellectual property cases. That a defendant set out to get as close as possible to the claimants' design, mark or invention as possible without infringing is considered relevant evidence but is of itself not determinative of infringement. So for example, Kitchin LJ in *Specsavers International Healthcare Ltd* v *Asda Stores Ltd* observed that,

far this is unjust depends on whether walking the line in this way is understood to be an objectionable social practice of itself rather than a legitimate manifestation of competition.[242]

In the normal course of events, courts have little choice but to accept this problem. As noted earlier in this chapter, rules provide a complete before-the-fact specification of legal outcomes such that, if the facts a rule stipulates are given, and the rule is valid, then the answer it supplies must be accepted. The court process is concerned only with establishing, on a balance of probabilities, what the relevant facts are. However, at the interim stage, the evidence is largely untested and the question of whether the defendant's activities fall within or without any rule remains unresolved. In *American Cyanamid Co* v *Ethicon Ltd*,[243] the House of Lords expressly rejected earlier authorities which held that a claimant to obtain an interim injunction had to show that she had a prima facie case, noting that the decision whether or not to grant an interim injunction had to be taken at a time when the existence of the right or the violation of it was uncertain:

> The use of such expressions as 'a probability,' 'a prima facie case,' or 'a strong prima facie case' in the context of the exercise of a discretionary power to grant an interlocutory injunction leads to confusion as to the object sought to be achieved by this form of temporary relief. The court no doubt must be satisfied that the claim is not frivolous or vexatious, in other words, that there is a serious question to be tried.
>
> It is no part of the court's function at this stage of the litigation to try to resolve conflicts of evidence on affidavit as to facts on which the claims of either party may ultimately depend nor to decide difficult questions of law

---

> it is important to distinguish between a defendant who takes a conscious decision to live dangerously and one who intends to cause deception and deliberately seeks to take the benefit of another trader's goodwill. It has long been established that if it is shown that a defendant has deliberately sought to take the benefit of a claimant's goodwill for himself the court will not 'be astute to say that he cannot succeed in doing that which he is straining every nerve to do' … A trader who has taken the decision to live dangerously is in a different position, however. He has appreciated the risk of confusion and has endeavoured to adopt a sign which is a safe distance away. All must depend upon the facts of the particular case

[2012] EWCA Civ 24 [115].

[242] Kelman is inclined to the former view: Kelman, above n.5, 41 2.

[243] [1975] AC 396.

> which call for detailed argument and mature considerations. These are matters to be dealt with at the trial.[244]

At this stage of the litigation process then, courts effectively turn a blind eye to any evidence establishing that a rule has, or has not, been infringed. This leaves them free to import notions such as justice into their decision making notwithstanding that such notions may be absent from the rule itself. One manifestation of this is that defendants who deliberately set out to 'walk the line' may find themselves disadvantaged at the interim stage.

How far this is a challenge to the principle of consistency depends on how far one understands courts' duty to give effect to binding and valid rules should extend to all stages of the litigation process. But the exercise of equitable discretion elsewhere, for instance in the informal acquisition of copyright and in the granting of springboard relief, on the face of it present clearer and more direct challenges to that principle. That matters are not necessarily ended even where Parliament 'spells things out' in clear statutory statements invites a reflection on form and its significance in the relationship between the legislature and the courts. That is the subject that I turn to in the chapter which follows.

---

244 Ibid., 407.

3. Legislative power and harmonization

Limits on law-making powers add a further crucial dimension to the functional arguments as to whether decisions in particular circumstances are better done by applying rules or standards. Where legal entitlements are set by rules, decision making regarding those entitlements requires only that the adjudicator determine the relevant facts and circumstances and then mechanically apply the rule to those facts so as to determine the outcome.[1] As noted in the previous chapter, legislation then, is par excellence, the process by which valid rules are made.[2] On the other hand, a legal direction framed so as to make adjudication subject to a standard intentionally demands of courts (or other body charged with the administration of the law) some degree of law-making power from the legislature to the courts. The choice between rules and 'rulelessness' can thus be seen as presenting a principal/agent problem, where the legislature, as principal, by the adoption of a certain form of legal direction, aims to control the decisions of its agents (the courts).[3]

A perfect division is, however, impossible if only because no legislature can hope to be omniscient and to draft legislation which covers every possible present and future eventuality. Almost any rule can prove to be ambiguous or unclear in relation to some disputed or disputable context of litigation.[4] In practice there are always unforeseen circumstances such

---

1 A regime of rules thus reduces the occasions of judicial law-making: Kennedy, D, 'Form and Substance in Private Law Adjudication' (1976) 89 Harvard L Rev 1685, 1690, 1705 and 1752.

2 MacCormick, N, *Legal Reasoning and Legal Theory* (Clarendon Press, 1978), 58.

3 Sunstein, C, 'Problems with Rules' (1995) 83 California L Rev 953, 1012. See also Ehrlich, I and Posner, R, 'An Economic Analysis of Legal Rulemaking' (1974) 3 J Legal Stud 257, 261; and Schauer, F, *Thinking like a Lawyer. A New Introduction to Legal Reasoning* (Harvard University Press, 2009), 191–3.

4 MacCormick, above n.2, 65–7; and Thomas, E W, *The Judicial Process. Realism, Pragmatism, Practical Reasoning and Principles* (Cambridge University Press, 2005), 115–17 and 120.

that the text of a rule fails to define the context in which it is to apply.[5] And even if the legislature were so gifted, the imprecision of language would inevitably lead to a misinterpretation of its will.[6]

Given the impossibility of perfect rules, even where legislation is detailed and meticulously drafted, it is inevitable then that some law will be made at the point of application and, in practice, the difference between rules and standards then may only be one of degree. Though they exist as polar opposites in the theoretical dimension, in the day-to-day adjudication of legal disputes whether a provision is classed as a rule or a standard more often turns on the question of how far decision makers are guided or constrained by that provision.[7] A legislative provision framed in general terms requires of tribunals that they spell out detail when it comes to specific applications. A detailed and specific provision is likely to require less of tribunals in routine application but may require creativity in interpretation so as to accommodate factual situations unforeseen by the legislature.[8]

The remainder of this chapter aims to evaluate the core factors which influence choice of form where that choice is seen as a principal/agent problem. It reflects then on the circumstances when decision making

---

[5] Schlag, P, 'Rules and Standards' (1985) 33 UCLA L Rev 379, 410 and 413.

[6] Thus it is that a legislative drafter can influence the development of legislative policy through the way in which they interpret their drafting instructions and in their choice of words to achieve a goal which may not only define that goal but may also subtly refine it: Lord Neuberger of Abbotsbury, Master of the Rolls, 'General, Equal and Certain: Law Reform Today and Tomorrow', Statute Law Society, Lord Renton Lecture 2011, accessed 20 January 2017 at https://www.judiciary.gov.uk/wp-content/uploads/JCO/Documents/Speeches/mr-speech-lord-renton-lecture-28112011.pdf, 12–13 citing Marcello, 'The Ethics and Politics of Legislative Drafting' [1996] Tulane L Rev 2437. See also Kennedy, above n.1, 1700.

[7] So for instance, Lord Mance in *Generics (UK) Ltd* v *Lundbeck A/S* commented that,

> Lord Walker of Gestingthorpe said in the case of *Synthon* that "In the interpretation and application of patent statutes judge-made doctrine has over the years done much to clarify the abstract generalities of the statutes and to secure uniformity in their application" ... while adding that: "Nevertheless it is salutary to be reminded, from time to time, that the general concepts which are the common currency of patent lawyers are founded on a statutory text, and cannot have any other firm foundation".

[2009] UKHL 12 [46].

[8] Goodrich, P, *Reading the Law. A Critical Introduction to Legal Method and Techniques* (Basil Blackwell, 1986), 38.

ought to be directed and constrained and when not, and on the tensions that arise when different factors influencing choice of form point to contradictory outcomes. The factors that push for the law to be certain or as the case may be flexible are not related to the principal/agent issue. There is no reason why certainty as an object should be peculiar to either legislation or judge-made law except perhaps that legislation is more visible and typically uses a canonical form of words, but these are just matters of convention. The remainder of this chapter explores form from three different perspectives which do relate to the relationship between the legislature as principal and the courts as its agent: the merits and demerits of *ex ante* versus *ex post* decision making; the avoidance of the perception of bias in decision making; and the demands and attendant costs of harmonizing the national intellectual property laws of European countries.

As to the first of these, noting that ability or inability to foresee relevant factual scenarios and responses favours respectively rules or standards, I set out to illustrate how standards tend to be preferred where the object of the law is to produce a fair outcome in any dispute between individuals by way of an exploration of how the law decides the question of priority in patent claims. In particular, insights in this respect are to be gained by comparing the rigid and rule-bound European first-to-file approach with the rather more flexible approach under the US's first-to-invent scheme for determining priority as it operated prior to the enactment of the America Invents Act (AIA). The analysis moves from there to trade mark law and comparison of the tests for, 'a likelihood of confusion', as a relative ground for refusal of registration of a sign and as a ground of infringement for a registered mark. Notwithstanding the conceptual links between the two tests I show that the test deployed in deciding infringement claims is more fact and situation sensitive than the test deployed in deciding whether a sign is registrable. That allows me to emphasize the fairly obvious point that rule-bound determinations are ill-suited to decisions where relevant factual scenarios and responses cannot easily be predicted. But rather less intuitively, I also show that standards applied in an *ex ante* context become coarsened and tend to become much more rule-like.

The second theme that is developed in this chapter starts with the observation that in the absence of rules, decisions can be perceived as prejudiced because they require evaluative and subjective judgements to be made. On the face of it, certain legal directions seem to require that personal convictions figure in the decision making process so bringing a risk of a perception of bias. The analysis I present aims to show why typically this is an unfounded concern but that fear has been fuelled by occasional instances in which the mechanisms that guard against the influence of personal convictions operate weakly. In intellectual property law this is particularly so where the condition of morality is incorporated into the law. Through an analysis of cases applying that condition in copyright, trade mark and patent law, I explain why it is problematic but equally why it is unusually so.

The final theme of this chapter looks at the relationship between legal form and the effort to harmonize national laws and practices amongst the member states of the European Union. The starting point here is the observation that the discretion afforded by standards can hinder efforts at harmonization and typically then rules are to be favoured to promote the object of consistency in the application of the law. Efforts to harmonize laws that for other reasons might be better framed as standards (for instance because the kind of foresight that rule-making requires is not possible) leads to an inevitable tension. A single example is used to illustrate the point: the law relating to the patentability of software-implemented inventions. I set out to show that the difficulties that European law-makers and courts have faced in deciding the form and content of the law governing the patentability of computer-implemented inventions can be seen as manifestations of conflicting demands as to form.

3.1 *EX ANTE* VERSUS *EX POST* DECISION MAKING

Rules and standards contemplate decisions made at different times. Under rules, the context of the rule, the circumstances when it is to be applied and the behaviours subject to the rule are all determined *ex ante*.[9] Effective rules demand foresight and it follows that the ability or inability to foresee relevant factual scenarios and responses favours respectively rules or standards.[10] Standards, by contrast, are preferable where the context over which the legal direction exercises control is such that the precise factual circumstances likely to arise are difficult to determine ahead of time. In these circumstances, the precise scope of the direction

---

[9] Sunstein, above n.3, 961.

[10] As Lord Diplock (writing extra-judicially) observed, when making law Parliament is 'inevitably indulging in crystal gazing. It is trying to foresee how human beings will react in the future to a new rule of conduct …': Diplock, K, 'The Courts as Legislators' (Holdsworth Club of the University of Birmingham, 1965), 13.

is better defined after an actual situation has occurred.[11] For this reason then, standards tend to be associated with judicial decision making.[12]

It is not hard to find instances of legal directions in intellectual property law that are framed as standards because of the difficulties and undesirability of defining, *ex ante*, precisely what the legal direction is to cover. Thus, under the Copyright Designs and Patents Act 1988, whilst the exclusive rights of the copyright owner are defined with some precision[13] and are exercisable without question in circumstances where the whole of a work is appropriated, it is much harder to say in advance whether a partial taking will count as an infringement. The Act says only that the exclusive rights of the copyright owner are enjoyed in respect of the whole or a substantial part of the copyright work and courts have repeatedly stressed that whether what has been taken constitutes a substantial part of the copyright work is a matter of impression and is determined by the quality of the part taken as much as the quantity.[14] No doubt it would be possible to create precise rules to determine the question of what part of a work must be taken for that taking to count as an infringement: a simple percentage test for instance. But such rules

---

11 As noted above, economic efficiency points towards the adoption of standards where there the costs of predicting future behaviour and thus of promulgating a detailed rule directed towards regulating this behaviour are high.

12 Given the doctrine of binding precedent and the consequential normative aspect of court judgements, this paints a slightly over-simplified picture in that court decisions can also make the law *ex ante*, though as explained above, courts typically have considerable explanatory discretion in deciding how to treat earlier decisions.

13 The acts restricted by copyright are listed in section 16 Copyright Designs and Patents Act 1988, whilst sections 17–21 go on to provide details of the restricted acts.

14 Under UK law the test has always been understood to be extremely subjective, depending much more on the quality of what has been taken, rather than the quantity: *Ladbroke (Football) Ltd* v *William Hill (Football) Ltd* [1964] 1 WLR 273, per Lord Reid, 276, Lord Hodson, 288, and Lord Pearce, 293. In light of a series of decisions of the European Court of Justice starting with C-5/08 *Infopaq International* v *Danske Dagblades Forening*, the UK Court of Appeal now understands that the test for determining whether a restricted act has been done in relation to a substantial part of a work is that the parts in question must contain elements which are the expression of the intellectual creation of the author of the work: *SAS Institute Inc* v *World Programming Ltd* [2013] EWCA civ 1482. The test is considered in more detail below at p. 204.

would be more likely to give rise to decisions that would look irrational than those involving the application of a vaguer standard.[15]

Similarly, courts have deliberately avoided coining definitions aimed at deciding, *ex ante*, whether the steps taken to arrive at a claimed invention would have been obvious to a person skilled in the relevant art. Decisions on the issue of obviousness do not lend themselves to the application of a particular verbal formula appropriate to all classes of claims.[16] Again, no doubt it would be possible to create precise rules to determine the question of obviousness in some contexts, but such rules would lead to irrational decision making in some (perhaps many) circumstances given the numerous ways in which creative people can be inventive.[17]

There are, of course, also provisions which are drafted as rules and where *ex ante* determinations of the context, the circumstances when the rule is to be applied and the behaviours subject to it are both desirable and practical. For instance, notwithstanding they are detailed and complex, the legal provisions relating to priority of patent claims are rules (or as close to the rule end of the rules/standards spectrum as it is possible to get). Intuitively, if any determination needs to be made *ex ante*, then it is the priority date of a patent application. But the priority date serves a number of functions and the desirability or otherwise of determining that date by way of a rule-based framework needs to be tested against each of these functions. First, the priority date provides the reference point for considering what is to be embraced in the state of the art in the context of deciding whether what is claimed is new and involves an inventive step. A related function is that the priority date is the date on which that described in an application itself becomes part of the state of the art for the determination of the novelty of later applications made before the date of publication of the prioritized application.[18] It is almost too obvious to say, but without a fixed reference point against which to judge

---

[15] Spence, M and Endicott, T, 'Vagueness in the Scope of Copyright' (2005) 121 LQR 657, 662. A simple percentage test would for instance be almost impossible to apply in any case involving 'non-literal' copying.

[16] *Johns-Manville Corp's Patent* [1967] FSR 327, 332, cited and expanded upon in *Conor Medsystems Inc* v *Angiotech Pharmaceuticals Inc* [2007] EWCA Civ 5 [46].

[17] On which note Lord Hoffmann's observations in *Biogen Inc* v *Medeva Plc* [1997] RPC 1 cited above p. 54.

[18] Under section 2(1) Patents Act 1977, an invention is said to be new if it does not form part of the state of the art. Section 2(2) goes on to provide that the 'state of the art in the case of an invention shall be taken to comprise all matter ... which has at any time before the priority date of that invention been made available to the public ...'

novelty and inventiveness, everything claimed becomes fragile and indeterminate. This then provides a strong ground for the clarity and certainty that comes from a rule-based determination.

The priority date also fixes the date after which, assuming that the applicant takes all relevant steps in due time, the invention can be published or publicly exploited without jeopardizing the grant of a patent for that invention. From the applicant's point of view then securing a priority date provides a signal: in effect it sounds the starting gun. Without wanting to strain the analogy, there is a good reason why a pistol shot is used to start races. Whilst the outcome of a race is uncertain and each competitor must accept the multiple uncertainties associated with any fair competition, when to start running is not one of these. The idea that rules are important in providing clear signals to claimants of intellectual property rights is one that will be returned to and developed in the final chapter of this book. For the moment, it is enough to note that so far as successfully securing a priority date provides a signal for the applicant, this too is a reason for welcoming the clarity and certainty that comes from a rule-based determination.

It is easy enough to see how these concerns have shaped UK law. So far as establishing a priority date is concerned, the default position is that the priority date of an invention to which an application for a patent relates is the date of filing the application.[19] It is hard to imagine a legal provision that could be any more rule-like than this. There are, however, exceptions to this very simple rule which add complexity but which are themselves rules rather than standards and for the same reasons that the default determination is a rule.[20] Rather than the filing date of an application, the Act allows an applicant to claim priority from an earlier relevant application.[21] A 'relevant application' can be an earlier one made under the Patents Act 1977, or it can be one made in a 'convention country'. These exceptions then are aimed at overcoming two very predictable undesirable consequences of a scheme where priority derives

19 Section 5(1) Patents Act 1977.

20 On the complexity of rules see Dworkin, R, *Taking Rights Seriously* (Harvard University Press, 1977), 25.

21 Under section 5 Patents Act 1977 a subsequent application may be deemed to have the priority date of an earlier application only so long as the subsequent application *is supported by matter disclosed in the earlier application.*

from the date of filing of an application and can be seen as contributing to the two core objectives identified above.[22]

Complex though these provisions are, they admit little if any discretion in decision making. An extraordinary example that illustrates the strictness of the rules regarding priority is that of 'poisonous priority'. Article 87(1) EPC requires that priority can only be accorded in respect of 'the same invention' as one in an earlier application. In case *R.* v *X/Same Invention* the EPO Enlarged Board of Appeal said that this meant,

> that priority of a previous application in respect of a claim in a European patent application ... is to be acknowledged only if the skilled person can derive the subject matter of the claim directly and unambiguously, using common general knowledge, from the previous application as a whole.[23]

In *Nestec SA* v *Dualit Ltd*[24] the patent claimed priority from an earlier published application. However, the terms of the claims of the patent in issue had been broadened between the priority document and the application as filed. The effect was that the claims covered some possibilities that were not present in the priority document. Arnold J, adopting the strict interpretation given to the term 'same invention' by the EPO, concluded that the broadened claims were not entitled to claim priority from the earlier application. However, since the earlier application was published and disclosed arrangements having all the features of the relevant claims, the earlier applicant anticipated the claimed invention which was thus invalid for lack of novelty.[25]

---

22 Allowing priority to be claimed from an earlier UK application recognizes that otherwise inventors might be inhibited from exploiting inventions at the earliest possible date by the necessity for complying with all the technical requirements of the Act and the Rules. Allowing priority to be claimed from applications made in convention countries gives effect to the UK's international obligations under the Paris Convention for the Protection of Industrial Property 1883 and the World Trade Organization's (WTO's) Agreement on Trade-Related Aspects of Intellectual Property Rights (the TRIPs Agreement), those conventions themselves recognizing the very considerable challenges that would otherwise face inventors if they had to file simultaneous applications in all of the countries in which they sought a patent.

23 [2002] EPOR 167, at reason [34].

24 *Nestec SA* v *Dualit Ltd* [2013] EWHC 923 (Pat).

25 [2013] EWHC 923 (Pat) [111].

The key question from our point is that, notwithstanding such occasional instances of the unfortunate consequences of a rule-bound framework,[26] whether this framework forces largely rational decision making as compared to one based on vaguer standards. If concern were only with the priority date as reference point and as signal to the applicant then the answer I think would be a clear 'yes'. But establishing a priority date is necessary for another reason that makes the answer to that question rather less clear. Establishing priority can also be about establishing a better claim to rights over an invention as compared to a competing claim of an independent deviser of the same invention. Though the determination of the priority date is necessary in both cases, competing claims to rights in the same invention differ from attacks founded on the assertion that what is claimed is not new or is obvious in light of the prior art. That a claimed invention must be new and involve an inventive step are conditions that serve the public interest. They are amongst the many features of patent system that are aimed at ensuring that, notwithstanding its undoubted costs, the system has a net social benefit. But a challenge to a patent application based on a rival claim to rights in the same invention is in purely individualistic terms. Rather than an individual claim being pitted against the public interest, an individual claim here is pitted against an individual objection. A rule-based determination will seem irrational if the operative rule does not require of the judge that she take account of the full range of factors thought appropriate to deciding who has the better claim, and demands that she give due weight to these factors in arriving at a decision. Put more simply, a rule-based determination risks being labelled as producing an unfair outcome. The issue is not merely an academic one so far as, until recently, the factors deemed relevant in deciding who has priority over rights in an invention differed as between the US and Europe. As is well known, prior to the reforms made by the America Invents Act, priority disputes in the US were decided according to who was the first to invent the claimed invention.[27]

---

[26] See for instance the critical commentary on the decision in *Nestec SA* v *Dualit Ltd* in the ipKat blog here: http://ipkitten.blogspot.co.uk/2013/05/poisonous-priority-how-many-ways-can.html; and http://ipkitten.blogspot.co.uk/2013/06/on-poisonous-priority-taking-debate.html, both accessed 20 January 2017.

[27] The US President signed the 'America Invents Act' (AIA) into law on 16 September 2011. With its coming into force, in priority disputes relating to applications with effective filing dates after 16 March 2013, priority will be given to the first inventor to file an application, or to the first inventor to disclose the invention to the public (assuming they then file within a year). For a brief

For decades the US resisted international pressure to change, on the grounds, amongst others, that any other way of deciding priority disputes was unfair.[28] More specifically it was felt that the first-to-file system created the possibility that a first inventor may be deprived of her invention.[29]

Under pre-AIA section 102(g) US Patents Act, a person would not be entitled to a patent where another inventor established that they had made the invention at an earlier time than the applicant and had not abandoned, suppressed or concealed it. Determinations of entitlement required consideration of the respective dates of both conception and reduction to practice of the invention, and also of the diligence of the first to conceive of the invention in reducing it to practice.[30] This is not the place for a comprehensive review of what historically was the position under US law.[31] It is sufficient to note that the pre-AIA US law on priority was less rule-like than its European equivalents. But, viewed solely in terms of the rule/standard dichotomy, care must be taken not to overstate the differences. Four simple tenets underpinned the pre-AIA US priority system:

1. the first to reduce the invention to practice usually had priority;
2. filing a valid application constituted a constructive reduction to practice;
3. the first to conceive might have prevailed over the first to reduce to practice if the first to conceive was diligent from a time prior to the other inventor's conception through to her own reduction to practice (either actual or constructive); and

---

overview of the changes to US law under the AIA from a European perspective, see Poore, A, 'The America Invents Act: Good News for Outsiders?' (2012) 7 JIPLP, 378.

28 See e.g. Macado, C, 'First-to-File: Is American Adoption of the International Standard in Patent Law Worth the Price?' (1988) Columbia Business L Rev 543, 544, 566 and 576–7; and Dickey, R, 'The First-to-invent Patent Priority System: An Embarrassment to the International Community' (2006) 24 Boston University International LJ 283, 288, 292 and 296.

29 Macado, above n.28, 576–7; Dickey, above n.28, at 299. Whether the pre-AIA system was in fact fairer is far from clear: see e.g. Mossinghoff, G, 'The First-to-Invent Rule in the US Patent System Has Provided No Advantage to Small Entities' (2005) 87 Journal of the Patent and Trademark Office Society 514; Lemley, M and Chien, C, 'Are the US Patent Priority Rules Really Necessary?' (2003) 54 Hastings LJ 1299; and Abrams, D and Wagner, R, 'Poisoning the Next Apple: How the America Invents Act Harms Inventors' (2012) 65 Stanford L Rev 517.

30 See e.g. Macado, above n.28, 549–50; and Dickey, above n.28, 294–5.

31 For such see the account published by the USPTO, accessed 20 January 2017 at http://www.uspto.gov/web/offices/pac/mpep/s2138.html.

4. any reduction to practice that had been 'abandoned, suppressed, or concealed' was disregarded.[32]

Only the third and fourth of these tenets admit the kind of discretion in decision making characteristic of standards. The usual state of affairs was that priority disputes under the pre-AIA framework were settled by answering the far more straightforward question: 'who first reduced the invention to practice?' On its own, this question is as likely to produce irrational outcomes as the question, 'who was the first to file a patent application?' This rule did not, however, operate in isolation and the third and fourth of the tenets qualified the rule in a way that brought nuance to the determination and allowed a conception of fairness to influence the outcome.

It is worthwhile here to return to the observation that sparked this line of analysis, specifically that rules and standards contemplate decisions made at different times. Effective rules demand foresight and it follows that the ability or inability to foresee relevant factual scenarios and responses favours respectively rules or standards. Standards will thus tend to be preferred where the object of the law is to produce a fair outcome in any dispute between individuals. It is precisely the individuality of such disputes that makes the foresight demanded by rules impossible if what it aimed at is a fair outcome. Of course, in some cases we may be prepared to sacrifice fairness where there are good reasons to adopt a rule. As noted above, there are indeed a number of very sound reasons why priority should be decided according to a simple rule and the pre-AIA US scheme for deciding priority reflects this in its typical rule-like character. But there is I think another reason why standards did not dominate decision making in pre-AIA priority disputes notwithstanding the individuality of such disputes. Priority claims, though in framed in individualist terms, are different from, for example, those where it is claimed that a particular right has been infringed or that a particular defence has been made out. Unlike priority claims, these latter claims require of decision makers that they think not just in terms of the rights being claimed but also in terms of correlative duties imposed on others. Thus decisions demand reflection not only on whether a particular right is a good sort of right to recognize and enforce but also whether the correlative duty is good sort of duty to impose.[33]

Ex ante vs *ex post* determinations and the relationship between rights and duties is particularly manifest in trade mark law where 'a likelihood

32 Dickey, above n.28, 295.
33 This observation is developed more fully below at p. 215.

of confusion' serves as a touchstone for both registrability and infringement of a mark. Thus, under section 5(2) Trade Marks Act 1994, a mark will be refused registration if, because of similarities between the mark and an earlier registered mark, and between the goods or services for which the two competing marks are (intended to be) registered, there exists a likelihood of confusion on the part of the public. A registered trade mark is infringed where a person, in the course of trade, uses a sign such that there exists a likelihood of confusion on the part of the public because of similarities between the registered mark and the sign and between the goods or services for which the mark and sign are associated.

On the face of it this scheme is a logical one. The relative grounds for refusing registration exclude from registration marks whose use would constitute infringement of a mark already on the register. For this reason courts have declared the relative grounds of refusal 'conceptually indistinguishable' from the grounds of infringement.[34] But manifestly the decision whether a mark should be refused registration is not taken at same time as a determination whether the registered mark has been infringed. The system of trade mark registration is intended to reduce the kind of evidential burdens facing claimants in typical passing off actions[35] and if evidence of actual confusion on the part of the public were demanded as a condition of refusing to register a mark on relative grounds, then one of the key benefits of the system would be lost. Normally, where the relative grounds are considered by the Registrar, the mark in issue will not have been used and there will be no evidence of actual confusion with marks already on the register. In the absence of evidence, the Registrar must necessarily make a speculative judgement about whether there is a likelihood of confusion assuming that the marks are used in a normal and fair way.[36] The comparisons thus are 'paper based' in that it is the representations on the register that are compared

---

[34] *Raleigh International TM* [2001] RPC 11 [15] relying on the comments of the Court of Justice in C–39/97 *Canon Kabushiki Kaisha* v *Metro-Goldwyn-Mayer Inc* [1999] RPC 117 [21]. See also C-291/00 *SA Société LTJ Diffusion* v *SA Sadas* [2003] ETMR 83 [41].

[35] Bently, L and Sherman, B, *Intellectual Property Law*, 4th edition (Oxford University Press, 2014), 812, who note that a system of trade mark registration reduced the difficulties of proving goodwill and distinctiveness that arose in a passing off action.

[36] Ibid., 993.

rather than the marks in use as perceived in fact by consumers.[37] That the Registrar must reach a decision in the absence of evidence is not remarkable. Even where evidence is presented courts have emphasized that the question of whether consumers are likely to be confused is to be decided by the judge and cannot be abdicated to witnesses.[38] What is remarkable is that the Registrar, in arriving at that decision, is invited to exercise foresight in anticipating how a mark will be used and whether, in the anticipated circumstances, the relevant public are likely to be confused. The point is that foresight here is demanded in the application of a standard. That is arguably also true where a *likelihood* of confusion is tested in the context of deciding whether there has been infringement.[39] However, as I shall show, in this context, courts adopt an *ex post* perspective, looking at how the mark and the conflicting sign have actually been used in deciding whether the relevant consumer is likely to be confused by that pattern of use.

The European Court of Justice has ruled in a series of cases that confusion, whether in the context of applying the relative grounds for refusing registration or whether in the context of infringement, is to be assessed by way of a standards-laden composite test.[40] As a test for infringement the form of the test reflects the difficulties and undesirability of defining, *ex ante*, precisely all the circumstances when use of a sign will infringe a trade mark. I would suggest that in large part the

---

[37] Dinwoodie, G and Gangjee, D, 'The Image of the Consumer in EU Trade Mark Law' in Leczykiewicz, D and Weatherill, S (eds) *The Images of the Consumer in EU Law. Legislation, Free Movement and Competition Law* (Hart Publishing, 2016), 364.

[38] See for instance *Marks & Spencer plc* v *Interflora Inc* [2012] EWCA Civ 1501 [59], [90] and [137]. Note also Morgan, J's scepticism regarding the value of survey evidence in *Enterprise Holdings* v *Europcar Group UK Ltd* [2014] EWHC 2498 (Ch) [34]. See also Davis, J, 'Revisiting the Average Consumer: An Uncertain Presence in European Trade Mark Law' (2015) IPQ 15, 26; and Dinwoodie and Gangjee, above n.37, 352 ('empirical evidence (of any type) merely informs the perceptions of the hypothetical or notional average consumer, which remains the legal benchmark').

[39] Dinwoodie and Gangjee, above n.37, 357–8.

[40] The key factors that must be taken into account are: (1) the degree of similarity between the marks; (2) the degree of similarity between the respective goods/services; (3) the distinctiveness of the claimant/earlier mark; and (4) the level of recognition of the claimants/earlier mark (its familiarity). These factors are interdependent and the global assessment of all the relevant factors involves an iterative process between all the relevant factors: *Esure Insurance* v *Direct Line Insurance* [2008] RPC 34 [46] citing C-342/97 *Lloyd Schuhfabrik Meyer & Co GmbH* v *Klijsen Handel BV* [2000] FSR 77 [19].

challenge is because infringement invites consideration of the duties imposed on others by recognition of the right. That perspective is absent or at best hypothetical at the registration stage. The difference acutely manifested itself in the litigation between the mobile telephone service providers O2 and Hutchinson 3G (H3G).[41]

Prior to the litigation and in what was a very successful campaign, much of O2's advertising material used images of bubbles showing different types and configurations of bubbles. Consistent with this use O2 had registered a number of trade marks including eleven depictions of bubbles. During the summer of 2004 the rival firm H3G ran a series of advertisements on national television to promote the launch of a new service. The advertisements compared the new service offered by H3G to those of its competitors, including O2. The advertisements made indirect reference to O2's services by showing bubbles and it was this use of imagery that provoked the claimants to bring an action for infringement of its bubble trade marks.

The parties disputed the specific comparison to be made in assessing similarity and hence the likelihood of confusion. The claimant argued that the relevant comparison was between the registered trade mark and the allegedly infringing sign without recourse to any extraneous material. In support, O2 observed that this was the approach taken under the Trade Marks Act 1938 and that it produced the manifestly desirable outcome that it was an infringement of the Rolex trade mark to sell watches described as 'imitation Rolexes'.[42] The judge, the claimant said, should thus assess the similarity between the bubble imagery used by H3G in its advertisement, and its registered bubble trade marks, without taking into account the other elements of the advertisement that indicated that the bubble imagery was used by H3G to refer to the claimant's services.[43] The argument advanced by the defendants, and which was accepted by the judge, was that the context in which the offending sign was used had to be taken into account. In accepting this, Lewison J reasoned that it was:

---

[41] *O2 Holdings Ltd* v *Hutchison 3G Ltd* [2006] EWHC 534 (Ch); [2006] EWCA Civ 1656; and C-533/06 *02 Holdings Ltd* v *Hutchison 3G Ltd* [2008] RPC 33.

[42] And there was authority, the claimant argued, that the law under the 1994 Act was essentially the same: *O2 Holdings Ltd* v *Hutchison 3G Ltd* [2006] EWHC 534 (Ch) [107]–[109].

[43] Specifically the voice-over, caption, soundtrack and the second half of the advertisement: ibid. [110].

> highly artificial to compare the mark and the sign through the eyes of the average consumer without considering what impact the overall use of the sign in context would have upon him. Moreover, as appears from the summary of the principles applicable to assessing the likelihood of confusion that follows, likelihood of confusion must be assessed 'globally'. Similarity and likelihood of confusion are intimately bound together. It would be illogical for a quite different approach to be taken to the question of similarity ... I conclude therefore that I should look at the advertisement as an integrated audio-visual presentation. This is, after all, how it was designed.[44]

The relationship between the test as it applied at registration and the test for infringement formed part of the argument advanced by the claimant on appeal. In arguing that the assessment of similarity called for a straight (acontextual) comparison between the sign complained of and the registered mark, the claimants noted that this was the operative test at the application stage where the mark applied for is devoid of any context of use and is to be compared with an earlier trade mark.[45] The Court of Appeal provisionally rejected this argument. Jacob LJ could see no good reason why the consideration should be limited to a comparison between the defendant's sign with the registered mark. He noted that the way the relevant provisions were framed clearly called for an examination of the context of the use. In particular, consideration of how the defendant was using the sign complained of was necessary to answer the basic question of whether it was being used 'in the course of trade'.[46]

The Court's assessment was provisional so far as it accepted that the position was unclear and referred the matter to the European Court of Justice. The European Court agreed that, for the purposes of assessing whether there was a likelihood of confusion, it was right to take into account the context in which the defendant's sign is used.[47] The Court added that although the notion of likelihood of confusion was the same whether applied at the registration stage or in claims of infringement, those contexts were different and accordingly different demands were placed on the decision maker:

> Once a mark has been registered its proprietor has the right to use it as he sees fit so that, for the purposes of assessing whether the application for registration falls within the ground for refusal laid down in that provision, it is necessary to ascertain whether there is a likelihood of confusion with the

44 Ibid. [118].
45 [2006] EWCA Civ 1656 [26].
46 Ibid. [34].
47 C-533/06 *O2 Holdings Ltd* v *Hutchison 3G Ltd* [2008] RPC 33 [64].

> opponent's earlier mark in all the circumstances in which the mark applied for might be used if it were to be registered.
>
> By contrast [in an infringement action], the third-party user of a sign identical with, or similar to, a registered mark does not assert any trade mark rights over that sign but is using it on an ad hoc basis. In those circumstances, in order to assess whether the proprietor of the registered mark is entitled to oppose that specific use, the assessment must be limited to the circumstances characterising that use, without there being any need to investigate whether another use of the same sign in different circumstances would also be likely to give rise to a likelihood of confusion.[48]

The decision in *Specsavers International Healthcare Ltd* v *Asda Stores Ltd*[49] went further in contextualizing the test in the infringement context in holding that it was appropriate to take into account not only the defendant's actual use of the complained of sign but the claimant's actual use of the registered mark and in particular the colour of the logo in actual use notwithstanding that the mark as it appeared on the register was monochrome. The CJEU held that it was appropriate to take into account this actual use in assessing whether there had been an infringement by way of a use likely to confuse consumers:

> At the very least where there is a trade mark which is registered not in a particular colour or characteristic, but in black and white, the colour or combination of colours in which the trade mark is later used affects how the average consumer of the goods at issue perceives that trade mark, and it is, therefore, liable to increase the likelihood of confusion or association between the earlier trade mark and the sign alleged to infringe it.[50]

Thus, notwithstanding the claim that the relative ground of refusal is 'conceptually indistinguishable' from the ground of infringement, the test deployed in deciding infringement claims is more fact and situation sensitive than the test deployed in deciding whether a sign is registrable.

---

[48] Ibid. [66]–[67]. See also the comments of Kitchin LJ in *Specsavers International Healthcare Ltd* v *Asda Stores Ltd* (No. 2) [2012] EWCA Civ 24 [87].

[49] C-252/12 *Specsavers International Healthcare Ltd* v *Asda Stores Ltd* [2013] ETMR 46 (the referral being made to the European Court by the UK Court of Appeal: [2012] EWCA Civ 24).

[50] C-252/12 *Specsavers International Healthcare Ltd* v *Asda Stores Ltd* [2013] ETMR 46 [37]. In this, the Court confirmed the provisional view expressed by the UK Court of Appeal: *Specsavers International Healthcare Ltd* v *Asda Stores Ltd* (No. 2) [2012] EWCA Civ 24 [96].

At the start of this line of analysis it was observed that rules and standards contemplate decisions made at different times. The ability to anticipate relevant factual scenarios and responses favours rule-bound decision making. Not only does this mean that rule-bound determinations are ill-suited to decision making where the context over which the legal direction exercises control is such that the precise factual circumstances likely to arise are difficult to determine ahead of time but, and as illustrated by the *O2 Holdings Ltd* v *Hutchison 3G Ltd* litigation, standard-based decision making is not well-suited to decisions which require foresight. When applied in such an *ex ante* context, the standard becomes coarsened, operating in an 'all or nothing' way: in short, operating something like a rule.

What the trade mark cases illustrate is that the difficulties of defining, *ex ante*, precisely what the legal direction is to cover applies not just to assessments of the right holders' interests but to assessments of how a right directs the actions of others by way of its correlative duty.[51] As noted in Chapter 2, under rules once the relevant facts are established the judge's role becomes one of merely stating the inevitable outcome dictated by deductive logic. What is absent in arriving at a rule-bound decision is any reflection, at the point when the rule is applied, on its consequences. Yet it is precisely in the consequences of a decision relating to the exercise of a right that the correlation between right and duty is exposed. The realm of duties being the testing ground for claims of right is a theme I shall return to later. For the moment it is enough to note that courts, because they are dispute settlement fora, are particularly well positioned to assess rights in terms of correlative duties. In this respect registration authorities, whether trade mark registries or patent offices, do not have the same advantages as courts.

3.2 AVOIDING PERCEPTIONS OF BIAS

Earlier in this chapter I noted that legal rulings are normative and are not merely exercises in discovery and description but rather ordain what consequences are to follow upon given conditions and so set patterns of future behaviour. To this extent the legislature does not have a monopoly on *ex ante* law-making. In many instances court decisions will involve an inductive process by which the court, in deciding a contemporary case, rationalizes earlier decisions as specific instances of an overriding

[51] On which analytic approach note Hohfeld, W, 'Fundamental Legal Conceptions as Applied in Judicial Reasoning' (1913) 23 Yale LJ 16.

general principle. The resulting declared general principle, though made *ex ante*, can be seen as in effect a summary of past wise decisions and can be defended precisely on the basis it is a good summary.[52] In this way, though made *ex ante*, such binding principles, because they are derived from individual decisions in which rights have been assessed in light of their correlative duties, avoid the difficulties of foresight normally associated with *ex ante* rule making.

Consequential reasoning is, however, intrinsically evaluative and subjective so far as different judges may differ in their perception of the degree of injustice or inconvenience which will arise from the adoption or rejection of a given ruling. This serves as an introduction to the second problem with standard-based decision making. In the absence of rules, decisions can be perceived as prejudiced precisely because they require evaluative and subjective judgements to be made[53] and with this comes the risk of a perceived breakdown in prospective, impersonal governance.[54] Rules, by contrast go some way to ensure that disputants perceive that the law treats each uniformly (if not fairly).

In principle, where entitlements are set by rules by a legislature entirely ignorant of the specific and personal circumstances of individual citizens, disputes regarding those entitlements can be said to be settled impartially and objectively, since the role of the judge is mechanically to apply the relevant rule to the fact situations in issue.[55] Where a rule is in place, the parties to a dispute who seek resolution by law may fear losing their case but not because they fear that the law or decisions made under that law will be influenced by any bias of the decision maker. Such impartiality in due process is essential if the expectation is that people will have recourse to the law to settle disputes. Further, the manifest

---

[52] Sunstein, above n.3, 969.

[53] Standards risk the abusive exercise of discretion and lack of predictability: Kelman, M, *A Guide to Critical Legal Studies* (Harvard University Press, 1987), 41; and Sunstein, above n.3, 958. Furthermore, without rules, decisions can be extremely expensive requiring the determination of both facts and law: Sunstein, C, *Legal Reasoning and Political Conflict* (Oxford University Press, 1996), 108.

[54] Although this risks a perception of injustice there are positive dimensions to this. In particular given the evils of industry-specific statutes, courts are better situated to engage in industry specific tailoring than the legislature: Burk, D and Lemley, M, 'Policy Levers in Patent Law' (2003) 89 Virginia L Rev 1575, 1668–9; and, more generally, Nard, C, 'Legal Forms and the Common Law of Patents' (2010) 90 Boston University L Rev 51.

[55] Sunstein, above n.3, 974.

fairness of the procedure makes it more likely that the losing party will comply with the decision.[56]

One way in which common law jurisdictions such as the United Kingdom aim to address the risk that judicial law-making is seen as damaging something as fundamental as the impersonal impartial governance guaranteed by 'the rule of law', is by way of a system in which there is a distinct hierarchy of courts in which law-making is an acknowledged role of the appellate courts.[57] Although the appellate courts in a sense make law in the context of deciding individual cases, there have developed rules and practices that in effect depersonalize this process: for instance by only allowing appeals where there is an issue of principle to be addressed; refusing to revisit findings of fact made by a court of first instance;[58] and basing decisions on the majority view of a panel of judges.

In a sense court decisions made by way of the inductive process by which the court rationalizes earlier decisions as specific instances of an overriding general principle is also a decision of a panel of judges though here the judges are separated in time. That separation also means that earlier decisions were necessarily made without knowledge of the particular circumstances of the contemporary case the outcome of which they are now influencing.

Drawing on past decisions is not always possible. When novel technology is involved there may be few if any relevant authorities that address the point in issue. So for instance, *Human Genome Sciences Inc* v *Eli Lilly & Co*[59] was concerned with the validity of a patent which claimed the nucleotide sequence of a gene encoding for a novel protein. The dispute centred on the way in which the requirement of industrial applicability applied in circumstances where the specification of the utility of that protein was speculative so far as it was based on the technique of bioinformatics and had not been confirmed or narrowed using *in vitro* and *in vivo* assays. The patent was attacked on the ground

---

[56] Not only do rules aim to ensure that decisions are reached impersonally, but more than that, they aim to ensure that law-making is done only by legitimate sources of authority: Kennedy, above n.1, 1707–8.

[57] Although wide issues of legislative policy are properly the concern of the political legislature, nevertheless it is widely acknowledged that a judicial power to make law is sometimes desirable and necessary: MacCormick, above n.2, 187.

[58] For instance by only allowing appeals where there is an issue of principle and not revisiting findings of fact made by the court of first instance, on which see above at p. 42.

[59] [2011] UKSC 51.

that the specification consisted of no more than sequence information for a polypeptide with broad, unspecific and inherently speculative statements about its biological activity and failed to characterize its function or any therapeutic or diagnostic utility for it. The Court of Appeal and High Court both found the condition of industrial applicability not satisfied. The Supreme Court came to a different conclusion. One very notable difference in the pattern of reasoning adopted by the Supreme Court was the overt influence of consequences. Lord Neuberger, at the outset of his speech, acknowledged that the outcome may give rise to potentially far-reaching consequences for scientific research, the biotech industry, and human health.[60] Similar sentiments were expressed by Lord Hope[61] and Lord Walker.[62] In allowing the appeal, the court took into account written interventions made by the BioIndustry Association (the BIA) which argued that adopting the Court of Appeal's reasoning would make it harder for patentees to satisfy the requirement of industrial applicability in the future so making it harder for UK bioscience companies to attract investment at an early stage in the R&D process.[63] No doubt conscious that taking into account the views of the BioIndustry Association might lead to a perception of bias, the Court emphasized that the Association had not set out to support either of the two parties to the appeal.[64]

This feature of the Supreme Court's decision allows me to make the point that perhaps the most important guard against the claim that an individual decision is biased is for a court to show that the decision is not

---

[60] Ibid. [2].

[61]

> [P]atent portfolios are often the most valuable asset of companies in the bioscience industry. So assessments of the value of a bioscience company's patent portfolio are likely to be a key consideration in deciding whether to acquire or invest in such a company. This in turn affects the funding that is made available for research and development, without which effective progress in putting a patented invention to practical use is likely to be very limited. The evaluation of a patent specification for this purpose will depend on whether it discloses an invention that is reasonably capable of industrial application.

Ibid. [141].

[62] '[This is] an important case: not only for the parties, but also for the bioscience industry generally (as the intervention of the BioIndustry Association makes clear) and, in some measure, for the future course of patent law in the United Kingdom': ibid. [167].

[63] Ibid. [100].

[64] Ibid.

arbitrary. Though often partnered, I understand bias and arbitrariness to be different types of failing. A biased decision is one I understand to favour one disputant over another for reasons that should not feature in the decision making process. So instances of bias might include the judge who finds for a claimant because they went to the same school or the academic who excuses plagiarism in a student essay on the grounds that the writer is pretty.[65] By contrast an arbitrary decision is one devoid of reason: it is a random, whimsical choice.[66] The judge who retires to his chambers and tosses a coin to decide who is to win in a dispute makes an arbitrary choice. They are common bedfellows because an absence of reason invites suspicions of bias. The judge who tosses a coin and finds in favour of his old school chum has no defence to the accusation of bias in decision making even though his decision was not in fact biased.

Entirely rule-bound decisions cannot be arbitrary though they might seem so precisely because judges deciding under a rule are under no obligation to reflect on whether the decision evidences the pursuit of intelligible and rational values. But despite this, decisions so taken are not arbitrary because it is reason enough for the judge to say that, 'I am bound to apply this rule.' The key point is that judicial decision making under a legislative rule requires of the judge only that they apply the rule. The judge may believe the rule to embody a particular value but applying that rule does not require her to identify or interpret its content. Rules then, in the same way they can help avoid perceptions of bias in judicial decision making can help to avoid the perception of arbitrariness. By contrast, without rules, judges must identify and apply principles and values as reasons for their decision. Thus, in *Human Genome Sciences Inc* v *Eli Lilly & Co*, any accusation that the decision is biased so far as it openly favours members of a particular class (members of the bio-pharmaceutical industry) is met with the argument that the decision is consistent with patent system's core objective of encouraging investment in R&D. This worked to head off any accusations of bias because the consequential reasons advanced worked to the advantage of both parties

---

65 It is possible for one or other of the parties to a dispute to make an application requesting that the trial judge recuse themselves on the ground of apparent bias (the test being whether the fair-minded and informed observer would conclude that there is a real possibility of bias). See e.g. *Resolution Chemicals Ltd* v *Lundbeck A/S* [2013] EWCA Civ 1515.

66 The term 'arbitrary' is also sometimes used to mean that a decision is 'unreasonable, capricious, despotic' rather than made without guidance of known principles or law: Davis, K, *Discretionary Justice. A Preliminary Inquiry* (Louisiana State University Press, 1969), 29.

to the dispute (both being members of the bio-pharmaceutical industry) notwithstanding that in the particular circumstances the outcome favoured the appellant over the respondent. In patent cases it will often be the case that parties to an individual dispute will have much in common despite being at loggerheads.[67] But in copyright and trade mark cases a wider range of interests are likely to be represented in legal disputes. In such circumstances advancing reasons for a decision may fuel accusations of bias as much as dispel them. This concern seemed to have influenced Jacob LJ's response in *L'Oréal SA* v *Bellure NV*[68] when invited to dispense with the 'outdated' requirement of some sort of misrepresentation to sustain a claim to passing off in favour of a tort of unfair competition which had no such requirement.[69] Jacob LJ rejected the idea observing that if the courts (or indeed Parliament) were to create such a tort it would be of wholly uncertain scope.[70] What is interesting is what Jacob LJ says about the difficulties of formulating, 'a clear and rational line', between that which is fair and that which is not:

> What one man calls 'unfair' another calls 'fair'. The market involves the interests of traders, their competitors and consumers. They all have different perspectives. An established trader would like the law to hold off all his competitors – and as far as possible. He would want to prevent all copying of his products and for as long as possible, preferably indefinitely. He would want as wide a gap as possible between his trade marks and those of others. He would oppose any form of comparative advertising. A newcomer will want to be able to copy – and to improve. He will want to be able fairly to advertise comparatively. And the consumer will want the best deal he can get. He would oppose anything deceptive, but probably nothing else.[71]

The emphasis here needs to be placed on Jacob LJ's concern that decision making be 'rational' and that object would be frustrated by adopting a touchstone such as fairness to assess liability. What makes decisions under the protean action of passing off rational in a way that he fears decisions under a tort of unfair competition would not be? The answer I would suggest is that Jacob LJ can see how reasons might be advanced to support developments in the law of passing off (for instance by accepting the claim that a contemporary business practice involves a

---

[67] They are what may be labelled as 'friendly strangers': Nard, above n.54, 99–100 (citing Lon Fuller).

[68] [2007] EWCA Civ 968.

[69] Ibid. [135].

[70] Ibid. [161].

[71] Ibid. [139].

new species of misrepresentation). But without some accepted measure or a least a list of factors deemed relevant to the assessment of fairness, a judge called upon to decide whether a particular business practice is or is not fair has only her personal convictions to advance as reasons for her decision.[72] It is this that brings the risk of a perception of bias in decision making.

Nowhere is reliance on personal conviction and with this the risk of perceived arbitrariness and bias in decision making a more acute issue than when the condition of morality is incorporated into a legal direction. For instance, in *Glyn* v *Weston Feature Films Co*,[73] Younger J could do little to disguise his personal views of the book, copyright in which, it was claimed, had been infringed by the defendant's film. The book, which had proved extremely popular with the public, contained a fictional account of the seduction of a young man by an older, and married, woman.[74] Younger J was of the view that the episode described in the novel was 'grossly immoral in its essence, in its treatment, and in its tendency'. His personal outrage is evident in his description of the work:

> Stripped of its trappings, which are mere accident, it is nothing more nor less than a sensual adulterous intrigue. And it is not as if the plaintiff in her treatment of it were content to excuse or palliate the conduct described. She is not even satisfied with justifying that conduct. She has stooped to glorify the liaison in its inception, its progress, and its results; and she has not hesitated to garnish it with meretricious incident at every turn.[75]

Although referring to no particular authority, and without any argument advanced by the claimants or defendants on the point, Younger J declared it as 'clear' that copyright could not exist in a work of a tendency so

---

[72] Of course the legislature could attempt to draft a set of factors as it did with section 41 Patents Act (on which see above at p. 38) but that would demand extraordinary foresight given the wide and unpredictable range of practices which such a tort might embrace and would unlikely be useful. No doubt over time, some guiding principles would emerge from a body of decided cases as it did with 'fair dealing'.

[73] [1916] 1 Ch 261.

[74] The book in issue was Elinor Glyn's *Three Weeks*. At the time of the trial it had sold many thousands of copies.

[75] Younger J was no more enamoured of the defendant's film which he described as 'vulgar to an almost inconceivable degree' and containing incidents and movements which were 'indecently offensive'.

grossly immoral.[76] What is particularly notable is the attempt to disguise that what is being dispensed here is a very personal view of the demands of justice. Younger J points out that copyright protection was to be denied, not because of his personal objection to the themes pursued in the novel, but because of the corrupting effect on those individuals of a less robust constitution than himself. The book, he said, was of 'a cruelly destructive tendency' and was:

> a glittering record of adulterous sensuality masquerading as superior virtue … calculated, with consequences as inevitable as they are sure to be disastrous, to mislead into the belief that she may without danger choose the easy life of sin many a poor romantic girl striving amidst manifold hardships and discouragements to keep her honour untarnished.

The patronizing terms in which the argument is advanced can be dismissed as reflecting the mores of the age. Much less excusable is the fact that the argument was unsupported by any evidence of the claimed corrupting effect. Rather the inevitability of the effect of reading the novel was entirely the product of the judge's imagination fed by his views of the popular literature of the time.[77] The final notable feature of the judgement is the extraordinary imputation of personality to the court with which it concludes. The court, Younger J said, 'owes it to its own

---

[76] At the time the case came to court it was reasonably well established that courts had the power to deny copyright protection to works which offended against public policy. Over a century earlier, Lord Eldon had declared that 'publications may be of such a nature, that the author can maintain no action at law': *Walcot* v *Walker* (1802) 32 ER 1. See also *Southey* v *Sherwood* 35 ER 1006; *Lawrence* v *Smith* 7 ER 928; and *Stockdale* v *Onwhyn* 108 ER 65. Only a few years before *Glyn* v *Weston Feature Films Co* was decided, the Court of Appeal had denied an interlocutory injunction directed to restraining the publication in the UK of two pictures originally published in France on the ground that they were too indecent to be entitled to copyright in England: *Baschet* v *London Illustrated Standard Co* [1900] 1 Ch 73. For an account of the development of the public policy as a ground for denying copyright protection see Sims, A, 'The Denial of Copyright Protection on the Public Policy Grounds' (2008) 30 EIPR 189.

[77] Younger J condemned the,

> injurious influence exercised upon the adventurous spirit of our youth by the penny dreadful which presents the burglar in the guise of a hero and so excites the imagination of the juvenile reader that, adopting in the spirit of true adventure the life of his idol, he presently finds himself in the dock branded by an unfeeling world as a common thief.

[1916] 1 Ch 261, 269–70.

self-respect' to render no assistance whatever to either of the parties in respect of the subject of their litigation.

This decision, perhaps more than any other, has fuelled the fear that applying a condition that a work be moral for it to be protected by copyright allows judges to indulge in their own idiosyncratic notions of deciding what is protected and so provoke almost inevitable dispute.[78] It is the kind of decision that advocates of rule-based decision making can point to showing how bias and arbitrariness feature decisions directed by standards.

Certainly morality as a condition is problematic in this respect and, I would suggest, is particularly so for the following reasons. First, morality as a condition, as it features in intellectual property laws, has been and continues to be applied extremely rarely. A contemporary judge faced with a decision as to whether an invention, sign or work is somehow immoral is limited in the extent she can co-opt the ghosts of judges-past to assist in the decision making. Secondly, as is often pointed out, societies' modal moral values change with time. The decision in *Glyn* v *Weston Feature Films Co* looks very dated not least of all because the kind of sensual adulterous intrigues that so vexed Younger J are nowadays the stock plot lines of the most popular television soap operas. Thus even where there are earlier decisions on which a contemporary judge can draw, their value in supporting decision making is likely to be limited. Certainly judges can reason inductively from earlier decisions so as to derive abstract statements as to the scope of the condition. For instance, Aldous LJ thought that the decision in *Glyn* v *Weston Feature Films Co* amongst others[79] could be made to stand for the general proposition that a court would be entitled to refuse to enforce copyright if the work in issue were immoral, scandalous or contrary to family life.[80] But the contemporary judge is still then faced with deciding whether in the circumstances, a particular work fits this description. A judge may set

---

[78] See for instance Sims, above n.76, at 195. Note also the comments of Jacob J in *Hyde Park Residence* v *David Yelland* that, 'there can certainly be dispute if the courts go too far in appointing themselves as moralists (a criticism often levelled at *Glyn*)': [1999] RPC 655, 665.

[79] Including *Attorney-General* v *Guardian Newspapers* (No. 2) [1990] 1 AC 109.

[80] *Hyde Park Residence Ltd* v *David Yelland* [2000] RPC 604 [65]; but c.f. the Court of Appeal's decision in *Ashdown* v *Telegraph Group Ltd* in which it was said that, 'we do not consider that Aldous LJ [in *Hyde Park* v *Yelland*] was justified in circumscribing the public interest defence to breach of copyright as tightly as he did': [2001] EWCA Civ 1142 [58].

out to give a decision that she thinks will reflect the moral values of contemporary society but since she is as much a member of that society as she is an impartial judge she will inevitably struggle to convince the cynic that she is not giving effect to her personal convictions. This observation brings to the third, and perhaps the most important, reason why applying morality as a condition in intellectual property law risks determinations being seen as biased or arbitrary in a way that does not apply to determinations made under standards more generally. In the preceding chapter I noted that decisions under standards, like all judicial decisions, must be coherent in that they must be seen to be rational and to pursue intelligible principles or policies. This requirement means that a judge, in applying a particular standard to meet a novel circumstance, must justify that decision by reference to the values, principles and policies that characterize the law in issue. Intellectual property law, I suggested, was partly autonomous such that a direction that an outcome be, for instance, 'fair' required of the judge that they apply that direction in a way that is rational and intelligible given the values, principles and policies that characterize patent, copyright and trade mark law. A judge is thus not free to give effect to their personal convictions, and the requirement of coherence acts as an important guard against any claim that decision making is biased. The problem it seems to me is that the values, principles and policies that characterize intellectual property law (i.e. those that make it partly autonomous) do not intersect with, and so cannot limit or qualify, the condition of morality. Judges are thus forced to make their judgements seem intelligible according to values, principles and policies that lie outside intellectual property law. Aldous LJ, for instance, in *Hyde Park Residence Ltd* v *Yelland*, held that the jurisdiction to refuse to enforce copyright comes from the court's inherent jurisdiction to refuse to grant an order where this would, 'offend against the policy of the law'. He cited in support of this principle an eighteenth century judgement in which a court had refused to enforce a contract for the sale of tea in circumstances where the seller knew the buyer intended to illegally import the tea into the UK.

It is giving effect to the requirement of coherence, as guard against any claim of bias or arbitrariness, that presents the greatest challenge to judges called upon to decide whether a sign, invention or work, in some way or another, offends the condition of morality. Consider for instance the assessment of the morality of an applied for trade mark. Under Article 3 Trade Marks Directive member states must under their national laws exclude from registrability trade marks which are contrary to public policy or to accepted principles of morality.[81] The UK Intellectual Property Office's Trade Marks Manual notes that in order to make the required assessment under the UK Act, the examiner must be objective, not subjective and that, '[o]bjectivity means being neither out of date nor a trend setter; not setting some kind of moral standard but also not being insensitive to public opinion'.

There is a corresponding provision in the Community trade mark Regulation,[82] described in the Office for Harmonisation in the Internal Market (OHIM) Guidelines as concerning subjective values, but values which must be applied as objectively as possible by the examiner.[83]

It is easy enough to provide hypothetical and extreme examples of the kind of sign the exclusion is intended to cover. The point about such extreme examples is that they brook no argument and so hide any suggestion that personal conviction may play a part in the decision making process. Often cited is Advocate General Ruiz-Jarabo Colomer's example of an application to register the trade mark BABYKILLER for a pharmaceutical abortifacient.[84] However, in practice drawing clear lines has proved challenging and there can be no surprise that the decisions where morality has figured in the reasoning have been criticized as lacking in consistency.[85] This element of trade mark law is, however, remarkable in providing an unusually clear instance of a perception of bias in decision making. In *Couture Tech Ltd's Application*[86] an application to register as a community trade mark a sign consisting of an exact

[81] Implemented by way of section 3(3)(a) Trade Marks Act 1994 which provides that a trade mark shall not be registered if it is contrary to public policy or to accepted principles of morality. For a review of decisions where this exclusion has been considered see Griffiths, J, 'Is There a Right to an Immoral Trade Mark?' in Torremans, P (ed.) *Intellectual Property and Human Rights* (Kluwer, 2008).

[82] Article 7.1.(f) of Council Regulation (EC) No. 207/2009 of 26 February 2009 on the Community trade mark.

[83] Guidelines for Examination in the Office for Harmonisation in the Internal Market (Trade Marks and Designs) on Community Trade Marks, Part B, Examination, Section 4: Absolute Grounds for Refusal, 7.

[84] C-299/99 *Phillips* v *Remington*, Opinion of Advocate General Ruiz-Jarabo Colomer [2001] ETMR 509 [18].

[85] Bently and Sherman, above n.35, 961.

[86] *Couture Tech Ltd's Application* (R 1509/2008-2) [2010] ETMR 774.

representation of the coat of arms of the Soviet Union[87] was refused as being contrary to public policy and morality because:

> This emblem was the official symbol of the Soviet Communist party that ruled the country according to the Soviet constitution. It is common knowledge that the Soviet Union was a totalitarian state that massively violated human rights, under the leadership of the Soviet Communist party, committed crimes against humanity, including summary executions, torture, sending innocent people to labour camps, involuntary settlement and stripping of citizens' rights. It is commonly accepted that the ethnicity-targeted population transfers in the Soviet Union led to [millions of] deaths due to inflicted hardships …
>
> Against this background, it is obvious that a sign which alludes to the Soviet totalitarian regime and its ideology which has tragically affected many countries, nations and individuals, is contrary to public policy and accepted principles of morality. In view of the genocide and other crimes committed by the Soviet regime under the leadership of the Soviet Communist party, it is clear that its official symbol may cause outrage in the minds of people in those Member States which have been directly affected. Particularly from Baltic States, where the majority of ordinary citizens whose values and standards would be offended when seeing the sign applied for in relation to the claimed goods and services, since it would be perceived by them as a glorification of the Soviet totalitarian regime.[88]

On appeal to the OHIM Second Board of Appeal, the applicant observed that the examiner's name was 'Lamsters', a Latvian name, and suggested that his view of the sign may thus have been biased.[89] Further, the appellant suggested that OHIM showed a general antipathy to the former Soviet symbols and similar signs.[90] The Board rejected the appeal and sought to counter the accusations of prejudice and bias by pointing to the objective criteria it relied on in forming a view as to how a sign would be perceived by the public. The Office, it said, did not have many options to find out how the sign would be perceived in various parts of the community. Without data from a survey, the only reliable ways of judging the public's view of a sign were general historical knowledge, national legal provisions regulating the use of that or similar signs, case law of the national courts concerning the use of that or similar signs and

---

87 Specifically the red star, sickle and hammer together with 15 ribbons containing the motto 'proletariats of the world, unite!' in all the 15 languages of the Soviet Socialist Republics of the Soviet Union.

88 [2010] ETMR 774, 779–80.

89 Ibid., 781.

90 Ibid., 784.

guidelines and decisions of national trade marks offices.[91] The Board argued that the laws and practices of Hungary, Latvia and the Czech Republic all, to a greater or lesser extent, showed that these types of signs would be viewed by consumers in those states at least, as being contrary to public policy and accepted principles of morality.

In *Couture Tech Ltd's Application* the examining office was forced to demonstrate a lack of bias in its decision making because the applicant and the staff populating the examining office had different values. But the trade mark office's perspective was rather wider than that of the applicant. The problem facing patent offices in Europe is for this reason rather different.

The morality condition is a particularly unhappy feature of patent law in that claims that office decisions are biased in favour of grant have proved difficult to defend against. The problem is linked to the feature that patent law shares with copyright and trade mark law: accusations of bias are typically met by justifying decisions as objectively rational and intelligible but according to values, principles and policies drawn from areas that lie outside intellectual property law. But whereas in trade mark law and copyright law, tribunals have been able to rely on values, principles and policies manifested in other areas of law, patent tribunals have cast their net wider still. To a degree this is because the morality condition is framed in a way that expressly limits the notice that can be taken of other laws in deciding whether the condition is satisfied.[92] Article 53(a) EPC provides that European patents shall not be granted in respect of inventions, 'the commercial exploitation of which would be contrary to ordre public or morality' but adds that the exploitation shall not be deemed to be so merely because it is prohibited by law or regulation in some or all of the Contracting States.[93] More significant

---

91 See e.g. in respect of Hungary: ibid., 795.

92 The tendency of the EPO to interpret the concepts of 'ordre public' and 'morality' detached from national and European law has been criticized as based on a misinterpretation of Art.53(a). The EPO's reading of the qualification would lead to the clearly erroneous conclusion that national laws could be in place that were immoral or without constitutional basis: Straus, J, 'Patenting Human Genes in Europe' (1995) 26(6) IIC 920, 931–2.

93 The EPO has indicated that whilst this exclusion may not be disregarded when assessing patentability it is to be narrowly construed consistent with the view that the concept of patentability must be as wide as possible: T19/90 *Harvard/Onco-Mouse* (OJ EPO, 1990, 476), at reason 5; V6/92 *Harvard/Onco-Mouse* (OJ EPO, 1992, 589), at reason 3; and T356/93 *Plant Genetic Systems/ Plant cells resistant to glutamine synthetase inhibitors* (OJ EPO, 1995, 545), at reasons 8 and 12. Most recently the EPO's Opposition Division has held that

still is the fact that the Patent Office is populated by individuals who are as much scientists and engineers as they are lawyers.

As I noted above that, as compared to trade mark law and copyright law, the law of patents is rather insular in that there are typically a relatively narrow range of interests represented in legal disputes. At the application stage there is still a greater alignment not just of interests but of values. Indeed in large part this is because of historical concerns of arbitrary decision making. An objection raised to the introduction of a system for the examination of patent applications when that was first being considered in the nineteenth century was that this would make the recognition of property rights subject to the discretion of government officials. By the time examination was introduced in the early twentieth century, fears of arbitrary decision making by examiners had been allayed by a growing trust in bureaucracy which was in part because of the increased use of experts.[94] This in large part was possible because of the emergence of social institutions which, amongst other things, gave credibility to claims of expertise and which were in turn supported by the establishment of a consistent and unified education and recognized qualifications.

It remains the case that both applicants and examiners are drawn from the ranks of scientists and engineers and, whatever their more specific roles (as research scientist in a commercial concern or examiner in a patent office), are members of the same social institutions and share formal qualifications and have common educational backgrounds. Faith in the decision making of experts is founded not just on a belief that the expert has extensive knowledge of a particular subject, but also a particular way of understanding and approaching that knowledge. This then perhaps explains the observation that one of the defining characteristics of patent law over the last century is its startling and marked isolation from cultural, political and ethical matters.[95] A consequence is that applicants then are unlikely to see any bias or prejudice in the decisions of examiners and still less to complain about it. But viewed through the eyes of those who are outside the scientific and engineering establishment, the system of patent examination can look skewed in

---

Article 53(a) EPC only applies in exceptional cases: *Harvard/Onco-Mouse*: Decision of the Opposition Division 7 November 2001 (OJ EPO, 2003, 419).

[94] Bently and Sherman, above n.35, 422.

[95] Bently, L and Sherman, B, 'The Ethics of Patenting: Towards a Transgenic Patent System' (1995) 3 Medical L Rev 275.

favour of grant over refusal. Nowhere is this more apparent than in the consideration of patent applications relating to biotechnological inventions.

Particularly notable in this regard is the decision of the EPO's Opposition Division in *Howard Florey Institute/Relaxin*[96] precisely because the opponents (a coalition of 'green' MEPs[97]) accused the EPO's Opposition Division of partiality in its conduct of the opposition proceedings. The claims in issue were to a DNA fragment encoding human H2-preprorelaxin; synthetic human H2-preprorelaxin; and the processes by which these were made. The opponents requested the revocation of the patent on the grounds that the subject matter was not patentable for lack of novelty and inventive step; that it represented a discovery; and that it offended against 'ordre public' or morality. At oral proceedings the opponents submitted a request to have the Opposition Division declared partial, contending that bias in favour of the proprietor of the patent was demonstrated in aspects of the Division's preliminary written opinion. This opinion contained the statement that the claimed H2-relaxin gene was in the form of a 'cDNA fragment'. According to the opponents, this was untrue since the claims referred to 'DNA' and not 'cDNA'. Given that one of the grounds of opposition was that what was claimed was a discovery, no doubt the opponents had in mind that cDNA differs from natural DNA in that the non-coding regions (introns) are removed from cDNA and therefore something indisputably new is artificially created when it is made.[98] The Opposition Division rejected the assertion that the 'mistake' was evidence of partiality and indeed that any mistake had been made at all. The Division noted that the claims related to a DNA fragment having a specified amino acid sequence and this sequence was encoded by a cDNA fragment derived from H2-relaxin mRNA. The Division observed that accordingly the claims were in fact directed to a cDNA sequence encoding preprorelaxin despite the fact that the word 'cDNA' was not used in the claim.

This aspect of the Opposition Division's decision in the *Relaxin* case serves to highlight the fact that the 'language' of patent law is the language of science and claims are read with the understanding of trained scientists. The same competencies inform the approach to morality. The

---

[96] *Howard Florey Institute/Relaxin*, Decision of the Opposition Division 8 December 1994 (OJ EPO, 1995, 388).

[97] The 'Fraktion der Grünen im Europäischen Parlament'.

[98] A point held to be of some significance in the decision of the US Supreme Court in *Association for Molecular Pathology* v *Myriad Genetics* 569 US __ (2013).

opponents in the *Relaxin* case contended that the subject matter of the disputed patent offended against the provisions of Article 53(a) arguing, amongst other things, that the patenting of human genes meant that human life was being patented which, they said, was intrinsically immoral. The Opposition Division emphatically rejected this argument:

> [T]he allegation that human life is being patented is unfounded. It is worth pointing out that DNA is not 'life', but a chemical substance which carries genetic information and can be used as an intermediate in the production of proteins which may be medically useful. The patenting of a single human gene has nothing to do with the patenting of human life. Even if every gene in the human genome were cloned (and possibly patented), it would be impossible to reconstitute a human being from the sum of its genes.[99]

As observed by Bently and Sherman, the EPO's treatment of the opponent's arguments in the *Relaxin* case illustrates the depth of the conflict between the logic of ethical objections and that of patenting.[100] From our perspective, what is interesting is that the decision to allow the patent was justified by way of reasons that looked to scientific principles rather than legal principles.

The dominant influence of the scientific mindset and the consequent insularity of decision making was also evident in the decision of the EPO's Technical Board of Appeal in *Plant Genetic Systems/Plant cells resistant to glutamine synthetase inhibitors*.[101] The patent claims in this case related to a process for genetically modifying plant cells and plants to make them resistant to herbicides based on a glutamine synthetase inhibitor, and to plant cells, plants and seeds so transformed. The patent was opposed by the environmental campaigning group Greenpeace on the grounds, inter alia, that the grant of a patent for plant life forms and the exploitation of the patent was contrary to morality and/or 'ordre public' under Article 53(a) EPC. The opponents appealed to the Technical Board of Appeal following a rejection of the opposition by the EPO's Opposition Division. The Board observed that the qualification to the prohibition in Article 53(a) meant that the assessment of whether or not a particular

---

[99] *Howard Florey Institute/Relaxin*, Decision of the Opposition Division 8 December 1994 (OJ EPO, 1995, 388), at reason 6.3.4.

[100] Bently and Sherman, above n.95, 281 and see also their comments at 284 ('it has not been possible to translate considerations such as risk to the environment, sacredness of humanity, or harm and suffering caused to animals, into a language that fits within the technical framework of patent law').

[101] T356/93 *Plant Genetic Systems/Plant cells resistant to glutamine synthetase inhibitors* (OJ EPO, 1995, 545).

subject matter was to be considered contrary to either 'ordre public' or morality was not dependent upon any national laws or regulations.[102] The opponents, however, pointed to a survey conducted among Swedish farmers in which the great majority of respondents declared themselves opposed to 'genetic engineering' (particularly 'super crops' such as herbicide-resistant plants); and an opinion poll carried out in Switzerland in which the majority of respondents opposed the patenting of animals and plants. This data, the opponents argued, indicated that the public was of the view that patents should not be granted for these kinds of inventions. The Board discounted both the evidence and the conclusions the opponents sought to draw from it.

In the Board's view, surveys and opinion polls were not reflective of the moral norms rooted in European culture. In part this was because the results of such surveys could fluctuate unforeseeably and within short time periods. For the Board then, like that generated in well-crafted scientific experiment, relevant data (even as to a concept as wayward as morality) needed to point to repeatable and immutable conclusions. The Board also challenged the validity of the methodology underpinning the data. Surveys, the Board said, could be very easily influenced and controlled by, for instance, the type of questions posed and the choice and the size of the representative sample.[103] The Board added that surveys of particular groups of people (such as for instance farmers) tended to reflect their specific interests and/or their biased beliefs. That is undoubtedly true, but at the same time an opinion does not become invalid simply because it is held by an individual who is a member of a particular group. That individual, and all the other members of the group, are also members of the public. In the Board's mind then, what counted were those moral norms shared by all and not merely by some. In this the Board seems to be demanding the kind of universality characteristic of scientific principles and laws.

Whether the results of surveys and opinion polls could ever constitute relevant evidence of whether a particular subject matter was contrary to morality was doubted by the Board. Each case had to be considered on its merits and consequently, if surveys and opinion polls were to be relied upon, they would have to be made ad hoc on the basis of specific

---

[102] Ibid., at reason 7.

[103] Of course, those who undertake this kind of empirical research are only too aware of such risks and accordingly exercise great care in the design of the data gathering exercise and in formulating the conclusions to be drawn from the data. For all that, social science methodology looks unsatisfactorily imprecise when set against the benchmarks typical of experiments in the natural sciences.

questions in relation to the particular subject matter claimed. Such a procedure, the Board said, was scarcely feasible. This highly reductive approach again is characteristic of a scientific mindset.

If laws and regulations are not determinative, nor the results of opinion polls, what then is left? The Board proceeded by giving a lecture on the merits of plant biotechnology, observing that its development led to a better understanding and control of the natural phenomena linked to plants. The technology, the Board said, was no more contrary to morality than traditional selective breeding. Traditional and modern techniques had in common the desire to change the property of a plant by introducing novel genetic material into it and genetic engineering techniques differed only in allowing more powerful and accurate control of such genetic modifications. Plant biotechnology was thus not per se immoral. The proselytizing done, the Board said that like any other tool, plant genetic engineering techniques could, however, be used for constructive or destructive purposes. Article 53(a) prohibited the grant of a patent only to inventions directed to a misuse or destructive use of a particular technology. But none of the claims of the patent in suit referred to subject matter which related to a misuse or destructive use of plant biotechnological techniques. The activities (production of plants and seeds, protection of plants from weeds or fungal diseases) and products (plant cells, plants, seeds) claimed could not be considered to be wrong as such in the light of conventionally accepted standards of conduct of European culture. By describing the subject matter of the patent in highly abstract terms (e.g. the production of plants and their protecting them from diseases), the Board avoided the need to state explicitly the basis of the 'conventionally accepted standards of conduct' on which it relied: norms relating to, for example, the protection of plants from disease, are taken as axiomatic. The Board thus seeks to justify its decision as grounded on an understanding of an external reference point rather than the decision merely reflecting the personal conviction of examiners. If our concern is the perception of bias, then the problem is that without being able to point explicitly to this external reference point it is impossible to distinguish between decisions based on objective and subjective values.

This then explains the apparent conflict with later decision of the Opposition Division in the *Harvard/Onco-Mouse* case.[104] The Opposition Division here noted that the Board of Appeal in *Plant Genetic Systems/*

---

[104] *Harvard/Onco-Mouse*, Decision of the Opposition Division 7 November 2001 (OJ EPO, 2003, 419).

Plant cells resistant to glutamine synthetase inhibitors had defined the concept of morality to be one which is related to the belief that some behaviour is right whereas other behaviour is wrong: a belief founded on the totality of the accepted norms which are deeply rooted in a particular culture. But the Opposition Division then went on to add that morality has to be assessed primarily by looking at laws or regulations which are common to most of the European countries. This, the Division said, was because these laws and regulations were the best indicator about what is considered right or wrong in European society. The reliance on laws and regulations as a reference point in this latter case, and in contrast to the former, might simply be because there were relevant laws and regulations on which to draw. Indeed the Opposition Division expressly stated that 'in so far as such laws or regulations concerning the relevant issue exist, it appears neither necessary nor appropriate to rely on other possible means of assessment ...' So far as the subject matter was concerned, the Division took the view that statutory law regulating the use of animals in research could be relied on to show whether the exploitation of the invention was prohibited or not. It went on to observe that the legal regulation of the use of animals for scientific purposes in most if not all of the states being party to the EPC, led to the conclusion that the use of animals for this purpose was allowed. Exploitation of the claimed invention then was not immoral for the purposes of Article 53(a).

Since the coming into force of the Biotech Directive,[105] some types of biological invention have been deemed to be immoral in a way that strips discretion from examiners where claims relate to the specifically listed biotechnological process and uses.[106] As is well known, the path to the enactment of this Directive was a rocky one. In October 1988 the first

[105] Directive 98/44/EC of the European Parliament and of the Council of 6 July 1998 on the legal protection of biotechnological inventions. In 1999, the Administrative Council of the EPO inserted a new chapter entitled 'Biotechnological inventions' into the EPC Implementing Regulations which effectively transposed the Directive into EPC law and practice. Of these, rule 28 EPC covers 'exceptions to patentability' and expressly refers to Article 53(a) EPC before then going on to list the specific instances mentioned in Article 6:2 of the Directive.

[106] Article 6:1 of the Directive reproduces the provisions of Article 53(a) of the EPC whilst Article 6:2 goes on to specify that on the basis of paragraph 6:1, that considered unpatentable are: (a) processes for cloning human beings; (b) processes for modifying the germ line genetic identity of human beings; (c) uses of human embryos for industrial or commercial purposes; (d) processes for modifying the genetic identity of animals which are likely to cause them suffering without any substantial medical benefit to man or animal, and also animals resulting from such processes.

draft of the Biotechnology Directive was presented by the European Commission to the Council. The aim was to clarify the European law on the patenting of biotechnological inventions which was then thought to be unclear. This first attempt at harmonizing legislation was rejected by the European Parliament in March 1995. Later that same year, the Commission put forward a second draft which provided the basis for the Directive as it came to be enacted.

During the brief period between the rejection of the first draft proposal and the submission of the second, the question was raised as to whether harmonizing legislation was by then necessary at all. The original proposal was introduced when biotechnology was a relatively new science and there was at the time legitimate concern as to whether the existing law under the EPC would be effective to cover biotechnological inventions. It was thus felt prudent to clarify the position by way of a harmonizing directive.[107] The position had changed by 1995 by which time the EPO had built up a considerable body of jurisprudence relating to biotechnological inventions and the general practice had emerged for patents for such inventions to be granted after testing them by the usual criteria for patentability.[108] Certainly by then it could have been argued that the existing provisions of the EPC (as interpreted by the various Boards of the EPO) provided an adequate and practical basis for deciding questions surrounding the morality of patents relating to biotechnological inventions.[109] Arguably then, the delays in the legislative process had rendered a harmonizing initiative unnecessary. There was, however, considerable pressure from both the Council and the Parliament to press ahead with a new draft and ultimately that pressure was yielded to and the Directive enacted. This observation provides a useful introduction to the final topic in this chapter: the relationship between European integration, harmonization and form.

---

107 Nott, R, 'The Biotech Directive: Does Europe Need a New Draft?' (1995) 17 EIPR 563, 564.

108 Ibid., 564.

109 Ibid., 565. Questions surrounding the morality of patents for biotechnological inventions featured heavily in the debates concerning this initiative, especially in the European Parliament.

3.3 EUROPEAN INTEGRATION, HARMONIZATION AND FORM

Intellectual property law is increasingly a cooperative venture amongst European states and efforts to codify and harmonize the law have already met with considerable success and are ongoing. The task of harmonization has fallen primarily to the national legislatures of the European Union and the EPC countries, requiring the enactment of legislation consistent with whatever is the agreed harmonized standard[110] but national courts (and patent authorities) have adopted interpretative practices that complement this effort.

Rules are the natural ally of codification[111] and this is all the more so where that codification is intended to underpin an objective of harmonization of national laws and practices.[112] The adoption of a standard at the supra-national level, whilst allowing flexibility in the interpretation of a provision, brings with it the risk of divergent interpretations and applications being adopted at the national level and the emergence of divergent national norms.[113] By contrast, the creation and application of

---

[110] Section 130(7) Patents Act 1977 for example, provides that certain specified provisions within the Act 'are so framed as to have, as nearly as practicable, the same effects in the United Kingdom as the corresponding provisions of the European Patent Convention'.

[111] Sunstein, above n.53, 16. See also Lord Neuberger of Abbotsbury, above n.6, 22 (making the reverse point that codification assists clarity and certainty).

[112] So for example and in respect of harmonization under the European Community regime,

> on the simplest model of legislative harmonisation, diverse national rules are eliminated in favour of a single Community rule. The harmonised rule promotes trade integration by virtue of its uniform EC-wide application while also transplanting to European level the imperative of respect of the variety of interests that have stimulated (different forms of) regulatory intervention over time in the Member States.

Weatherill, S, 'Pre-emption, Harmonisation and the Distribution of Competence to Regulate the Internal Market' in Barnard, C and Scott, J (eds) *The Law of the Single European Market. Unpacking the Premises* (Hart Publishing, 2002), 51. So far as harmonization of the national laws of European Union member states is concerned, rules may also be favoured because 'Continental Europeans' share an autonomous view of the law; a view which favours rules over standards: Lundmark, T, 'Legal Science and European Harmonisation' (2014) 130 LQR 68.

[113] The same point has been made in relation to the notion of the average consumer as that is deployed in trade mark law: Dinwoodie and Gangjee, above n.37, 369. As observed by the American jurist Karl Llewellyn: 'in law your

clear general rules at the supra-national level serves to guide and constrain decision making by national authorities so promoting a uniform understanding and application of the law.[114] The attempts to harmonize intellectual property law provide a useful perspective from which to view the opposition between rules and standards in highlighting certain constraints on rule-making and the costs of sacrificing flexibility under rules.

Although not a uniquely European problem,[115] the European experience is particularly illuminating in this respect because the efforts to

---

logical system refuses to remain on the level of description, of arranging existing observation. Backed by the fact and doctrine of precedent, your logical system shifts its content to the level of ought': Llewellyn, K, *The Bramble Bush. On Our Law and its Study* (Oceana Publications, 1951), 78. Llewellyn's argument is supported by the recent observation of the Court of Appeal that under 'the old law' patents were refused only where on no reasonable view could the subject matter be patentable. Despite that being the rule, in practice a decision of the Office or on appeal to the Appeal Tribunal was taken to decide the matter once-and-for all: *Aerotel Ltd* v *Telco Holdings Ltd and Macrossan's Application* [2006] EWCA Civ 1371 [5]. Note also Craig Allen Nard's observation that in the area of patent law, the US Supreme Court may be more inclined to adopt a standard rather than a rule because the Federal Circuit alone is the arbiter on the contours of the standard following the creation of the CAFC (a court which now has exclusive appellate jurisdiction in patent matter, rather than 13 appellate courts): Nard, above n.54, 87.

[114] So for example, the Committee on Legal Affairs and the Internal Market said that the proposed Directive to harmonize member states' laws regarding the patentability of computer-implemented inventions set out,

> to provide a restrictive restatement of the law as it has been applied by the Boards of Appeal of the European Patent Office, in order to ensure that patents for computer-related inventions are granted on the same basis everywhere in the European Union and that the national courts deal with contested patents on the basis of uniform principles.

Committee on Legal Affairs and the Internal Market, *Report on the proposal for a directive of the European Parliament and of the Council on the patentability of computer-implemented inventions*, 18 June 2003 (A5-0238/2003).

[115] It has been observed that the codification of the obviousness standard in the 1952 US Patents Act failed to remedy divergence between the lower courts. Ullrich suggests that,

> [d]ivergence of jurisprudence is unavoidable and will never be remedied, since the concept of non-obviousness, by its very nature, cannot be applied to a given invention by a simple mechanical operation but only be rendering individual judgements not on the inventive effort or on the quality or superiority of the product resulting from the invention, but on the issue of whether the invention discloses differences from prior art that an ordinary

harmonize patent law throughout Europe have involved two harmonization mechanisms. The Biotechnology Directive is one instance of harmonizing legislation originating in the European Union. The European Union's influence has been largely overshadowed by that of the EPC, which has had a more comprehensive harmonizing effect on European patent law albeit through softer enforcement mechanisms than those operating under the EU scheme.[116] The EPC's expressed core purpose is to strengthen cooperation between the states of Europe in respect of the protection of inventions. The mechanisms by which this is to be achieved are twofold and made clear in the preamble which provides that members entered into the Convention 'desiring that such protection may be obtained in those States by a single procedure for the grant of patents, and by the establishment of certain standard rules governing patents … granted'.

The European patent system is not immune from the impossibility of drafting perfect rules and the EPO Boards thus have a law-making role: a role that is recognized and acted upon by national courts. In *Merrell Dow*

> expert would not have bridged by his skill. The 'level of patentability' remained open to judicial discretion since a determination of the reach of the ordinary skill of an expert in the relevant field always constitutes a matter of personal, though limited interpretation.

Ullrich, H, *Standards of Patentability for European Inventions: Should an Inventive Step Advance the Art?* Vol 1 of IIC Studies in Industrial Property and Copyright Law (Max Planck Institute, 1977), 74–5. This is a manifestation of a much broader problem. Douglas North, using historical examples, has illustrated what happens when a common set of rules is imposed on two different societies. He observed that the,

> common imposition of a set of rules will lead to widely divergent outcomes in societies with different institutional arrangements' because, 'although the rules are the same, the enforcement mechanisms, the way enforcement occurs, the norms of behaviour, and the subjective models of the actors are not. Hence, both the real incentive structures and the perceived consequences of policies will differ as well.

North, D, *Institutions, Institutional Change and Economic Performance* (Cambridge University Press, 1991), 101.

[116] As observed by Graeme Dinwoodie, albeit in his reflections regarding the harmonization of trade mark law, 'harmonization (even of similar subject matter) is a project that can occupy a wide spectrum of possibilities in terms of detail or granularity … it is possible … to achieve through looser arrangements some of the same goals that tight EU harmonization is pursuing': Dinwoodie, G, 'The Europeanization of Trade Mark Law' in Ohly, A and Pila, J (eds) *The Europeanization of Intellectual Property Law: Towards a European Legal Methodology* (Oxford University Press, 2013), 79.

Pharmaceuticals Inc v *Norton*,[117] Lord Hoffmann, noting that the Patents Act 1977 had been enacted to bring the law of the UK into conformity with the corresponding provisions of the EPC and that section 130(7) of the Act provides that various sections of the Act are, 'so framed as to have, as nearly as practicable, the same effects in the United Kingdom as the corresponding provisions of the [EPC]', considered it the duty of UK courts to construe these various sections, as far as possible, so as to give them the same effect as the corresponding articles of the EPC. He added that for the purpose of construing the 1977 Act regard must be taken of the decisions of the European Patent Office on the construction of the EPC. Lord Hoffmann acknowledged that while these decisions were not technically binding upon UK courts, they were of great persuasive authority because:

> they are decisions of expert courts (the Boards of Appeal and Enlarged Board of Appeal of the EPO) involved daily in the administration of the EPC and secondly, because it would be highly undesirable for the provisions of the EPC to be construed differently in the EPO from the way they are interpreted in the national courts of a Contracting State.

The UK Court of Appeal has since gone further holding that the special circumstances arising from the creation of the European patent system require a further exception to the general rule that the Court of Appeal is bound to follow its own decisions.[118] In *Actavis Ltd* v *Merck & Co Inc*,[119] Jacob LJ indicated that the Court of Appeal is free but not bound to depart from the *ratio decidendi* of its own earlier decision if it is satisfied that the EPO Boards of Appeal have formed a settled view of European Patent law which is inconsistent with that earlier decision. Generally he said, the Court of Appeal would follow such a settled view.[120]

---

117 [1996] RPC 76.

118 Under the rule expressed in *Young* v *Bristol Aeroplane Company* [1944] KB 718, the Court of Appeal is bound to follow previous decisions of its own except: (1) the court is entitled and bound to decide which of two conflicting decisions of its own it will follow; (2) the court is bound to refuse to follow a decision of its own which, though not expressly overruled, cannot, in its opinion, stand with a decision of the House of Lords; and (3) the court is not bound to follow a decision of its own if it is satisfied that the decision was given *per incuriam.*

119 [2008] EWCA Civ 444.

120 Extra-judicially, Sir Robin Jacob has observed that 'in the absence of a full European Patent Court, the Boards of Appeal are the closest thing to it': Jacob, R, 'The Relationship between European and National Courts in Intellectual Property Law' in Ohly, A and Pila, J (eds) *The Europeanization of*

Motivated then by their understanding of the purpose of the European patent project and the attendant value of a commitment to consistency in respect of EPO decisions regarding the proper construction of the EPC, UK courts seemed prepared to accept that they are bound to follow EPO decisions.[121] UK courts recognize and expect that the EPO's Boards of Appeal will lay down 'principles of law': that is to say, statements of law that are to be interpreted as not only deciding the case in issue but in deciding how future cases falling within the principle are to be decided.[122]

However, notwithstanding the early enthusiasm for the European project, UK courts' commitment to a harmonized understanding of patent law under the direction of the EPO has become tempered. For instance, the Court of Appeal in *Human Genome Sciences Inc* v *Eli Lilly & Co*[123] said that:

> in the UK the key importance of the [EPO Technical Board of Appeal's] case law is well settled. We follow any principle of law clearly laid down by them, only reserving the right to differ if we are sure that the commodore is steering the fleet on to the rocks.[124]

Lord Neuberger in the Supreme Court was rather more expansive in his explanation:

> [W]hile national courts should normally follow the established jurisprudence of the EPO, that does not mean that we should regard the reasoning in each decision of the Board as effectively binding on us. There will no doubt sometimes be a Board decision which a national court considers may take the law in an inappropriate direction, misapplies previous EPO jurisprudence, or

Intellectual Property Law: Towards a European Legal Methodology (Oxford University Press, 2013), 194.

[121] See also the comments of Nichols LJ in *Gale's Application* [1991] RPC 305, 323; Laddie J in *Fujitsu's Application* [1996] RPC 511, 524; Aldous LJ in *Fujitsu's Application* [1997] RPC 608, 611; Jacob J in *Bristol Myers Squibb Co* v *Baker Norton Pharmaceuticals Inc* [1999] RPC 253, 272–3; and Jacob LJ in *Aerotel Ltd* v *Telco Holdings Ltd and Macrossan's Application* [2006] EWCA Civ 1371 [6]. Of course the courts of other countries of the European Patent Union also follow EPO jurisprudence: Jacob, above n.120, 195.

[122] As Sir Robin Jacob puts it, 'because consistency is so important, the higher UK courts have for at least twenty years made it plain that the principles laid down in the decisions of the Boards of Appeal should be followed in the UK courts': Jacob, above n.120, 194.

[123] [2010] EWCA Civ 33.

[124] Ibid. [39].

> fails to take a relevant argument into account. In such cases, the national court may well think it right not to apply the reasoning in the particular decision. While consistency of approach is important, there has to be room for dialogue between a national court and the EPO (as well as between national courts themselves). Nonetheless, where the Board has adopted a consistent approach to an issue in a number of decisions, it would require very unusual facts to justify a national court not following that approach.[125]

In 1996 Lord Hoffmann was of the view that the EPO's decisions were not 'technically binding' on UK courts. Lord Neuberger's formulation of the same commitment as one in which the EPO's decisions were not 'effectively binding' evidences rather more caution. What then has prompted this reflection on the relationship between the EPO and UK courts?

It is well-enough known that the most profound disagreements between UK courts and the EPO have centred on the criteria governing the patentability of software-implemented inventions. Amongst EPC member states, national legislative provisions on patentable subject matter correspond to those contained in Article 52 EPC which expressly excludes 'programs for computers' from the European conception of invention, together with various other abstract, intellectual and mental subject matters.[126] However, the exclusion operates only to the extent to which an application or patent relates to the specified subject matter 'as such',[127] a qualification which has admitted some variation in understanding the precise scope of the exclusion. The EPO's first opportunity to test the boundaries of the exclusion arose in *Vicom Systems Inc/Computer-related invention*[128] which concerned a claim relating to a computer-implemented method of processing digitally

---

125 *Human Genome Sciences Inc* v *Eli Lilly & Co* [2011] UKSC 51.

126 Specifically, (a) discoveries, scientific theories and mathematical methods; (b) aesthetic creations; (c) schemes, rules and methods for performing mental acts, playing games or doing business, and programs for computers; and (d) presentations of information: Article 52(2) EPC. The corresponding UK provisions are contained in section 1(2) Patents Act 1977.

127 Article 52(2) EPC.

128 T208/84 *Vicom Systems Inc/Computer-related invention* (OJ EPO, 1987, 14). The decision in *Vicom* was preceded by an amendment to the EPO Guidelines for Examination, issued on 6 March 1985, and which laid out the basic test for patentability as whether a claimed invention had 'technical character': van Voorthuizen, J, 'The Patentability of Computer Programs and Computer-Related Inventions under the European Patent Convention' (1987) 18 IIC 627, 628–9.

encoded images.[129] The EPO's Technical Board of Appeal held that a claim directed to a technical process carried out under the control of a computer program could not be regarded as relating to that program as such, as it was the application of the program for which in effect protection was sought.[130] The Board held that it was inappropriate to make a distinction between embodiments of the same invention carried out in hardware or in software, pointing out that that digital image filters and conventional analogue filters were both concerned with the manipulation of images, and that decisive to patentability was rather the 'technical contribution' the claimed invention made to the known art.[131]

This 'technical contribution' approach informed decision making for the best part of 20 years. However, the EPO's Technical Board of Appeal moved away from using this approach, significantly but partially in *PBS Partnership/Controlling Pension Benefits System*,[132] and completely in *Hitachi/Auction Method*.[133] The EPO's current understanding is that what matters having regard to the concept of 'invention' within the meaning of Article 52(1) EPC is the presence of technical character; a characteristic which can be implied by the physical features of an entity or the nature of an activity and, most significantly, which can be conferred to a non-technical activity by the use of technical means, even if that means is known and of itself makes no contribution to the art.[134] The consequence of the *PBS Partnership/Controlling Pension Benefits System* and *Hitachi/Auction Method* decisions is that the requirement that what is claimed is 'an invention' within the meaning of Article 52 EPC is now so easily satisfied as to be an insignificant bar to patentability. All that is required to impart the requisite technical character to a claimed method is the

[129] The EPO's Examining Division rejected the claim as being directed to a mathematical method on the basis that digital image processing was just a calculation carried out on two-dimensional arrays of numbers: T208/84 *Vicom Systems Inc/Computer-related invention* (OJ EPO, 1987, 14), at reason 2.

[130] Ibid., at reason 12.

[131] Ibid., at reason 16.

[132] T931/95 *PBS Partnership/Controlling Pension Benefits System* (OJ EPO, 2001, 441).

[133] T258/03 *Hitachi/Auction Method* (OJ EPO, 2004, 575) and confirmed in T424/03 *Microsoft/Data transfer with expanded clipboard formats* [2006] EPOR 414.

[134] T258/03 *Hitachi/Auction Method* (OJ EPO, 2004, 575), at reason 4. See also T424/03 *Microsoft/Data transfer with expanded clipboard formats* [2006] EPOR 414, at reason 5. This means that, for example, the use of a pen would confer technical character on a claimed method of writing: ibid. See also *CFPH LLC's Application* [2005] EWHC 1589 [87].

specification of some technical implementing means, however banal or well known[135] including, for instance, activities which are so familiar that their technical character tends to be overlooked, such as the act of writing using pen and paper.[136]

Labelling this 'the any hardware approach' the UK Court of Appeal in *Aerotel Ltd* v *Telco Holdings Ltd*[137] rejected this approach as simply 'wrong':

> Some examples outside the context of computer programs and methods of doing business show why it must be wrong. Consider for instance the following:
>
> i) a claim to a book, e.g. to a book containing a new story the key elements of which are set out in the claim;
> ii) a claim to a standard CD player or iPod loaded with a new piece of music.
>
> Everyone would agree that the claims must be bad – yet in each case as a whole they are novel, non-obvious and enabling. To deem the new music or story part of the prior art (the device of *Pension Benefits*) is simply not intellectually honest. And, so far as we see, the *Microsoft* approach, which discards that device, would actually lead to patentability.[138]

In T154/04 *Dun's Licensing/Estimating Sales Activity*,[139] which decision came only months after that in *Aerotel*, the EPO's Technical Board of Appeal not only confirmed the 'any hardware approach' as correct, but described the UK Court of Appeal's decision in *Aerotel* as not consistent with a good-faith interpretation of the EPC and added that the approach advocated in *Aerotel* was irreconcilable with the EPC.

At one level this can be understood as simply a disagreement between two expert courts as to the preferred reading of a particular legislative

---

[135] Only activities falling within the notion of a non-invention 'as such' will typically represent purely abstract concepts devoid of any technical implications: T258/03 *Hitachi/Auction Method* (OJ EPO, 2004, 575), at reason 4.5.

[136] T258/03 *Hitachi/Auction Method* (OJ EPO, 2004, 575), at reason 4.6. However, the involvement of technical considerations is not sufficient for a method, which may exclusively be carried out mentally, to have technical character: T914/02 *General Electric Company/Method for determining nuclear core loading arrangement* [2006] EPOR 143, at reason 2.3.3. Only if implemented by way of a 'suitably programmed computer' does such a claim become 'technical': ibid., at reason 3.

[137] [2006] EWCA Civ 1371.

[138] *Aerotel Ltd* v *Telco Holdings Ltd and Macrossan's Application* [2006] EWCA Civ 1371 [27].

[139] [2007] EPOR 38.

provision. But this is an overly simplistic reading and the saga also usefully illustrates how functional criteria, attempts to constrain legislative power and the preference for the rule form in harmonization initiatives compete for influence in this area of the law.

Before going on to illustrate that point, it is necessary to expose the Court of Appeal's misrepresentation (or perhaps misunderstanding) of the EPO's approach in the *PBS Partnership/Controlling Pension Benefits System* and *Hitachi/Auction Method* decisions. Contrary to the Court of Appeal's assertion, and openly recognized by the Board, the any hardware approach does not lead to the conclusion that all methods involving the use of technical means are patentable. Rather, to be patentable they still have to be new, represent a non-obvious technical solution to a technical problem, and be susceptible of industrial application.[140] Crucially, as pointed out by the Board in *PBS Partnership/Controlling Pension Benefits System*, the former test for patentability (the technical contribution approach advocated in *Vicom Systems Inc/Computer-related invention* and subsequent cases) was closely related to test for whether a claimed invention involved an inventive step.[141] Thus under the any hardware approach the contribution approach effectively survives but in the context of determining whether a claimed invention involves an inventive step rather than in determining whether what is claimed is 'an invention'.[142] In a case decided a year earlier than *Aerotel*, Peter Prescott QC, sitting as a deputy judge in the UK High Court[143] summarized the EPO's any hardware approach thus:

> [The European Patent Office] look at the applicant's claim, and ask themselves: does it have any 'technical features'? If there are no 'technical features' at all they reject the application, for not being an 'invention'. But they consider it is an invention if there is any 'technical feature' at all. They take it very far. Even paper, or ink, can count as a technical feature. I suppose

---

140 Ibid.

141 T931/95 *PBS Partnership/Controlling Pension Benefits System* (OJ EPO, 2001, 441), at reason 7.

142 Indeed in *Actavis Ltd* v *Novartis AG*, Jacob LJ himself endorsed this aspect of the test for whether a claimed invention involves an inventive step in saying that, 'although "inventive step" is defined as being one which is not obvious, one must always remember the purpose of that definition – to define what is inventive. That which is not inventive by any criteria is not made so by the definition'. Thus, an element of a claim that is purely arbitrary and non-technical and solves no problem and advances the art not at all is to be *treated* as obvious: [2010] EWCA Civ 82 [37].

143 [2005] EWHC 1589.

> a detective story, written on paper with ink, would pass that part of their test. What they then go on to do is to ask themselves, 'Yes, but is it old, or obvious?' And in deciding if it is old or obvious, they ignore anything that is not a 'technical feature'.[144]

Thus, it is the case that subject matter which was unpatentable prior to the decisions in *PBS Partnership/Controlling Pension Benefits System* and *Hitachi/Auction Method* remains so, but changed by these decisions is the ground for refusing the grant of a patent.[145]

I have argued elsewhere that the primary significance of the decisions in *PBS Partnership/Controlling Pension Benefits System* and *Hitachi/Auction Method* is in inviting a reappraisal of the nature of the problem under consideration, changing it from one of interpretation to classification and, in consequence, how decisions of the EPO should be understood by later tribunals.[146]

The inability of any legislature to be able to foresee how technology will evolve creates a strong functional preference for a standards-dominated definition of what should be patentable subject matter.[147] Indeed UK law prior to the introduction of the 1977 Act contained no definition of patentable subject matter and courts were largely free to decide what properly fell within the scope of the patent system. Courts adopted a conception of invention that varied through the application of a social policy aimed at encouraging the introduction and making available of useful new products or processes in light of changing conditions in the field of technology and the sciences.[148]

---

[144] Ibid. [45].

[145] Certainly Peter Prescott in *CFPH LLC's Application* felt that both approaches led to the same end result in practice: ibid. [47]. See also the comments of Mann J in *Macrossan's Application* [2006] EWHC 705 [23]. However, the Court of Appeal has suggested that the approach to obviousness adopted by the EPO in T424/03 *Microsoft* differed, and was more liberal, than that in T258/03 *Hitachi/Auction Method*: *Aerotel Ltd* v *Telco Holdings Ltd and Macrossan's Application* [2006] EWCA Civ 1371 [26]. Whether or not this is so, it is clear that the EPO in T424/03 *Microsoft* saw the question of whether the claimed invention involved an inventive step as one of fact which turned on the particulars of that case: T424/03 *Microsoft/Data transfer with expanded clipboard formats* [2006] EPOR 414, at reason 7.

[146] Booton, D, 'The Patentability of Computer-implemented Inventions in Europe' (2007) IPQ, 92.

[147] Duffy, J, 'Rules and Standards on the Forefront of Patentability' (2009) 51 William & Mary L Rev 609, 616–17.

[148] See e.g. the comments of Lord Diplock in *American Cyanamid Co (Dann's) Patent* [1971] RPC 425, 452.

The framers of the EPC sought to harmonize the conditions of patentability and the flexible and versatile policy-driven approach to patentable subject matter that characterized the 1949 Act was abandoned in favour of a codified list of things specifically said not to be inventions.[149] The EPO's creative interpretation of the exclusion has meant that tens of thousands of claims to software-implemented inventions have been granted under the EPC. But a search of the EPO's jurisprudence on software-related inventions reveals little clear definitive guidance – nothing that can properly be called a 'rule' – that determines what is or is not patentable under the EPC. The EPO has been consistent in demanding that what is claimed is 'technical' in some way (first, in requiring of an invention it makes a 'technical contribution' and latterly in requiring that it have 'technical character'), but precisely what is meant by technical in either context has remained obscure.[150]

That patentability rather turns on a rather vague concept suits the EPO very well in its role as administrator of the EPC, allowing as it does a flexible policy-driven approach to the fundamental concept of 'invention'. Indeed in *PBS Partnership/Controlling Pension Benefits System*, the EPO Technical Board of Appeal openly acknowledged that the meaning of the terms 'technical' and 'technical character' was not particularly clear but added that this was also true of the term 'invention'.[151] The idea that the uncertain boundaries of 'technical character' inevitably flow from the inherently vague parent notion of 'invention' was taken up and expanded upon by the UK patent court in *CFPH LLC's Application.*[152] Peter Prescott QC, sitting as a deputy judge, argued that the use of the word 'technical' as a shorthand expression in order to identify patentable subject matter, whilst often convenient, merely restated the problem of

---

[149] Article 52(2) EPC and implemented into the Patents Act in Section 1(2).

[150] See e.g. the comments of the Principal Examiner in *Fujitsu's Application* who was prepared to accept as a workable description of what might constitute a technical contribution: 'something of a technical character, having some practical and technical impact, as opposed to some mere thought process', but crucially was not convinced that this provided a complete definition: [1996] RPC 511, 516. On appeal, Aldous LJ observed that the principle that to be patentable a thing must make a technical contribution lay 'at the heart of patent law' but the principle's application was far from straightforward and there were 'difficulties in identifying clearly the boundaries between what is and what is not a technical contribution': [1997] RPC 608, 614 and 616.

[151] T931/95 *PBS Partnership/Controlling Pension Benefits System* (OJ EPO, 2001, 441), at reason 6.

[152] [2005] EWHC 1589.

defining 'invention' in different and more imprecise language[153] and that problem was irresolvable because:

> we are dealing with a rather peculiar branch of human knowledge. First, what is an 'invention' is no more than a convention of human culture. Secondly, it is about legislating for ideas that have not yet been thought of and which, perhaps, at present, cannot be conceived ... By its very nature, therefore, the subject cannot be reduced to a precise verbal formula.[154]

A degree of obscurity in respect of the boundaries of patentable subject matter has thus been justified by some tribunals as essential given that, as a policy tool aimed at encouraging innovation, the patent system must be capable of accommodating currently unforeseeable developments in science and technology. As noted above, whilst clarity and predictability are features of rule-based judgement in that ideal rules provide a complete or nearly complete before-the-fact specification of legal outcomes, so defined rules are poorly suited to new circumstances arising because of unanticipated developments and can thus become hopelessly anachronistic.

Whilst there is some strength in such arguments, the relatively open standard that they advocate sits uncomfortably with the intention that the EPO not having a wide-ranging discretion in respect of the identification of patentable subject matter.[155]

There are a number of reasons why substantive patent examination in Europe is generally rule based, which reasons are independent of the patent system's overall *raison d'être* and which have exerted a pressure to formulate or understand the criterion of 'technical character' as a rule notwithstanding that there may be good reasons not so to do. Individually and collectively, these reasons have raised an expectation that the criterion of 'technical character' should be a rule with known and fixed content. Not only is this expectation at the root of the complaints and

---

153 Ibid. [14]

154 Ibid. [16]–[17].

155 Kolle, G, 'The Patentable Invention in the European Patent Convention' (1974) 5 IIC 140, 144 and 151. If this was the intention of the delegates to the Conference then it manifestly failed though it is far from clear that this was the intention given the complexity of the negotiations, on which see Pila, J, 'Article 52(2) of the Convention on the Grant of European Patents: What Did the Framers Intend? A Study of the Travaux Preparatoires' (2005) 36 IIC 755, 769–70.

criticism that the law lacks clarity,[156] but, as will be shown below, has also led to a determined though ultimately fruitless search for meaning, which effect has been encouraged by attempts by the EPO to disguise decision making as involving the application of a rule when the actual state of affairs is otherwise.

One key reason for trying to make the stages of substantive examination and grant as rule based as possible is that the very inflexibility of rules produces huge efficiency gains in decision making. Without rules, decisions can be extremely expensive requiring the determination of both facts and law. Efficiency is an important concern given the volume of work undertaken by patent offices in that *all* patent applications are subject to examination, and the number of decisions required of patent offices in any given period is thus far greater than that of, for example, the patent court.[157] This concern no doubt underpinned the Munich Diplomatic Conference's desire that the EPO should not be called upon to examine and make decisions where the claimed subject matter was doubtful or controversial.[158]

But it is also the case, at least within Europe, that clear rules further the goal of harmonization. The European patent system is a cooperative venture between the countries of Western Europe, which aims at codifying, where possible, established laws and which intends, to a significant degree, to harmonize the conditions for the grant of a patent.[159] As has

---

[156] For the users of the patent system, questions of novelty and inventiveness are routine matters and that their determination is rule based raises an expectation of rule-based clarity generally in substantive examination and grant. For an example of this type of expectation-led criticism see Cook, T, 'Patents for Business Methods and Computer Program Related Inventions' (2000) 6(5) CTLR 123, 123.

[157] According to the most recently published of the EPO's annual reports, 278 867 filings were made in 2015 and 160 022 applications. However, the most important statistic from our perspective is the number of examinations which in 2015 was 122 949 (European and International): accessed 20 January 2017 at https://www.epo.org/about-us/annual-reports-statistics/annual-report/2015.html.

[158] It also underpins the EPO Enlarged Board's view that the 'referral procedure' under Art.112 (which allows the President of the EPO to refer a point of law to the Enlarged Board of Appeal where two Boards of Appeal have given different decisions on the same question) is only intended to allow a referral to be made to the Board when there is a conflict in the case law, making it difficult if not impossible for the Office to bring its patent granting practice into line with the case law of the Boards of Appeal: G03/08 Opinion of 12 May 2010, at reason 7.2.6.

[159] Accepting that the primary objective of the EPC is the provision of a unitary patent application and examination procedure and harmonization of

already been noted, national tribunals, in interpreting their national laws, look to decisions of the EPO Boards of Appeal for authoritative guidance on the interpretation of the corresponding provisions of the EPC because it is seen as undesirable for the provisions of the EPC to be construed differently in the EPO from the way they are interpreted in the national courts.[160] Although not strictly binding upon national courts and authorities, decisions of the EPO are considered to be of great persuasive authority and to this extent have 'precedential' status.[161]

In principle, if the objective of harmonization imposes a duty on national tribunals to look to decisions of the EPO, then there is a corresponding obligation on the EPO to provide authoritative guidance in that, if a decision of the EPO on the particulars of a case is to be authoritative, it ought to be justified on generic grounds which can then provide the basis for decisions in future similar cases.[162] Steeped in the common law tradition of binding precedent and familiar with the mechanisms of harmonization that operate under European Community law, UK patent authorities have engaged in a frustratingly unrewarding trawl through EPO decisions in search of some generically applicable rule that may guide their own decisions.[163] The criticism directed at the EPO by the Court of Appeal in *Aerotel* was as much about an absence of clarity as it was about muddled thinking. Indeed Jacob LJ took the extraordinary step of formulating a series of questions, aimed at forcing clarity in the law, and asking that the President of the EPO refer these

---

national patent laws is a secondary objective not essential to the first. The purpose of the Convention is reflected in the wording of its Preamble which provides that members entered into the Convention, 'desiring to strengthen co-operation between the states of Europe in respect of the protection of inventions', and, 'desiring that such protection may be obtained in those States by a single procedure for the grant of patents, and by the establishment of certain standard rules governing patents … granted'.

160 See above at p. 127.

161 It is notable that at one point in the negotiations leading up to the conclusion of the EPC, the goal of harmonization was set up as an overriding objective precisely to overcome the difficulties of arriving at an agreed text that balanced certainty with flexibility: Pila, above n.155, 772. The drafters of the EPC also anticipated that precedent would play an important role in setting the balance between certainty and flexibility, though there was disagreement as to how the legislative framework should be drafted best to achieve this: ibid., 769.

162 In relation to common law precedent see MacCormick, above n.2, 75–9.

163 A further contributory factor may also be 'the lawyer's natural tendency to associate law and rules, and to think of "the law" as a collection or system of rules': Dworkin, above n.20, 38.

questions to the EPO's Enlarged Board of Appeal. In effect then, the Court of Appeal, was asking for a 'preliminary ruling' from the EPO's Enlarged Board of Appeal on the correct approach to adopt in determining whether an invention relates to subject matter that is excluded under Article 52 EPC and how those elements of a claim that relate to excluded subject matter should be treated when assessing whether an invention is novel and inventive under Articles 54 and 56 EPC.[164] The then EPO President, Alain Pompidou, rejected this request holding there was no legal basis for a referral to the Enlarged Board.[165]

Of course, the EPO itself went some way to inviting the expectation that the requirement that an invention have 'technical character' should be a generic rule with a known and fixed content in arguing that 'technical character' was the unifying characteristic common to all phenomena called 'inventions' and that the apparently diverse group of things said not to be inventions in Article 52(2) EPC were, in fact, related by its absence. In particular, in *IBM/Document abstracting and retrieving*[166] a claim relating to a computer-implemented means of abstracting, storing and retrieving documents was refused on the grounds that it lacked 'technical character' and fell within the excluded category of schemes, rules and methods for performing mental acts. In reaching this decision, the Board argued that whatever their differences, the various types of subject matter excluded under Article 52(2) had in common that they referred to activities which did not aim at any direct technical result but were rather of an abstract and intellectual character.[167]

The scene was thereby set for 15 years of fruitless pursuit of this elusive notion.[168] The futility of that pursuit is now made manifest in

---

[164] This, the Court said, was done in the hope that there was a spirit of cooperation between national courts and the EPO and notwithstanding that it was formally no business of the Court to define questions to be asked of an Enlarged Board: *Aerotel Ltd* v *Telco Holdings Ltd and Macrossan's Application* [2006] EWCA Civ 1371 [75] and [76]. The influence of precedent is evident at [29] of this decision. Sir Robin Jacob has since admitted that this was an attempt to invent something like 'a reference system': Jacob, above n.120, 196.

[165] Unlike the arrangements for providing for a consistent interpretation of European Union law, there is no 'preliminary reference' procedure under the EPC system under which a national court might obtain authoritative guidance on the meaning of supra-national legal provision.

[166] T22/85 *IBM/Document abstracting and retrieving* (OJ EPO, 1990, 12).

[167] Ibid., at reason 2.

[168] So for example, the UK Comptroller of Patents in *Fujitsu's Application* complained that whilst decisions of the EPO appeared to distinguish between inventions which provided a 'technical advance' and were thus patentable and

that, whilst the justificatory arguments advanced by the EPO in *IBM/Document abstracting and retrieving* pointed to the question of whether claimed subject matter was 'an invention' as one of interpretation, the decisions in *PBS Partnership/Controlling Pension Benefits System* and *Hitachi/Auction Method*, in shifting the inquiry into the determination of obviousness, suggest that the EPO now treat it as one of classification. This change sends an important signal indicating that a decision of the EPO as to whether certain claimed subject matter is or is not a patentable invention should not be regarded as a ruling in a point of law but rather as a matter of evidence.[169]

In understanding this change, it is important to appreciate that the obligation of the EPO to promote and further harmonization, whilst undoubtedly influential in shaping its decisions and their interpretation, exists only in the exercise of its primary obligation of administering the grant of European patents. The EPO's primary responsibility is to decide individual cases and it is in this context that it interprets the EPC. Allowable discretion in the exercise of this role imports an essential flexibility into the determination of patentable subject matter. This explains why, even within the EPO itself, decisions of the Technical Board of Appeal are not understood to be binding on future decisions and

---

those which did not, in practice it was often very difficult to determine whether a particular invention did as a matter of fact involve the sort of technical contribution alluded to in the cases and added that the difficulty 'has been compounded by the fact that there are recent decisions of the EPO Technical Board of Appeal in which the question of what constitutes a technical advance or contribution seems to have been rather more flexibly interpreted than has hitherto been the case': *Fujitsu's Application* [1996] RPC 511, 521. The Court of Appeal in that case was similarly perplexed. Aldous LJ, although attaching considerable weight to the authority of decisions of the EPO, admitted to having difficulty in identifying the boundary between what was and what was not a technical contribution: [1997] RPC 608, 614.

[169] On the importance of the classification of problems as ones of interpretation or classification see above at p. 63. The Court of Appeal has recently observed that any pure question of law should be decided during prosecution and that it is not enough to get a patent past the application stage to show that as a matter of law it merely arguably covers patentable subject matter. But if a debatable question of pure fact is or may be involved at the application stage, things are different – one cannot then say that the decision at that point must be the last word on the subject: *Aerotel Ltd* v *Telco Holdings Ltd and Macrossan's Application* [2006] EWCA Civ 1371 [5].

examiners are free to ignore parts of Board of Appeal decisions that 'they don't like'.[170]

It is illuminating in this respect to compare certain efforts aimed at providing some clarity to this area of the law. A significant opportunity presented itself on the occasion of the Diplomatic Conference, held in Munich in November 2000, which undertook a modernizing revision of the EPC. The process of reform had been initiated in 1999 at an intergovernmental conference of the member states of the EPC which generated a request for the EPO to prepare a revision conference.[171] After consultation, the Administrative Council of the EPO produced a draft Basic Proposal, the first iteration of which proposed that Article 52(2) be deleted completely since it was essentially superfluous;[172] an amendment to the EPC supported by the EPO itself.[173] The reasoning behind this proposal was that:

> The list of items found in Article 52(2) EPC are simply examples of non-technical 'inventions', which would remain unpatentable even in the absence of this provision. Simultaneously, the deletion of Articles 52(2) and (3) EPC would avoid all the problems the interpretation of any statutory exception entails. Thus, it should be incumbent on Office practice and case law to determine whether subject-matter claimed as an invention has a technical character and to further develop the concept of invention in an appropriate manner, in light of technical developments and the state of knowledge at the time.[174]

Because this rather radical rewriting of Article 52 did not find universal support, the Administrative Council simultaneously put forward an alternative proposal that revision involve only the deletion of computer programs from Article 52(2)(c). This narrower amendment, the Council said, had met with broad consensus. The current exception, it said, had become de facto obsolete in light of the way in which it had been interpreted and applied by the EPO.[175] Had this alternative proposal been

---

170 Alton, A, 'Forum on Software Inventions at the EPO' (2003) 32 CIPA Journal 643, 644, reporting the comments of an EPO panel of experts.

171 'Report of the Intergovernmental conference of the member states of the European Patent Organisation on the reform of the patent system in Europe, Paris, 24 and 25 June 1999' (22 OJ EPO 1999, 545), 545 and 549.

172 Basic Proposal for the Revision of the European Patent Convention, CA/100/00 e [6].

173 Ibid.

174 Ibid.

175 Revision of the European Patent Convention, CA/100/00 e [2]. See also G3/08 *President's Reference/Computer program exclusion* [2009] EPOR 9 [63].

adopted it would no doubt have satisfied the objective of enhanced clarity in so far as it would have gone some way to align the express wording of the EPC with the EPO's interpretation of it. But it is notable that this species of clarifying amendment would not have come at the expense of fettered EPO decision making; rather quite the opposite.

Notwithstanding that it had been initiated by the EPO itself, the conference rejected this proposal.[176] In particular there was close to united opposition from the EU member states.[177] With the single exception of the Austrian delegation, the EU member states advocated postponing any decision pending further consideration and consultation.[178] The EU delegates' position was informed by the fact that the European Commission had launched a consultation exercise on the patentability of computer-implemented inventions raising then the possibility of harmonization of this aspect of the law within the Community. Any action relating to the EPC, it was argued, should be postponed pending the outcome of this EU initiative. There was also the concern that the deletion of computer programs from Article 52(2) might be misunderstood as broadening the scope of patentable subject matter.[179]

The stage was thus set for the entrance of the institutions of the European Union as *dramatis personae*. The Commission's 1997 Green Paper[180] had identified the removal of computer programs from the list of non-patentable inventions as one of the issues facing the Community and referred specifically to the developments in the United States. Although by no means one-sided, the Consultation which the Green Paper and its follow-up[181] initiated indicated widespread support for the removal of the prohibition on the patentability of computer programs.[182] Soon after the

---

[176] Conference Resolution (OJ EPO 2001, Special Edition No. 1, 50), 11–12.

[177] The delegations of the EU member states had met in Brussels on 17 November 2000 (three days before the Diplomatic Conference) in order to agree on a common standpoint and to coordinate their voting with regard to computer programs: Nack, R and Phélip, B, *AIPPI Report on the Diplomatic Conference for the Revision of the European Patent Convention Munich, November 20–29, 2000*.

[178] Ibid.

[179] Ibid. See also G3/08 *President's Reference/Computer program exclusion* [2009] EPOR 9 [65].

[180] European Commission, *Promoting Innovation through Patents: Green Paper on the Community Patent and the Patent System in Europe*, COM (1997) 314 final.

[181] Ibid.

[182] Booton, D and Mole, P, 'The Action Freezes? The Draft Directive on the Patentability of Computer-implemented Inventions' (2002) IPQ 289.

'failure' of the Munich Diplomatic Conference in this respect, the Commission put forward a proposal for an EU Directive aimed at harmonizing the law on the patentability of computer-implemented inventions.[183] The Commission in justifying the need for Community action argued that the law and administrative practices of the member states relating to the grant of patents in this field were divergent[184] and that the legal situation was ambiguous and lacked certainty.[185] The implication then was that, notwithstanding the harmonization mechanisms operating under the EPC and the commitment of national patent authorities and courts to follow the lead of the EPO, divergent national approaches had nevertheless evolved.[186]

Under the proposed Directive, member states were required to ensure that computer-implemented inventions were patentable, subject only to the conditions of industrial applicability, novelty and inventiveness. The Directive, however, specified that to involve an inventive step, a computer-implemented invention had to make a 'technical contribution', by which was meant a contribution to the state of the art in a technical field which was not obvious to a person skilled in the art. The term 'technical' was not defined in the Directive but no doubt had the proposal come into force then the Court of Justice, under the preliminary ruling procedure, would soon after have been called upon to provide authoritative guidance as to what was meant.

The proposed directive was not intended to extend patent protection to inventions which did not meet the established criteria for patentability under the EPC, but only to make those criteria more transparent.[187] As is well documented, this attempt to concretize established conditions was met with considerable opposition,[188] the upshot of which led to the

---

[183] Proposal for a Directive of the European Parliament and of the Council on the Patentability of Computer-implemented Inventions, COM (2002) 92 final.

[184] Ibid., Explanatory Memorandum, 2.

[185] Ibid.

[186] Whether this was in fact true was open to question at the time; however, with hindsight it is clear that the risk was always there and that the UK has now moved away from the EPO's position and presumably that in other EPC member states.

[187] Proposal for a Directive of the European Parliament and of the Council on the Patentability of Computer-implemented Inventions, COM (2002) 92 final, Explanatory Memorandum, 3 and 11.

[188] Particularly from academics, start-up companies, software engineers and students who championed an 'open source' approach to software development. The opponents' voices were coordinated through the EuroLinux Alliance. The overriding concern of the opponents was that the monopolistic nature of patents

rejection of the proposal by the European Parliament[189] ending any prospect of the directive coming into force.

A final attempt at producing clarity came in in 2008 when the then President of the EPO, Alison Brimelow, published a reference which drew attention to inconsistencies and conflicts in the EPO jurisprudence concerning the patentability of software-implemented inventions, and in which she referred her own set of questions to the Enlarged Board of Appeal.[190] For the purpose of the current argument, the precise content of the questions referred is not relevant save perhaps for noting the fundamental character of the first: 'can a computer program only be excluded as a computer program as such if it is explicitly claimed as a computer program?' More interesting were her observations on the tensions at play:

> As the EPC was drafted, the feeling was that it was better not to define the exclusion precisely in law, but rather that the matter should be left in the hands of the EPO and the national courts. This flexibility is important as technology develops and new technologies emerge. Nevertheless, to quote a working group in 1972: 'it was stressed that a matter as important as computer programmes should not be left in a state of prolonged uncertainty pending legal developments'. Diverging decisions of the boards of appeal have indeed created uncertainty, and answers to the questions arising from these decisions are necessary to enable the further, harmonious development of case law in this field.[191]

In its response, the Enlarged Board noted that the object and purpose of a referral by the President was to ensure the uniform application of the law within the Organisation in the interest of legal certainty.[192] The Board drew a distinction between 'different decisions' and 'divergent

---

would bring the European programming industry to a halt by proprietizing the building blocks of the programmer's trade: Attridge, D, 'Challenging Claims! Patenting Computer Programs in Europe and the USA' (2001) 1 IPQ 22, 26.

[189] On 6 July 2005, the European Parliament voted to reject the Council's common position on the directive Patentability of computer-implemented inventions: European Parliament legislative resolution on the Council common position with a view to the adoption of a directive of the European Parliament and of the Council on the patentability of computer-implemented inventions (P6_TA(2005)0275).

[190] G3/08 *President's Reference/Computer program exclusion* [2009] EPOR 9.

[191] Ibid. [2] (footnotes omitted).

[192] G03/08 *Programs for Computers*, Opinion of the Enlarged Board of Appeal, 12 May 2010, at reason 6.

decisions'.[193] The former, the Board said, could be ones that are far apart in time, regardless of whether they actually still have a claim to validity in view of intervening changes in case law, whereas the latter, by contrast, were ones which varied in their substantive content while being close together in time.[194] Having regard to the purpose of the referral process, the Board took the view that the right of the President to refer legal questions to the Enlarged Board was confined to circumstances where there could be said to be 'divergent' rather than 'different' decisions of Boards of Appeal (i.e. when there is a conflict in the case law).[195] Importantly the right of referral did not allow the President to use an Enlarged Board referral as a means of replacing Board of Appeal rulings with the decision of a putatively higher instance.[196] The Enlarged Board understood its role as concerned with promoting effective decision making within the Organisation. Its job was thus to resolve conflicts in the case law that would otherwise make it difficult for the Office to bring its patent granting practice into line with the case law of the Boards, but it did not see itself as a grand engineer of harmonization except perhaps coincidentally:

> Even the essentially commendable desire for harmonisation expressed by Lord Justice Jacob in the *Aerotel/Macrossan* judgment can be taken up by the Enlarged Board only to the extent possible under the EPC, even if his suggestion might significantly advance the cause of legal uniformity in Europe. When judiciary-driven legal development meets its limits, it is time for the legislator to take over.[197]

This prolonged and ongoing saga in Europe amounts to a debate as to the appropriate level of constraint that should operate on decisions relating to the patentability of computer-implemented inventions. It highlights a significant problem facing the law-makers of Europe to the extent that harmonization is set up as a primary and overriding objective. The risk is

---

[193] A distinction that Sir Robin Jacob has since described as 'purposeless': Jacob, above n.120, 195.

[194] G03/08 *Programs for Computers*, Opinion of the Enlarged Board of Appeal, 12 May 2010, at reason 7.1.

[195] Ibid., at reason 7.2 and 7.3.1.

[196] Thus for example, the Board said that, 'a presidential referral is not admissible merely because the European Parliament and Council have failed to adopt a directive on CII [computer-implemented invention] patenting or because consistent Board rulings are called into question by a vocal lobby': G03/08 *Programs for Computers*, Opinion of the Enlarged Board of Appeal, 12 May 2010, at reason 7.2.7. See also ibid., reasons 7.3.5 and 7.3.8.

[197] Ibid., at reason 7.2.7.

that rules become rules maintained simply for rules' sake. This raises the prospect of a system in which the law is clear, and discretion restrained in individual cases, but meaningless factual distinctions govern the outcomes in turn leading to a sense that the law lacks a rational basis.[198] Fuelled by sensationalist stories in the popular press and mainstream media, it is a commonly held view that EU law-making is frequently irrational. I have no doubt that this perception influenced the decision of those citizens who voted in favour of the UK leaving the European Union.

---

198 On which point note Kelman, above n.53, 47.

4. A conflict at the foundation

The aim of this chapter is to show that, in something as fundamental as marking out the boundaries of protectable subject matter, form matters. As I noted in Chapter 2, decision making according to rules is appropriate when certainty, uniformity, stability or security are particularly valued but that the certainty of a rule depends on the context over which it is said to exercise control.[1] This chapter focusses on the single foundational context: defining that which is protected. I will show that invariably the security of expectation that rules generate in this context is compromised by the simultaneous operation of a standard that occupies the same territory as the rule. This chapter then serves as a foundation for exploration of the social, political and theoretical dimensions of the analysis that follow in Chapters 5 and 6.

The analysis starts with patent law and in particular a brief historical account outlining how the conditions that a claimed invention be new and that it involve an inventive step became discrete elements in establishing patentability. I show that as a matter of contemporary law there is no significant qualitative difference between the tests: a conclusion supported by noting their evolution from a single test that asked only and in fairly non-specific terms whether what was claimed was patentable subject matter. That the difference between the two contemporary tests lies only in the degree of difference demanded between what is claimed and what is known means that something which is not new is a fortiori obvious. That observation invites consideration of why two discrete tests emerged and have remained. At this stage I only hint at the argument advanced in later chapters that the test for novelty remains and is useful precisely because it is a rule.

I then go on to consider copyright law and in particular the condition that a work must be original if it is to enjoy copyright protection. Many readers will instinctively baulk against my claim that the test for whether a work is original is much more rule than it is standard-like. To head off

[1] Schlag, P, 'Rules and Standards' (1985) 33 UCLA L Rev 379, 407. Of course this observation applies not only to certainty but the other consequential characteristics of rules.

counterarguments I spend some time establishing that in the great majority of cases originality is assessed by asking only whether the claimed work was copied. Of course I accept that although this test is that which operates in the great majority of cases, sometimes courts have adopted an alternative formulation which looks to the exercise of skill, labour and judgement. I set out to show both that these are indeed different tests (rather than alternative ways of expressing the same thing) and that the latter test only applies where copyright is claimed in works which are, to a greater or lesser extent, copies of existing productions. And lest any readers think my head in the sand, I also take an opportunity to note the influence of the European Court on the originality standard but reserve making any critical assessment of this development until the chapter which follows. The central theme of the chapter is returned to by showing that the rule-like originality condition looks superfluous given that its effect is entirely subsumed by the standard-like test applied in establishing whether a work has been infringed by copying. In particular I note that courts have held that there can be no infringement of work which is itself copied nor can an infringement claim be made out where the alleged infringement is in copying a part of a work which part is itself copied. To arrive at a conclusion that there is here a rule and a standard in simultaneous operation and occupying the same territory requires, however, that I establish that in copyright law it is more artificial to treat subsistence and infringement as discrete contexts than to consider them together. I feel confident making that claim given that the question of whether a work is original is almost invariably considered where there is some dispute and typically where an alleged infringer argues that what they have taken is not the claimant's original work. In this respect I draw a contrast between copyright law and patent law, and show that in respect of patents, validity and infringement are discrete contexts. In justifying this I need readers to forgive a small digression from the central line of argument but one that allows me to explaining the relationship between patent validity and infringement historically and then as a matter of contemporary law.

The chapter concludes with an account of trade mark law which I suggest most clearly demonstrates the significance of form. In particular I note that refusal of registration of a sign under section 5(1) Trade Marks Act 1994 on the grounds that it is identical to a mark already on the register is a rule requiring, for instance, no assessment of whether the relevant consumer is likely to be confused between the sign and the mark. By contrast, much more standard-like is the test operating under section 5(2) of the same Act, by which registration of a sign will be refused if its use would produce in the minds of average consumers a likelihood of confusion as to the trade origin of the goods and services associated with the sign. I argue that the tests for whether there is identity under section 5(1) and whether there is a likelihood of confusion under section 5(2) are not qualitatively different: they are both directed to establishing whether a sign is relatively distinctive. This again raises the question of why have the rule at all if its effects are embraced by the simultaneous operation of a standard.

In the case of tangible property, the starting point for marking out the boundaries of protectable subject matter can be informed by 'real world' physical boundaries.[2] This anchoring of property claims is absent where the claim is to intellectual property. How the object of property is identified and how its limits are defined is entirely determined by the various schemes, rules and concepts that are as artificial as any other element of the law.[3] And it follows that what certainty or uncertainty there is as to the limits of property claims is entirely the product then of conscious efforts by law-makers. If the boundaries are clear or unclear, they have been fashioned to be so to further some end.[4] This matters to two classes of person: right owners and users as potential licensees or infringers.

In various contexts right owners must make decisions based on what they believe they have rights over. For instance, and perhaps most obviously, the decision whether to bring an action for infringement is informed in part by the understanding of the security and scope of the rights on which the intended action is grounded. And of course there is a correlative understanding that informs the actions of potential licensees and potential infringers. To the extent that the boundaries of the protectable subject matter are unclear, both classes are forced to make decisions under conditions of uncertainty. At the same time, where a degree of certainty is introduced by way of a rule the risk adverse can be motivated

---

[2] See e.g. Gordon, W, 'An Inquiry into the Merits of Copyright: The Challenges of Consistency, Consent, and Encouragement Theory' (1989) 41 Stanford L Rev 1343, 1379; and Drahos, P, *A Philosophy of Intellectual Property* (Ashgate, 1996), 155.

[3] Bently, L and Sherman, B, *Intellectual Property Law*, 4th edition (Oxford University Press, 2014), 3. That said 'the view that property is a thing is nowadays seen as quaint and false, or at least not helpful. Property is thought to be a rights relation between one person and another … or between one person and many others': Drahos, above n.2, 4. All the same whilst it may be that all rights are incorporeal, some property is not: ibid., 16.

[4] See in relation to copyright: Barron, A, 'Copyright Law and the Claims of Art' (2002) IPQ 368, 381; and Griffiths, J, 'Dematerialization, Pragmatism and the European Copyright Revolution' (2013) 33 OJLS 767.

to act believing that the consequences of their actions are largely predictable.

It is almost too obvious to say so, but decisions made under standards only contribute to uncertainty up to the point when a decision is actually made. From then on legal rights and correlative duties are clear. So far as marking out the boundaries of protectable subject matter is concerned, this matters because certain intellectual property rights such as patents and trade marks are protected conditional on a formal examination preceding registration whereas others, such as copyright, are not.[5] A register does two important things. If it is accessible, it communicates information to the public. What information depends on what is contained on the register. Typically, this would include the name of the right holder and some indication of the subject matter over which they claim dominion. A publically accessible register can thus deter individuals from pursuing courses of action that they fear would infringe an enforceable right. How far they are deterred will depend in part on their understanding that the registered right would be recognized and enforced if tested. This observation brings me on to the second important thing that a register does. All intellectual property rights require the person claiming the right to demonstrate that what is being claimed satisfies certain essential criteria related to the nature of the right claimed (novelty and inventiveness in the case of a claim to a patentable invention; originality in the case of a claim to copyright in a work; and so on and so forth). Registration that requires an examination as to whether these criteria have been met enhances security of expectation both for the right holder and for the public. That security of expectation can be undermined if the decisions made by the examining body can be reviewed and overturned such that the right in issue is limited in scope or revoked entirely.

Patents are registered rights. A patent may be granted only for an invention which is new, which involves an inventive step and which is capable of industrial application. Although phrased in terms of conditions to be satisfied if an invention is to qualify for protection, the qualities of novelty, inventiveness and industrial applicability have been held rather to be elements of an 'invention' as that term in normally understood.[6]

---

[5] Although the US operates a register of copyright works, copyright registration is not a condition of copyright protection: section 408 US Copyright Act (Title 17 USC). An owner is nevertheless wise to register a work since doing so establishes a public record of the copyright claim and registration is necessary before an infringement suit may be filed: section 411 US Copyright Act.

[6] Per Lord Hoffmann in *Biogen Inc* v *Medeva Plc* [1997] RPC 1, 42 but c.f. Hobhouse LJ in *Biogen Inc* v *Medeva Plc* [1995] RPC 25, 88.

Thus, for the purposes of patent law, that which is novel, inventive and capable of industrial application *is* an invention.[7]

In the great majority of cases, the significant hurdles are to show that what is claimed is new and involves an inventive step.[8] As I noted earlier in this book, the question of whether something is new and whether it is obvious are both understood to be ones of fact. But, though both are questions of fact, the question of whether a claimed invention is new is more 'rule-like' than the one of whether it involves an inventive step. Whether a claimed invention is new is determined objectively in the sense that it is irrelevant whether the novelty destroying prior art has in fact been seen or acted upon by anyone. It is enough to anticipate a claimed invention that it is available to the public.[9] The effect is to operate a 'bright line' test which avoids subjectivity and most questions of degree and notwithstanding that the test sometimes produces harsh results.[10] This is not to say that there are not discretionary elements to the test for novelty: the test is not entirely free from matters requiring the exercise of judgement. In particular, only information that a person skilled in the art is able to derive from the prior art without 'undue burden' can defeat a claim to novelty.[11] But the notion of 'undue burden' does not allow an inquiry into such subjective matters as the cost of carrying out the analysis or the time taken to find the relevant information.[12]

Although the adoption of structured approaches to the question of whether what is claimed involves an inventive step are attempts to make

---

[7] Except that subject matter which is expressly said not to be an invention under Article 52 EPC (and the corresponding provisions in section 1(2) Patents Act 1977).

[8] The condition that an invention must be industrially applicable is rarely a hurdle not least of all because, in many cases, an invention which passes (or fails) the test for industrial application under section 4(1) will equally pass (or fail) the test for patentability under section 1(2): Intellectual Property Office, *Manual of Patent Practice*, accessed 30 January 2017 at https://www.gov.uk/government/publications/patents-manual-of-patent-practice, [4.03]. The question of the industrial applicability of a gene was considered by the Supreme Court in *Human Genome Sciences Inc* v *Eli Lilly & Co* [2011] UKSC 51.

[9] *Lux Traffic Controls Ltd* v *Pike Signals Ltd* [1993] RPC 107, 134; and G1/92 *Availability to the Public* [1993] EPOR 241, 243.

[10] *Milliken Denmark* v *Walk Off Mat* [1996] FSR 292, 310–11.

[11] Ibid., 310–11.

[12] G1/92 *Availability to the Public* [1993] EPOR 241, 243–4. See also Bently and Sherman, above n.3, 536.

the question more tractable,[13] at root the question cannot be approached with rigorous objectivity and deciding whether a claimed invention is obvious is an evaluative exercise such that reasonable people can easily reach different conclusions.[14] It has been described as a qualitative rather than quantitative test[15] and one that is difficult to answer with confidence.[16]

Predictably, the obviousness standard has been criticized for its uncertainty.[17] And as with all decision making under standards, decisions have been criticized for seeming arbitrary. Bochnovic, for instance, argues that in many cases courts disguise what he labels as their 'true approach' under the guise of obviousness and that, 'in many cases the court carries

---

[13] The EPO routinely employs the so-called problem and solution approach, which, as noted by Szabo, was an approach developed to achieve consistency in practice so rendering the outcome of the assessment as predictable as possible. The broad aim was to overcome the influence of various national practices by providing a method that was sufficiently reliable, uniform and convincing: Szabo, G, 'The Problem and Solution Approach in the European Patent Office' (1995) 26(4) IIC 457, 459. In the UK, the four-stage *Windsurfing/Pozzoli* test is used, though UK courts have emphasized that the test is not peculiarly English and have sought to de-emphasize the differences between this and the EPO's problem and solution approach: *Generics (UK) Ltd* v *Daiichi Pharmaceutical* [2009] EWCA Civ 646; and *Actavis Ltd* v *Novartis AG* [2010] EWCA Civ 82. For a detailed consideration of the differences in the approaches see: Cole, P, 'Inventive Step – Meaning of the EPO Problem and Solution Approach, and Implications for the United Kingdom' (1998) 20 EIPR 214 (Part 1) and 267 (Part 2).

[14] Singer, R, *The European Patent Convention*, revised English edition by Raph Lunzer (Sweet & Maxwell, 1995), 176–7 where it is observed that 'the practitioner is confronted with the issue of obviousness or inventiveness more often than with any other single issue'. See also Ullrich, H, *Standards of Patentability for European Inventions: Should an Inventive Step Advance the Art?* Vol 1 of IIC Studies in Industrial Property and Copyright Law (Max Planck Institute, 1977), 38 ('the question of whether the invented device comes so close to a prior art device or the combined teaching of several prior art elements that it is obvious is a matter of individual appraisal by the judge of last instance, be he a lawyer or a technical expert himself. Therefore, the non-obviousness issue will always require a genuine value judgement') and Griffiths, A, 'Windsurfing and the Inventive Step' (1999) IPQ 160, 169.

[15] *Mölnlycke AB* v *Procter & Gamble* [1994] RPC 49, 112.

[16] Ibid., 114. In *Conor Medsystems Inc* v *Angiotech Pharmaceuticals Inc* [2008] UKHL 49 [42], Lord Hoffmann approved the case-by-case approach to the question that had previously been advocated by Kitchin J in *Generics (UK) Ltd* v *Lundbeck A/S* [2007] RPC 32. See above at p. 38.

[17] Ullrich, above n.14, 39; and Griffiths, above n.14, 160.

out what amounts to a subconscious determination of whether the invention is deserving of a patent, and then having reached a conclusion, proceeds to perfunctorily apply the obviousness requirement to achieve the desired result'.[18]

Yet it is clear that the requirement of inventiveness, in addition to novelty, did not emerge by accident. This is not the place for a comprehensive historical review and I intend only to give an account of the historical path trodden by English courts to demonstrate that from very early in the evolution of the law, courts were not minded to adopt a simple conception of patentable subject matter under which patentability would have turned only on whether what was claimed was objectively new in light of the available prior art. Rather they adopted in addition an evaluative standard of obviousness notwithstanding that this added a 'miasma of uncertainty around patents'.[19]

Although there are now clear distinctions between the tests for whether a claimed invention is new and whether it involves an inventive step,[20] these have only emerged and crystallized during the modern age. Prior to 1905, examination of patent applications in the UK was confined to formalities. In 1905, the Office began to search prior literature and examine against the search results. Cornish identifies this change in examination practice as marking the point when the question of novelty became separated from the inquiry into obviousness so far as examination was confined to novelty, but once a patent had been granted it could be attacked for obviousness.[21] But the grounds on which a patent could be revoked were themselves not codified until the Act of 1932.[22] Prior to

---

[18] Bochnovic, J, *The Inventive Step: Its Evolution in Canada, the United Kingdom and the United States*. Vol 5 of IIC Studies in Industrial Property and Copyright Law (Max Planck Institute, 1992), 65.

[19] Cornish, W, Llewelyn, D and Aplin, T, *Intellectual Property: Patents, Copyrights, Trademarks & Allied Rights*, 8th edition (Sweet & Maxwell, 2013), 126. There are numerous statements to similar effect, but the most colourful describes the test as it was understood on the other side of the Atlantic. Judge Learned Hand in *Harries* v *Air King* 183 F2d 158, 162 (1950), described the obviousness standard as 'as fugitive, impalpable, wayward, and vague a phantom as exists in the whole paraphernalia of legal concepts'.

[20] See e.g. the comments of the Court of Appeal in *Mölnlycke AB* v *Procter & Gamble* [1994] RPC 49, 114.

[21] Cornish et al., above n.19, 126.

[22] Gratwick, S, 'Having Regard to What Was Known and Used' (1972) 88 LQR, 341, 341. The Patents and Designs Act 1932 provided that a patent could be invalidated when, 'the invention is obvious and does not involve any inventive step having regard to what was known or used prior to the date of the patent'.

that, a patent was always liable to be revoked under the common law for 'want of subject matter', a ground that did not always clearly differentiate between anticipation and obviousness.[23] As observed by Fox, the 1932 Act, in providing that a patent was liable to be revoked on the ground that the claimed invention was obvious and did not involve any inventive step provided statutory authority for a doctrine which the courts had been exercising for nearly a century prior to this.[24] It could be said then that it wasn't until 1932 and the codification of the grounds upon which a patent could be revoked, that lack of novelty and obviousness became clearly separate grounds.[25]

Fox traces the origin of the doctrine that a patent can be attacked for obviousness to the argument advanced in *Crane* v *Price*,[26] that 'the quantity or degree of invention was so small that it could not become the subject of a patent'.[27] Although the argument was rejected, Fox asserts that a new idea was thereby injected into the law of patents and it was

---

Similarly section 32(1)(f) Patents Act 1949 provided that a patent was liable to be revoked on the ground, 'that the invention, so far as claimed in any claim of the complete specification, is obvious and does not involve any inventive step having regard to what was known or used, before the priority date of the claim, in the United Kingdom'.

[23] Gratwick asserts that although it was clear by 1890, and the decision of Lord Herschell in *Longbottom* v *Shaw* (1891) 8 RPC 333, that courts understood the importance of dealing with the issues of novelty and inventiveness separately, the language used in the judgements was not always chosen as carefully as it might have been: Gratwick, above n.22, 341. For instance Romer LJ in *Cooper* v *Baedeker* said that a 'peculiar patentable novelty' is a condition for good subject matter for a patent: (1900) 17 RPC 209, 213. Hamilton LJ in *Place* v *Blackburn* observed that the 'novelty sufficient to support' a patent required a development that was 'beyond the competence of the ordinary machinist's draftsman': (1912) 29 RPC 656, 664. Fletcher Moulton LJ in *Wilson* v *Wilson Bros* said that 'there is no practical difference between novelty and subject-matter': (1911) 28 RPC 733, 737. Lord Herschell in *Thomson* v *American Braided Wire* suggested that the question 'whether a patent is invalid by reason of the invention not being new', and 'whether that for which a patent has been obtained is a mere adaptation of known materials to uses analogous to those to which they had been applied before involving no invention and therefore not capable of being the subject matter of a patent' were not really different questions but the same question in different form: (1889) 6 RPC 518, 526–7. See also Bochnovic, above n.18, 2 and 18.

[24] Fox, H, *Monopolies and Patents: A Study of the History and Future of the Patent Monopoly* (University of Toronto Press, 1947), 239–40.

[25] Ibid.

[26] (1842) 4 MAN & G 580.

[27] Ibid., 605.

merely a matter of time until a jury or a court would be found which would hold that the subject matter of a particular patent was not of sufficient significance to be dignified by the grant of letters patent.[28] He observes that whilst the following half-century demonstrated a degree of confused thinking in the decisions of English courts, there eventually emerged an understanding that in order for a patent to have proper subject matter, the invention which it disclosed must be such as would have required an inventive act of the mind to have produced it.[29]

No doubt the motivation was a concern over the consequences of making patents 'too easy' to obtain.[30] That fundamental concern not only predated the decision in *Crane* v *Price* but indeed predated the Statute of Monopolies and is arguably evident in the reported decisions of the Privy Council from the 1570s which expressed the rule that the king could not grant patent monopolies for 'mere improvements'.[31] At the same time, the patent system from the outset was understood as a system for encouraging the setting up of new manufactures rather than a system for rewarding inventive acts.[32] The consequence was that it did not matter whether a particular individual had worked long and hard in order to arrive at her claimed invention or that she had incurred great expense to make it available. What mattered was only that the claimed invention was new and useful to the public. There is a challenge in reconciling these core understandings which no doubt contributed to the confused path taken to incorporating obviousness into the test for patentability. So for instance, in *Crane* v *Price* itself, Tindall CJ in rejecting the argument that the degree of invention was too small for what was claimed to be the subject of a patent, observed:

> [W]e think, if it were necessary to consider the labour, pains and expense encountered by the plaintiff in bringing his discovery to perfection, that there is evidence in this cause that the expense was considerable and the experiments numerous; but, in point of law, the labour of thought or experiment, and the expenditure of money, are not the essential grounds of consideration upon which the question whether the invention is or is not the subject matter of a patent, ought to depend; for if the invention be new and useful to the

---

28 Fox, above n.24, 235.

29 Ibid.

30 Cornish et al., above n.19, at 126; and Griffiths, above n.14, 162.

31 On which see the account of *Matthey's case* (1571) and *Bircot's case* (1572) in Mossoff, A, 'Rethinking the Development of Patents: An Intellectual History, 1550-1800' (2001) 52 Hastings LJ 1255, 1263. See also Bochnovic, above n.18, 17; and Cole (Part 2), above n.13, 267.

32 Fox, above n.24, 233.

> public, it is not material whether it is the result of long experiments and profound research, or whether of some sudden and lucky thought, or of mere accidental recovery.[33]

The solution was in adopting a test that did not ask how the inventor produced the invention but rather asked whether the invention could have been brought about by a person of ordinary skill, where the focus is shifted from the activity leading to the invention to the result of that activity.[34] Although there are some relatively contemporary statements to the effect that the requirement of an inventive step is linked to the policy of rewarding inventors for their efforts,[35] the better view, in the sense of being more in accord with evolution of the requirement in English law, is that the requirement serves to prevent the too-ready grant of patents from hampering those skilled in the relevant art in the ordinary technical development that must take place in an industry.[36] For my purpose, there

---

[33] (1842) 4 MAN & G 580, 605. On the other side of the Atlantic this aspect of the decision in *Crane* v *Price* influenced the dissenting opinion of Woodbury J in *Hotchkiss* v *Greenwood* 52 US 248 (1850).

[34] This was the solution arrived at by the US Supreme Court in *Hotchkiss* v *Greenwood* 52 US 248 (1850). That US courts were ahead of those in the UK in this respect might be because, unlike the courts in the UK, US courts were not obliged to deal with the terminology used in the Statute of Monopolies: Bochnovic, above n.18, 27.

[35] Perhaps most notably, Hoffmann LJ (as he was at the time) in *Société Technique De Pulverisation Step* v *Emson Europe Ltd* did not distinguish between the concepts of reward and incentive when he said that,

> the words 'obvious' and 'inventive step' involve questions of fact and degree which must be answered in accordance with the general policy of the Patents Act to reward and encourage inventors without inhibiting improvements of existing technology by others. The question is therefore whether in accordance with this policy the patent discloses something sufficiently inventive to deserve the grant of a monopoly.

[1993] RPC 513, 519. This understanding stands in contrast to that of Sir Donald Nicholls V-C, sitting in a differently constituted Court of Appeal who observed that,

> the criterion for deciding whether or not the claimed invention involves an inventive step is wholly objective … [and we] do not consider that it assists to ask whether 'the patent discloses something sufficiently inventive to deserve the grant of a monopoly'. Nor is it useful to extract from older judgments expressions such as 'that scintilla of invention necessary to support a patent'.

Mölnlycke AB v *Procter & Gamble* [1994] RPC 49, 112.

[36] Paraphrasing what was said by Pumfrey J in *Conor Medsystems Inc* v *Angiotech Pharmaceuticals Inc* [2006] EWHC 260 (Pat) [34].

is no better articulation of the policy behind the requirement of an inventive step than that of Oliver LJ in *Windsurfing International Inc* v *Tabur Marine (Great Britain) Ltd*:

> [T]he notion behind anticipation is, as we understand it, that it would be wrong to enable the patentee to prevent a man from doing what he has lawfully done before the patent was granted. No doubt, the philosophy behind [the requirement of non-obviousness] is different to this extent, that a patent is granted only for an invention and that which is obvious is not inventive, but it also must, we think, take into account the same concept as anticipation, namely that it would be wrong to prevent a man from doing something which is merely an obvious extension of what he has been doing or of what was known in the art before the priority date of the patent granted.[37]

I am aware that I have relied on the same quotation earlier in this book, and justify this repetition on the grounds that Oliver LJ's explanation has value because it explicitly recognizes the connections between the requirement of non-obviousness, that of novelty and the concept of 'invention' and, importantly, leads us to the observation that there is no significant qualitative difference between the tests for whether what is

---

[37] Per Oliver LJ in *Windsurfing International Inc* v *Tabur Marine (Great Britain) Ltd* [1985] RPC 59, 75. This was not some fundamentally new way of thinking about the requirement of non-obviousness. The Court of Appeal in support of its view cited the speech of Lord Moulton in the much earlier case of *Gillette Safety Razor Co Ltd* v *Anglo-American Trading Co Ltd* (1913) 30 RPC 465. It might also (though it did not) refer to the still earlier decision in *Harwood* v *The Great Northern Railway Company*, in which Lord Westbury said that,

> there would be no end to the interference with trade and with the liberty of adopting any mechanical contrivance, if every slight difference in the application of a well-known thing should be held to constitute ground for a patent … you cannot have a patent for a well-known mechanical contrivance merely when it is applied in a manner or to a purpose, which is not quite the same, but is analogous to the manner or the purpose in or to which it has been hitherto notoriously used.

(1865) XI House of Lords Cases (Clark's) 654, 682–3. More recently, the court in *Brugger* v *Medic-Aid* observed that,

> [t]he policy behind the law in this area is that one trader should not be prevented by a statutory monopoly from doing something which, at the date of the patent, is obvious. A trader must be free to adopt a product, process or design which is the, or one of the, obvious modifications over what has gone before without the need to look over his shoulder to consider whether it is protected by patent.

[1996] RPC 635, 653.

claimed is new and whether it is obvious. Both invite a comparison between what is claimed and what is known and an assessment, through the eyes of a person skilled in the relevant technical field, of the extent of the difference. The upshot is that something which is not new is a fortiori obvious. If the prior art contains clear and unmistakeable directions that would enable the skilled person to arrive at the claimed invention, then the steps from prior art to invention are minuscule and the path between the two manifestly clear. Of itself this is not an original observation. John Bochnovic, for instance, puts is thus:

> The two requirements are necessarily related in the form of analysis which must be used with both. An invention may be viewed as a movement along a line comprising a continuum of novelty, or difference from that theretofore known. At one extreme one can visualize a body of known art. This may be represented by what today is acknowledged to be prior art. The novelty requirement is a strict requirement, which can be viewed as existing on a one-to-one basis with individual pieces of prior art, in the sense that within the pieces of prior art must be found a piece of prior art identical to the alleged invention in order to negative novelty. Virtually any variation in the alleged invention from an individual piece of prior art is sufficient. If the alleged invention is not matched by any individual piece of prior art then there is novelty ... The requirement of inventive step can be viewed as existing on this continuum of novelty. Once the threshold novelty requirement is satisfied, and one moves (with the alleged invention) along the continuum, the requirement that a balance may be maintained between the public interest and the inventor demands that there be a point along that continuum which serves as a demarcation between non-patentability and patentability. This is a point, representing a significant departure from the prior art, at which the public interest deems that the alleged invention merits a patent monopoly.[38]

---

[38] Bochnovic, above n.18, 36–7. To similar effect, Andrew Griffiths has suggested that the inventive step requirement 'acts as a supplementary or "constructive" novelty requirement and ensures that the public receive something valuable as well as something new in return for the award of a patent': Griffiths, above n.14, 163–4. However, c.f. Bently and Sherman, above n.3, who suggest, at 529, that,

> novelty requires that the invention be quantitatively different from what has been disclosed previously; that is, that the technical information disclosed by the patent is not already available to the public. In this sense, novelty is different from the requirement that to be patentable an invention must have involved an inventive step ..., which is basically a qualitative examination to ascertain whether the contribution is creative enough to warrant a monopoly.

The shared form of analysis has been also recognized by the courts. So, for instance, the Court of Appeal in *General Tyre and Rubber Co* v *Firestone Tyre and Rubber Co Ltd* observed that:

> If ... the prior publication contains a direction which is capable of being carried out in a manner which would infringe the patentee's claim, but would be at least as likely to be carried out in a way which would not do so, the patentee's claim will not have been anticipated, although it may fail on the ground of obviousness ...[39]

It is hard then to argue with Bochnovic's conclusion that the nature of the inventive step requirement is one of degree and the degree is the degree of novelty or the difference from the prior art.[40] If this is right and something which is not new is a fortiori obvious, then we need to ask why it is that, through conscious effort of those who shaped the law, two discrete tests emerged and have remained. Put another way, if the scope of the requirement that a claimed invention involve an inventive step embraces the requirement that a claimed invention be new, then why have the novelty requirement at all?[41] There would be no increase (or decrease) in the number of successful applications for patents, nor would the public be more or less hindered by granted patents, if the condition of novelty were dispensed with and all that was demanded was that a claimed invention involve an inventive step. Indeed as illustrated above, this hypothetical situation was the one that existed and operated prior to 1932 and the codification of the grounds upon which a patent could be

---

[39] Per Sachs LJ in *General Tyre and Rubber Co* v *Firestone Tyre and Rubber Co Ltd* [1972] RPC 457, 485. Lord Hoffmann in *Synthon BV* v *Smithkline Beecham plc* made the same point but in a different way when he said that,

> it is [the] requirement that performance of an invention disclosed in the prior art must necessarily infringe the patent which distinguishes novelty from obviousness. If performance of an invention disclosed by the prior art would not infringe the patent but the prior art would make it obvious to a skilled person how he might make adaptations which resulted in an infringing invention, then the patent may be invalid for lack of an inventive step but not for lack of novelty

[2005] UKHL 59 [25]. See also the speech of Oliver LJ in *Windsurfing International Inc* v *Tabur Marine (Great Britain) Ltd* [1985] RPC 59, 75.

[40] Bochnovic, above n.18, 37.

[41] Bochnovic goes some way to recognize the issue without really addressing it. Rather he seems to argue that the novelty requirement has survived because it predated even the Statute of Monopolies and its nature and application has never been questioned: Bochnovic, above n.18, 36.

revoked. The argument I want to advance is that the novelty condition survives and is useful because, as it has evolved in parallel with the evolution of the condition of non-obviousness, so it has become more rule-like and it is its form that gives it utility. Here, in something so fundamental as how the law sets boundaries around what is patentable, form matters. Of course in this patent law may be unusual or unique and how far form matters in other areas of intellectual property law must be explored before arriving at a general conclusion.

Any analysis of copyright law is potentially devalued by its current state of flux. The rather fragmented and uncoordinated legislative and judicial efforts directed towards harmonizing the copyright laws of the member states of the European Union make it hard to predict where we will end up and how much of the landscape will be familiar. So much more so given that whilst the UK is now very likely to leave the EU, it is equally likely that UK courts will still be obliged to give effect to European legislation under any post-exit agreement reached with the EU. In this and the chapter that follows I set out to draw evidence for my argument from 'traditional' UK copyright law whilst acknowledging that a new law is emerging.

The Copyright Designs and Patents Act 1988, in common with its twentieth-century predecessors, on the face of it provides an exhaustive list of the subject matter protected by copyright.[42] So far as literary, dramatic, musical and artistic works are concerned, whether copyright subsists in a work turns on whether that work is 'original' and, secondly, whether it falls within one of the defined categories, which alone constitute the subject matter in which copyright can be claimed.[43] On the one hand, these two elements can be seen as functioning in the same way as the elements of novelty and inventive step function in patent law but only so far as all are hurdles which if surmounted allow the respective right to be claimed in the subject matter to which the elements relate. There are, however, differences. Certainly, like the requirements of novelty and inventive step, the condition of originality (as it applies to claims that copyright subsists) applies universally. It is thus a fundamental condition, an analysis of which should tell us something useful

---

[42] Bently and Sherman, above n.3, 59.

[43] Only literary, dramatic, musical and artistic works are required to be 'original' for copyright to subsist in them under section 1 Copyright Designs and Patents Act 1988. However, copyright will not subsist in sound recordings, films, broadcasts or typographical arrangements to the extent that they are copies of existing works (see sections 5A(2); 5B(4); 6(6); and 8(2) of the Act respectively).

about the rights which turn on its satisfaction. In contrast, the second element, that of defined subject matter, defines the boundaries of copyright in a rather different way. A combination of statutory provision and judicial pronouncement have produced a set of definitions which are self-contained: each more or less complete and independent and which show little if any evidence of any coherent policy or rationale other than all relate to works which might broadly be classified as belonging to 'the arts' and all aim to make the boundaries they set justiciable. Other than that, these definitions are arrived at by the pursuit of policies unique to each class of work.[44]

As far as the condition of originality is concerned, this is ostensibly a standard if what is understood is that 'skill, labour and judgement' be exercised in the production of a work as a condition of claiming copyright.[45] But in the great majority of cases this is not how the

---

[44] This reflects the historical development of copyright law in the UK. Until the codification effected by the Copyright Act 1911, there were a variety of copyrights each protected by a different piece of legislation. For an outline account of the early history of copyright law in the UK see Cornish et al., above n.19, 389–96. The policy objects are not of course unique to UK law but other jurisdictions use different mechanisms to achieve similar ends on which see for example, van Gompel, S and Lavik, E, 'Quality, Merit, Aesthetics and Purpose: An Inquiry into EU Copyright Law's Eschewal of Other Criteria than Originality' (2013) 236 Revue Internationale du Droit d'Auteur 100. On the face of it the UK's obligations under EU law do not require any change in the way in which copyright works are categorized and indeed Jacob LJ in *Nova Productions Ltd* v *Mazooma Games Ltd* noted that these specific categories were, 'an aspect of UK copyright law untouched by any EU law': [2007] EWCA Civ 219 [11]. However, Eleonora Rosati has argued that the CJEU's judgement in C-393/09 *Bezpečnostní softwarová asociace – Svaz softwarové ochrany* v *Ministerstvo kultury* can be interpreted as meaning that European law demands that the only condition for the subsistence of copyright in a work is that it its author's own intellectual creation. The argument hinges on the court's comments regarding the graphical user interface of a computer program and whether this can be protected by the 'ordinary law of copyright'. The court held that it could be protected observing that copyright is liable to apply only in relation to a subject matter which is original in the sense that it is the author's own intellectual creation ([2011] ECDR 3 [44]–[46]): Rosati, E, 'Towards an EU-wide Copyright? (Judicial) Pride and (Legislative) Prejudice' (2013) IPQ 47, 59.

[45] It has rightly been observed that there is an imprecision in courts' use of these terms. Bently and Sherman say that,

> while the phrase 'labour, skill, or judgment' may be a useful label by which to describe the traditional British test of originality, it should be noted that it is a

condition has been understood and applied. Rather, much more typically what has been demanded is that the work originate from the author, that is to say it must not itself be copied from another work.[46] In the great majority of cases no judicial discretion need be exercised in establishing that the condition is satisfied: either there will be evidence that the work is copied or the evidence will indicate that the work originated from its author.

Although in the great majority of cases it is typically understood and applied as a rule, there are circumstances where courts have adopted an alternative formulation of the originality condition; one which allows the exercise of judicial discretion. 'Originality', meaning the exercise of skill, labour and judgement rather than simply 'not copied', is a variation of the originality condition which has its origins in cases where copyright has been claimed in works which are, to a greater or lesser extent, copies of existing productions but where courts have nevertheless found good reasons for entertaining the claim to copyright in these derivative works.[47] Often cited in this regard, and the fountainhead for this reading of the originality condition is *MacMillan* v *Cooper*:[48] a case concerning a claim to copyright in textbooks comprised of abridgements of existing literary works to which had been added notes and commentary for students. The later case of *Ladbroke (Football) Ltd* v *William Hill (Football) Ltd*[49] also concerned a claim to copyright in compilations: specifically betting coupons. More recently, the test has been applied in relation to simplified naval navigation charts derived from more detailed Admiralty charts;[50] to 'arrangements' of existing musical works;[51] and to modern 'performing editions' of the out-of-copyright music of the seventeenth-century composer Michel-Richard de Lalande.[52]

---

form of words that is not used with great precision (and thus should not be viewed as if it were a statutory phrase).

Bently and Sherman, above n.3, 97.

46 *University of London Press Ltd* v *University Tutorial Press Ltd* [1916] 2 Ch 601, 609.

47 These 'good reasons' are explored more fully below at p. 197.

48 (1924) 40 TLR 186.

49 [1964] 1 WLR 273. The link between the skill, judgement and labour test and compilations is made at 277–8 where it is distinguished from the normal 'not copied' test.

50 *MacMillan Publishers* v *Reed* [1993] FSR 455.

51 *Fisher* v *Brooker* [2006] EWHC 3239.

52 *Hyperion Records Ltd* v *Sawkins* [2005] EWCA Civ 565. The Court of Appeal here relied in large part on the earlier decision of the House of Lords in

That these should be understood as different tests rather than variations of a single standard of originality emerges from an analysis of the Privy Council's decision in *Interlego* v *Tyco Industries*.[53] Here, the claimants asserted copyright in the engineering drawings of its plastic brick-shaped blocks and in particular in those drawings which recorded minor modifications to the design and methods of manufacture of these bricks. The legal issue was summarized by Lord Oliver thus:

> [T]he primary question on Tyco's appeal can be expressed in this way: can Lego, having enjoyed a monopoly for the full permitted period of patent and design protection in reliance upon drawings in which no copyright any longer subsists, continue their monopoly for yet a further, more extensive period by re-drawing the same designs with a number of minor alterations and claiming a fresh copyright in the re-drawn designs?[54]

This issue translated into a clash as to the meaning of 'original'. Because they were copied from earlier drawings, the defendants argued that no copyright subsisted in the drawings in issue whereas the claimants pointed to the considerable labour and skill involved in their production. The court found for the defendants holding that skill, labour or judgement merely in the process of copying cannot confer originality.[55] Lord Oliver observed that, although there were a number of well-known cases in which it had been said that originality depended upon the degree of skill, labour and judgement involved, these cases involved literary compilations of one kind or another. He continued:

> it is stressed that the amount of skill, judgment or labour is likely to be decisive in the case of compilations. To apply that, however, as a universal test of originality in all copyright cases is not only unwarranted by the context in which the observations were made but palpably erroneous.[56]

There is a third meaning of originality that occasionally also now operates in UK law. Originality meaning the product of author's own intellectual creation is the product of the European Union legislature's attempts to formulate harmonized conditions for the subsistence of copyright. The Court of Appeal in *Football Dataco Ltd* v *Brittens Pools*

Walter v *Lane* [1900] AC 539, itself a case concerning a claim to copyright in the reports of speeches that the reporters themselves had not written.

[53] [1988] RPC 343.

[54] Ibid., 365.

[55] Ibid., 367 and 371–2.

[56] Ibid., 371.

Ltd[57] has ruled that no independent UK copyright in compilations or databases has survived the implementation of the European Database directive since, if it were otherwise, this would undermine the Directive's object of harmonizing national laws.[58] A consequence is that compilations and databases, to enjoy copyright protection, must by reason of the selection or arrangement of their contents, constitute the author's own intellectual creation.[59] How far this differs in substance from a test of originality based on 'skill, labour and capital' is a little uncertain but the tests are different.[60] What is clear is that for a database or compilation to count as original and so to enjoy copyright protection, some form of 'creativity' must be exercised in the selection and arrangement of constituent elements.[61]

By reason of European harmonizing legislation the originality of photographs and computer programs also turn on whether these productions can be said to be the author's own intellectual creation.[62] The CJEU has held that an intellectual creation is an author's own if it reflects the

---

[57] [2010] EWCA Civ 1380.

[58] Ibid. [14]. This view was confirmed by the European Court of Justice on referral in C-604/10 *Football Dataco Ltd* v *Yahoo! UK Ltd* [2013] FSR 1.

[59] Article 3 Directive 96/9/EC on the legal protection of databases.

[60] In *Football Dataco Ltd* v *Yahoo!*, the UK Court of Appeal referred to the CJEU the question of whether the 'author's own intellectual creation' requires more than significant labour and skill from the author and if so what? The CJEU replied that significant labour and skill on the part of the author cannot as such justify the protection of a database by copyright if that labour and that skill do not express any originality in the selection or arrangement of that data: C-604/10 *Football Dataco Ltd* v *Yahoo! UK Ltd* [2013] FSR 1 [38]–[39].

[61] Thus and for instance, in *Forensic Telecommunications Services Ltd* v *Chief Constable of West Yorkshire* it was held that a database listing the memory addresses where user data was stored in mobile phones did not enjoy copyright. This data had been obtained through trial and error and the originator of the database thus did not select the contents, but rather they were acquired as a matter of happenstance over time, and the arrangement was the most obvious and basic one possible: [2011] EWHC 2892 (Ch) [88]–[90].

[62] Under Article 6 Directive 2006/116/EC on the term of protection of copyright and certain related rights, 'photographs which are original in the sense that they are the author's own intellectual creation' are protected by copyright. Article 1.3 Directive 2009/24/EC on the legal protection of computer programs similarly provides that 'a computer program shall be protected if it is original in the sense that it is the author's own intellectual creation'.

author's personality and this is so if the author is able to express her creative abilities in the production of a work by making free and creative choices.[63]

In respect of other types of work, whether the UK test of originality has survived European harmonization is a matter of some debate. Formally, the originality requirement has been harmonized only in respect of computer programs, photographs and databases. However many commentators believe that the CJEU's interpretation of the so-called 'Information Society Directive'[64] requires a harmonized conception of originality across all types of works. As its full name suggests, this Directive was chiefly intended to modernize copyright in light of advances in information technology in a uniform manner. Amongst other things it introduced a comprehensive code for defences to copyright infringement. Article 2 of the Directive is headed 'reproduction right' and provides that member states shall provide for the exclusive right to authorize or prohibit direct or indirect, temporary or permanent reproduction by any means and in any form, in whole or in part, of relevant works. The ECJ, in *Infopaq International* v *Danske Dagblades Forening*,[65] called upon to interpret Article 2 indicated that, 'the various parts of a work … enjoy protection under art 2(a) of Directive 2001/29, provided that they contain elements which are the expression of the intellectual creation of the author of the work'.[66]

The statement is ambiguous. The court might here be saying that to be protected under copyright law, a work must be the intellectual creation of the author: that is to say this is a statement about originality. Or the court might be saying that where a part of a work is taken, that part must contain an element of the intellectual creation of the author if a partial taking is to qualify as infringement. Although the context of the reference may suggest the latter interpretation is to be preferred, that the court meant the former is suggested by its later decision in *Bezpečnostní softwarová asociace – Svaz softwarové ochrany* v *Ministerstvo kultury*[67] in which the court said, in relation to a claim to copyright in a graphical user interface, that copyright is liable to apply only in relation to a subject matter which is original in the sense that it is the author's own

63 C-145/10 *Painer* v *Standard Verlags GmbH* [2012] ECDR 6 [87]–[89] and [94].

64 Directive 2001/29/EC of 22 May 2001 on the harmonisation of certain aspects of copyright and related rights in the information society.

65 Case C-5/08 [2010] FSR 495.

66 Ibid. [39].

67 [2011] ECDR 3.

intellectual creation. And in the joined cases C-403/08 *Football Association Premier League* v *QC Leisure* and C-429/08 *Murphy* v *Media Protection Services*,[68] the CJEU ruled that, '[s]porting events cannot be regarded as intellectual creations classifiable as works … That applies in particular to football matches, which are subject to rules of the game, leaving no room for creative freedom for the purposes of copyright'.[69]

The implications of the adoption of the European conception of originality will be considered in the chapter following this one. For the moment it is enough to note that, like the UK's occasional assessment of skill, labour and judgement, this European test is more standard-like and requires the exercise of judicial discretion.

Though there are exceptions, historically certainly and arguably as a matter of contemporary law, in the great majority of cases the condition of originality operates as a rule in that in these cases whether something is original turns on whether it is copied or not. There are instances where it does not, and why this is will be considered later. Although things may change if the 'European' standard makes further incursions, for the moment at least it can be said that, for much of the history of UK copyright law, the test for whether something is 'original' in copyright law is thus like the test for whether something is new in patent law in being rule-like.

Above it was argued that the novelty rule in patent law was instrumentally superfluous in that its scope was entirely embraced by the more standard-like test for obviousness. The conclusion was that form must therefore matter. To reach the same conclusion in respect of copyright requires then to find a standard that embraces all that is covered by the originality rule (at least as it is understood to mean only not copied) which renders it instrumentally superfluous.

So far as subsistence is concerned, in copyright law there is no parallel to inventive step. Unlike the novelty condition then, originality operates alone: there is no other universally applicable condition which must be satisfied for copyright to be claimed in a work. Certainly an original work will only qualify for copyright protection if it is of a kind in which copyright can subsist. But within the statutory and common law definitions one can find no implicit or explicit element which is common to all

---

68 [2012] FSR 5.

69 Ibid. [98].

types of work and which does, or could, function as a justiciable condition for establishing a right.[70]

But the originality condition does look instrumentally superfluous once one examines how courts approach the question of whether a copyright work is infringed and in particular whether a 'partial taking' amounts to an infringement. In short, there can be no infringement of work which is itself copied nor can an infringement claim be made out where the alleged infringement is in copying a part of a work which part is itself copied.

Courts approach the question of whether a work has been infringed in two stages. Each allows courts to find there has been no infringement on the ground that the element of the claimant's work allegedly taken is itself copied. The first step is an evidential one – courts compare the alleged infringing work with the work in which copyright is claimed looking for similarities as indicators that copying has taken place:

> The purpose of the examination is not to see whether the overall appearance of the two designs [sic] is similar, but to judge whether the particular similarities relied on are sufficiently close, numerous or extensive to be more likely to be the result of copying than of coincidence. It is at this stage that similarities may be disregarded because they are commonplace, *unoriginal*, or consist of general ideas ...[71]

The point is that the similarity may be because the defendant's and claimant's work are both copied from a common source. If a defendant has access to the same source material as a claimant, then those elements of the claimant's work which are themselves copied cannot contribute to the evidence that the defendant has copied the claimant's work.

If it is found that a defendant's work incorporates features taken from the claimant's work, then the second stage is to ask whether what has been taken constitutes all or a substantial part of the copyright work.

---

[70] It is interesting to speculate whether this would change if, as has been argued, the UK's approach to the categorization of copyright works is inconsistent with European law (see above at n.44). The current definitions serve as coarse filters excluding from copyright protection those products of human ingenuity which cannot be classed as works in which copyright can subsist. If all that were demanded for copyright to subsist in a work were that it was 'the author's own intellectual creation' this would potentially open copyright's doors to a vast range of productions unless courts could devise some common and necessary characteristic (in addition to the exercise of the intellect) that could serve to define the products of the 'the arts'.

[71] Lord Millet in *Designer Guild Ltd* v *Russell Williams (Textiles) Ltd* [2001] FSR 113 [39] (emphasis added).

Under the Copyright Designs and Patents Act 1988, the exclusive rights of the copyright owner are enjoyed not only in the copyright work as a whole but in any substantial part of it.[72] That is what the legislation says but this now needs to be understood in light of the changes effected by the Information Society Directive.[73] Article 2 of the Directive is headed 'reproduction right' and provides that member states shall provide for the exclusive right to authorize or prohibit direct or indirect, temporary or permanent reproduction by any means and in any form, in whole or in part, of relevant works. The Directive differs from section 16 Copyright Designs and Patents Act 1988 in not specifying that a partial taking must be 'substantial' to count as an infringement. I shall have more to say about that difference and the European Court's interpretation of the Directive in the chapter which follows. For the moment it is sufficient to note that whether we are talking about the traditional UK approach or that now demanded under the Directive, whether infringement has occurred turns on whether a defendant appropriates the protected parts of the claimant's work. Crucially, under this test, taking that part which is itself copied is no infringement:

> The reproduction of a part which by itself has no originality will not normally be a substantial part of the copyright and therefore will not be protected. For that which would not attract copyright except by reason of its collocation will, when robbed of that collocation, not be a substantial part of the copyright and therefore the courts will not hold its reproduction to be an infringement.[74]

This can be seen as a manifestation of a broader principle articulated by Lord Hoffmann in *Newspaper Licensing Agency* v *Marks & Spencer*,[75] that the qualitatively important part of a work is identified 'by reference to the reason why the work is given copyright protection'.

What then would be the effect of dispensing with originality as a condition for copyright to be claimed? Such a move would not strengthen or otherwise significantly alter copyright owners' individual claims that their work has been infringed nor would the class of potential defendants – that is, those individuals restrained in their actions by the subsistence of copyright – be increased. The requirement that a defendant must take a substantial part of a work to infringe embraces all that is demanded if the

---

[72] Section 16(3)(a) Copyright Designs and Patents Act 1988.

[73] Directive 2001/29/EC of 22 May 2001 on the harmonisation of certain aspects of copyright and related rights in the information society.

[74] *Ladbroke (Football) Ltd* v *William Hill (Football) Ltd* [1964] 1 WLR 273, 293 and applied in *Warwick Film* v *Eisenger* [1969] 1 Ch 508, 532–3.

[75] [2001] UKHL 38.

work in issue is to be considered original. Yet the 'rule-like' originality condition persists notwithstanding that its instrumental effects are entirely embraced within the scope of the substantial taking standard.

The critic will quickly point out that the test for whether a work is original and that for whether it is infringed do not occupy the same territory and that suggesting so is to introduce the artefact that can arise if the context over which the relevant legal provision exercises control is drawn too widely.[76] By way of counter I would argue that, in copyright law, it is more artificial to treat subsistence and infringement as discrete contexts than to consider then together. The question of whether a work is original is almost invariably considered where there is some dispute, typically and as the examples given illustrate, where an alleged infringer argues that what they have taken is not the claimant's original work. Whilst courts are prepared to consider applications for declarations of non-infringement of copyright, this is very rarely done and such applications are approached cautiously and conservatively. In particular, courts have indicated that they will be slow to require a party who has made no allegation of copying to answer a negative case of non-copying.[77] Generally speaking, declaratory relief cannot be obtained against a person who had not asserted any right, courts taking the view that a party should be allowed to choose his own proceedings at a time and manner of his own choosing and should not be brought into court by the opposing party to resist a claim for a declaration of non-liability.[78] More significantly from our perspective, applications for declarations will only be considered if the question is real and not theoretical and the person raising the question must have a real interest to raise it.[79] Thus, whilst there is no reason why an application cannot be made seeking a declaration of non-originality of a claimed copyright work, the person

---

[76] An artefact discussed above at p. 27.

[77] *Point Solutions Ltd* v *Focus Business Solutions Ltd* [2005] EWHC 3096 [68].

[78] Ibid. [67] following *Wyko Group Plc* v *Cooper Roller Bearings Co Ltd* [1996] FSR 126. However, an assertion of a right can be made expressly or by implication and it has been held that a letter that implicitly asserts that copying has taken place is a sufficient assertion to found an application for a declaration of non-infringement: [2005] EWHC 3096 [71]–[74].

[79] *Point Solutions Ltd* v *Focus Business Solutions Ltd* [2005] EWHC 3096 [67] following *Russian Commercial and Industrial Bank* v *British Bank of Foreign Trade Ltd* [1921] 2 AC 438. The position is essentially the same in the United States on which see *Klinger* v *Conan Doyle Est Ltd* No. 14-1128 (7th Cir 2014).

making the application must put the question surrounding originality into a specific context that demonstrates why they have an interest in the question.

Having now raised the issue of the significance of context, I need to return to patent law to reflect on the choice of context made in the preceding analysis. The key observation is that in patent law validity and infringement are independent issues. This is most evident in the fact that, in contrast to copyright, any person can seek revocation of a patent on the grounds that what is claimed is not a patentable invention.[80] There is no requirement that the person applying should have any particular interest in revoking the patent[81] and the applicant's motive for applying to revoke is irrelevant.[82]

This is not to say that alleged infringers' particular interests are disregarded in patent law. An alleged infringer has a wider range of options compared with the disinterested third party in that the grounds available for revocation of the patent are also available as defences in proceedings for infringement.[83] Thus a defendant faced with a claim that they have infringed a patent can escape liability if they can show that what they have taken is not protected subject matter because it is not new, or because it is an obvious development of the prior art. And of course, the alleged infringer can also respond with a counter-claim seeking revocation of the patent.

This does not, however, detract from the fact that patent law differs from copyright law in that infringement is not the only circumstance in which the validity of a patent may be put in issue. But even where an action for infringement is met with a counter-claim seeking revocation,

---

[80] Section 72 Patents Act 1977 provides that,

> (1) Subject to the following provisions of this Act, the court or the comptroller may by order revoke a patent for an invention on the application of any person … on (but only on) any of the following grounds, that is to say – (a) the invention is not a patentable invention.

Note, however, that under section 74(2) an action cannot be brought claiming only a declaration that a patent is invalid, the proper course being to claim for revocation. See also *North-Eastern Marine Engineering Co* v *Leeds Forge Co* (1906) 23 RPC 529; *Traction Corp* v *Bennett* (1908) 25 RPC 819; and c.f. *Killen* v *MacMillan* (1932) 49 RPC 258, 260.

[81] Thus in *Cairnstores Ltd* v *Aktiebolaget Hassle* [2002] FSR 35 an 'off-the-shelf' property company, which had no assets and did not trade, was permitted to pursue revocation proceedings for a pharmaceutical patent. So too a firm of patent agents in *Oystertec's Patent* [2003] RPC 29.

[82] *TNS Group Holdings Ltd* v *Nielsen Media Research Inc* [2009] FSR 23.

[83] Section 74(1)(a) Patents Act 1977.

courts treat the question of whether a claim is valid and whether it is infringed as distinct. This was not always so in that, under the '*Gillette* defence', courts elided questions of validity and infringement following what Lord Moulton said in *Gillette Safety Razor Co Ltd* v *Anglo-American Trading Co Ltd*:

> [T]he defendant's right to succeed can be established without an examination of the terms of the Specification of the Plaintiffs' Letters Patent ... It is impossible for an ordinary member of the public to keep watch on all the numerous Patents which are taken out and to ascertain the validity and scope of their claims. [A manufacturer] ... is entitled to feel secure if he knows that that which he is doing differs from that which has been done of old only in non-patentable variations, such as the substitution of mechanical equivalents or changes of material shape or size. The defence that 'the alleged infringement was not novel at the date of the Plaintiff's Letters Patent' is a good defence in law, and it would sometimes obviate the great length and expense of Patent cases if the defendant could and would put forth his case in this form, and thus spare himself the trouble of demonstrating on which horn of the well-known dilemma the plaintiff had impaled himself, invalidity or non-infringement.[84]

In understanding this decision, it is important to appreciate that it came less than a decade after the Patent Office began to search prior literature and examine against the search results. Furthermore, the particular patent in issue had been granted on 30 December 1902 and was thus granted without examination of the invention's claimed novelty.[85] Lord Moulton's expression of concern regarding the capacity of ordinary members of the public to assess the validity and scope of issued patents thus came at a time when there remained a high degree of scepticism regarding the information contained in the patent register, even as to whether what was claimed was new in the strict modern sense of that requirement. The approach advocated in *Gillette* is premised on the assumption that the defendant will be cognisant of the prior art and should enjoy a certain security of expectation in acting on that knowledge. By contrast, what the defendant knows, or should know, of the patent and the patent register is considered irrelevant. To this extent the *Gillette* defence can be seen as a product of its age and in particular of a time where the information contained in the patent register could not be relied upon.

---

84 *Gillette Safety Razor Co Ltd* v *Anglo-American Trading Co Ltd* (1913) 30 RPC 465, 480–81.

85 It was not until 1905 that the UK Patent Office began to search prior literature and examine against the search results: see above at p. 153.

The approach advocated in *Gillette* continued for a considerable period notwithstanding its anachronistic foundations. There are two reasons for this. The first is pragmatic. Concern over the length and expense of patent cases is as much of a contemporary concern as it was in the early twentieth century. Thus in *Société Technique de Pulverisation Step* v *Emson Europe Ltd*[86] the Court of Appeal described the approach taken in *Gillette* as 'a useful short cut' but added that it was useful only in cases where the questions of obviousness and infringement both turned upon the same point of construction.[87] The second reason the approach has retained its credibility is because it is nowadays seen as a particular manifestation of the fundamental principle that that it would be wrong to enable a patentee to prevent a man from doing what he has lawfully done before the patent was granted. So for instance, Birss J in *Koninklijke Philips Electronics NV* v *Nintendo of Europe GmbH* noted that,

> [i]t has been well understood in English law for over a century (see *Gillette Safety Razor* v *Anglo American* …) that those working in industry are entitled to be sure that they are not infringing any valid patent if all they do is make obvious improvements to the prior art.[88]

However, under the EPC and the corresponding national laws, although it remains extant, the principle that a patent should not prevent someone from doing that which was lawful before the patent was granted is, however, no longer given effect by way of the rules concerning validity. This emerges most clearly from Lord Hoffmann's account in *Merrell Dow Pharmaceuticals Inc* v *Norton*[89] of the difference between the old and current law as that relates to attacks on novelty based on prior 'uninformative' use. The question in *Merrell Dow* was whether a patent was anticipated by a prior use which made the claimed invention available to the public but in a way that conveyed no information to the public about the nature of the product or how to make it. Lord Hoffmann observed that under the Patents Act 1949 and following the decision of the House of Lords in *Bristol-Myers Co (Johnson's) Application*,[90] such 'uninformative use' would invalidate the patent.[91] Lord Hoffmann observed that the 'old law' was founded on two principles: the first, that

---

[86] [1993] RPC 513.
[87] Ibid., 518–19.
[88] *Koninklijke Philips Electronics NV* v *Nintendo of Europe GmbH* [2014] EWHC 1959 (Pat) [33].
[89] [1996] RPC 76.
[90] [1975] RPC 127.
[91] [1996] RPC 76, 85.

the Crown could not grant a patent which would enable the patentee to stop another trader from doing what he had done before; and the second that the test for anticipation before the priority date was in this respect co-extensive with the test for infringement afterwards.[92] By contrast, under the Patents Act 1977 and the EPC, to be part of the state of the art, the invention must have been made available to the public. Lord Hoffmann continued:

> An invention is a piece of information. Making matter available to the public within the meaning of section 2(2) therefore requires the communication of information. The use of a product makes the invention part of the state of the art only so far as that use makes available the necessary information.[93]

From the understanding that an invention is a piece of information, Lord Hoffmann concludes that the 1977 Act not only introduced a substantial qualification into the old principle that a patent cannot be used to stop someone doing what he has done before[94] but also created a gap between the tests for infringement and anticipation in that acts done secretly or without knowledge of the relevant facts, which would amount to infringements after the grant of the patent, will not count as anticipations before.[95]

Thus, under the current law it is no longer possible to say that a person is entitled to feel secure if he knows that that which he is doing differs from that which has been done of old only in non-patentable variations. If what has been done communicates no information to the public then such a person will have no defence to a claim of patent infringement nor will there be grounds to revoke the patent. This makes sense if the patent system is understood to be primarily concerned with providing new information to the public rather than being concerned with providing the public with new products and processes. Not only must an applicant fully disclose their invention as a condition of grant, but there can be no

---

92 Ibid., 86.

93 Ibid.

94 Although under the 1977 Act, secret or uninformative use no longer invalidates a patent, rights are given under section 64 to any person who in the UK before the priority date of the invention does in good faith an act which would constitute an infringement of the patent if it were in force, or makes in good faith effective and serious preparations to do such an act.

95 Ibid. Lord Hoffmann found support for this conclusion in the dicta of Aldous J in *PLG Research Ltd* v *Ardon International Ltd* [1993] FSR 197 and in the reasoning of the EPO's Enlarged Board of Appeal in G02/88 *Mobil/Friction reducing additive* [1990] EPOR 73.

challenge to validity only on the grounds that the public had access to the claimed product or process before the priority date of the patent. In such circumstances, the prior use is not deemed to be a relevant contribution to the public welfare (this despite the fact that the public have the benefit of actual use of the product or process before the patent application is filed). Only if the prior use amounts to an enabling disclosure is there a relevant contribution to the public welfare. Whether an infringer does or does not fully disclose the invention to the public by way of their infringing use of it is immaterial. The public have already benefited from the disclosure made by the patentee and the infringer's actions thus add nothing relevant to the public welfare (this despite the fact that the supply to the public of the product or process is increased by the infringer's activities). Validity and infringement are separate issues then because patent law has a communication function that is not shared with copyright law. Both patent and copyright provide incentives in the form of an opportunity to profit from a limited monopoly. A copyright owner cannot take advantage of that opportunity except by making available the information that is the subject matter of protection: no one would buy a book that they were unable to read. But sometimes a patent owner can profit from sales of a product incorporating an invention without disclosing the invention.

Patent validity, then, is a discrete context. Not only is it the case that validity can be put in issue other than as a counter to a claim of infringement, but even where an action for infringement is met with a counter-claim seeking revocation, the questions of validity and infringement are no longer elided. And over this discrete context, the novelty rule and the inventiveness standard exercise control.

Perhaps of all the major intellectual property rights, the significance of form is most apparent in relation to trade marks. Under UK and European trade mark law, a sign will be refused registration if it falls foul of either the 'absolute' or 'relative' grounds of refusal. The absolute grounds, contained in sections 3 and 4 Trade Marks Act 1994, implement specific policies: they essentially operate in the same way as for instance the provisions in patent law that direct what is to be regarded as an invention and the statutory and judge-made definitions of subject matter in copyright law. By contrast, the relative grounds laid out in section 5 Trade Marks Act 1994 implement a general policy: in effect conditions that all trade marks must satisfy to be registrable. It is here, in these generally applicable relative grounds, that the now familiar pattern is found of a 'rule-like' condition whose instrumental effects are entirely embraced within the scope of standard.

On the face of it the ground of refusal under section 5(1) Trade Marks Act 1994 that disallows registration of an identical marks to one already on the register in relation to identical goods or services is a straightforward rule-like provision. Crucially from our perspective, although the Court of Justice has indicated that the perception of identity between the sign and the trade mark must be assessed globally with respect to an average consumer,[96] there is no need to show that the similarities between the mark and sign and the goods to which they are applied would generate any confusion in the mind of such an average consumer.

This then is in contrast to the relative ground of refusal contained in section 5(2) Trade Marks Act 1994, where a sign is to be refused registration if use of the sign would produce in the minds of average consumers a likelihood of confusion as to the 'trade origin' of the goods and services associated with the sign. The European Court of Justice has ruled in a series of cases that confusion is to be assessed by way of a standards-laden composite test requiring an overall assessment of the claimant's mark and defendant's sign. The factors taken into account are interdependent and the global assessment of all the relevant factors involves an iterative process between all the relevant factors.[97] For example, a lesser degree of similarity between the goods or services may be offset by a greater degree of similarity between the marks, and vice versa.[98]

The tests for whether there is identity under section 5(1) and whether there is a likelihood of confusion under section 5(2) then are not qualitatively different: they are both directed to establishing whether a sign is relatively distinctive. Indeed absolute, unconditional protection in the case of identity was not envisaged in the original Commission proposal for the Directive. Rather, under that original proposal, the protection afforded was bound up with the concept of similarity of signs, similarity of goods and services and the possibility of confusion arising therefrom.[99] The conceptual overlap between the two tests (as those tests have been understood and applied by the Court of Justice) was explicitly recognized by the Court of Appeal in *Reed Executive Plc* v *Reed*

96 Deemed to be reasonably well informed, reasonably observant and circumspect: C-291/00 *SA Société LTJ Diffusion* v *SA Sadas* [2003] ETMR 83 [52]. See also *Miss World Ltd* v *Channel Four Television Corp* [2007] EWHC 982 (Pat).

97 *Esure Insurance* v *Direct Line Insurance* [2008] RPC 34 [46] citing *Lloyd Schuhfabrik* [2000] FSR 77 [19].

98 [2008] RPC 34 [46].

99 C-291/00 *SA Société LTJ Diffusion* v *SA Sadas* [2003] ETMR 83, Opinion of Advocate General Jacobs [A34].

Business Information Ltd[100] and by AG Jacobs in *SA Société LTJ Diffusion* v *SA Sadas* when he said:

> Where rigorously identical signs or marks are used in the course of trade for identical goods or services, it is difficult if not impossible to conceive of circumstances in which all likelihood of confusion could be ruled out. In such cases, it would be both redundant and extravagant to require proof of that likelihood.[101]

The conclusion is that if the rule in section 5(1) were dispensed with, instrumentally nothing would change. An identical sign, applied for in respect of goods or services identical to those for which an identical trade mark has been registered would simply be seen as an instance of extreme similarity leading to inevitable confusion and could comfortably be accommodated within the standard-like provision of section 5(2) without significantly altering the scope of what can be registered.

That validity is a discrete context is even more pronounced in trade mark law than it is in patent law. Section 47(2) Trade Marks Act 1994 allows for the registration of a trade mark to be declared invalid on the ground that there is an earlier trade mark in relation to which the conditions set out in section 5(1), (2) or (3) obtain. Although section 47(3) provides that any person may make an application for a declaration of invalidity, where the application relates to the relative grounds, only the proprietor of an earlier mark or right can bring an application for invalidity.[102]

In conclusion, in respect of patents, copyright and trade marks, the boundaries of protectable subject matter are marked by a combination of rules and standards. In all cases, where there is a rule, the territory that this occupies is fully embraced by a corresponding standard. Intuitively it seems reasonable to suppose that, in the context over which they exercise control, the rules in patent law, copyright and trade mark law must contribute to a desirable certainty of expectation and stability. That a

---

100 [2004] EWCA Civ 159.

101 [2003] ETMR 83 [A37]. See also the Opinion of AG Ruiz-Jarabo Colomer in C-206/01 *Arsenal Football Club Plc* v *Matthew Reed* [2003] RPC 144 [AG51] and the comments of Arnold J in *OCH-ZIFF Management Europe Ltd* v *OCH Capital LLP* [2010] EWHC 2599 (Ch) [88]. All of these opinions draw support from Article 16(1) of the WTO's Agreement on Trade-Related Aspects of Intellectual Property Rights which provides that a likelihood of confusion shall be presumed in the case of the use of an identical sign for identical goods or services.

102 Under Article 5 Trade Mark (Relative Grounds) Order 2007.

standard simultaneously exercises control over the same context suggests with equal force that flexibility and dynamism are desirable features of the law. A step towards understanding what is going on, if not the key, lies in the observation that intellectual property, like all private property, is a form of both private and public power. The private nature of this power lies in the relation between the right holder and a specific duty bearer (whether licensee or alleged infringer). But property, it is said, gives the right holder the right to exclude the world and the public power of property lies in the right's influence on the actions of an indefinite number of persons.[103] The legal provisions that go into defining the boundaries of a claim to a right have a hortatory function that gives them a particular significance in the exercise of this public power. These provisions provide right holders with the means of signalling to the world the boundaries of the territory over which they claim dominium. The behaviours induced depend in part on the perception of the certainty of any claim to a protected territory. Thus form has significance in understanding the relationships between right holders, duty bearers and the wider public. Form and this interpersonal/social dimension of intellectual property law is the subject matter of the chapter which follows.

---

[103] Drahos, above n.2, 149 and to similar effect Kennedy, D, 'Form and Substance in Private Law Adjudication' (1976) 89 Harvard L Rev 1685, 1767–8.

5. Form and the interpersonal/social dimension

Although the precise content of the arguments has varied, there has never been a period in history when intellectual property law has been free from political debate. There has been a tendency to caricature these debates as highly polarized arguments between opponents advocating extreme positions.[1] Meaningful argument is typically rather more nuanced and reflects a diversity of opinion between extremes. But it is useful in the interests of clarity and as a starting point to describe the conflicting positions in relatively stark terms. On the face of it, the intellectual property system is one which allows an individual right owner to pursue their self-interests with indifference to the effect that this has on others in society. This is unremarkable so far as this is a characteristic of all private property. The institution of property confers private domain over some things and within certain parameters the owner of property is entitled to suit herself as to what she does with her property. Whatever reasons the owner may have for dealing with her property in a particular way, whether she is motivated by envy, strategy or perverseness, she can do as she pleases with what she owns. The institution of private property is thus one that emphasizes individuality.[2]

1 Bently, L and Sherman, B, *Intellectual Property Law*, 4th edition (Oxford University Press, 2014), 4.

2 Harris, J, *Property and Justice* (Oxford University Press, 2002), 65. See also Gordon, W, 'An Inquiry into the Merits of Copyright: The Challenges of Consistency, Consent, and Encouragement Theory' (1989) 41 Stanford L Rev 1343, 1360; Drahos, P, *A Philosophy of Intellectual Property* (Ashgate, 1996), 200–202; and Merges, R, *Justifying Intellectual Property* (Harvard University Press, 2011), 5. This 'liberal model' is the dominant ideology of property and has been for some time; however, it is not the only model and the 'stewardship model' has been put forward as an alternative and one in which the owner of the property must consider the interests of the community with rights and duties being constructed accordingly: Howe, H, 'Copyright Limitations and the Stewardship Model of Property' (2011) IPQ, 183.

Private property owners are certainly not generally obliged to share their wealth or to transfer it to others. One reason is that, where there is rivalry in consumption of the property in question, any redistribution scheme, whatever its core motivation, would need to address the issue of entitlement since the forced taking of property from one diminishes their estate to the extent that it enriches another. Unless we were being purely tyrannical we would need to advance reasons for any hierarchy of entitlements. For instance, we might choose to say that an entitlement claim based on an individual's desert must give way to a rival claim based on another individual's need. Or we might not. The difficulty in balancing such rival claims increases the complexity of the exercise and naturally then tends to create inertia.

That complexity does not arise in the case of intellectual property rights and this perhaps explains the persistence and vigour of the political debates surrounding this form of property in societies where it is understood that individuals can generally do as they will with their own private property even in the face of others' pressing need.[3] As is often observed, there is no rivalry in the consumption of 'intellectual goods' and typically the costs of their transmission are very low. Because there is no rivalry in consumption, we do not need to pitch different bases of claims to entitlement against one another in order to arrive at a justified allocation of rights. A decision that someone should be allowed to use a piece of information without the right owner's consent does not require us to disentitle the right owner. That is an option but it is not necessary. And similarly, the successful claimant need not be given rights co-extensive with those of the owner. The satisfaction of their immediate needs might require less.

---

[3] For instance in *Southwark LBC* v *Williams* the Court of Appeal refused to accept necessity as a counter to an order for immediate possession where the defendants, in dire need of housing accommodation, had entered empty houses owned by the local authority. Lord Denning MR observed that,

> when a man, who is starving, enters a house and takes food in order to keep himself alive … English law does not admit the defence of necessity. It holds him guilty of larceny. Lord Hale said that 'if a person, being under necessity for want of victuals, or clothes, shall upon that account clandestinely, and animo furandi, steal another man's food, it is felony …': Hale, *Pleas of Crown,* i. 54. The reason is because, if hunger were once allowed to be an excuse for stealing, it would open a way through which all kinds of disorder and lawlessness would pass.

[1971] Ch 734, 744.

Furthermore, information is shareable at little or no cost to the person in possession of it and that has become all the more so with modern means of electronic copying and distribution. Typically the transaction costs of a forced or voluntary transfer are negligible. An individual thus cannot defend a decision to keep certain information to themselves (by keeping it secret) or to exercise a legal right so as to prevent others from using that information on the grounds that they are unwilling or unable to bear the cost of distributing the information more widely. Intellectual property is not then like the unused bicycle that slowly rusts in the back of the garage because the costs of disposing of it exceed what it is worth to its owner. The owners of intellectual property keep the protected information to themselves only because they hope that by so doing they will gain some advantage by having exclusive use of it.

The intellectual property system, in allowing individuals to appropriate ideas using the force of law, thus seems bound to provoke a debate in which will feature the opposed attitudes of individualism and altruism. Those particular terms are chosen because they correspond with those adopted by Duncan Kennedy in his exploration of form and adjudication in private law in which he sought to show that in private law disputes, arguments surrounding choice of form had 'powerful overtones' of substantive debates about values.[4] Kennedy asserted that whilst concepts such as liberty, equality, justice, welfare are deeply ingrained in culture, they make two senses of the world, one altruist and the other individualist.[5] Before going on to give an account of Kennedy's attempt to show a correspondence between form and values, it is necessary to expand a little on the values that characterize the opposing attitudes of individualism and altruism.[6]

---

4 Kennedy, D, 'Form and Substance in Private Law Adjudication' (1976) 89 Harvard L Rev 1685, 1685 and 1710.

5 Kennedy, above n.4, 1766. Kennedy apparently later expressly recanted 'the whole idea of individualism and altruism': Gabel, P and Kennedy, D, 'Roll over Beethoven' (1984) 36 Stanford L Rev 1, 15. However, this recantation was contained in a conversational form that did not facilitate the clear identification of either the constituent elements of the argument nor the conclusions arrived at and Alan Hunt has convincingly argued that Kennedy did not set out to reject the specific concepts of individualism and altruism but rather the form of theory that employed or produced these concepts: Hunt, A, 'The Theory of Critical Legal Studies' (1986) 6 OJLS 1, 20–25.

6 Kennedy said of his construction of these positions that both, 'have been assembled from diverse legal, moral, economic, and political writings, and I can give no plausible description of the principle of selection at work. As a result, it

For Kennedy, a commitment to individualism brings with it a sharp distinction between the interests of the individual and those of others in society and a belief that it is legitimate to express a preference in conduct for those interests. Self-interest is partnered by conduct characterized by self-reliance whereby an individual's objectives are defined and achieved without an expectation of help from others. But it follows that an individual has no corresponding obligation to share or sacrifice anything to further the interests of others.[7] This reciprocity is further manifested in the individualist's respect for the laws that make it possible to coexist with others similarly self-interested.[8]

The political paradigm of altruism as conceived of by Kennedy is a marginally richer concept. A commitment to altruism brings with it recognition of a duty to share advantages with others, which is founded on a belief that one ought not to indulge a preference for one's own interest over those of others:

> The simplest of the practices that represent altruism are sharing and sacrifice. Sharing is a static concept, suggesting an existing distribution of goods which the sharers rearrange. It means giving up to another gains or wealth that one has produced oneself or that have come to one through some good fortune. It is motivated by a sense of duty or by a sense that the other's satisfaction is a reward at least comparable to the satisfaction one might have derived from consuming the thing oneself. Sharing may also involve participation in another's losses: a spontaneous decision to shift to oneself a part of the ill fortune, deserved or fortuitous, that has befallen someone else. Sacrifice is the dynamic notion of taking action that will change an ongoing course of events, at some expense to oneself, to minimize another's loss or maximize his gain.[9]

Kennedy admitted that it was difficult even to identify a counter-ethic to individualism because the rhetoric of individualism so dominated legal discourse at the time he was writing. Forty years on, and the counter-ethic of altruism seems to me quite visible at least in arguments surrounding the existence and exercise of intellectual property rights. One thing that has manifestly changed in the intervening period is

is impossible to "prove" or "disprove" the validity of the two constructs': Kennedy, above n.4, 1722–3.

[7] Ibid., 1713.

[8] Ibid.

[9] Ibid., 1717.

an enhancement of political engagement mediated by electronic communications. Even in its relatively brief history, the internet has been particularly influential in the way it allows individuals with shared interests to identify one another, communicate, share information and coordinate activities.[10] The internet has thus allowed new forms of social organization and with it the emergence of a new way of exercising political power outside the conventional societal hierarchies. At least in certain spheres, this has allowed traditionally under-represented interests to gain political power.[11] The perceived negative effects of intellectual property rights have been the focus of newly emerged, electronically mediated social institutions which have a strong commitment to the altruist political vision. The internet is home to a very vocal community committed to the politics of altruism and the expression 'information wants to be free' has become something of a slogan for what may broadly be called the open access movement.[12] Copyright law in particular has been subject to scrutiny so far as the internet, by giving a voice to certain classes of the users of copyright, has acted to raise awareness of the duties that correspond to claims to copyright. There are many who think that copyright stifles our ability to make the most of the internet and related technology.[13] The internet, I would argue, has also changed

---

[10] Studies in social psychology suggest a significant social influence on the commitment to either individualism or altruism. In individualist societies, reward allocation is such as to enable those members who made a greater contribution to claim a larger share of the reward. By contrast, in collectivist societies, more emphasis is put on group membership and within groups rewards tend to be allocated equally: Hofstede, G, *Culture's Consequences: Comparing Values, Behaviors, Institutions, and Organizations Across Nations*, 2nd edition (Sage, 2001), 227, 241 and 244–5.

[11] Cass Sunstein has argued that rules can emerge when one group of interests is well-organized or otherwise powerful, and when its adversaries are not. In such circumstances, he suggests, the well-organized interests can press the government body in the direction of rules: Sunstein, C, 'Problems with Rules' (1995) 83 California L Rev 953, 1013–14.

[12] Merges, above n.2, 77.

[13] This was certainly one of the core conclusions of the 2011 Hargreaves Review. The review found that copyright law in particular was obstructing innovation and economic growth. The report's authors observed that,

> [c]opyright, once the exclusive concern of authors and their publishers, is today preventing medical researchers studying data and text in pursuit of new treatments. Copying has become basic to numerous industrial processes, as well as to a burgeoning service economy based upon the internet. The UK cannot afford to let a legal framework designed around artists impede vigorous participation in these emerging business sectors.

the perception of the interests protected by copyright. Digitization and internet-mediated distribution has made the costs of publishing negligible. Importantly, the relevant technology is as much in the hands of the general public as it is in those of commercial publishers. If publishers ever benefited from asymmetry of information in their assertions regarding the necessity of copyright, that is not now the case. The widely recognized negligible costs in reproducing and disseminating copyright works have worked to undermine one of the central justifications for copyright protection.[14] Thus it is commonly argued that widespread illegal copying on the internet can be explained by reference to the fact that the public is not persuaded by the rationales offered for copyright.[15]

Within this rather nebulous 'open access' movement are pockets of organization with a clear common political standpoint. For instance, and perhaps most notably the Pirate Party is a political party whose growth resulted directly from the rise in legal action against online copyright 'piracy', in particular the successful 2009 case against the *Pirate Bay* in the Stockholm District Court.[16] Also notable is the Open Rights Group, a campaigning group that amongst other things made representations to the Hargreaves Committee. As one might expect given the character of the internet, other coalitions are rather less formal in nature but one way or

---

Foreword, Hargreaves, I, *Digital Opportunity. A Review of Intellectual Property and Growth*, May 2011, accessed 24 January 2017 at http://webarchive.nationalarchives.gov.uk/20140603093549/http://www.ipo.gov.uk/ipreview.htm.

[14] On publishers and copyright see: Breyer, S, 'The Uneasy Case for Copyright: A Study of Copyright in Books, Photocopies, and Computer Programs' (1970) 84 Harvard L Rev 281.

[15] Garon, J, 'Normative Copyright: A Conceptual Framework for Copyright Philosophy and Ethics' (2003) 88 Cornell L Rev 1278, 1335 *et seq*; Strahilevitz, L, 'Charismatic Code, Social Norms, and the Emergence of Cooperation on the File-swapping Networks' (2003) 89 Virginia L Rev 505, 538 *et seq*; and Chapter 6 in IviR, *Recasting Copyright for the Knowledge Economy* (Amsterdam: Institute for Information Law, University of Amsterdam, 2006), accessed 24 January 2017 at http://ec.europa.eu/internal_market/copyright/docs/studies/etd2005imd195recast_report_2006.pdf.

[16] Verdict B 13301-06, Stockholm District Court, Division 5, Unit 52. English translation available from the International Federation of the Phonographic Industry, accessed 24 January 2017 at http://www.ifpi.org/content/library/pirate-bay-verdict-english-translation.pdf. For a brief history of the Pirate Party, accessed 24 January 2017 at http://www.businessinsider.com/pirate-party-germany-elections-2012-4?op=1&IR=T.

another are characterized by a commitment to sharing and/or sacrifice. For instance, in 2001 several thousand scholars from around the world put their names to an open letter, directed to the publishers of scientific materials and calling for: 'the establishment of an online public library that would provide the full contents of the published record of research and scholarly discourse in medicine and the life sciences in a freely accessible, fully searchable, interlinked form'. The signatories pledged not to publish in, or peer review for, journals that were not open access.[17] The Creative Commons organization makes freely available an infrastructure comprising a set of copyright licences and tools that allow individuals to grant licences to others facilitating the sharing, use and development of copyright works.[18] There are also sharing initiatives that focus on inventions and patents for inventions. For instance, there are (admittedly few) examples of coordinated voluntary licensing of patents via so-called patent pooling aimed at the sharing of information to meet acute and chronic public health needs[19] and other data sharing initiatives

---

[17] The letter itself has disappeared from the PLOS archives but an account of the history of the movement including an account of the letter is available, accessed 24 January 2017 at https://www.plos.org/history. As UK researchers are aware, the four UK higher education funding bodies are committed to making the products of academic research freely accessible to all and have introduced an open access requirement in the next Research Excellence Framework, accessed 24 January 2017 at http://www.hefce.ac.uk/rsrch/oa/.

[18] The creative commons website explains that it,

> is a nonprofit organization that enables the sharing and use of creativity and knowledge through free legal tools. Our free, easy-to-use copyright licenses provide a simple, standardized way to give the public permission to share and use your creative work – on conditions of your choice. CC licenses let you easily change your copyright terms from the default of 'all rights reserved' to 'some rights reserved.' Creative Commons licenses are not an alternative to copyright. They work alongside copyright and enable you to modify your copyright terms to best suit your needs.

Accessed 24 January 2017 at https://creativecommons.org/about/.

[19] For instance, the Medicines Patent Pool (MPP) is

> a United Nations-backed public health organisation working to increase access to HIV, viral hepatitis C and tuberculosis treatments in low- and middle-income countries. Through its innovative business model, the MPP partners with governments, industry, civil society, international organisations, patient groups and other stakeholders to forecast, prioritize and license needed medicines. The organisation encourages generic manufacture and the development of new formulations through patent pooling.

Accessed 24 January 2017 at http://www.medicinespatentpool.org/about/.

directed to the same end[20] as well as those aimed at fostering scientific research.[21]

The account so far might suggest that I see society as populated by two distinct groups, but whilst it may be that in some contexts the political paradigms of individualism and altruism might be caricatures of the positions adopted in contests between individuals, it is also the case that these values compete within an individual so far as everyone is to some degree ambivalent in their feelings about the conflict.[22]

Kennedy sought to show that advocating rules over standards or vice versa could be seen as an invitation to choose between sets of values such that the rule form was associated with individualism and the standard form with altruism.[23] In particular he argued that one can draw an analogy between the arguments that lawyers make when they are defending a 'strict' interpretation of a rule and those they put forward when they invite a judge to rule in a way that is substantively individualist. Likewise, he said, the rhetoric in which lawyers engage when arguing for a relaxation in the rigour of a regime of rules is similar to that put forward in support of substantively altruist law-making.[24]

I cannot hope to capture the full depth of Kennedy's argument in this brief introduction but I must at least attempt a summary account of the chief reasons he advanced in support of his conclusion. The correspondence was, he said, evident as between formal and substantive moral,

---

For commentary see: Dionisio, D (ed.) Pooling ARV Drug Patents: A Pro-Access Fitting Strategy? The Open Aids Journal, Special Issue (2010); 't Hoen, E, Berger, J, Calmy, A and Moon, S, 'Driving a Decade of Change: HIV/AIDS, Patents and Access to Medicines for All' (2011) 14 Journal of the International AIDS Society, 1–47; and Cox, K, 'The Medicines Patent Pool: Promoting Access and Innovation for Life-saving Medicines through Voluntary Licenses' (2012) 4 Hastings Science and Technology Law Journal 291.

[20] See for instance the account of the WIPO Re:Search initiative in Bombelles, T, Dent, J, Sharafudeen, M, Stevens, P, Graef, K and Krattiger, A, *WIPO Re:Search: Sharing Innovation in the Fight against Neglected Tropical Diseases*, Global Challenges Brief (WIPO, 2015); and Bombelles, T and Dent, J, 'Neglected Tropical Disease Research: Re-thinking the Drug Discovery Model' (2015) 7(6) Future Medicinal Chemistry 693, accessed 24 January 2017 at http://www.future-science.com/doi/pdf/10.4155/fmc.15.29.

[21] Hayden, E, 'Geneticists Push for Global Data-sharing' (2013) 498 Nature, 16.

[22] Kennedy, above n.4, 1710.

[23] Ibid., 1745. This is a variation on the claim made by Hayek that there is a close association between the rule of law and free markets so far as both require generality, on which see Sunstein, above n.11, 981–2.

[24] Kennedy, above n.4, 1738.

economic and political arguments; the correspondence being clearest in the moral dimension. As to that, Kennedy observed that individualist rhetoric makes a virtue of self-reliance which underpins the claim that people ought to be willing to accept the consequences of their own actions. So it follows that whilst they ought to enjoy the fruits of those actions, they must equally bear any consequent costs and losses and ought not to rely on others to bail them out if they suffer ill fortune. In the formal debate about rules and standards, this finds a parallel in the rule-proponent's blasé acceptance of the consequences of the over- and under-inclusiveness of rules.[25]

Kennedy asserted that there is a historical basis to the connection between economic individualism and rule advocacy founded in the Classical theory of laissez-faire which favoured a legal regime in which the state systematically refused to intervene ad hoc to achieve particular economic results.[26] Kennedy saw the correspondence between formal and substantive economic arguments as more intricate than that in the moral dimension and comprising three elements. The first related to substantive arguments as to the scope of legal intervention. Kennedy argued that, in other than a state of nature (i.e. given some form of state intervention), favouring rules over standards was inherently non-interventionist and so inherently individualist. The claim that rules are less interventionist than standards rests on the fact that rules are less result oriented than standards.[27] Outside a particular rule's scope of operation, individuals are free to do as they please, even if this activity frustrates the rule's purpose. Secondly, Kennedy observed that one fundamental premise of economic individualism is that the forced sharing of wealth undermines the goal of maximizing wealth creation. In substantive debates, the individualist thus opposes welfare programmes financed through the tax system. In the sphere of private law there is corresponding support for the various doctrines that operate to allow individuals to refuse to share superfluous wealth with those who have a greater need. This position is replicated in

---

25 Ibid., 1739–40. Kennedy's suggestion that the argument of the advocate of 'relaxation' of a rigid rule ultimately rests on the assertion that there is a moral duty on the part of the private beneficiary of the over- or under-inclusion to forego their advantage is I think less convincing as a general statement though the argument stands up well in relation to formalities (on which see above at p. 72).

26 Ibid., 1745–8. This is I think a variation on the claim made by Hayek that there is a close association between the rule of law and free markets so far as both require generality, on which see Sunstein, above n.11, 981–2.

27 Kennedy, above n.4, 1741–2.

arguments relating to form in which the rules advocate, in rejecting adjudication that takes account of the particularities of the case, adopts a position analogous to that of substantive economic individualism.[28] The third and final element to the parallel between substantive economic and formal dimensions is linked to ideas associated with Social Darwinism and the belief that conflict increases net social welfare. The substantive argument is far from simple and I accept the risk that I misrepresent here in my summarized account. The starting point is that in a competitive environment there will be winners and losers. State intervention in the form of insurance against loss caused by the activities of the aggressively competitive would have the effect of perpetuating the weakly competitive whilst not allowing the strongly competitive to reap the full benefits of their actions. The assumption is that non-intervention yields a net social benefit: the harm that is suffered by the weak is more than offset by the social value arising from the actions of the strong (though the precise mechanism by which so favouring the actions of the strongly competitive leads to a net social benefit is obscure). The substantive argument is thus not so much individualist as anti-altruist. It finds expression in Laddie J's now famous dictum that: 'the courts are not a branch of social services whose job is to help the infirm or the unwise'.[29] The parallel argument in the realm of form rests on the assertion that the 'security' provided by rules (over standards) encourages transactions. Kennedy argues that this formal argument in favour of rules rests on the same implicit Social Darwinism as the substantive in that the security of transaction is purchased at the expense of tolerating breach of altruistic duty on the part of the beneficiary of the mechanical arbitrariness of rules.[30]

Kennedy saw the formal and substantive political arguments as close to identical, both centring on the debate surrounding the limits of judicial activism. So far as the rules advocate was concerned, a regime in which judges were confined to the formulation and application of rules minimized both the institutionally inappropriate investigation of the likely results of decision and the inherently legislative activity of making value judgements. The advocate of rules saw the former as undesirable because judges are not equipped to determine the wide-ranging social consequences of their decisions: only the legislature was competent to carry

---

28 Ibid., 1742–3.

29 *Merck & Co Inc* v *Generics (UK) Ltd* [2003] EWHC 2842 (Pat) [47].

30 Kennedy, above n.4, 1745.

out such investigations. The latter was seen as undesirable because the value judgements of the kind required by standards are inherently arbitrary and subjective and should thus be made only according to majority vote.[31]

Kennedy saw the chief value in relating form to substance as rendering the contribution of 'policy' in decision making more intelligible.[32] But it is important to appreciate the limits of what is being claimed, both by Kennedy and in this chapter. That there is a general and close connection between preferences for the form of adjudication and substantive values cannot survive even the most rudimentary scrutiny if this is understood to mean that it is generally the case that advocating a rule-based solution to a particular legal dispute shows a political commitment to individualism whereas a corresponding political commitment to altruism leads to a demand for a standards-based solution.[33] But that is not what is being claimed here. Kennedy himself recognized this and whilst concluding that there is a sound analytical basis for the intuition of a connection between individualism and rules, described that connection as 'structural' rather than 'contextual' by which he meant that it lay in the correspondence between the structures of the formal and substantive arguments. As

---

31 Ibid., 1751–3.

32 Ibid., 1724 and in more detail at 1732. As a central figure in the critical legal studies movement, Kennedy had a wider object. That these values compete within an individual is in many ways the most significant aspect of the 'fundamental contradiction' to 'critical theorists' in that it 'provides an account of the contingency and indeterminacy of the legal process. The existence of competing principles creates the ever-present possibility of judicial choice': Hunt, above n.5, 21. In this book I do not set out to go further than using the individualist/altruist distinction to try to understand the role of policy in decision making.

33 This is acknowledged even amongst Kennedy's champions. Mark Kelman, for instance, observes that there are three distinct sorts of critiques of the claim that the rule form is individualistic and the standard form altruistic: first, that it is frequently irrelevant; second that it is sometimes more or less correct depending on whom one views as the relevant disputants; and third that it is hopelessly and needlessly ambiguous on the distinction between selfish quasi-altruism and genuine selflessness: Kelman, M, *A Guide to Critical Legal Studies* (Harvard University Press, 1987), 56 *et seq.* See also Schlag, P, 'Rules and Standards' (1985) 33 UCLA L Rev 379, 420.

such it was not one that was necessary in practice or verifiable empirically.[34] Mark Kelman has suggested then that the observed correspondence should be understood as aesthetic.[35] The rule form, Kelman says, may appeal to the substantive individualist because its formal virtues match up aesthetically with the virtues she is inclined to admire. The aesthetically grounded argument is thus that it is the image projected by the invocation of the need for a more rule-like solution in any case which resonates with the substantively individualistic ideological position, even though individualism does not ultimately rest on a rule-bound regime.[36] And even then Kelman acknowledged that a claim that the rule form resonates aesthetically with substantive individualist values will sometimes (perhaps often) be irrelevant. The kind of functional arguments explored in Chapters 2 and 3 that rest on the observation that certain characteristics of rules and standards make them well- or ill-suited to resolve particular disputes in particular circumstances, exist independently and are powerful in their own terms.[37]

The claim that I aim to advance in the remainder of this chapter is that, understood and qualified in this way, an exploration of form in intellectual property law goes some way to render the contribution of 'policy' in decision making more intelligible in this area of the law. My starting premise is that if there is a relationship between form and substance in intellectual property law, then at first blush one would expect to find the rule form to be associated with securing claims and strengthening the

---

[34] Kennedy, above n.4, 1724. He also says 'individualism and altruism can be reduced neither to facts nor to logic, [and] … cannot be used with any degree of consistency to characterize personalities or opinions or the outcomes of lawsuits': ibid.

[35] In this Kelman may have simply articulated more clearly what Kennedy intended to say. That Kennedy understood the relationship to be essentially an aesthetic one is indicated when he says that,

> there is a sound analytical basis for the intuition of a connection between individualism and rules. The connection is structural rather than contextual. It is not a connection that is necessary in practice, or even verifiable empirically. It consists in the exact correspondence between the structures of the two arguments

(Kennedy, above n.4, 1745)

[36] The argument that the rule form is individualistic only in its aesthetic form means that it is perfectly consistent to argue both that rule-bound regimes are impossible and that a commitment to rules represent the working out of an ideological programme.

[37] Kelman, above n.33, 56. Note, however, that Kennedy asserted that choice of form is seldom purely instrumental or tactical: Kennedy, above n.4, 1710.

position of right holders whereas the standard form to be associated with limiting scope and facilitating public access.[38] As I shall show, how far that is the case depends on whether we are talking of copyright, patents or trade marks.

The account of copyright starts by returning to the condition that a work must be 'original'. Normally this condition is assessed by way of a rule (asking only whether the work is copied or not) and this rule is clearly associated with securing the position of right holders. However, the greater part of the analysis is given over to showing how the occasional and more standard-like test that looks to skill, effort and judgement, applies where the claimant has reworked material typically in the public domain. Where this is so, a claim to copyright succeeds only if that reworking enhances access, appreciation or otherwise improves the usefulness of the publicly available material. These observations go some way to support Kennedy's thesis that the rule form is associated with individualism and the standard form with altruism.

Following on from the point pressed in the previous chapter that copyright subsistence and whether it has been infringed are issues that cannot be divorced, there follows an account of how courts approach the question of infringement. I note that whether a substantial part of a claimant's work has been copied is a test that is standard-like in form being described by courts as a matter of impression. I argue that how courts decide whether a taking is substantial is a means of restricting rather than extending rights. That is particularly clear in the way in which courts have drawn a distinction between ideas and expression and especially in cases involving literary works that are not works of fiction and those where it is claimed that copyright in an artistic work has been infringed by the reproduction of technical features of a design. I suggest that the test for infringement by substantial taking implements the idea/expression dichotomy by way of a standard because it looks to the impact of the property claim on the freedom of others. This impact and the interests at stake are hard to assess *ex ante* given the diverse social and economic reach of copyright. They are much more concrete where an individual right is pitched against a corresponding individual duty in an infringement action. This line of analysis allows me to conclude the section on copyright with a brief digression from the main theme by way of a critical appraisal of the contemporary reshaping of copyright law

---

[38] As will be demonstrated in the following chapter, these expectations are a key element in those justificatory theories that draw on Immanuel Kant's view of rights to property being essential for achieving personal autonomy.

effected by the judicial interpretations of the obligations contained in the EU's Information Society Directive.

I start the account of patent law by observing that because patentability requires that what is claimed is both new and inventive (the tests being rule-like and standard-like respectively), the law is hard to square with the thesis that the rule form is associated with securing claims whereas the standard form is associated with limiting scope. However, I suggest that it would be wrong to see securing a patent as solely an individualistic act. The requirement that a patentee disclose the invention as a condition of grant is a significant sacrifice and one that distinguishes patent law from copyright law in terms of the control exercisable over the claimed subject matter by the right owner. Furthermore, because applications are subject to substantive examination, the patent applicant cannot secure protection for a claimed invention by dishonestly exaggerating the extent of its contribution to the relevant technical field. The conclusion is that the process of application and examination itself shows a simultaneous commitment to individualism and altruism so far as it is concerned both with securing individual rights and with limiting scope and facilitating public access.

The concluding section dealing with trade marks starts by attempting to show how, perhaps counterintuitively, the notions of sacrifice and sharing are relevant concerns in the competitive marketplace that being the milieu in which trade marks function. In this environment altruism has an application when that means sharing the right to use a particular sign with users who are not the mark owner's direct competitors. I go on to outline the European Court's fabrication of that limitation on the scope of trade mark rights that confines owners' rights to preventing only those unauthorized uses that affect, or are liable to affect, the functions of the mark. The court, I note, has held that this limitation applies even in circumstances where there is a precise identity between the mark and the complained of sign and the goods or services to which these are attached. In such circumstances liability cannot be assessed mechanically but rather requires the court to assess the impression that the complained of use makes on the mind of the consumer.

Although this analysis goes some way to establish the correspondence between form and substance in trade mark law, I acknowledge that the correspondence is nevertheless relatively weak and suggest that this is because the rights in marks are justified by reference to the interest of consumers. The key point is that the relationship between form and substance is obscured in trade mark law by the fact that owners' rights to exclude on the one hand, and the limits on scope on the other, are viewed through the filter of consumer interest. This interest itself embodies a simultaneous commitment to individualism and altruism, trade marks being a central means by which consumers satisfy their simultaneous desires to emulate others whilst at the same time attempting to construct an individual identity through acts of consumption.

5.1 COPYRIGHT LAW

To claim copyright in a work requires the claimant to show that the work is original. However assessed, whether under the European or UK tests, the condition of originality is one that on the face of it looks to the author's contribution to the creation of the work rather than what the work contributes to the stock of human knowledge.[39] Given this, it is easy to see a claim to enjoy copyright in a work as an act politically aligned with individualism. As was pointed out in the preceding chapter, under UK law and in the great majority of cases the condition of originality has operated as a rule turning on whether a work is copied or not: that is to say whether the work originated from the claimed author. To this extent the rule form here is thus indeed associated with securing claims and strengthening the position of right holders.

But as also noted in the previous chapter, whether a work is original is not invariably decided according to a rule and there are circumstances where courts have adopted an alternative formulation of the originality condition; one which allows the exercise of judicial discretion. The proposition that in copyright law the rule form is associated with securing claims and strengthening the position of right holders whereas the standard form is associated with limiting scope and facilitating public access suggests a reason why that should be so. 'Originality', meaning the exercise of skill, labour and judgement rather than simply 'not copied', is a variation of the originality condition which has its origins in cases where copyright has been claimed in works which are, to a greater or lesser extent, copies of existing productions but where courts have nevertheless entertained the claim to copyright in such reworkings. A finding that the requisite skill, labour and judgement have been expended in the production of the reworking validates the claim over this reworked territory. The contrary finding leaves the claimant empty-handed. The possible outcomes in a copyright case where in a response to a claim of infringement, the defendant asserts that what they have taken is not original are:

---

[39] In contrast to for example the requirement of novelty in patent law, which concerns the relationship of the claimed invention with the state of the art.

1. Copyright is infringed: the defendant copied the claimant's original work.
2. There is no infringement: the defendant did not copy the claimant's work.
3. There is no infringement: the defendant copied an unoriginal part of the claimant's work.

The matrix is different where the claim to copyright turns on a test for originality that looks to skill, labour and judgement rather than simply asking whether the claimed work is copied. In such cases the possibility exists of the court declaring that the work as claimed lacks originality and that the claimant has no rights over the work in issue (the equivalent outcome to a finding that a patent claim is invalid in a counter-claim to a patent infringement action).[40] In such cases, typically the claimant will have reworked material that is in the public domain. The claim to copyright in such circumstances is supportable so far as the reworking enhances access or otherwise improves the usefulness of material available to all. So for instance, positioning material in a thoughtful compilation can make the information contained more useful by contextualizing it in a particular way.[41] An abridgement of an ancient text can make it more intelligible and so accessible to modern students as in *Macmillan* v *Cooper*, where Lord Atkinson held that, '[t]he mere process of selecting passages from works readily accessible to the public is not [sufficient], but that difficulty in obtaining access to the originals or skill manifested in making or arranging the selection is sufficient to give the character of an "original literary work" to the selection'.[42]

Consider for instance the decision of the Court of Appeal in *Hyperion Records Ltd* v *Sawkins*.[43] Here the claimant was a musicologist who had prepared modern 'performing editions' of works originally composed by the French baroque composer Michel-Richard de Lalande. The defendant record company used four of the claimant's editions when recording those works for a compact disc. Whilst it had agreed to pay the claimant

40 Of course that outcome is hypothetically possible in any copyright case, but only a dishonest or delusional claimant would claim rights over work knowing it to be copied.

41 As in *MacMillan* v *Suresh Chunder Deb* ILR 17 C 951 which concerned a claim to copyright in the book *The Golden Treasury of Songs and Lyrics* which contained a selection from the poems of many English authors of various periods.

42 *MacMillan* v *Cooper* (1924) 40 TLR 186.

43 [2005] EWCA Civ 565.

a fixed fee for his work on the scores, it denied that he had any copyright in the performing editions as original musical works and refused to pay him any royalty. The defendant record company contended that the editions were no more than transcriptions of Lalande's music and did not involve the creation of new music in the form of notes or sounds.

The court noted that it was the aim of the claimant, so far as was possible, to reproduce faithfully Lalande's music in the form of an accurate edition close to the composer's original intentions. This involved consulting and drawing on manuscript and printed sources dating from the late seventeenth and early eighteenth centuries. Work was necessary in order to select a version and to produce a score and a series of parts which would be playable. That involved transcription of the music from the original scores into modern notation and interpretation of the original manuscripts. The court accepted that the work of the claimant did not, in general, involve recomposition of Lalande's music or making an 'arrangement' of it but concluded that the production of the performing editions required substantial effort, skill and time on the part of the claimant. This was sufficient to satisfy the originality requirement even though the claimant worked on the scores of existing musical works composed by another person whose works were out of copyright; and the claimant had no intention of adding any new notes of music of his own. Importantly the Court of Appeal emphasized the general policy of copyright and noted that if the claim of the claimant to copyright in the performing editions were upheld, that would not prevent other musicologists, composers, performers or record companies from copying Lalande's music directly or indirectly or from making fresh performing editions of their own. All that the claimant could prevent them from doing, without his consent, was taking the short-cut of copying his performing editions in order to save themselves the trouble that he went to in order to produce them.[44]

There is no doubt that this version of the originality test, assessed according to the exercise of skill, labour and judgement, is more standard-like than rule-like. Lord Atkinson in *MacMillan* v *Cooper* put it thus:

---

[44] Ibid. [30]. In consequence, and as succinctly put by Whitford J in *LB (Plastics) Ltd* v *Swish Products Ltd*, '[t]wo compilers covering the same area may produce identical, or nearly identical street directories; two artists drawing or photographers photographing Nelson's column nearly identical representations, but each is entitled to copyright in his particular representation of the work in question': [1977] FSR 87, 92.

> What is the precise amount of the knowledge, labour, judgment or literary skill or taste which the author of any book or other compilation must bestow upon its composition in order to acquire copyright in it … cannot be defined in precise terms. In every case it must depend largely on the special facts of the case, and must in each case be very much a question of degree.[45]

Whilst in *Ladbroke (Football) Ltd* v *William Hill (Football) Ltd*, Lord Pearce observed that directories, catalogues and the like have been held to be original and to acquire copyright but there is no copyright where the work of compilation was not substantial but negligible and that, 'in each case it is a question of degree whether the labour or skill or ingenuity or expense involved in the compilation is sufficient to warrant a claim to originality in a compilation'.[46]

This form of the originality requirement is not stringent, however, and requires only a minimal level of creativity. The vast majority of compilations and the like will pass the test and the cases where copyright has been denied are accordingly comparatively few. The claimants in *Cramp & Sons Ltd* v *Smythson Ltd*[47] were the publishers of a pocket diary. The diary published by the claimants contained the usual diary pages accompanied by pages containing information of the kind usually found in diaries at that time, including: a calendar for the year; postal information; a selection of 'days and dates' for the year; tables of weights and measures; and comparative time tables. The claimants asserted that the defendants by copying seven of these tables and inserting them into their own diary infringed the claimants' copyright.

The claimants made no claim to copyright in any one of the seven tables individually nor to the order in which the seven tables were arranged in their diary. Rather the claim was in the selection of the seven

---

[45] (1924) 40 TLR 186. See also the speech of Lord Simon in *Cramp & Sons Ltd* v *Smythson Ltd* [1944] AC 329.

[46] [1964] 1 WLR 273, 292 and to the same effect Lord Reid at 277–8 ('it is not disputed that, as regards compilation, originality is a matter of degree depending on the amount of skill, judgment or labour that has been involved in making the compilation'). Note also the comments of Whitford J in *LB (Plastics) Ltd* v *Swish Products Ltd* [1977] FSR 87, 93 ('[i]f in relation to any work, be it literary, dramatic, musical or artistic, the question being asked is, "is this an original work", the answer must depend on whether sufficient skill or labour or talent has gone into it to merit protection under the Act. It is always a question of degree'); and Jacob J in *Ibcos Computers Ltd* v *Barclays Mercantile Highland Finance Ltd* [1994] FSR 275, 290 ('there is no reason why a compilation of computer programs should not itself acquire a separate copyright … it is all a question of degree, just as it is in the case of any other compilation').

[47] [1944] AC 329.

tables for publication. The choice they made, they maintained, showed knowledge and skill and expended labour sufficient to entitle the collection to qualify as an original literary work. The House of Lords rejected the claim on the grounds that insufficient labour had gone in to the selection. Lord MacMillan, for instance, said this:

> The inclusion or exclusion of one or more of the tables constituting the ordinary stock material of the diary-compiler seems to me to involve the very minimum of labour and judgment. As I have said, and as the authorities remind us, the question must always be one of degree and on questions of degree different minds may naturally reach different conclusions. For myself, I should say that, if any compilation could be held to fall short of displaying the qualities requisite to attract copyright, the respondents' collection of seven tables is such a one.[48]

In *Leslie* v *Young & Sons*,[49] the House of Lords rejected a claim to copyright in a local version of a railway timetable. It was observed that the information given was derived from the ordinary railway timetables issued by relevant railway companies and available to everyone. Certainly the claimants' local timetable provided a convenient arrangement of the information for people starting from the particular location of Perth, and was more readable so far as it gave information only in respect of the more prominent stations instead of giving the whole list of stations as they appeared in the timetables issued by the railway companies. But, the House of Lords said, the labour and ingenuity required to produce the local timetable was insufficient to make the timetable the subject matter of a copyright. However, that part of the claimant's work containing information regarding excursions and 'circular tours' was the product of considerable independent labour and thus enjoyed copyright.

In both *Cramp & Sons Ltd* v *Smythson Ltd* and *Leslie* v *Young & Sons* the success of the claim to copyright turned only on the degree of skill and labour exercised in the production of the relevant works. Because such decisions focus on the efforts of the author, they can easily lead to the conclusion that copyright is here given as a reward for those efforts. That, however, is certainly not an inevitable conclusion and indeed I would go further and say that there is evidence that it is a mistaken one. The difficulty is that because subsistence is conditional on a test of originality which examines the author's contribution to a work, this admits the possibility of a claim to copyright being recognized as a desert-based reward or as incentive. The normative argument, based on

---

48 Ibid., 338.

49 [1894] AC 335.

the moral imperative that the unpleasantness of undertaking effort to the individual requires that individual is rewarded by way of a property,[50] is not the only argument that can support a claim to a right based on the exercise of effort. There is an equally strong instrumental argument that supposes that an individual's reluctance to engage in the unpleasantness that is labour can be overcome if there is incentive enough for this to happen. The property right then provides this incentive.[51] It is important to see that these two normative bases as distinct. Jeremy Waldron offers the following a powerful illustration:

> The overall social good is served by senators – keeping in touch with their constituents. But keeping in touch with constituents involves travelling back and forth to one's home state, and that can be dreary and exhausting as well as expensive. Even if senators were given free air travel, they might not do it often enough. So let's suppose we provide them with free first class travel as an incentive: they can now enjoy themselves with free drinks as they fly back and forth between Washington D.C. and North Dakota or wherever. This incentive – the benefit of free first-class travel – might be seen as a necessary reward to the senators for keeping in touch with their constituents. But would we therefore infer that they morally deserve first class travel? Clearly not. Offering the benefit is simply a matter of behavioral manipulation of a class of individuals who have shown that they can be relied on to promote the public interest only when it is made coincident with their own.[52]

In this and the chapter which follows, I intend to demonstrate that in its form and substance, the originality condition serves the public interest, chiefly in channelling the incentive provided by copyright. As a first step in that direction, I want to show that in circumstances where the claimant has reworked material, and typically material in the public domain, a claim to copyright succeeds only if that reworking enhances access, appreciation or otherwise improves the usefulness of the publicly available material. This policy is not always clearly articulated in the judgements, not least of all because it is given effect through the test of originality, that being the only vehicle available to the courts but one which is ill-suited to the task because it is framed in a way that invites

---

[50] On which see Justin Hughes' consideration of the significance of labour in: Hughes, J, 'The Philosophy of Intellectual Property' (1988) 77 Georgetown LJ 287, 303. If we were to attempt to devise some evaluative measure of a law so grounded, then I supposed that this would require comparing the size of the reward with the degree of the author's effort.

[51] Ibid., 303.

[52] Waldron, J, 'From Authors to Copiers: Individual Rights and Social Values in Intellectual Property' (1992–93) 68 Chicago-Kent L Rev 841, 852.

only an examination of the author's contribution to a work. Thus, in the case of compilations the condition of originality is said to be satisfied if skill, labour and judgement has been exercised in the reworking of the material forming the compilation. That the degree of effort expended by an author is not, however, the sole point of focus is revealed by comparing those cases where a claim to copyright fails because the labour required to produce a work is held insufficient, such as *Cramp & Sons Ltd* v *Smythson Ltd* and *Leslie* v *Young & Sons*, with those where a claim fails because, although the claimant can demonstrate the exercise of skill, labour and judgement, this is wrongly directed: it is said to be of 'the wrong kind'. In particular, courts have held that the exercise of skill, labour and judgement merely in the process of copying cannot confer originality.[53] This was so in *Interlego* v *Tyco Industries*.[54] It will be recalled from the previous chapter that the claimants here asserted copyright in engineering drawings of its plastic brick-shaped blocks. The relevant drawings all had the characteristic that they were modifications of and were very largely copies of earlier drawings and represented an updating of the pre-existing designs which incorporated only small (but technically significant) modifications. Their claim to copyright was rejected, Lord Oliver commenting:

> Take the simplest case of artistic copyright, a painting or a photograph. It takes great skill, judgment and labour to produce a good copy by painting or to produce an enlarged photograph from a positive print, but no one would reasonably contend that the copy painting or enlargement was an 'original' artistic work in which the copier is entitled to claim copyright. Skill, labour or judgment merely in the process of copying cannot confer originality ... copying, per se, however much skill or labour may be devoted to the process, cannot make an original work. A well executed tracing is the result of much labour and skill but remains what it is, a tracing.[55]

In *Hyperion Records Ltd* v *Sawkins* the record company pointed to the similarities between the exercise of Dr Sawkins' musical labour and skill and the artistic endeavours of the claimants in *Interlego*. In particular, Hyperion contended that Dr Sawkins had not utilized 'the right kind' of skill and labour to acquire an independent copyright, as he had not

---

[53] Without wishing to labour the point I am not convinced that there is a clear distinction between the skills and judgements involved in for example, attempting to accurately portray a person's face in a drawing where that person is sitting for the artist and attempting the same but working from a photograph.

[54] [1988] RPC 343 and see the account of this case above at p. 163.

[55] [1988] RPC 343, 371–2.

produced original music. Rather he had done no more than reproduce the musical contents of the Lalande source material and the editions in which he claimed copyright were no more than transcriptions of Lalande's music, not involving the creation of new music in the form of notes or sounds. The court rejected this argument noting that none of Lalande's music could have been played or performed by a modern orchestra by using any of the earlier extant Lalande scores.

The difference between these two cases then does not lie in different degrees of effort being expended: in both cases it was accepted that the relevant production required the application of significant skill and labour. Nor does the difference lie in that skill and labour being directed to a transformation of the source material: in both cases the claimants set out to make no more than a faithful reproduction of the earlier work. Where there is a difference is in the fact that that the exercise of skill and labour in *Interlego* was directed to extending an existing monopoly and to this extent restricting public access to the source material[56] whereas Dr Sawkins' skill and effort enhanced the public's access to and appreciation of the music of Lalande (by making Lalande's work more readily performable and recordable). In particular, Jacob LJ observed that Dr Sawkins' efforts had the practical value of making the Lalande's music playable and that the sort of work done by Dr Sawkins should be encouraged as a matter of public policy since it saved others the time and trouble of re-creation of near-lost works, but did not create a monopoly in them.[57]

Of course one could argue that there is a relevant difference linked to the kind of works in issue: that in terms of originality, somehow copying

---

[56] Lord Oliver in *Interlego* observed that copyright,

> confers protection on an original work for a generous period. The prolongation of the period of statutory protection by periodic reproduction of the original work with minor alterations is an operation which requires to be scrutinized with some caution to ensure that that for which protection is claimed really is an original artistic work.

[1988] RPC 343, 372.

[57] *Hyperion Records Ltd* v *Sawkins* [2005] EWCA Civ 565 [85]–[86]. I should add that Jacob LJ doubted that the decision in *Interlego* could be read as standing for the general proposition that there can never be copyright in a copy. Rather he said, 'the true position is that one has to consider the extent to which the "copyist" is a mere copyist – merely performing an easy mechanical function. The more that is so the less is his contribution likely to be taken as "original".': ibid. [82]. For commentary on this aspect of the *Sawkins* decision see Ong, B, 'Originality from Copying: Fitting Recreative Works in the Copyright Universe' (2010) IPQ 165, 188.

an artistic work to produce something visually identical differs from copying a musical work to produce something aurally identical. That seems unlikely and courts do not make this kind of distinction. Thus, the reasoning and outcome in *Sawkins* was heavily influenced by the much earlier decision of the House of Lords in *Walter* v *Lane* which concerned a literary work.[58] In that case the House of Lords held that copyright subsisted in shorthand writers' reports of speeches which had been delivered in public when reporters were present. The reporters made notes in shorthand, transcribed them, corrected, revised and punctuated them. The reporters were held to be the authors of the published verbatim reports of the speeches so produced. The Court of Appeal in *Sawkins* observed that these reports has been held by the House of Lords to be 'original' literary works, even though the intention of the reporters was to produce as accurate a report as possible of a work of which they were not the authors. Citing the speech of Lord Halsbury in particular, the Court of Appeal noted that the House of Lords had reasoned that the law did not permit a person to make profit and appropriate to himself the labour skill and capital of another.[59] However, the House of Lords in *Walter* v *Lane* also reasoned that the public benefit anchored the claim to copyright in the reports. Lord Halsbury, for instance, and drawing an analogy with patent law, suggested that those who preserve the memory of spoken words, of value to the public, are entitled to a merit analogous to that attributed to the importer of foreign inventions.[60] In this, it is possible that the court was influenced by a vestigial memory of the Statute of Anne 1710: 'an Act for the Encouragement of Learning'.[61]

The assertion that copyright can only subsist in a copy of an existing work if that copy somehow enhances access, appreciation or otherwise improves the usefulness of the copied work serves to explain the apparent paradox implicit in the test for originality of photographic copies. As pointed out by Lord Oliver in *Interlego*, an individual who, with brushes,

[58] *Walter* v *Lane* [1900] AC 539. In *Hyperion Records Ltd* v *Sawkins*, the decision in *Walter* v *Lane* was heavily relied upon by Mummery LJ but rather less so by Jacob LJ: [2005] EWCA Civ 565 [33]–[36].

[59] *Hyperion Records Ltd* v *Sawkins* [2005] EWCA Civ 565 [35] referring to the speech of Lord Halsbury in *Walter* v *Lane* [1900] AC 539, 545 and 547.

[60] *Walter* v *Lane* [1900] AC 539, 549 and see also the speech of Lord James, 555. Note also the comments of Lord Atkinson in *MacMillan* v *Cooper* (1924) 40 TLR 186. For commentary see: Pila, J, 'Compilation Copyright: A Matter Calling for "a certain … sobriety"' Oxford Legal Research Paper Series, Paper No. 45/2008, November 2008, accessed 1 February 2017 at https://papers.ssrn.com/sol3/papers.cfm?abstract_id=1299012, 11; and Ong, above n.57, 176.

[61] An objective then repeated in the Sculpture Acts of 1798 and 1814.

paint and canvas, produces a good copy of an existing painting does not thereby produce an original artistic work notwithstanding the skill, judgement and labour involved: the copy is not 'original'.[62] If, however, the copyist comes armed with a camera rather than the tools of the painter, then the outcome is different. In terms of what is original, for the purpose of determining whether copyright subsists in a photograph, the requirement of originality has traditionally been set low, demanding little more than the opportunistic pointing of the camera and the pressing of the shutter button.[63] The distinction is hard to justify in terms only of the skill and labour involved. Certainly it can be argued that the photographer exercises judgement in matters such as the angle from which to take the photograph, the lighting, the correct film speed and what filter to use and so on[64] or that creativity consists precisely in the fidelity with which the photograph reproduces the impression created by the original.[65] But such observations hardly explain why the painter's efforts do not count whereas the photographer's do. The real difference is that the photographer's efforts count because a photograph of an existing work can serve to enhance access and appreciation of the copied work whereas the painter's efforts cannot. For the great majority of us, exposure to works of art comes initially and perhaps only through viewing photographic

---

[62] C.f. Jacob LJ in *Hyperion Records Ltd* v *Sawkins* [2005] EWCA Civ 565 [79]–[82] (citing in support the authors of the *Modern Law of Copyright*).

[63] *Antiquesportfolio.com Plc* v *Rodney Fitch & Co Ltd* [2001] FSR 23 citing *Copinger and Skone James on Copyright*, 14th edition (Sweet & Maxwell, 1999) at para 3.104. Mark Rose pertinently observes that, 'because copyright is conceived as protecting original works of authorship, the products of new technologies such as photography must be represented as the work of authors in order to be brought under its umbrella'. He goes on to note that 'in the discourse of copyright … the goal of protecting the rights of the creative author is proudly asserted even as the notion of author is drained of content': Rose, M, *Authors and Owners: The Invention of Copyright* (Harvard University Press, 1993), 136.

[64] *Antiquesportfolio.com Plc* v *Rodney Fitch & Co Ltd* [2001] FSR 23. Note now C-145/10 *Painer* v *Standard Verlags GmbH* [2012] ECDR 6 [91] ('in the preparation phase, the photographer can choose the background, the subject's pose and the lighting. When taking a portrait photograph, he can choose the framing, the angle of view and the atmosphere created. Finally, when selecting the snapshot, the photographer may choose from a variety of developing techniques the one he wishes to adopt or, where appropriate, use computer software').

[65] See e.g. Landes, W and Posner, R, 'An Economic Analysis of Copyright' (1989) 18(2) Journal of Legal Studies 325, 357. Note also Ong, above n.57, 167.

reproductions of those works. It would take a lifetime and very considerable resources to see all the original works contained in a typical 'coffee table' published edition.[66] Unlike the photographer, the painter copyist enhances public access and appreciation hardly at all.

It could be argued that the requirement that a work originate from the author, reduced to the question of whether a work is copied or not, brings with it the implicit demand that skill, labour and judgement be exercised in the production of a work.[67] From this standpoint, asking whether a work is copied is in effect a convenient shorthand way of deciding whether making it called for the exercise of skill, labour and judgement. Leaving aside the point that if this is so then the decision in *Interlego* is rather hard to explain,[68] the much greater problem with the argument is that copying and the exercise of skill and effort are manifestly not opposites. Given the character of the subject matter protected by copyright (broadly 'the arts'), if 'not copied' is understood as convenient shorthand way of demanding anything, then it is surely that the work is new.[69] If I take a paint brush and casually scrawl a few lines across a

---

[66] The authors of one of the leading practitioner texts extend the argument to all photographs observing that merit can lie in capturing a scene that is unlikely to occur again: May, C, Onslow, R, Lane, L, Whyte, J, Clark, F, Alexander QC, D, Tappin QC, M, Vitoria QC, M, Berkeley, I and Speck QC, A, *Laddie, Prescott and Vitoria: The Modern Law of Copyright and Designs*, 4th edition (Butterworths, 2011), 254. Without wanting to fully argue the point, there is perhaps here a parallel in the arguments advanced as to why naturally occurring products if artificially synthesized in a way that makes them available for practical use count as 'novel' for the purposes of patent law: see e.g. the decision of the EPO Opposition Division in *Howard Florey Institute/Relaxin*, Decision of the Opposition Division 8 December 1994 (OJ EPO, 1995, 388).

[67] For instance see Ong, above n.57, 170–71.

[68] Though it may well be an aberrant decision. Ong suggests that the dicta in *Interlego* need to be understood in the narrow factual context of that case and 'should not be taken as unqualified statements of broad principle': Ong, above n.57, 172. So too Jacob LJ in *Hyperion Records Ltd* v *Sawkins* [2005] EWCA Civ 565 [79]–[82]. I disagree.

[69] Of course there is no actual inquiry into the novelty of what is produced but that is because it is not necessary. As observed by Learned Hand J in *Sheldon* v *Metro-Goldwyn Pictures Corp*, 'if by *some magic* a man who had never known it were to compose anew Keats's Ode on a Grecian Urn, he would be an "author," and, if he copyrighted it, others might not copy that poem, though they might of course copy Keats's': 81 F2d 49 (2d Cir. 1936), 54 (emphasis added). There is some historical support for the view that copyright law and doctrine embodies an implicit novelty condition so far as the requirement of originality was first introduced expressly into UK copyright law in the Sculpture Copyright

substrate it will not be copied but there will be little if any skill or effort involved. Yet it can be said with some confidence that the painting so produced will be objectively new.[70] Not so of course if, with the same tools, I copy with fidelity an existing painting, though the skill in making such a copy is considerably greater than that involved in the daubing.

From my perspective, a more important point is that this argument overlooks the importance of form. Whatever claims may be made as to the correspondence of the substantive demands placed on authors by the two tests for originality, it cannot be denied that in form they are different: one is a simple rule; one a standard. Put another way, the scheme that is in place invites us to consider why we have a 'shorthand' test at all and why sometimes we don't. The reasoning and the outcomes of the cases on originality go some way to support Kennedy's thesis that the rule form is associated with individualism and the standard form with altruism. In all cases, a claim to copyright in a work requires the claimant to show that the work is original and this on the face of it describes the author's contribution to the creation of the work. Normally it is sufficient for the work to originate from the author in the sense of not being copied. The test, 'not copied' is a rule and is clearly associated with securing the claims of right holders. On the other hand, the standard form of the originality test, which looks to the degree of skill, labour and judgement exercised in producing the work, is much more clearly associated with facilitating public access: with seeing copyright as encouraging individuals to direct their labour for the benefit of others.[71] I explore the

---

Act 1814 and which protected 'any new and original sculpture, or model, or copy, or cast'.

[70] This would be true even if, rather than attempt something so abstract, I set out to portray a commonly portrayed object or person. For instance, all of the portraits of the current monarch are manifestly representations of the same woman but none is so alike as to be indistinguishable from another. As observed by Oliver Wendell Holmes J on the portraits painted by Velazquez and Whistler,

> others may try their hand on the same face. Others are free to copy the original. They are not free to copy the copy. The copy is the personal reaction of an individual upon nature. Personality always contains something unique. It expresses its singularity even in handwriting, and a very modest grade of art has in it something irreducible, which is one man's alone. That something he may copyright.

Bleistein v *Donaldson Lithographing Co* 188 US 239 (1903), 249–50.

[71] As will be demonstrated in the following chapter, these expectations are a key element in those justificatory theories that draw on Immanuel Kant's view of rights to property being essential for achieving personal autonomy.

correspondence between formal and substantive economic arguments more fully in the final chapter.

If we hope to understand how the political paradigms of individualism and altruism compete for influence within copyright law then, as I explained in the preceding chapter, it would be wrong to divorce the question of whether a work is original from the question of whether it is infringed.[72] Whether a substantial part of a claimant's work has been copied is a test that is standard-like in form being a matter of impression based on the quality of what has been taken rather than the quantity. The question then is whether the test for infringement, as a standard, also manifests a commitment to altruism?

What then is required to establish infringement? The Copyright Designs and Patents Act provides little by way of concrete guidance in this respect. The exclusive rights of the copyright owner (the so-called 'acts restricted by copyright') are laid out in section 16(1) and include for instance the right to copy the work. Section 16(2) goes on to provide that copyright is infringed by a person who without the licence of the copyright owner does, or authorizes another to do, any of the acts restricted by the copyright. Crucially, the Act makes clear that a defendant does not need to copy all of the work for this to count as infringement. Rather, section 16(3) provides that references to the doing of an act restricted by the copyright in a work are: 'to the doing of it … in relation to the work as a whole or any substantial part of it …'

Although the precise formulation of the test applied by courts has varied, courts have repeatedly stressed that what is protected from appropriation is the skill, judgement and labour which goes into the

---

[72] Expressly recognized by Mummery LJ in *Hyperion Records Ltd* v *Sawkins* when he said that,

> the important point is that copyright can be used to prevent copying of a substantial part of the relevant form of expression, but it does not prevent use of the information, thoughts or emotions expressed in the copyright work. It does not prevent another person from coincidentally creating a similar work by his own independent efforts. It is not an intellectual property monopoly in the same sense as a patent or a registered design. There is no infringement of copyright in the absence of a direct or indirect causal link between the copyright work and the alleged copy. Thus, if the claim of Dr Sawkins to copyright in the performing editions were upheld, that would not prevent other musicologists, composers, performers or record companies from copying Lalande's music directly or indirectly or from making fresh performing editions of their own.

[2005] EWCA Civ 565 [29]–[30].

production of a work. For instance, Lord Scott in *Designer Guild Ltd v Russell Williams (Textiles) Ltd* stated that it was an underlying principle of copyright law that a copier is not at liberty to appropriate the benefit of another's skill and labour.[73]

It is important to appreciate, however, that what flexibility there is in deciding whether what has been done amounts to an infringement is not typically (if ever) judged according some meaning of 'originality' or indeed to its components of 'skill and labour'. This is a necessary consequence of the test of originality being a rule. If there is no serious argument to be had as to whether a work originated from the claimant (i.e. that it has not been copied) then that is that; the work is deemed original and implicitly to have involved the exercise of skill and labour. Thus in most cases courts take for granted the boundaries of the work and that the work as a whole is protected.[74] What discretion there is arises in the way in which courts give effect to the legislative direction that a defendant's actions must relate to a substantial part of a work to count. Thus Lord Scott in *Designer Guild Ltd v Russell Williams (Textiles) Ltd* went on to say that in deciding whether there had been an infringement it was useful to ask whether, 'the infringer [has] incorporated a substantial part of the independent skill, labour etc. contributed by the original author in creating the copyright work ...'[75]

It follows that merely showing that a defendant has copied part of a work and in so doing made use of the skill and labour of a claimant, whilst necessary, is not sufficient to establish infringement.[76] Whilst the original purpose may have been to enhance rights by allowing copyright

---

[73] To the same effect and frequently cited is a passage from the speech of Lord Hoffmann in *Newspaper Licensing Agency* v *Marks & Spencer* [2001] UKHL 38 [19] and on which see below at p. 213.

[74] Bently and Sherman, above n.1, 203.

[75] *Designer Guild Ltd* v *Russell Williams (Textiles) Ltd* [2001] FSR 113 [64] citing Laddie, H, Prescott, P and Vitoria, M, *Laddie, Prescott and Vitoria: The Modern Law of Copyright and Designs*, 2nd edition (Butterworths, 1975). In the same case Lord Bingham observed that,

> [t]he law of copyright rests on a very clear principle: that anyone who by his or her own skill and labour creates an original work of whatever character shall, for a limited period, enjoy an exclusive right to copy that work. No one else may for a season reap what the copyright owner has sown.

[2001] FSR 113 [2]. See also *Krisarts SA* v *Briarfine Ltd* [1977] FSR 557, 561–2; *Cantor Fitzgerald International* v *Tradition (UK) Ltd* [2000] RPC 95, 132; and *Baigent* v *Random House Group* [2007] EWCA Civ 247 [6].

[76] At least this was the position before the changes effected by the Information Society Directive and the interpretation afforded that by the CJEU in

owners to restrain the activities of unscrupulous copyists who sought to escape liability by introducing minor variations into an otherwise copied work,[77] the notion of substantial taking has been more notably effective in restricting rather than extending rights. So for instance, until recently courts often took the view that to infringe, the part taken had to be essential, vital or important to count as 'substantial'.[78]

The way in which the notion of substantial taking operates to limit copyright's scope is particularly manifest in those cases where a defendant has blatantly copied and undoubtedly taken advantage of the claimant's skill and labour but chiefly in the sense of extracting ideas from the claimant's work. Copyright, it has been said, protects the detail with which ideas are presented.[79] The more abstract and simple the copied idea, the less likely it is to constitute a substantial part of the work in which it is expressed.[80] The reason advanced for this is that, at a certain level of abstraction, an idea, though expressed in a work does not represent sufficient of the author's skill and labour as to attract copyright protection.[81] There are many examples of the kind of test involved. In the *Designer Guild* case itself, Lord Hoffmann was of the view that the mere notion of combining stripes and flowers in a design of wallpaper would not have amounted to a substantial part of the claimant designer's work.

Such decisions can easily lead to the conclusion that the test for copyright infringement is chiefly concerned with ensuring that authors receive a just reward for the exercise of their skill and labour. Protection is thus denied only where there is insufficient effort on the author's part.[82] On the other hand, as Jonathan Griffiths pertinently observes, 'in

---

C-5/08 *Infopaq International* v *Danske Dagblades Forening*, on which see above at p. 93.

[77] See Bently and Sherman, above n.1, 195.

[78] Ibid., 199 (citing as an example Slesser LJ in *Hawkes* v *Paramount* [1934] 1 ChD 593, 606).

[79] *Designer Guild Ltd* v *Russell Williams (Textiles) Ltd* [2001] FSR 113 [26].

[80] Ibid.

[81] As Drahos observes, 'judgments of identity and recognition lie at the heart of infringement issues in intellectual property …' Conclusions, he observes, 'are underpinned by a complex dynamic of social, psychological and ideological factors' and 'judges are necessarily involved in a process of abstraction in which they … create the abstract object that then form the basis of their … judgement': Drahos, above n.2, 154. See also Griffiths, J, 'Dematerialization, Pragmatism and the European Copyright Revolution' (2013) 33 OJLS 767.

[82] This accords with Landes and Posner's economic analysis and their assertion that the costs involved in coming up with the kind of new idea normally

reality, a designer's labour and skill will not necessarily be expended on the detail of a work rather than on its more general conception. Sometimes it may be but, on other occasions, it may not'.[83] And as Lord Hoffmann himself observed in *Designer Guild Ltd* v *Russell Williams (Textiles) Ltd*:

> the original elements in the plot of a play or novel may be a substantial part, so that copyright may be infringed by a work which does not reproduce a single sentence of the original. If one asks what is being protected in such a case, it is difficult to give any answer except that it is an idea expressed in the copyright work.[84]

Rather the operation of the test for infringement is concerned with limiting the scope of copyright in a way that ensures that at least some of what the author has done is available to others. That policy is particularly clear in the way in which courts have drawn a distinction between ideas and expression in two classes of case: those claiming infringement of literary works that are not works of fiction; and those claiming infringement of artistic works where the defendants have blatantly copied and undoubtedly taken advantage of the claimant's skill and labour but chiefly in extracting information from a claimant's work.

As to the former, the policy that the test for infringement is concerned with limiting the scope of copyright arguably manifests itself in those cases where the literary work contains a set of instructions for making something. I say arguably because the policy is obscured because judges can reason by reference to the difference between a thing and the

---

embodied in an expressive work usually are low relative to the costs in time and effort of expressing the idea: Landes and Posner, above n.65, at 348. However, these authors clearly do not attach much to the notion of 'idea' as it applies in the arts insofar as they express the view that, '[w]hat passes for "ideas" in the case of most expressive writing normally is not comparable to the sort of inventions, costly to develop, that receive protection under the patent laws'.: ibid., at 350. Justin Hughes expresses much the same view when he observes that,

> [p]rotection of expression and not of ideas can be understood as protection for that part of the idea-making process that we are most confident involves labor. In a world in which we cannot definitely separate idea and execution, we still find ways to emphasize that property protection goes to execution and less to the ideas themselves.

Hughes, above n.50, 314.

83 Griffiths, above n.81, 774.

84 *Designer Guild Ltd* v *Russell Williams (Textiles) Ltd* [2001] FSR 113 [24].

representation of that thing so avoiding finer distinctions between ideas and the expression of ideas. For instance, in *Foley* v *Ellot*[85] it was held that there was no infringement of copyright in knitting guides[86] by making garments according to the instructions therein. Megarry VC thought it quite plain:

> that there is no reproduction of the words and numerals in the knitting guides in the knitted garments produced by following the instructions. The essence, I think, of a reproduction (and I do not attempt to be exhaustive) is that the reproduction should be some copy of or representation of the original.[87]

In finding for the defendants on this point he might equally have said that the skill and labour that the claimants invested in the design of the garments was 'not of the right kind'. More clear then, are cases where the copyright work and alleged infringement are the same type of work. In *Baigent* v *Random House Group*, the authors of a low-brow history book claimed their work had been copied by the author of a best-selling fictional work that adopted similar themes. Mummery LJ observed that:

> it takes time, effort and skill to conduct historical research, to collect materials for a book, to decide what facts are established by the evidence and to formulate arguments, theories, hypotheses, propositions and conclusions. It does not, however, follow … that the use of items of information, fact and so on derived from the assembled material is, in itself, 'a substantial part' of [a claimant's work] simply because it has taken time skill and effort to carry out the necessary research.
>
> … Original expression includes not only the language in which the work is composed but also the original selection, arrangement and compilation of the raw research material. It does not, however, extend to clothing information, facts, ideas, theories and themes with exclusive property rights, so as to enable … claimants to monopolise historical research or knowledge and prevent the legitimate use of historical and biographical material, theories propounded, general arguments deployed, or general hypotheses suggested (whether they are sound or not) or general themes written about.[88]

---

85 [1982] RPC 433.

86 Pieces of paper with various words and numerals on them which constitute detailed instructions intelligible to anyone who understands the production of knitwear.

87 [1982] RPC 433, 434.

88 [2007] EWCA Civ 247 [155]–[156]

In *Ravenscroft* v *Herbert*[89] Brightman J called upon to decide whether the literary copyright in a published account of the history of a spear (part of the Hapsburg treasure in the Hofburg Museum in Vienna) was infringed in a fictional account of the post-war fate of the spear, accepted that:

> a historical work is not to be judged by precisely the same standards as a work of fiction. The purpose of a novel is usually to interest the reader and to contribute to his enjoyment of his leisure. A historical work may well have that purpose, but the author of a serious and original historical work may properly be assumed by his readers to have another purpose as well, namely to add to the knowledge possessed by the reader and perhaps in the process to increase the sum total of human experience and understanding. The author of a historical work must, I think, have attributed to him an intention that the information thereby imparted may be used by the reader, because knowledge would become sterile if it could not be applied. Therefore, it seems to me reasonable to suppose that the law of copyright will allow a wider use to be made of a historical work than of a novel so that knowledge can be built upon knowledge.[90]

On the facts, Brightman J nevertheless found there to have been an infringement. There has been a wholesale pillaging of not only theme but also incident and language. Importantly from our perspective, Brightman observed that the claimant's work was rather idiosyncratic, disjointed and unmethodical, and a very personal insight into history.[91] To this extent the claimant could not be said to be clothing information, facts, ideas, theories and themes with exclusive property rights. As illustrated by the decision in *Ravenscroft* and notwithstanding the generality of the statements made both in that case and in *Baigent*, courts have not adopted the simple position that copyright in a non-fictional literary work is never infringed if all that is taken is the theme or 'plot'. Rather it is always a question of degree.[92]

The other type of case where it is clear that the test for infringement operates to limit the scope of copyright involves artistic works and claims that the defendants have taken key information from the work. An example is *Catnic Components Ltd* v *Hill and Smith Ltd.*[93] The claimants

89 [1980] RPC 193.

90 [1980] RPC 193, 206.

91 [1980] RPC 193, 203 and 205.

92 On which see the comments of Pumfrey J in *Sandman* v *Panasonic* [1998] FSR 651, 662. Note also the decision in *Elanco Products* v *Mandops* [1979] FSR 46.

93 [1982] RPC 183.

here were manufacturers of steel lintels of a novel design for use in the building industry. The defendants, intending to enter the market, examined the brochure issued by the claimants and copied it by making their own drawings and then manufacturing lintels in accordance with the design recorded in the claimants' brochure. The claimants contended that their design of lintel embodied a novel idea the development of which had involved much skill and labour on their part, and that by taking that idea the defendants had taken advantage of that skill and labour which had been embodied in the brochure drawings and, because of its intrinsic importance, had constituted a substantial part of the brochure drawings. The Court of Appeal rejected this argument holding that there had been no infringement of copyright in the claimants' artistic work. Buckley LJ, whilst accepting that it was the quality rather than the quantity of the part taken that mattered in deciding whether there had been an infringement, observed that what was protected by copyright was the claimants' 'artistic work' as such and not any information which it may be designed to convey. He continued:

> If it is said that a substantial part of it has been reproduced, whether that part can properly be described as substantial may depend upon how important that part is to the recognition and appreciation of the 'artistic work'. If an 'artistic work' is designed to convey information, the importance of some part of it may fall to be judged by how far it contributes to conveying that information, but not, in my opinion, by how important the information may be which it conveys or helps to convey. What is protected is the skill and labour devoted to making the 'artistic work' itself, not the skill and labour devoted to developing some idea or invention communicated or depicted by the 'artistic work'.[94]

To similar effect, in *Rose Plastics GmbH* v *William Beckett & Co (Plastics) Ltd*, Whitford J held that the defendants could not be said to have copied a substantial part of the claimant's design drawings by copying a visually insignificant feature that recorded a technically important aspect of the claimant's product,[95] whilst the Court of Appeal in *Johnstone Safety Ltd* v *Peter Cook (Int) Plc* observed that a claim that a substantial part of a work has been taken was not made more potent by demonstrating that the part, in functional terms, was an important design feature.[96]

---

[94] Ibid., 223. See also *Burke and Margot Burke Ltd* v *Spicers Dress Designs* [1936] Ch 400, 406.

[95] [1989] FSR 113, 123.

[96] [1990] FSR 161, 177.

The decisions in *Catnic Components* and *Rose Plastics* both use the vehicle of 'substantial taking' to make the distinction between ideas and the expression of ideas. In both cases the defendants had taken ideas which, whilst expressed by drawings, were not artistic ideas. Rather the ideas were of a functional character directed to solving particular technical problems. These decisions then can be seen as attempts by courts to define and limit the application of copyright to subject matter within the territory that they consider properly the province of patent law.[97] But the dichotomy between ideas and protectable expression as it is manifested in the test for substantial taking has been used by courts more generally in such a way as to set the merit in recognizing an individual claim against the cost of thereby restraining access to what may be called the building blocks of culture, communication, innovation, creativity and expression.[98] So, in addition to considering how far an infringement claim might limit access to functional ideas, courts have also considered how particular claims to copyright, if upheld, would impact on matters such as techniques, methods and styles.[99]

In all these cases courts are engaged in a balancing exercise. The upshot is that sometimes an infringement claim will succeed; in other instances it will not. Outside the most routine instances of total and unaltered copying, whether copyright is infringed is judged according to

---

97 As observed by Lord Hoffmann, 'a literary work which describes a system or invention does not entitle the author to claim protection for his system or invention as such. The same is true of an inventive concept expressed in an artistic work. However striking or original it may be, others are (in the absence of patent protection) free to express it in works of their own': *Designer Guild Ltd* v *Russell Williams (Textiles) Ltd* [2001] FSR 113 [25].

98 As expressed by Bently and Sherman, above n.1, 214.

99 See e.g. the comments of Laddie J in *IPC Media* v *Highbury Leisure* [2004] EWHC 2985 [14] concerning a claim to 'design, subject matter, theme and presentational style' of a magazine. See also *Jones* v *London Borough of Tower Hamlets* [2001] RPC 379 (claim to an architectural style). In relation to computer programs, courts have rejected claims to the 'business logic' (in effect the detailed function or functions that the program performs) notwithstanding that this is a necessary step in the production of a computer program and one that typically involves considerable skill, effort and judgement, on which see in particular *Navitaire Inc* v *Easy Jet Airline* [2005] EWHC 0282 (Ch) and note also *Nova Productions Ltd* v *Mazooma Games Ltd* [2006] EWHC 24 (Ch) and [2007] EWCA Civ 219. Landes and Posner argue that technique is harder to copy well than a work embodying the technique and with copies likely to be costly, slow to appear and imperfect, the originator of a technique will be able to recoup his fixed costs even if he has no property right in the technique: Landes and Posner, above n.65, 353.

a standard. So for instance, and despite what was said and decided in *Catnic Components* and *Rose Plastics*, one cannot say that there can never be copyright in a functional idea. Jacob J in *Ibcos Computers Ltd* v *Barclays Mercantile Highland Finance Ltd*, commenting on those cases where a claim to copyright might be said to be an attempt to protect functional ideas, rejected the simple proposition that, 'if there is only one way of expressing an idea that way is not the subject of copyright' and said rather that:

> The true position is that where an 'idea' is sufficiently general, then even if an original work embodies it, the mere taking of that idea will not infringe. But if the 'idea' is detailed, then there may be infringement. It is a question of degree. The same applies whether the work is functional or not, and whether visual or literary.[100]

Whilst in *Sandman* v *Panasonic*, Pumfrey J dismissed as unhelpful the kind of a priori approach embodied in the general proposition that copyright protects only embodiments of a principle, not the principle itself which can be protected, if at all, by a patent.[101] And more generally, Laddie J observed in *IPC Media* v *Highbury Leisure* that it is impossible to define the boundary between mere taking of general concepts and ideas on the one hand and copying in the copyright sense on the other.[102]

How far copyright protects 'ideas' then is always a question of degree regardless of the nature of the idea. Certainly the claimed subject matter must be the product of the claimant's skill and labour and certainly it must have been copied by the defendant. But it is never enough simply to show that a particular work is original and the defendant has copied some aspect of the claimant's original work.[103] Whether there has been

---

[100] [1994] FSR 275. This understanding needs re-evaluating in light of the decision of the European Court in *Bezpečnostní softwarová asociace – Svaz softwarové ochrany* v *Ministerstvo kultury* [2011] ECDR 3 on which see below at p. 221.

[101] [1998] FSR 651, 661–2.

[102] [2004] EWHC 2985 (Ch) [14].

[103] Although copying is an essential element in infringement to provide a causal connection between the claimant's work and the alleged infringement, it does not follow that any copying will infringe. Indeed whilst the well-known rough practical test, 'that what is worth copying is prima facie worth protecting' (*University of London Press Ltd* v *University Tutorial Press Ltd* [1916] 2 Ch 601, 610) remains frequently cited, nowadays this typically done to illustrate how not to approach the question of infringement. Jacob J, for instance, in *Ibcos Computers Ltd* v *Barclays Mercantile Highland Finance Ltd* observed that the aphorism, if taken literally,

copyright infringement cannot be reduced to a simple rule-like formula.[104] In all of these cases, we again see how the political paradigms of individualism and altruism map on to and influence form. The test for infringement by substantial taking implements the idea/expression dichotomy by way of a standard because it looks to the impact of the property claim on the freedom of others.[105] It is for this reason that Lord Hoffmann's dicta in *Newspaper Licensing Agency* v *Marks & Spencer* must be treated with caution when he said that:

> the question of substantiality is a matter of quality rather than quantity ... But what quality is one looking for? That question, as it seems to me, must be answered by reference to the reason why the work is given copyright protection. In literary copyright, for example, copyright is conferred (irrespective of literary merit) upon an original literary work. It follows that the quality relevant for the purpose of substantiality is the literary originality of that which has been copied ...[106]

Neither as a description nor as a normative statement is this account complete. Although it identifies the basis of an author's claim, it fails to

---

> would mean that all a plaintiff ever had to do was to prove copying. Originality, appropriate subject matter for copyright and a taking of a substantial part would all be proved in one go. One would not need the Act if the aphorism represented the law. It proves too much.

[1994] FSR 275, 289. See also the decision of Pumfrey J in *Cantor Fitzgerald International* v *Tradition (UK) Ltd* [2000] RPC 95, 133.

[104] Thus in *Cantor Fitzgerald International* v *Tradition (UK) Ltd,* Pumfrey J held that copyright protection could extend to a computer program's 'architecture' if a substantial part of the programmer's skill, labour and judgement went into it. The term 'architecture', he said, in the relevant sense (what he called 'functional architecture'), referred to the overall structure of the system of operation of the program at a very high level of abstraction (i.e. matters such as the information stored and the operations carried out on that information): [2000] RPC 95, 134. Note also *Jones* v *London Borough of Tower Hamlets* [2001] RPC 407 ('conflicting answers could without error be given to the questions – is that plan or house only a copy of the concept or style of the original and hence legitimate, or is it a copy of the author's manifestation of that concept or style and hence an infringement?').

[105] Bently and Sherman say that, 'the exclusion of ideas from the scope of protection is an important judicial technique that is used to reconcile the divergent interests of copyright owners with those of users, creators, and the public more generally': Bently and Sherman, above n.1, 213.

[106] [2001] UKHL 38 [19]. For criticism see Griffiths, above n.81, particularly at 775–9.

articulate the interests ranged on the other side which, in the context of infringement, go to defining the scope of the claim.

We are left with the question of why it is that the dichotomy between ideas and expression has been most keenly felt in the test for whether copyright has been infringed rather than in the test for whether a claimed work is original. The reason, I would argue, is that, as with the recognition and exercise of any legal right, balancing competing interests (whether public or private) figures in decision making. Because there is no rivalry in the consumption of the abstract objects that are the subject of intellectual property, they are capable of 'universal accessibility' and the exercise of an intellectual property right thus has the capacity to interfere with the freedoms of others in a way that is far greater than the exercise of a property right relating to some physical object.[107]

In the case of copyright, identifying the interests that are at stake *ex ante* is extremely challenging given the hugely diverse social contexts into which copyright law reaches. The creation and use of the kind of subject matter covered by copyright law (let us say 'the arts') tends not to be carried out in identifiable and discrete social contexts and still less in identifiable social institutions (whether formal or informal). This is partly because of the diversity of the subject matter covered by copyright law, both within classes of protected subject matter and in the range of classes, and partly because, within 'the arts', what social institutions there are tend towards the informal. The landscape of creation and use in the arts is not one which will, with time, tend towards predictable stable relationships. If it ever were, information technology and the impact of the internet have made that outcome even less likely.[108]

---

107 See Drahos, above n.2, 211.

108 The 2011 Hargreaves Review for instance, observed that,

> digital technology is probably the most important and transformative technology of our time … and has pushed content and communication technology into new uses, meaning the IP system has become part of people's daily lives. This has transformed us all into regular, if not daily, copyright creators …

Hargreaves, I, *Digital Opportunity. A Review of Intellectual Property and Growth*, May 2011, accessed 24 January 2017 at http://webarchive.nationalarchives.gov.uk/20140603093549/http://www.ipo.gov.uk/ipreview.htm, [1.17]. The Australian Law Reform Commission, in its report on *Copyright and the Digital Economy*, recommended the adoption of a 'fair use' exception precisely because, as a standard rather than a rule, it is more flexible and better able to adapt to new technologies: ALRC Report 122, 2013, at 4.39, accessed 1 February 2017 at http://www.alrc.gov.au/publications/copyright-report-122.

So far as the UK is concerned, the solution has been for interests to be typically defined by way of a process that pitches an individual right against an individual correlative duty.[109] In most cases an author knowing the history of production of a particular work can be confident that the work in which they are claiming to enjoy copyright is original (in the more usual sense of 'originality' meaning only 'not copied'). But the right so gained is concrete only insofar as it secures for the originator of the work a right to bring an action at law. The precise contours of the right are defined only when the claimed right is exercised with a view to restraining the actions of an alleged infringer.[110] This provides adjudicators with an important and useful perspective. As observed by Jeremy Waldron:

> legal duties are hard things for people to have – since they constrain conduct and in that sense limit freedom – we should expect the realm of duties to be the testing ground for claims of right. The realm of duties – the propositions about duty that a given claim of right entails – is where we should expect the problems with the right (if there are any) to surface. It is true that not all the problems of a legal institution are connected with the duties it imposes. But the duties are a good place to start, since they will take us to whatever hardships are most intimately involved in the immediate recognition and enforcement of the rights.[111]

In UK copyright law, the realm of duties traditionally has indeed been the testing ground for claims of right in an approach in which claims are assessed in the context of deciding whether copyright in a work has been infringed.

For all its strength, there is a risk to this approach, especially in a common law system. Without care such an approach risks fact-specific

---

[109] Hohfeld, W N, *Fundamental Legal Conceptions as Applied in Judicial Reasoning* (1913) 23 Yale LJ 16. For Hohfeld, a right was a claim for which there was a correlative duty. Property relations are arguably core examples of the right/duty correlativity thesis: Drahos, above n.2, 148. One advantage of this analytical scheme is that it exposes how far the exercise of a property right directs the actions of others. It is for this reason that Drahos observes that the, 'rights, powers, privileges and immunities of the property holder can be thought of as being in microcosm the structural analogue of the sovereign's power to regulate conduct through commands, prohibitions and permissions': ibid., 148.

[110] Most obviously in an infringement action, but also in for example licence negotiations or in disputes over the ownership of rights such as between business partners; employers and employees; and commissioners and commissioned.

[111] Waldron, above n.52, 844. See also Dworkin, R, *Taking Rights Seriously* (Harvard University Press, 1977), 194.

elements that relate to the behaviour of a particular defendant generating general norms that relate to the right in issue. The risk is that a 'good' duty is seen as one that does not allow or encourage bad behaviour. The aphorism, 'what is worth copying is worth protecting', is a prime example in that it suggests the normative basis for according rights is that it is wrong to copy. This is no doubt what concerned Laddie J in *Autospin (Oil Seals) Ltd* v *Beehive Spinning* when he said:

> many copyright cases involve defendants who have blatantly stolen the result of the plaintiff's labours. This has led courts, sometimes with almost evangelical fervour, to apply the commandment 'thou shalt not steal'. If that has necessitated pushing the boundaries of copyright protection further out, then that has been done. This has resulted in a body of case law on copyright which, in some of its further reaches, would come as a surprise to the draughtsmen of the legislation to which it is supposed to give effect.[112]

In an adversarial system claimants in advancing their case can be expected to draw attention to any morally doubtful behaviour on the part of the defendants. As suggested by Laddie J, sometimes judges look sympathetically on such arguments; at other times they do not.[113] The tensions at play were nicely encapsulated by Hoffmann J in *Billhöfer Maschinenfabrik* v *Dixon* when he said that, '[i]n these matters the law must strike a balance. On the one hand, wholesale copying is not fair competition. On the other hand, all technological progress depends upon the adaptation and improvement of other people's ideas. Not everyone may agree about where the line should be drawn …'[114]

---

[112] [1995] RPC 683, 700. Note also the comments of Whitford J in *Davis (J&S) Holdings* v *Wright Health Group*, who observed that,

> [o]ver the years, in the absence of any developed law of unfair competition in this country, the words to be found in the various sections of the Copyright Act have been extended by judicial decision, sometimes followed by statutory redefinition to a point where their meaning bears very little relation to the meaning which those not familiar with the law would give to these words.

[1988] RPC 403, 410.

[113] So for instance in *MacMillan* v *Cooper* (1924) 40 TLR 186, Lord Atkinson said that an infringer of copyright disobeyed the injunction 'thou shalt not steal'. In contrast, Lord Templeman in *CBS Songs* v *Amstrad*, observing that a claimant's rights derive from statute and not from the Ten Commandments, said that such a consideration could not enhance the rights of owners of copyright or extend the ambit of infringement: [1988] AC 1013, 1057. See also *Baigent* v *Random House Group* [2007] EWCA Civ 247 [97].

[114] [1990] FSR 105. See also the comments of Evershed MR in *Purefoy Engineering* v *Sykes Boxall* (1955) 72 RPC 89, 99.

In this briefest of statements, Lord Hoffmann shows a simultaneous commitment to the values associated with the political paradigms of individualism and altruism. As noted above, an acceptance that unregulated competition is good thing is a value associated with the political paradigm of individualism.[115] Acceptance that there is a benefit to sharing on the other hand (and this must I think include the sharing of ideas) is a value aligned to altruism. Predictably then, Hoffmann does not advocate that copyright owners should benefit from the mechanical arbitrariness of rules in a way that would favour security of transaction over altruistic duty.

The analysis so far has been confined to the approach to infringement, and for that matter originality, that had been developed in the UK prior to European harmonization initiatives. The copyright landscape has undoubtedly changed and there is now certainly a new European test for assessing infringement and arguably a new European standard of originality. Having outlined the strengths and weaknesses of the 'traditional' UK approach I feel in a better position to comment on the 'Europeanization' of UK copyright law.

As I have already noted on a number of occasions, Article 2 of the 'Information Society' Directive[116] is headed 'reproduction right' and provides that member states shall provide for the exclusive right to authorize or prohibit direct or indirect, temporary or permanent reproduction by any means and in any form, in whole or 'in part', of relevant works. The wording suggests that the unlicensed reproduction of any part (rather than a substantial part) of a work should qualify as an infringement. This would seem to be the view of the Court of Justice. In *Infopaq International* v *Danske Dagblades Forening*,[117] called upon to interpret Article 2, the Court observed that the need for uniform application of Community law and the principle of equality required that where provisions of Community law made no express reference to the law of the member states for the purpose of determining their meaning and scope then normally the provisions must be given an autonomous and uniform interpretation throughout the Community. This was the case with Article 2.[118] As to the circumstances when a partial taking amounted to a reproduction, the court held that regard had to be taken of the wording

---

[115] And in particular the belief that conflict increases net social welfare, on which see above at p. 187.

[116] Directive 2001/29/EC of 22 May 2001 on the harmonisation of certain aspects of copyright and related rights in the information society.

[117] [2010] FSR 495.

[118] Ibid. [27].

and context of Article 2 and in the light of the objectives of the Directive and of international law. Copyright, the court said, is liable to apply only in relation to a subject matter which is original in the sense that it is its author's own intellectual creation. In this respect, parts are to be treated in the same way as the whole and, 'the various parts of a work … enjoy protection under art 2(a) of Directive 2001/29, provided that they contain elements which are the expression of the intellectual creation of the author of the work'.[119]

This formula was repeated by the Grand Chamber of the Court in joined cases C-403/08 *Football Association Premier League* v *QC Leisure* and C-429/08 *Murphy* v *Media Protection Services*.[120]

As I write there have been few opportunities for English courts to consider the implications of this. In *SAS Institute Inc* v *World Programming Ltd*[121] Arnold J in an attempt to relate what was said in *Infopaq* to the UK's legislative framework held that when considering whether a substantial part has been reproduced it is necessary to consider whether the part reproduced expresses the author's own intellectual creation.[122] The Court of Appeal agreed:

> Our domestic legislation confines the doing of a restricted act (e.g. copying) to doing that act in relation to the work as a whole or any 'substantial part of it' … It has long been the position in domestic law that what is substantial is a question to be answered qualitatively rather than quantitatively. In *Infopaq* the court said that parts of a work are entitled to the same protection as the work as a whole. But the parts in question must 'contain elements which are the expression of the intellectual creation of the author of the work' … This is now the test for determining whether a restricted act has been done in relation to a substantial part of a work.[123]

UK courts have repeatedly stressed that whether what has been taken constitutes a substantial part of the copyright work is a matter of impression and is determined by the quality of the part taken as much as the quantity.[124] What is now demanded is that the quality of the part taken is to be assessed by reference to the intellectual creativity expended by the author in the creation of that part.

---

119 [2010] FSR 495 [39].

120 [2012] FSR 5 [154]–[157].

121 [2010] EWHC 1829 (Ch)

122 Ibid. [243]. Later in his judgement Arnold J equated 'intellectual creation' with 'skill, judgement and labour': ibid. [263].

123 [2013] EWCA civ 1482 [38].

124 See above at p. 205.

But this is to gloss over a more profound change. Whereas previously whether there had been an infringement turned on the question of whether the alleged infringer incorporated a substantial part of that independent skill and labour, now it is sufficient to show that the infringer has taken any element of the intellectual creativity of the work's author. The first and obvious point is that the test for infringement by partial taking has thus become much more 'rule-like' in stripping from decision makers the discretion allowed them in deciding whether the part taken embodied a substantial part of the skill and labour of the author.[125] This is no great surprise: as explained at some length above, rules are the natural ally of harmonization.[126] Surprise or not, this change requires some radical rethinking of the way in which UK courts assess copyright infringement claims. No doubt moved by the spirit of harmony and cooperation and the laudable desire to further European integration, UK courts have since the decision in *Infopaq* understated the degree of change required. But some indication of the degree of rethinking that needs to be done is to be found in Jacob LJ's dicta in *Nova Productions Ltd* v *Mazooma Games Ltd*: a case that required the court to interpret UK copyright law in light of the Directive on the legal protection of computer programs. Jacob LJ observed:

> The Directive defines 'restricted acts' as reproduction 'in any form, in part or in whole' (Art. 4(a)). The UK Act does not say 'in part or in whole'. It uses the well-established language 'in relation to the work as a whole or any substantial part', s.16(3)(a). [Counsel for the claimants] wisely decided that he could not make any point based on this difference of language. He accepted that although the Directive did not say 'substantial part' its meaning must be so limited. Otherwise it would require the copying of insubstantial parts to be an infringement – which is so absurd as to be assuredly wrong.[127]

This stands in stark contrast to the relatively sanguine attitude to the same issue adopted by the Court of Appeal in *SAS Institute Inc* v *World Programming Ltd*. The difference, I would suggest, is in recognizing that the approach advocated by the European Court to infringement by partial taking is 'absurd and assuredly wrong' in a system in which originality is

---

125 Griffiths, above n.81, 787. As observed by Bently and Sherman, 'in an era in which there is increased international norm setting in the definition of the right of the copyright owner, the non-protection of ideas represents one of the few avenues by which the courts can take account of the individual circumstances and merits of particular decisions': Bently and Sherman, above n.1, 214.

126 Above at p. 125.

127 [2007] EWCA Civ 219 [29].

typically assessed by way of the simple 'not copied' rule. In *SAS Institute Inc*, the Court of Appeal openly embraced the European Court's test for whether the criterion of originality is satisfied (a work must be the intellectual creation of the author) and recognized that, following the decisions of the European Court in *Infopaq*, *Bezpečnostní softwarová asociace – Svaz softwarové ochrany* v *Ministerstvo kultury* and *Football Association Premier League* v *QC Leisure*, that this test was demanded under the Information Society Directive and so applied to all authorial works notwithstanding that the Directive did not expressly deal with the scope of copyright protection.[128]

Although *SAS Institute Inc* was the first occasion where a UK court explicitly adopted the European test for originality for all authorial works, this development was to an extent heralded by Proudman J in *Newspaper Licensing Agency* v *Meltwater Holding BV* when she observed that the European Court in *Infopaq* seemed to be saying that there was no distinction to be made between the part and the whole. She went on to observe that a part must contain elements which are the expression of the intellectual creation of the author if its taking is to amount to an infringement.[129] The logical other side of the coin is that a work must contain an expression of the author's intellectual creation to be protected.[130]

At this point in my narrative I am all too aware that engaging in speculation at such an early stage in the development of European

---

[128] *SAS Institute Inc* v *World Programming Ltd* [2013] EWCA civ 1482 [29]–[37].

[129] *Newspaper Licensing Agency* v *Meltwater Holding BV* [2010] EWHC 3099 (Ch) [69].

[130] The Court of Appeal, however, did not, at this point, take the opportunity to reconsider the UK's approach to originality but took the view that the decision in *Infopaq* had not qualified the long standing test established by UK authorities: *Newspaper Licensing Agency* v *Meltwater Holding BV* [2011] EWCA Civ 890 [20]. And in all this the groundwork was arguably done by Lord Hoffmann in the decade prior to the European Court's decision in *Infopaq*: Griffiths, above n.81, 771–4. The adoption of the European standard of originality would not lead to a different outcome in the majority of cases though some decisions, especially those relating to 'subcreative literary works (such as the leaflet that was the subject matter in *Elanco Products* v *Mandops* [1979] FSR 46), would have been decided differently under the European standard: see Derclaye, E, 'Infopaq International A/S v Danske Dagblades Forening (C-5/08): Wonderful or Worrisome? The Impact of the ECJ Ruling in Infopaq on UK Copyright Law' (2010) 32 EIPR 247, 248–50. Note also Rahmatian, A, 'Originality in UK Copyright Law: The Old "Skill and Labour" Doctrine under Pressure' (2013) 44(1) IIC 4.

copyright law carries with it a considerable risk of being proved wrong. All the more so given that on 23 June 2016 the citizens of the UK voted to leave the European Union. As I write it seems then that the UK is very likely to leave the EU. It is also likely that under any post-exit agreement UK courts will be obliged to give effect to at least some European legislation though it is impossible to say what the precise nature and extent of this obligation will be. There is, however, little risk in observing that, given the diverse social contexts in which the relevant activities occur, striking an appropriate balance between the interests of creators and users of copyright works will continue to present challenges to the creation of bright line rules and courts will endeavour to arrive at new solutions to what is a very old problem. As things stand what seems to have changed is the hunting ground for these solutions: where previously this was in the notion of 'substantial taking' it lies now in the notion of originality. The most profound change then will be that duties will cease to be the testing ground for claims of right and with this change, a significant dimension is lost. That is not entirely a bad thing if it means that the commandment 'thou shalt not steal' ceases to influence decisions that push at the boundaries of copyright protection. What is lost, however, is that which is lost when the 'public interest' is used as a measure of the limits of a claimed right rather than the interests of a particular user (as defendant). Dworkin, for instance, draws a distinction between abstract and concrete rights observing that, '[a]bstract rights, like the right to speak on political matters, take no account of competing rights; concrete rights, on the other hand, reflect the impact of such competition'.[131]

I fear that copyright law will become more certain but more abstract and decisions more remote.[132] By way of illustration of things to come, consider for instance what was said by the Advocate-General and the Court in *Bezpečnostní softwarová asociace – Svaz softwarové ochrany* v *Ministerstvo kultury*[133] in relation to the question of whether a graphic user interface, which enabled a computer user to communicate with a computer program, was a copyright work protectable under the Information Society Directive. The Advocate-General, though acknowledging that such an interface required considerable intellectual effort on the part

---

131 Dworkin, above n.111, 98.

132 This I think is essentially the same conclusion as that reached by Jonathan Griffiths when he says of the law post-*Infopaq* that it appears, 'to be concerned with the protection of creativity per se rather than creativity in any particular context': Griffiths, above n.81, 784.

133 [2011] ECDR 3.

of its author, nevertheless indicated that it was not 'original' in a copyright sense because the majority of the elements which comprise the interface have a functional purpose and the form of expression thus dictated by the technical function which those elements fulfil. In such cases, he said:

> the criterion of originality is not met, since the different methods of implementing an idea are so limited that the idea and the expression become indissociable. If such a possibility was offered, it would have the consequence of conferring a monopoly on certain companies on the computer program market, thus significantly hampering creation and innovation on that market, which would run contrary to the objective of ['the Information Society'] Directive 2001/29.[134]

The court agreed as to the approach to be adopted holding that where expression is dictated by a technical function, the author is not permitted to express his creativity in an original manner and achieve a result which can be said to be the intellectual creation of that author.[135] In *SAS Institute Inc* v *World Programming Ltd*, the UK Court of Appeal interpreted this as meaning, '(a) that if expression is dictated by technical function then the criterion of originality is not satisfied; and (b) that, where that is the case, the product is not an intellectual creation of the author at all'.[136]

As noted above, the Court of Appeal then went on to say that the test for determining whether a restricted act has been done in relation to a substantial part of a work was now whether the parts in question contained elements which are the expression of the intellectual creation of the author of the work.[137] Something of the flexibility of the previous position has thus been lost in that, whilst it has certainly always been the case that courts have scrutinized copyright claims that embrace functional ideas, the simple proposition that, 'if there is only one way of expressing an idea that way is not the subject of copyright' has not been favoured. Rather, and as noted above, it has always been a matter of degree and courts have in the past looked to the detail of what has been taken in deciding whether there has been an infringement.

In sum and to the extent that it is provable at all, the hypothesis that the rule form is associated with securing claims and strengthening the position of right holders whereas the standard form is associated with

---

134 Ibid. [AG76].
135 Ibid. [49].
136 [2013] EWCA civ 1482 [33].
137 Ibid. [38].

limiting scope and facilitating public access is largely true in the case of copyright law.

5.2 PATENT LAW

Patent law on the other hand does not on the face of it fit so comfortably with the idea that the rule form is associated with securing claims whereas the standard form is associated with limiting scope, not least of all because securing a patent is conditional not only on the claimed invention being new (which is assessed by way of a rule) but also whether it involves an inventive step (a test which is more standard-like in form). That said, the 'obviousness' standard is applied differently at the application stage than post-grant and is more rule-like in the former than the latter. In an approach endorsed by the courts, the UK Patent Office has traditionally adopted a low standard for applicants to satisfy and has resolved any doubts in the applicant's favour.[138] In an appeal from a decision of the Patent Office that had refused an application on the grounds that what was claimed was obvious, Jacob J in *Petra Fisher's Application* observed that the case was one which turned on evidence and in relation to that, 'it is right to say that the Comptroller, before he refuses a patent for obviousness, should be particularly careful and should be satisfied that it is a clear case ...'[139]

In this, he was maintaining the approach that had been adopted under the Patents Act 1949 and which had been considered and endorsed by the Divisional Court in *Swift & Co's Application*[140] and by the Court of Appeal in *General Electric Company's Applications*[141] in which it was observed that, unlike an action for revocation, examiners must make decisions based on a limited range of evidence (normally only written evidence) and without the benefit of being able to cross-examine the relevant parties.[142] Alan White, writing in the fifth edition (2001) of the CIPA's *Guide to the Patents Act* offers the following explanation of this approach:

---

[138] Cornish, W, Llewelyn, D and Aplin, T, *Intellectual Property: Patents, Copyrights, Trademarks & Allied Rights*, 8th edition (Sweet & Maxwell, 2013), 186.

[139] *Petra Fisher's Application* [1997] RPC 899, 905.

[140] [1962] RPC 37.

[141] [1964] RPC 413.

[142] On which see the speech of Diplock LJ in *General Electric Company's Applications*, in which he notes the differences between the statutory wording

> obviousness first comes to be judged by an examiner in ex parte examination … In such an examination, the examiner necessarily has to try and assume the position of a man skilled in the art and therefore in practice is forced to make somewhat hypothetical pronouncements on obviousness or unobviousness based on his own perception of what the man skilled in the art would have thought at the relevant time. Perhaps because of this, the philosophy within the British Patent Office has traditionally been to give an applicant the benefit of the doubt so that he has a chance to bring infringement proceedings under it before a court at the risk that the court may hold the patent not to have been validly granted and therefore revoke it. Thus, in the substantive examination … it has been stated that the Comptroller should be particularly careful before he refuses a patent for obviousness and should be satisfied that it is a clear case; i.e. that he should have no reasonable doubt that a valid patent cannot arise from the application …[143]

The key point is that the question of whether a claimed invention is obvious is approached with rather less subtlety at the examination stage than it is post-grant. At the examination stage the test is coarsened and is more rule-like than when it is applied in a revocation action. In this, there is a comparison to be made with the respective tests for assessing whether a sign which is the subject matter of a trade mark application is confusingly similar to an already registered trade mark and the test for whether a sign used in the course of trade is confusingly similar to a registered trade mark. In Chapter 3 above it was observed that the test as applied by the trade mark registry was coarser and more rule-like than the test applied by courts in infringement proceedings. I there argued that this was because the foresight demanded by *ex ante* decision making tended to make rules of what in an *ex post* context would be standards and was a feature of the fact that rules and standards contemplate decisions made at different times. That argument does not seem to explain why the form of the test for obviousness at the application stage differs in being more rule-like, from the same test applied in a revocation action. The question is always whether the purported invention would have been obvious to the notional skilled addressee at the priority date of the application. Both examiner and courts are thus required to form a judgement relating to the same past event (the devising of the claimed invention at the priority date). Unlike the position in trade mark law, no foresight seems to be required of examiners in assessing obviousness.

and the procedure for opposing an application under section 14 Patents Act 1949 and that for bringing an action for revocation under section 32 of the Act: [1964] RPC 413, 452–3.

[143] CIPA, *Guide to the Patents Act*, 5th edition (Sweet & Maxwell, 2001), 76–7. This suggestion does not appear in later editions of the Guide.

But in one important respect that is not true: examiners can only speculate as to how a particular invention might fare in the market once commercialized.

That matters because courts have repeatedly warned that, with the benefit of hindsight, that which was inventive when first done can seem obvious now. Aldous LJ for instance, in *Beloit Technologies* v *Valmet Paper Machinery Inc* observed that whether an alleged inventive step would be obvious to a person skilled in the art:

> is a jury type question which inevitably requires the Court and usually the witnesses to look back with knowledge of the invention. Such an advantage was not available to the inventor and therefore, when deciding the jury type question, the Court must be careful not to be wise after the event. The Court must put on 'the spectacles' of the notional skilled addressee at the priority date of the patent and, using such contemporary evidence as there may be, make sure that any conclusion reached is not the result of hindsight.[144]

In this, decision makers face two challenges. The first is in understanding the attitudes and thinking of those in the art at the priority date. In this, courts look to what was happening in the relevant technical field at the time of the invention.[145] So far as this challenge is concerned, examiners are advantaged over courts because their decisions are typically taken at a time which is closer to that of the devising of the invention.[146] But the greater challenge is not in divining and then adopting a historical mindset in a general way, but rather in attempting to imagine a creative environment without knowledge of the invention in issue. In this examiners are

144 *Beloit Technologies* v *Valmet Paper Machinery Inc* [1997] RPC 489, 494. See also the judgement of Fletcher Moulton LJ in *British Westinghouse* v *Braulik* (1910) 27 RPC 209; Lord Diplock in *Technograph Printed Circuits Ltd* v *Mills & Rockley (Electronics) Ltd* [1972] RPC 346, 362; and Kitchen J in *Abbott Laboratories Ltd* v *Evysio Medical Devices UCL* [2008] EWHC 800 (Ch) [180] (cited with approval by the Court of Appeal in *Apimed Medical Honey Ltd* v *Brightwake Ltd* [2012] EWCA Civ 5 [54]); *Nokia Oyj (Nokia Corp)* v *IPCom GmbH & Co KG* [2012] EWCA Civ 567 [128]); and *Rovi Solutions Corp* v *Virgin Media Ltd* [2015] EWCA Civ 781 [9]).

145 See e.g. *Lucas* v *Gaedor* [1978] RPC 297, 358; *Chiron Corporation* v *Organon Teknika* (No. 3) [1994] FSR 202, 223; *Schlumberger Holdings Ltd* v *Electromagnetic Geoservices AS* [2010] EWCA Civ 819 [81]–[82]; and *Actavis Ltd* v *Eli Lilly and Co* [2015] EWHC 3294 (Pat) [95]–[98].

146 For instance, in *Actavis Ltd* v *Eli Lilly and Co,* Carr J explicitly acknowledged the difficulties in avoiding hindsight when the priority date was over two decades before the trial date and much had changed in the state of knowledge of the relevant field: [2015] EWHC 3294 (Pat) [98].

disadvantaged partly because they must make decisions without hearing oral evidence or being able to cross-examine witnesses[147] but chiefly because certain evidence pointing towards inventiveness can emerge and strengthen with the passage of time. In a judgement that was subsequently described as 'a masterpiece' by the Court of Appeal,[148] Laddie J in *Haberman* v *Jackel International Ltd*[149] listed nine matters that were of value in helping to determine whether a particular development was obvious. Most of these related to events and issues at the priority date,[150] but the commercial success of the invention, once it had been commercialized, could also provide a useful guide:

> (h) How well has the patentee's development been received? Once the product or process was put into commercial operation, to what extent was it a commercial success? In looking at this, it is legitimate to have regard not only to the success indicated by exploitation by the patentee and his licensees but also to the commercial success achieved by infringers. Furthermore, the number of infringers may reflect on some of the other factors set out above. For example, if there are a large number of infringers it may be some indication of the number of members of the trade who were likely to be looking for alternative or improved products.
>
> (i) To what extent can it be shown that the whole or much of the commercial success is due to the technical merits of the development, i.e. because it solves the problem? Success which is largely attributable to other factors, such as the commercial power of the patentee or his licensee, extensive advertising focussing on features which have nothing to do with the development, branding or other technical features of the product or process, says nothing about the value of the invention.[151]

---

[147] As observed by Diplock LJ in *General Electric Company's Applications* [1964] RPC 413, 452–3.

[148] *Schlumberger Holdings Ltd* v *Electromagnetic Geoservices AS* [2010] EWCA Civ 819.

[149] [1999] FSR 683.

[150] Such as the problem that the invention addressed, how long that problem had existed, how significant it was seen to be and how widely known it was.

[151] Per Laddie J in *Haberman* v *Jackel International Ltd* [1999] FSR 683, 700–701 and cited with approval by the Court of Appeal in *Aerotel Ltd* v *Wavecrest Group Enterprises Ltd* [2009] EWCA Civ 408 and later described as 'a masterpiece' in *Schlumberger Holdings Ltd* v *Electromagnetic Geoservices AS* [2010] EWCA Civ 819. On UK Courts' approach to evidence of inventiveness see: Cole, P, 'Inventive Step – Meaning of the EPO Problem and Solution Approach, and Implications for the United Kingdom' (1998) (Part 2) 20 EIPR 267, 268–9.

Nevertheless, although the test for whether a claimed invention is obvious when applied at the examination stage is coarser and more rule-like than the test applied by courts in a revocation action, it nevertheless differs from the test for whether a claimed invention is new. The test for obviousness, at whatever stage it is applied, is not a rule.

Where then does this leave the hypothesis that the rule form is associated with securing claims and strengthening the position of right holders whereas the standard form is associated with limiting scope and facilitating public access? I think that is still broadly true for patent law, but its veracity is obscured because it is easy to assume that securing a patent is solely an individualistic act when in fact it is both an individualistic and an altruistic act. In one sense of course securing a patent is clearly individualistic in character: it is a claim made by an individual to exclusive rights in an invention. Certainly an invention is a piece of information[152] and as such is shareable at little or no cost to the person in possession of it. It is for this reason that those scientific researchers who claim a strong commitment to 'open science' see a conflict between that idea and the values implicit in the patent system.[153] Although it has been suggested that the prospect of obtaining a patent discourages publication and/or data sharing,[154] what empirical evidence is available does not support these claims[155] and is hard to square with the condition that, to secure patent protection, an invention must be

---

[152] See for instance Lord Hoffmann's account in *Merrell Dow Pharmaceuticals Inc* v *Norton* [1996] RPC 76, 86.

[153] See for instance the report of The Royal Society on 'Keeping Science Open' in which the report's authors note that 'a climate of secrecy' limits the free flow of ideas and information that are vital for successful science: The Royal Society, *Keeping Science Open: The Effects of Intellectual Property Policy on the Conduct of Science* (The Royal Society, April 2003), v.

[154] Andrews, L, 'Genes and Patent Policy: Rethinking Intellectual Property Rights' (2002) 3 Nature Reviews Genetics 803, 804; The Royal Society, *Keeping Science Open*, above n.153, [2.11]. It has also been suggested that researchers are induced to delay publication of their findings to allow time for the preparation of patent applications: David, P, 'Can "Open Science" be Protected from the Evolving Regime of Intellectual Property Rights Protections?' (2004) 160 Journal of Institutional and Theoretical Economics 9, 17. That argument does not seem credible in light of the possibility of filing provisional applications. For instance, section 14(2) Patents Act 1977 provides that the provisions on form and content of an application shall not prevent an application being initiated by documents complying with the rather more informal demands of section 15(1).

[155] Nicol, D and Nielson, J, 'Patents and Medical Biotechnology: An Empirical Analysis of Issues Facing the Australian Industry', Centre for Law and Genetics, Occasional Paper No. 6 (Centre for Law and Genetics, Faculty of Law,

described in the patent specification.[156] This disclosure must be enabling: it must be clear and complete enough such that a person skilled in the relevant art could perform the claimed invention without the burden of an undue amount of experimentation or the application of inventive ingenuity.[157] If this requirement is not met at the application stage it will lead to a refusal and if found to have been breached post-grant will lead to the revocation of the granted patent.[158] A patent then represents a quid pro quo: 'the quid to the patentee is the monopoly; the quo is that he presents to the public the knowledge which they have not got'.[159]

A complete disclosure of the claimed invention as condition for the grant of a patent has long been a feature of patent law. As early as the late eighteenth century, courts recognized the role of the patent specification in providing instruction to the public. In 1778, in the case of *Liardet* v *Johnson*, Lord Mansfield showed a remarkably modern understanding of this function in his direction to the jury regarding the condition that the specification must instruct others how to make the claimed invention:

> For the condition of giving encouragement is this: that you must specify upon record your invention in such a way as shall teach an artist, when your term is out, to make it – and to make it as well as you by your directions; for then at the end of the term, the public have the benefit of it. The inventor has the benefit during the term, and the public have the benefit after.[160]

University of Tasmania, 2003), 126–30; and The Royal Society, *Keeping Science Open*, above, n.153, v.

[156] For instance under section 14(3) of the UK Patents Act 1977 it is required that 'the specification of an application shall disclose the invention in a manner which is clear enough and complete enough for the invention to be performed by a person skilled in the art'. See also Article 83 EPC and section 112 US Patents Act (Title 35 USC).

[157] Section 14(3) Patents Act 1977. See also *Novartis* v *Johnson & Johnson* [2010] EWCA Civ 1039; *Mentor* v *Hollister* [1993] RPC 7; and *Valensi* v *British Radio Corporation* [1973] RPC 337.

[158] Section 72(c) Patents Act 1977.

[159] *Pope Appliance Corporation* v *Spanish River Pulp and Paper Mills* [1929] AC 269, 281.

[160] *Liardet* v *Johnson* reported in the *Morning Post* of 23 February 1778 (No. 1667, p. 2, col 4) and reproduced by Hulme, E, 'On the History of Patent Law in the Seventeenth and Eighteenth Centuries' (1902) 18 LQR 280, 285. Hulme has elsewhere argued that the decision in *Liardet* v *Johnson* was a landmark in this respect and invested the patent specification with a character and function distinct from that with which it had originally been introduced: Hulme, E, 'On the Consideration of the Patent Grant, Past and Present' (1897) 13 LQR 313,

But long before the specification was understood to perform this teaching function, it was a typical condition of grant that the patentee promise to train apprentices in the relevant method.[161]

The publication of the application and the granted patent[162] facilitate sharing in two ways. First and most obviously, publication of a clear and complete disclosure of the claimed invention allows the public to learn of and from what the patentee has done. Obviously during the term of the patent, the extent to which anyone can make use of the information publicly disclosed in a patent specification is limited.[163] But once the patent has expired, anyone is then free to use the information contained in the patent specification and to exploit the formerly protected invention. Secondly, from the moment an application is published others are prevented from being granted a patent for the same invention[164] whether or not the first inventor decides to pursue her application.

---

317. Others have argued that this overstates the significance of the case, that times for filing specifications were stipulated prior to *Liardet* and that from the 1740s onwards, the filing of drawings and plans for many mechanical inventions was on the increase: Adams, J and Averley, G, 'The Patent Specification the Role of *Liardet* v *Johnson* (1986) 7(2) Journal of Legal History 156; and see also Mossoff, A, 'Rethinking the Development of Patents: An Intellectual History, 1550–1800' (2001) 52 Hastings LJ 1255, 1292–3.

[161] Mossoff, above n.160, 1261. Note also Drahos, who observes that 'one finds early on in the evolution of patent law the view that patentees had a duty to work the patent in the realm so that relevant industrial expertise was made accessible to all': Drahos, above n.2, 223.

[162] Under UK law the application is published as soon as possible after a period of eighteen months from the filing date or priority date (section 16(1) Patents Act 1977 and Patents Rules 2007, rule 26(1)). Under section 24(1) and (3) of the Act a patent is published as soon as practicable after grant.

[163] The mandated disclosure of the details of an invention might have some utility to the patentee's competitors even during the patent term. In large part this depends on the scope of the monopoly of a particular patent and it is generally the case that 'the greater patent protection is, the smaller the benefit to competitors from the information contained in the patent grant because the less they can do with it': Landes, W and Posner, R, *The Economic Structure of Intellectual Property Law* (Belknap, 2003), 299.

[164] Under section 2(3) Patents Act 1977,

> the state of the art in the case of an invention to which an application for a patent or a patent relates shall be taken also to comprise matter contained in an application for another patent which was published on or after the priority date of that invention, if the following conditions are satisfied, that is to say – (a) that matter was contained in the application for that other patent both as filed and as published; and (b) the priority date of that matter is earlier than that of the invention.

How effective the patent system is in facilitating the sharing of ideas that inventors might otherwise keep to themselves is open to question,[165] but nevertheless, the policy of making the patent system a source of technical information has been deliberately pursued[166] and the procuring of information is often advanced at least as a partial justification of it.[167] In this respect patent law differs notably from copyright in that the exclusive rights of the copyright owner are not exercisable only on condition that a work is published. Indeed the exclusive rights to copy and publish a work are frequently relied on by copyright owners precisely to prevent the publication of their work.[168] The difference is an

---

165 Critics point out that inventors will be inclined to disclose, via the patent system, only those of their inventions which could not be kept secret if exploited. If an invention can be fully exploited and its value appropriated by its owner whilst keeping it secret, obtaining a patent is unnecessary and unappealing. The great majority of patented inventions are thus those that are largely (or fully) disclosed by being exploited: typically by putting products incorporating the invention onto the market. The forced disclosure of an invention in the patent specification contributes nothing useful to the public domain if a skilled man can learn of and from the invention by examining products that incorporate it: see e.g. Machlup, F, *An Economic Review of the Patent System. Study No. 15 of The United States Subcommittee on Patent, Trade Marks and Copyrights* (US Government Printing Office, 1958), 24. In this respect it is notable that product innovations are far more likely to be patented than process innovations: Cohen, W, Nelson, R and Walsh, J, *Protecting Their Intellectual Assets: Appropriability Conditions and Why US Manufacturing Firms Patent (or Not)*, NBER Working Paper 7552 (National Bureau for Economic Research, 2002), 16 and see also Kingston, W, 'Patent Protection for Modern Technologies' (1997) IPQ 350, 358 (noting that the great majority of European firms that used the patent system were in production industries).

166 Cornish et al., above n.138, 149.

167 Machlup, above n.165, 24; and Fisher, M, 'Classical Economics and the Philosophy of the Patent System' (2005) IPQ 1, 20. More elaborate mandated disclosures make the public communication more unmistakeable which is efficient because the clear public definition of property rights lowers transaction costs and tends to optimize investments: Landes and Posner, above n.163, 34.

168 See e.g. *Hubbard* v *Vosper* [1972] QB 84; *Hyde Park Residence* v *Yelland Ltd* [2000] RPC 604; and *Ashdown* v *Telegraph Group* [2001] EWCA Civ 1142. In *HRH Prince of Wales* v *Associated Newspapers Ltd* [2006] EWCA 1776 the defendant newspaper raised an 'interesting and novel argument' linked to the evidence that the claimant had no intention of publishing the literary work in issue and consequently there was no commercial interest at stake. In these circumstances, the defendant argued, the claimant's only purpose in invoking copyright was to protect his privacy. If the claimant were not in a position to complain of publication by the assertion of right to privacy (under Article 8 of

important one[169] though overlooked by even the most astute of commentators. James Penner, for instance, in reflecting on claims to property rights in information, says this:

> A true property right in an idea or an expression would constitute a right of exclusion from that idea or that expression itself. Subjects of the law would have a duty not to read about or understand an invention or take in the expression in a book or a painting (a funny notion since patents are published when granted, and a copyright is a right exclusively to disseminate).[170]

Penner is correct so far as copyright does indeed give the owner the exclusive right to reproduce and disseminate a work. But there is no obligation for the owner so to do as a condition of claiming the right. The exclusive rights of the copyright owner include the right not to disseminate the work. Unlike the patent owner then, the copyright owner can keep her ideas to herself and can rely on her legal rights to prevent anyone else from disclosing them more widely. As Harris observes, in copyright law, a private domain is reserved:

> It consists of an open-ended set of use-privileges, control powers, and powers of transmission … It is not specifically enacted that the copyright owner may (if he chooses) license only members of his family to make copies, or transact only with publishers whose politics match his own, or keep the work unpublished until some turn in public affairs which makes it topical and

---

the European Convention on Human Rights (ECHR)) then, the defendant said, it could not be right that he should be able to rely upon his copyright in order to protect his privacy. The Court of Appeal did not consider this argument because it found that the claimant had a valid claim based on breach of confidence and interference with his right of privacy: [2006] EWCA 1776 [83]–[84]. In the US (where copyright's incentive function has a constitutional basis), authors who do not allow access to their works after first publication may find their exclusive rights vulnerable to the fair use doctrine: Gordon, above n.2, 1376.

169 As noted by Justin Hughes,

> [a]s long as complete exclusion cannot or does not happen, ideas will be available to people in their own thoughts even though these ideas already have become someone else's property. Through this availability, one idea can lead to still more ideas. In other words, once a 'new' idea has been put into intellectual commerce, once people know about it, it leads to an 'expansion' of the common, or of the accessible common.

Hughes, above n.50, 316

170 Penner, J, *The Idea of Property in Law* (Clarendon Press, 1977), 119.

> profitable, or read passages from it aloud at a charity bazaar. He may do these and countless other things with the work because he is its owner.[171]

In the previous chapter I noted that patent law has a communication function that is not shared with copyright law and this provided an explanation of why validity and infringement are separate contexts in patent law but are not so in copyright law. The patent system requires the invention be disclosed because otherwise the patent owner might be able to benefit from the shelter of a monopoly grant by marketing products incorporating the protected invention in a way that does not fully disclose that invention (a strategy that is not available to the copyright owner). There is a risk associated with forced public disclosure however. An accessible register acts not only to inform the public of what the invention is but also what is claimed to be protected. Information contained on the register acts to deter potential competitors from replicating an already claimed invention so benefiting the patent owner.[172] But without a robust examination of what is claimed the patent owner could benefit in this way without actually having devised a patentable invention. Although it is natural to think that the process of application and examination is concerned with securing individual rights, a robust examination of what is claimed is an important means of limiting scope and facilitating public access and the hypothesis that the standard form is associated with limiting scope and facilitating public access is thus not fatally undermined, though the greater challenge now becomes how to explain the rule form of the novelty requirement. I shall attempt to explain that in the final chapter of this book.

5.3 TRADE MARK LAW

The law concerned with protection of marks shares with patents and copyright the feature that it grants individuals rights to control information, specifically that which signals to consumers the trade origin of goods and services. But on the face of it the tension between individualism and altruism is less acute so far as trade mark law is concerned. Prima facie, the notions of sacrifice and sharing, which are the essence of

---

171 Harris, above n.2, 46.

172 There is also a public benefit here in that the information contained on the register deters potential competitors from the wasteful investment involved in replicating an already claimed invention. On the *in terrorem* effect of patents see below at p. 274.

altruism, have little relevance in the context of a claim to a legal right over the use of a mark, the function of which is to distinguish the goods or service of the owner's undertaking from those of its competitors in a free market. It is competition rather than cooperation that defines markets: a situation that trade mark law is designed to bolster. That said, even within this environment, some degree of sharing is necessary if competition is not to be stifled. So for instance and most obviously, subject to a number of conditions being satisfied, a firm is allowed to use a rival's registered mark in order to compare goods or services meeting the same needs or intended for the same purposes.[173]

But sometimes rights in marks are exercised in ways that limit activities outside the competitive marketplace and in such circumstances there emerge parallels between trade mark law and copyright law in terms of the conflict between the individualist and altruist paradigms. The notion of altruism has an application if that means sharing the right to use a particular sign with a community of actual or potential users other than the mark owner's competitors in a particular market.

Trade marks are a ubiquitous feature of modern Western societies: they have 'invaded our popular culture'.[174] As has been noted elsewhere, contemporary marketing practices have imbued marks with a significance that extends far beyond signalling trade origin.[175] Marks in contemporary use not only inform the consumer who made the product but often also enhance the product or become a functional part of it.[176] As observed by distinguished chief judge of the US Ninth Circuit Court of Appeals, Judge Alex Kozinski, in his iconic article, 'Trade Marks Unplugged', it is no accident that trade marks play a significant role in public discourse, often providing vivid metaphors and compelling imagery:

> Trade marks are often selected for their effervescent qualities, and then injected into the stream of communication with the pressure of a firehose by means of mass media campaigns. Where trade marks come to carry so much

---

[173] Under Article 3(a) Directive 2006/114/EC concerning misleading and comparative advertising. See also *L'Oréal SA* v *Bellure NV* [2007] EWCA Civ 968 [50]–[70]; and *O2 Holdings Ltd* v *Hutchison 3G Ltd* [39]–[57].

[174] Kozinski, A, 'Trade Marks Unplugged' (1993) 68 New York University L Rev 960, 965.

[175] See for instance the detailed historical account given in Drescher, T, 'The Transformation and Evolution of Trade Marks – From Signals to Symbols to Myth' (1992) 82 Trademark Reporter 301.

[176] Kozinski, above n.174, 962.

communicative freight, allowing the trade mark holder to restrict their use implicates our collective interest in free and open communication.[177]

Kozinski sees such active marketing as effecting a partial transfer of ownership of the signs and symbols around which such efforts centre. The originators of such powerful symbols must, he says, be prepared to give up some measure of control over their use, because in a sense they also belong to all the other minds that have received and integrated them.[178]

There are two contexts in which allowing its owner to restrict the use of a mark has implications for a collective interest in free and open communication, each of which has generated a different legal response. The first is the use of marks in what might be called 'general public discourse'. One consequence of the communicative freight carried by marks is that representations of life in modern Western societies must necessarily include marks if they are not to be incomplete and unrealistic portrayals.[179]

I have very little to say about this context and the legal response. The primary means by which the European legislation sets out to prevent trade mark owners from restricting uses of their marks outside the commercial environment lies in the condition that, to infringe a mark, there must be some use of the mark done 'in the course of trade'.[180] This has been interpreted as meaning that the use of a sign must take place in the context of some commercial activity with a view to gaining economic advantage if it is to count.[181] The rights conferred by a trade mark can be relied on only against 'economic operators'[182] and private uses do not satisfy the condition and cannot then be infringements. This is so even if

---

177 Ibid., 973.

178 Ibid., 975.

179 A fact commercially exploited to their mutual benefit by the advertising industry and movie makers in the phenomenon of product placement.

180 A condition under all the heads of infringement specified in section 10 Trade Marks Act 1994. Note also that Section 10(4) provides a non-exhaustive list of what amounts to a relevant 'use' in this context.

181 C-206/01 *Arsenal Football Club Plc* v *Reed* [2003] RPC 144 [40]; C-48/05 *Adam Opel AG* v *Autec AG* [2007] ETMR 33 [18]; and C-17/06 *Céline SARL* v *Céline* [2007] ETMR 1320 [17]. Thus the use of another's trade mark by a political party in an election broadcast which aimed at encouraging viewers to vote for that party is not 'use in the course of trade': *Unilever plc* v *Griffin* [2010] EWHC 899 (Ch) [11]–[14].

182 C-324/09 *L'Oréal SA* v *eBay International AG* [2011] ETMR 52 [54].

such uses are done for financial gain.[183] It is also the case that, using a sign in purely internal communications, for instance in internally circulated emails, does not qualify as a use in the course of trade, either because such use is private or because it is not a 'use' of a trade mark at all.[184]

Much more interesting from my perspective are instances where there is no question that a mark is being used in the course of trade, but the circumstances are such that the owner's right to restrict that use has been pitched against a claimed right to free use of the mark. There is some degree of overlap with the previous context insofar as some businesses are concerned with providing accurate representations of features of the modern world and want to use trade marks to enhance the quality of their reproductions. For instance, the defendants in *Adam Opel AG* v *Autec AG*[185] were manufacturers of remote-controlled toy-scale model cars, whilst the claimant was a large European car manufacturer. Amongst the defendant's products was a replica of one of the claimant's cars. That replica reproduced the claimant's trade mark on the radiator grille, as on the original model of the vehicle of reference. AG Colomer recognized that a basic characteristic of numerous toys is the representation of something and that the essence of a toy is recreating the objects and events of history in order to adapt them to the mentality of children or

183 This includes private sales on internet sales platforms such as eBay. There is some discretion exercisable here, in that whether such selling activities are properly considered private depends on their volume, frequency and 'other characteristics': ibid. [55].

184 It follows that purely internal use of a trade mark (for instance in internally circulated emails) is not a 'use' of that mark: *OCH-ZIFF Management Europe Ltd* v *OCH Capital LLP* [2010] EWHC 2599 (Ch) [55]–[66]. As a consequence, the Court of Justice, in a decision that has important implications for the current business model applied to the provision of internet search facilities, has held that a referencing service provider (i.e. the operator of a search engine, such as Google) does not use a sign in the course of trade when it stores as keywords, for certain of its clients, signs which are identical with trade marks and arranges for the display of advertisements when those keywords are used as search terms by a user of the search engine. In such circumstances, a referencing service provider does not itself use the signs because they do not appear in its own commercial communications: joined cases C-236/08; C-237/08; and C-238/08 *Google France and Google Inc* v *Louis Vuitton Malletier*; *Google France* v *Viaticum Luteciel*; and *Google France* v *CNRRH* [2010] ETMR 30 [55]–[58].

185 C-48/05 *Adam Opel AG* v *Autec AG* [2007] ETMR 33.

those requiring more imaginative contact with their postulates.[186] Later in his opinion he commented on the significance of accuracy in representation:

> In the toy industry, the manufacture and marketing of model cars on a smaller scale than the original real car has been widespread since 1898 ... The little cars have become the 'Proustian madeleine' of adults who relive their childhood experiences while still in short trousers, giving free rein to their dreams.
>
> If, at the outset, the objective was to reproduce reality in miniature for a very specific group, children, in order to bring the adult world within their reach, adapted to their size, the target group has little by little widened, to include also adult collectors. This latter group has probably increased the demands in the quality of the reproduction, requiring the greatest possible accuracy in the model. The design of this type of article does not therefore rely on copying the most significant characteristics, but also in replicating even the tiniest ones.[187]

Another instance of circumstances giving rise to a consideration of competing interests in the use of a mark arises because commerce has extended its sphere of operation such that established and well-known institutions and organizations that traditionally have not traded in goods or services have sought to take commercial advantage of their reputations built outside the sphere of commerce. One way in which they do this is by converting signs with which they are associated into trade marks. Common examples are sports clubs and organizations; broadcasters and programme makers; and musicians and performers. This can create tensions between those that attach only the traditional meaning to a sign (for instance, that the wearer is a supporter of Real Madrid; is a fan of *Dr Who*; who also enjoyed a performance by Madonna during her last European tour) and those who see it in its adopted modern role as a mark signifying trade origin.[188] This tension most famously manifested itself in litigation connected with *Arsenal FC*, one of the most successful football ('soccer') clubs in England. The club was founded in 1886 (by a group of workers from the Woolwich Arsenal Armament factory) and for many decades supporters have signified their allegiance to the club either by wearing its shield or by holding signs bearing its name or nickname, 'the

---

186 Ibid. [AG3]

187 Ibid. [AG37]–[AG38].

188 Identified as the essential function of a trade mark by the European Court in C-39/97 *Canon Kabushiki Kaisha* v *Metro-Goldwyn-Mayer Inc* [1999] RPC 117 [28].

Gunners'. However, it was not until the early 1990s that the club began to take trading in souvenirs and memorabilia seriously[189] and as a prelude to this, 1989 saw the club register various words and logos as trade marks.[190] The defendant, Matthew Reed, was the proprietor of a football merchandise company which sold a range of souvenirs and memorabilia: a business which he had been in long before the club itself entered that market.[191] Without the club's licence, he sold goods identical to those for which the football club had registered its marks featuring signs that were identical to some of these marks (so-called 'unofficial merchandise'). In response to the claim that his activities amounted to trade mark infringement, the defendant argued that the Arsenal signs on his products would be perceived as a badge of support, loyalty or affiliation to those to whom they are directed and would not be perceived as trade marks (i.e. as signs indicating trade origin).[192]

A related circumstance which yields similar tensions arises because of the modern phenomenon of brand extension. Owners of trade marks have extended their operations into new markets relying on the reputational capital of existing trade marks to enhance their competitive position in a way that offsets the disadvantages normally encountered by new entrants to a market.[193] Such moves into new markets can create conflicts where previously there were none. Apple Corps is the record company synonymous with the Beatles. Indeed, the company started life as The Beatles Ltd in 1963 but changed its name in the late 1960s. The first apple trade mark was registered in 1968.[194] Apple Computer was founded in 1976 and has since become extremely well known as a manufacturer of computer-based electronic devices and as a software developer. It too adopted apple trade marks: the word 'apple' and a stylized apple with a bite taken out of it.[195] Inevitably the huge success of Apple Computer led

---

189 *Arsenal Football Club Plc* v *Reed* [2001] RPC 922 [7].

190 Ibid. [50].

191 Ibid. [3].

192 An argument accepted by Laddie J at first instance: [2001] RPC 922 [58].

193 Griffiths, A, 'The Law and Economics of Trade Marks' in Bently, L, Davis, J and Ginsburg, J, *Trade Marks and Brands: An Interdisciplinary Critique* (Cambridge University Press, 2008), 249. The directions of such extensions can be surprising: I doubt for instance that anyone would have predicted that the well-known road haulage firm Eddie Stobart would have entered the legal services market following the deregulation of that industry in the UK, accessed 24 January 2017 at http://www.legalfutures.co.uk/latest-news/keep-on-trucking-eddie-stobart-enters-legal-services-market-yes-really.

194 *Apple Corps Ltd* v *Apple Computer Inc* [2006] EWHC 996 (Ch) [2].

195 Ibid. [3].

to a tension between the mark owners and in 1981 and then again in 1991 the two companies arrived at agreements concerning the fields of use of their respective marks. Under these agreements and in general terms Apple Computer was allowed to use its marks in relation to computer goods and services, but not in relation to equipment specifically adapted for use in the recording or reproduction of music, or in relation to operational services relating to music. Apple Corps, on the other hand, could use its marks in relation to sound and video recording, and reproducing apparatus and instruments, and sound and video records, but not computers and computing systems. Under both agreements, musical content was the exclusive preserved of Apple Corps, an element of the agreement that was strained to breaking point with the introduction, by Apple Computer, of the iTunes music store in 2003.[196] In an action claiming breach of the agreement reached in 1991, Apple Corps argued that Apple Computer's use of its Apple mark in relation to the iTunes Store (the mark was present when a user accessed the Store) produced an association with the music content making its use one which is 'in connection' with the music content. To a contemporary consumer the clash perhaps seems inevitable. But the extension of Apple Computer's business into music distribution must have seemed unlikely even in 1991 and all the more so in 1976 when it was founded. As noted by the court, at the time of the 1991 agreement, the large scale transmission of computer data down ordinary telephone lines to consumers was unknown: in short this aspect of the internet did not exist. Furthermore personal computers' capacity to reproduce music with any fidelity was typically poor.[197]

The circumstances leading to the dispute in *Adam Opel AG* v *Autec AG*;[198] *Arsenal* v *Reed*;[199] and *Apple Corps Ltd* v *Apple Computer Inc*[200] in one way or another invited courts to consider the proper boundaries of trade mark protection in light of the ubiquity and cultural significance of contemporary trade marks.

Certain unauthorized uses undertaken in the course of trade fall within the scope of the statutory defences to a claim of trade mark infringement

196 Ibid. [4]–[8].

197 Ibid. [54].

198 C-48/05 *Adam Opel AG* v *Autec AG* [2007] ETMR 33.

199 *Arsenal Football Club Plc* v *Reed* [2001] RPC 922; C-206/01 *Arsenal Football Club Plc* v *Reed* [2003] RPC 144; *Arsenal Football Club Plc* v *Reed* (No. 2) [2002] EWHC 2695 (Ch); and *Arsenal Football Club Plc* v *Reed* (No. 2) [2003] EWCA Civ 696.

200 [2006] EWHC 996 (Ch).

but these are specific and rather narrow in scope.[201] A far more significant limitation on the scope of trade mark rights arises because the European Court has held that European trade mark law does not entitle the proprietor of a mark to prohibit all uses in the course of trade. Rather, the court said, the right of prohibition presupposes the existence of a specific interest of the proprietor as trade mark proprietor and that the use of a sign by a third party must affect or be liable to affect one of the functions of the mark if it is to infringe. This is particularly significant, not only in providing another opportunity to assess the veracity of the claim that the rule form is associated with securing claims and strengthening the position of right holders whereas the standard form is associated with limiting scope and facilitating public access, but because in trade mark law the court has taken something that on the face of it is a clear rule and made it subject to a standard.

The legislative scheme does not, on the face of it, provide adjudicators with any flexibility in cases of so-called 'double identity' where a sign identical to a registered mark is attached to goods identical to those for which the mark is registered. Such cases of 'double identity' are covered by Article 5(1) Trade Mark Directive. That this provision admits no discretion in its application is indicated by the tenth recital in the Preamble to the Directive, which provides that, 'the protection afforded by the registered trade mark, the function of which is in particular to guarantee the trade mark as an indication of origin, is absolute in the case of identity between the mark and the sign and goods or services ...'[202]

---

201 Thus an owner cannot rely on her rights in a mark so as to prevent a third party from using, in the course of trade, his own name or address: Art. 6(1)(a) Trade Marks Directive. Nor can she prevent the mark being used descriptively; nor to indicate the intended purpose of a product or service: Art. 6(1) (b) and (c) respectively. And in all cases, for the defence to be available, the use must be 'in accordance with honest practices in industrial and commercial matters': Art. 6(1). As derogations, these uses are given a restrictive interpretation: C-48/05 *Adam Opel AG* v *Autec AG* [2007] ETMR 33 [AG34]. For a fuller account see Bently and Sherman, above n.1, 1061–71; and see also Ramsey, L P and Schovsbo, J, 'Mechanisms for Limiting Trade Mark Rights to Further Competition and Free Speech' (2013) 44(6) IIC 671, 676.

202 As it appeared in the original First Council Directive 89/104. Recital (11) of the subsequent version (Directive 2008/95/EC) contains the same wording except that, for reasons that are unclear, the latter recital says that the protection afforded by the registered trade mark 'should be' absolute in the case of identity (rather than previously 'is' absolute). This change is probably of no significance: Morcom, C, 'Trade Marks and the Internet: Where Are We Now?' (2012) 34(1) EIPR 40, 52.

It appears then that Article 5(1) is framed as and intended to operate as a rule where the role of the adjudicator is confined to establishing only, as a matter of fact, whether there is identity between the mark and the sign and the goods or services to which these are attached.[203] However, the Court of Justice in C-206/01 *Arsenal Football Club Plc* v *Reed*[204] observed that the tenth recital to the Trade Marks Directive stated that the aim of the protection afforded was to guarantee the trade mark as an indication of origin and it followed that the rights were given so that the trade mark proprietor could protect her interests as proprietor, that is, to ensure that the trade mark can fulfil its functions. In light of this, the Court said that, '[t]he exercise of that right must therefore be reserved to cases in which a third party's use of the sign affects or is liable to affect the functions of the trade mark, in particular its essential function of guaranteeing to consumers the origin of the goods'.[205]

Thus the judgement in *Arsenal* made an effect (or likelihood of an effect) on one of the functions of the trade mark a prerequisite for the exercise of the exclusive right laid down in Article 5(1)(a). Notwithstanding the lack of a legislative basis, the court has placed this condition on an equal footing with the express legislative demands. In *Céline SARL* v *Céline*,[206] the court declared that four conditions had to be satisfied if a right holder is to prevent the use of a sign by a third party which is identical to his mark:

- that use must be in the course of trade;
- it must be without the consent of the proprietor of the mark;

---

[203] Accepting that the Court, in requiring that 'identity' be assessed from the perspective of the 'average consumer' introduced an element of judgement into what is otherwise a strict rule: C-291/00 *SA Société LTJ Diffusion* v *SA Sadas* [2003] ETMR 83 [52] and *Miss World Ltd* v *Channel Four Television Corp* [2007] EWHC 982 (Pat).

[204] C-206/01 *Arsenal Football Club Plc* v *Reed* [2003] RPC 144.

[205] Ibid. [51] and repeated by the Court of Justice in the later cases of C-245/02 *Anheuser-Busch* v *Budejovický Budvar, Národní Podnik* [2005] ETMR 27 at [59]; and C-48/05 *Adam Opel AG* v *Autec AG* [2007] ETMR 33 [21]. The *Arsenal* ruling, though couched in more general terms, was anticipated by the earlier decision in C-2/00 *Hölterhoff* v *Freiesleben* [2002] ETMR 79, in which it was held that the owner of a trade mark could not object if a third party, in the course of commercial negotiations, used the sign solely to denote the particular characteristics of the goods he is offering for sale in a way that there can be no question of the trade mark used being understood as a sign indicating trade origin.

[206] C-17/06 *Céline SARL* v *Céline* [2007] ETMR 1320.

- it must be in respect of goods or services which are identical to those for which the mark is registered; and
- it must affect or be liable to affect the functions of the trade mark, in particular its essential function of guaranteeing to consumers the origin of the goods or services.[207]

These conditions then are cumulative and of equal weighting: the fourth, the product of judicial interpretation, being according equal status to those specified in the legislation.[208] Furthermore, AG Colomer has indicated that, unlike the legislative defences, the scope of uses outside the function of a mark should not be interpreted restrictively because these are not 'derogations but rather limitations on the use of *jus prohibendi*'.[209]

That this makes the assessment under Article 5(1)(a) much less rule-like becomes clear from an examination of the Court's indication of how compliance with the condition might be tested. That issue was left open by the Court in *Arsenal*[210] but subsequently, in *Anheuser-Busch* v *Budejovický Budvar, Národní Podnik,* the court declared that the use of a sign is liable to affect the essential function of guaranteeing to consumers the origin of the goods where the use of that sign is such as to create the

207 Ibid. [16]. This weighting has been adopted by UK courts, although both the Court of Appeal and Arnold J in the High Court have summarized the Court of Justice's case law as six conditions, with the premise to these four conditions providing the additional two: *Interflora Inc* v *Marks & Spencer plc* [2014] EWCA Civ 1403 [67]; and *Supreme Petfoods Ltd* v *Henry Bell & Co (Grantham) Ltd* [2015] EWHC 256 (Ch) [83].

208 Senftleben argues that the court is using the function theory as a meta norm which functions as a general yardstick for assessing trade mark claims such that without a showing of adverse effect on at least one protected function, a trade mark infringement action cannot succeed: Senftleben, M, 'Function Theory and International Exhaustion: Why it is Wise to Confine the Double Identity Rule in EU Trade Mark Law to Cases Affecting the Origin Function' (2014) 36 EIPR 518, 520. On the importance of according weight and value to limitations in order to produce a 'balanced' system note the comments in Ramsey and Schovsbo, above n.201, 676.

209 C-48/05 *Adam Opel AG* v *Autec AG* [2007] ETMR 33 [AG34].

210 Although arguably the court indicates that what was required was evidence of confusion on the part of the consumer as to the source of origin of the marked goods or services. This would seem to be implicit from the Courts comments that, 'the essential function of a trade mark is to guarantee the identity of origin of the marked goods or services to the consumer or end user by enabling him, without any possibility of confusion, to distinguish the goods or services from others which have another origin'. C-206/01 *Arsenal Football Club Plc* v *Reed* [2003] RPC 144 [48].

impression, in the minds of consumers, that there is a material link in trade between the third party's goods and the undertaking from which those goods originate.[211]

The decade following the *Arsenal* decision saw a significant increase in commercial activity on the internet which predictably led to litigation as trade mark owners and their competitors sought to map out rights and liabilities in this new trading environment. The inevitable referrals from national courts for preliminary rulings on how European trade mark law is to be understood in these novel circumstances has given the European Court an opportunity to clarify and refine the test for establishing whether an unauthorized use of a registered mark is liable to affect its function.

Most of the referrals have sought guidance on the law in relation to the practice by referencing service providers (most notably Google) of selling search 'keywords', which are identical to registered trade marks, to internet-based traders other than the trade mark owner. When a user undertakes a search using a referencing service provider such as Google, two types of result will typically be provided in response to the keyword(s) entered by the user. The first are the 'natural results', which are the range of sites determined as most relevant to the keyword according to the objective criteria written into the operating algorithms of the search engine. The second are advertisements which appear in the results because the advertisers have paid the referencing service provider to display their advertisements in response to specified keywords being included in a search.[212] The sale of keywords corresponding to registered trade marks prompted consideration of the extent to which keywords corresponding to trade marks can be used outside the control of the proprietors of the trade marks.

Understanding this context is necessary only to understand the terms in which the court expressed the test for establishing whether the essential function of a trade mark was adversely affected when an internet user was shown, on the basis of a keyword identical with a mark, a third party's advertisement. In the first of the internet trading cases, *Google France* v *Louis Vuitton*, the court held that this depended on the manner

---

[211] C-245/02 *Anheuser-Busch* v *Budejovický Budvar, Národní Podnik* [2005] ETMR 27 [60].

[212] See the opinion of AG Poiares Maduro in joined cases C-236/08; C-237/08; and C-238/08 *Google France and Google Inc* v *Louis Vuitton Malletier*; *Google France* v *Viaticum Luteciel*; and *Google France* v *CNRRH* [2010] ETMR 30 [AG1]–[AG5].

in which that advertisement was presented, and that the function of indicating the origin of the mark would be adversely affected if:

> the ad does not enable normally informed and reasonably attentive internet users, or enables them only with difficulty, to ascertain whether the goods or services referred to by the ad originate from the proprietor of the trade mark or an undertaking economically connected to it or, on the contrary, originate from a third party ...[213]

This basic formula has since been repeated by the Court on a number of occasions,[214] most recently in *Interflora Inc* v *Marks & Spencer plc.*[215] Although phrased in fact-specific terms (in particular 'ad' and 'internet user'), the court arrived at this formula by way of analogy with the earlier cases of *Céline*, *Anheuser-Busch* and *Arsenal.*[216] It is probable then that the same test would be applied *mutatis mutandis*, to determine whether, for instance, the sale of toy cars, the sale football memorabilia or the provision of music streaming services, would be such as to affect the essential function of a registered trade mark. On the other hand, that it would be easy enough to arrive at a more general formulation suggests that there may be significance in the fact that the Court has not done so.[217]

---

[213] Joined cases C-236/08; C-237/08; and C-238/08 *Google France and Google Inc* v *Louis Vuitton Malletier*; *Google France* v *Viaticum Luteciel*; and *Google France* v *CNRRH* [2010] ETMR 30 [84].

[214] C-278/08 *Die BergSpechte Outdoor, Reisen und Alpinschule Edi Koblmüller GmbH* v *Günter Guni, trekking.at Reisen GmbH* [2010] ETMR 33 [35]; C-558/08 *Portakabin Ltd* v *Primakabin BV* [2010] ETMR 52 [34]; and C-324/09 *L'Oréal SA* v *eBay International AG* [2011] ETMR 52 [94].

[215] C-323/09 *Interflora Inc, Interflora British Unit* v *Marks & Spencer plc, Flowers Direct Online Ltd* [2012] ETMR 1 [45].

[216] Joined cases C-236/08; C-237/08; and C-238/08 *Google France and Google Inc* v *Louis Vuitton Malletier*; *Google France* v *Viaticum Luteciel*; and *Google France* v *CNRRH* [2010] ETMR 30 [84]–[85].

[217] AG Kokott in C-46/10 *Viking Gas A/S* v *Kosan Gas A/S* was not so reticent when she said that:

> the function of indicating the origin of the mark is adversely affected if the use thereof does not enable reasonably well informed and reasonably observant and circumspect consumers, or enables them only with difficulty, to ascertain whether the goods or services thus labelled originate from the proprietor of the trade mark or an undertaking economically connected to it or, on the contrary, originate from a third party.

[2011] ETMR 58 [AG38]. Alice Blythe argues that it is, 'likely that the jurisprudence underpinning the test in *Google France* v *Louis Vuitton* will be

One reason for this reticence may be that such a general formulation would openly disclose how far the court has come to blur the distinction between identity under Article 5(1)(a) and confusing similarity under Article 5(1)(b) notwithstanding that the court has refrained from explicit use of the word confusion.[218] I do not intend to join with that criticism as such. The key observation so far as the current analysis is concerned is that the overt rule-like character of Article 5(1), a rule associated with securing the claims of right holders, has been significantly qualified by a standard limiting the scope of trade mark rights in a way that ensures that at least some free use can be made of the protected mark. That remains true notwithstanding that, since the decision in *Arsenal*, right owners' interests have been enhanced by the Court's explicit recognition that the owners can exercise their rights in circumstances where a third party's use of a sign affects functions other than the essential function of indicating trade origin.

The court in *Arsenal* referred rather cryptically and ambiguously to the 'functions of a trade mark' whilst only specifically identifying the signalling function of indicating trade origin to consumers. Later, in *L'Oréal SA* v *Bellure NV* the Court of Justice confirmed that rights in a mark were conferred to enable the proprietor to protect her specific interests as proprietor, that is, to ensure that the trade mark can fulfil its functions, but added that these functions included not only the essential function of the trade mark but others and in particular those of guaranteeing the quality of the goods or services to which it was attached and of communication, investment or advertising.[219]

---

subsequently expanded and refashioned in order to be useful in relation to Article 5(1)(a) claims which range beyond the use of adwords': Blythe, A, 'In Search of Mr Average: Attempting to Identify the Average Consumer and His Role within Trade Mark Law' (2013) 37(11) EIPR 709, 713.

218 In this respect note the comments of Kitchen LJ in *Interflora Inc* v *Marks & Spencer plc* [2014] EWCA Civ 1403 [84]. See also Morcom, above n.202. Further, it has been observed that the European Court's recognition of the communication, investment and advertising functions of marks in *L'Oréal SA* v *Bellure NV* blurs the distinction between general protection against confusion and specific protection against dilution: Senftleben, above n.208, 519.

219 C-487/07 *L'Oréal SA* v *Bellure NV* [2010] RPC 1 [58]. This formula was taken from the opinion of AG Jacobs in C-337/95 *Parfums Christian Dior SA* v *Evora BV* [1997] ECR I-6013 which was considered by AG Mengozzi in C-487/07 *L'Oréal SA* v *Bellure NV* [2010] RPC 1 [AG51].

The court has since repeated this particular list of protected functions on a number of occasions,[220] most recently in *Interflora Inc* v *Marks & Spencer plc*, when it noted that trade marks were often instruments of commercial strategy used for advertising purposes or to acquire a reputation in order to develop consumer loyalty. In light of this, a trade mark's function of indicating origin was not the only function of the mark worthy of protection against injury by third parties and the proprietor of a trade mark could exercise her exclusive right:

> where there is, or is liable to be, an adverse effect on one of the functions of the trade mark, irrespective of whether the function concerned is the essential function of indicating the origin of the product or service covered by the trade mark or one of the other functions of the mark, such as that of guaranteeing the quality of that product or service or that of communication, investment or advertising.[221]

Clearly this increases the richness of the test over that first articulated in the *Arsenal* decision by multiplying the range of factors that courts must weigh in the balance in order to decide whether, in a case of identity, a trade mark owner can restrain the activities of a third party. But this development has not changed the test's character to something more rule-like and indeed the development has had quite the opposite effect. By increasing the complexity of the inquiry, the court has moved the law even further from the clarity and predictability of a rule-based test.[222] This has led to manifest frustration in the English Court of Appeal, Jacob LJ expressing the view that the functions other than the essential function were conceptually vague and ill-defined, with the consequence that it was difficult if not impossible to draw a line between a use that was merely descriptive and so lay outside the range of uses that could be restricted by the owner, and a use that strayed into the territory of advertising and so

---

220 Joined cases C-236/08; C-237/08; and C-238/08 *Google France and Google Inc* v *Louis Vuitton Malletier*; *Google France* v *Viaticum Luteciel*; and *Google France* v *CNRRH* [2010] ETMR 30 [77] and [79]; and C-558/08 *Portakabin Ltd* v *Primakabin BV* [2010] ETMR 52 [30].

221 C-323/09 *Interflora Inc, Interflora British Unit* v *Marks & Spencer plc, Flowers Direct Online Ltd* [2012] ETMR 1 [38].

222 Kokott AG in her opinion in C-46/10 *Viking Gas A/S* v *Kosan Gas A/S* goes further in suggesting that, 'not every adverse effect on those functions justifies the application of Article 5(1) … The protection of those functions on the basis of that provision, first, must not undermine the requirements of specific protective rules and, second, must respect overriding other interests': [2011] ETMR 58 [AG59]. For criticism of the uncertainty created see Senftleben, above n.208, 521.

could be restrained.[223] He concluded by expressing regret at the fact that the court had not adopted a clearer and more direct route to the outcome.[224]

Criticism has also come from the European Commission on the grounds that aspects of the Court's case law concerning trade mark functions other than the indication of origin function are erroneous and problematic from the point of view of legal certainty.[225] Indeed in its proposed revisions to European trade mark law published in March 2013, the Commission suggested that, in the interests of legal certainty and consistency, the legislation be amended to make clear that in cases of double identity, only the origin function matters.[226]

These criticisms are fair so far as the court has undoubtedly made the law less clear and predictable but, at the same time, has introduced a flexibility that might allow the law to adapt to unforeseeable developments in the use of trade marks (by owners and third parties). It is safe to predict, for instance, that their use as 'keywords' will not be the only novel use found for trade marks in the online trading environment.[227]

---

223 *L'Oréal SA* v *Bellure NV* [2010] EWCA Civ 535 [30]–[31].

224 Ibid. [32].

225 See the opinion of AG Jääskinen in C-323/09 *Interflora Inc, Interflora British Unit* v *Marks & Spencer plc, Flowers Direct Online Ltd* [2012] ETMR 1 [AG9] recommending legislative reform to meet these criticisms.

226 Proposal for a Regulation of the European Parliament and of the Council amending Council Regulation (EC) No. 207/2009 on the Community trade mark (COM(2013) 161 final) (in particular recital (15) and Art 9(2)(a)); and Proposal for a Directive of the European Parliament and of the Council to approximate the laws of the member states relating to trade marks (COM(2013) 162 final) (in particular recital (19) and Art 10(2)(a)). In this respect the Commission's recommendations followed those of the Max Plank Institute report: Max Planck Institute for Intellectual Property and Competition Law, *Study on the Overall Functioning of the European Trade Mark System*, 15 February 2011, accessed 24 January 2017 at http://ec.europa.eu/internal_market/indprop/docs/tm/20110308_allensbach-study_en.pdf, 103–4. These proposed amendments were, however, opposed by the Parliament (see European Parliament legislative resolution of 25 February 2014 on the proposal for a directive of the European Parliament and of the Council to approximate the laws of the member states relating to trade marks) and did not make it into the finally agreed reform package: see Regulation (EU) 2015/2424 amending Council Regulation (EC) No 207/2009 on the Community trade mark; and Directive (EU) 2015/2436 to approximate the laws of the member states relating to trade marks.

227 Ramsey and Schovsbo observe that, 'the EU's explicit statutory limitations alone may not achieve the correct balance between trade mark rights and other important public interests in many trade mark disputes, especially in cases

But this standards-based flexibility is important more generally insofar as, outside the most routine instances of counterfeiting, deciding whether an owner should be able to restrict the unauthorized use of a mark in a particular case demands the exercise of judicial discretion in a way that strikes an appropriate balance between the competing interests and such that the results may be largely case specific.[228] The judicial role is not then to arrive at a state of affairs which promote competition: the competing interests are already there. It is rather to ensure that what competition there is, is undertaken fairly. And as with copyright law, sharing and altruism are understood to be essential characteristics of *fair* competition. This serves to explain the rather paradoxical statement made by the Court in *Interflora Inc* v *Marks & Spencer plc*, that, although the legal protection of trade marks is an essential element in a system of undistorted competition, this does not mean that trade mark owners are protected against practices inherent in competition.[229] What it had in mind is perhaps indicated later in the judgement when it explained that:

> it cannot be accepted that the proprietor of a trade mark may – in conditions of fair competition that respect the trade mark's function as an indication of origin – prevent a competitor from using a sign identical with that trade mark in relation to goods or services identical with those for which the mark is registered, if the only consequence of that use is to oblige the proprietor of that trade mark to adapt its efforts to acquire or preserve a reputation capable of attracting consumers and retaining their loyalty. Likewise, the fact that that use may prompt some consumers to switch from goods or services bearing that trade mark cannot be successfully relied on by the proprietor of the mark.[230]

So in the Court's view, where an advertisement displayed on the internet on the basis of a keyword corresponding to a trade mark does no more than put forward an alternative to the goods or services of the proprietor of the trade mark, such use falls within the ambit of fair competition and cannot be restrained by the owner of the trade mark.[231] This conclusion reflects the Court's judgement as to, on balance, what is fair competition

involving new technologies where legislators may not have predicted the different ways a mark may be used by third parties': Ramsey and Schovsbo, above n.201, 673 and see also their comments at 684–5.

[228] Kozinski, above n.174, 977. See also the Opinion of AG Colomer in C-48/05 *Adam Opel AG* v *Autec AG* [2007] ETMR 33 [AG34]; and Ramsey and Schovsbo, above n.201, 684–5.

[229] [2012] ETMR 1 [57].

[230] Ibid. [64]

[231] Ibid. [91] and see also [81] and [95].

and finds a parallel in Hoffmann J's dicta in *Billhöfer Maschinenfabrik* v *Dixon* on copyright law and fair competition.[232] But as always, the flexibility of a standard comprises clarity and certainty, an effect which is all the more acute in circumstances where the legal direction is intended to provide authoritative guidance to national tribunals in the interests of harmonization.[233] That the chief critics of the Court's jurisprudence are the Commission and national courts, both one way or another voicing the complaint that the law as developed by the court lacks clarity,[234] is hardly surprising then and the tensions in evidence here are essentially the same as those that have influenced the European attempts to harmonize the rules regarding the patentability of computer-implemented inventions.[235]

Earlier in this chapter I aimed to show that in copyright law and patent law, it is indeed the case that the rule form is associated with securing claims and strengthening the position of right holders whereas the standard form is associated with limiting scope and facilitating public access. The same is true of trade mark law but only to an extent. A critic would no doubt point out that whilst that association may well hold up in cases of identity, it is not present in circumstances where right holders seek to protect their interests against uses and/or signs which are merely similar, or where they seek to restrain activities which they believe harm reputation or take unfair advantage. Unlike copyright law, in trade mark law it cannot be said that there is a general correspondence between form and a commitment to a particular political paradigm. The explanation of the difference allows me to introduce an interesting further dimension to

---

232 Above at p. 216. Annette Kur argues that it would be wrong to conclude that the Court of Justice's decisions on double identity will automatically lead to enhanced protection of trade marks. Rather, she says, protection will be given only where the interests of the trade mark holder are seriously jeopardized by 'conduct that is incompatible with fair and sound competition': Kur, A, 'Trade Marks Function, and Don't They? CJEU Jurisprudence and Unfair Competition Principles' (2014) 45 IIC 434, 442.

233 Ramsey and Schovsbo observe that,

> there will be less harmonization of domestic trade mark laws if national courts have flexibility to implement new limitations on trade mark rights that further the public interest. There is disagreement about the proper competition policy and scope of the right to freedom of speech, and thus the content of the limitations on trade mark rights will likely differ among courts and nations.

Ramsey and Schovsbo, above n.201, 697.

234 Kur, above n.232, 444.

235 On which see above at p. 130 *et seq.*

the conflict between the political paradigms of individualism and altruism that finds expression in the role of the public interest in trade mark law.

In some very limited respects the individualist/altruist conflict lies at the heart of trade mark law as much as it does copyright. Certainly the legal protection of marks allows individuals to claim exclusive rights over the use of signs which have the potential to impact on the public interest in freedom of expression. Given, however, the limits placed on the exercise of trade mark rights outlined above, one might question how far this concern needs to be taken seriously. The greater impact of a claim to exclusive rights over a particular sign is on other traders and only indirectly on the wider public (which has an interest in free and fair competition amongst traders). When the public interest is raised as an objection to a claim made by a trade mark owner, typically the immediate and direct impact that is complained about relates to the restrictions placed on other traders.[236] For instance, the Court in C-108/97 *Windsurfing Chiemsee* v *Huber* observed in relation to the exclusion from registration of descriptive marks under Article 3(1)(c) of the Directive,[237] that:

> Article 3(1)(c) of the Directive pursues an aim which is in the public interest, namely that descriptive signs or indications relating to the categories of goods or services in respect of which registration is applied for may be freely used by all … Article 3(1)(c) therefore prevents such signs and indications from being reserved to one undertaking alone because they have been registered as trade marks.[238]

---

236 Davis, J, 'Between a Sign and a Brand: Mapping the Boundaries of a Registered Trade Mark in European Union Trade Mark Law' in Bently, L, Davis, J and Ginsburg, J (eds) *Trade Marks and Brands: An Interdisciplinary Critique* (Cambridge University Press 2008), 75–6.

237 Article 3(1)(c) of the Directive is entitled 'Grounds for refusal or invalidity' and provides that trade marks:

> which consist exclusively of signs or indications which may serve, in trade, to designate the kind, quality, quantity, intended purpose, value, geographical origin, or the time of production of the goods or of rendering of the service, or other characteristics of the goods or service' shall not be registered or if registered shall be liable to be declared invalid.

238 Joined cases C-108/97 and C-109/97 *Windsurfing Chiemsee Produktions- und Vertriebs GmbH* v *Boots und Segelzubehör Walter Huber and Franz Attenberge* [1999] ETMR 585 [25]. That Article 3(1) must be understood in light of this public interest has been repeated by the court on a number of occasions: C-191/01 *OHIM* v *Wrigley* ('Doublemint') [2004] ETMR 121 [31]; joined cases

This pattern of reasoning seems to manifest the individualist/altruist conflict in a straightforward way. What disrupts the relationship is the fact that an individual can secure rights in a descriptive mark if that mark acquires a distinctive character through the use made of it.[239] The question of whether the use of a mark has led to it acquiring distinctive character is answered by reference to the relevant customer's perception and in particular:

> in order to demonstrate that a sign has acquired distinctive character, the applicant or trade mark proprietor must prove that, at the relevant date, a significant proportion of the relevant class of persons perceives the relevant goods or services as originating from a particular undertaking because of the sign in question (as opposed to any other trade mark which may also be present).[240]

Crucially then, if consumers perceive the mark as an indication of trade origin then the interest that other traders may have in using the mark is overridden. This is but one illustration of instances where, when set in the balance against competing interests, the rights of trade mark owners are referred to in a way that indicate that these rights are aligned with the interests of consumers and it is the interest of consumers that justifies the right claimed. The same argument is put forward where the owner of a mark is claiming that use of the mark by a third party harms the essential function of the mark. The essential function of a mark was said by the

---

C-53/01 to C-55/01 *Linde AG; Winward Industries Inc; and Rado Uhren AG Applications* [2003] ETMR 963 [73]; C-265/00 *Campina Melkunie BV* v *Benelux-Merkenbureau* [2004] ETMR 821 [34]–[36]; and C-363/99 *Koninklijke KPN Nederland NV* v *Benelux-Merkenbureau* [2004] ETMR 771 [54]–[55]; [68]; [94]–[95]; and [102].

[239] Under Article 3(3) Trade Marks Directive. See also Davis, above n.236, 79.

[240] *The London Taxi Corporation Ltd* v *Frazer-Nash Research Ltd* [2016] EWHC 52 (Ch) [178] and *Société des Produits Nestlé SA* v *Cadbury UK Ltd* [2016] EWHC 50 (Ch) at [57], interpreting and applying C-215/14 *Société des Produits Nestlé SA* v *Cadbury UK Ltd* [2015] ETMR 50, at [58]–[67]. See also joined cases C-108/97 and C-109/97 *Windsurfing Chiemsee Produktions- und Vertriebs GmbH* v *Boots- und Segelzubehör Walter Huber and Franz Attenberge* [1999] ETMR 585 [47]–[48]. Note also Dinwoodie, G and Gangjee, D, 'The Image of the Consumer in EU Trade Mark Law' in Leczykiewicz, D and Weatherill, S (eds) *The Images of the Consumer in EU Law. Legislation, Free Movement and Competition Law* (Hart Publishing, 2016), 346 ('to be "distinctive" in doctrinal language – trade marks must be understood by consumers as pointing to a particular producer as the source of the goods (even if the consumers could not specifically name the producer)').

Court in *Arsenal*, is 'to guarantee the identity of origin of the marked goods or services to the *consumer or end user*'.[241] By way of application, typical is what was said by the court in *Google France* v *Louis Vuitton*[242] in its observation that an adverse effect on the function of indicating origin would occur in circumstances where, because of the way in which advertisements were displayed in response to that trade mark being used as a search term by an internet user, the user would err as to the origin of the goods or services in question.[243] And, as observed by Graeme Dinwoodie and Dev Gangjee, even where trade mark protection is justified on terms such as protecting goodwill or investment, consumer interests play an 'epistemic' role, for example:

> where third parties make unauthorised use of a sign that is the same as or similar to a registered trade mark, confused consumers are unable to claim in their own right. Their actual or presumed reaction to the third party use will however determine whether the trade mark owner's action to protect its property interest is successful. Indeed, consumer perceptions and interests function as the litmus test both for the existence and scope of protection; there are few areas of trade mark law where the concept of the consumer is not relevant.[244]

---

241 C-206/01 *Arsenal Football Club Plc* v *Reed* [2003] RPC 144 [48] (emphasis added).

242 Joined cases C-236/08; C-237/08; and C-238/08 *Google France and Google Inc* v *Louis Vuitton Malletier*; *Google France* v *Viaticum Luteciel*; and *Google France* v *CNRRH* [2010] ETMR 30.

243 Ibid. [85]. More specifically the court said that there would be an adverse effect where a third party's ad suggested an economic link between that third party and the proprietor of the trade mark ([89]) or where the ad was vague to such an extent on the origin of the goods or services that a normally informed and reasonably attentive user would be unable to determine whether the third party was economically linked to the proprietor ([90]). See also C-323/09 *Interflora Inc, Interflora British Unit* v *Marks & Spencer plc, Flowers Direct Online Ltd*, [2012] ETMR 1 [44]–[45]. The so-called 'advertising function' can be seen as parasitical on the essential origin function so far as the court has indicated that the advertising function would be harmed in circumstances where the proprietor of a mark was denied the opportunity of using the mark effectively to inform and win over consumers: ibid. [59]. So too the so-called 'investment function', which though distinct, overlaps the advertising function and which the court has said is harmed in circumstances where there is a substantial interference with the proprietor's use of its trade mark to acquire or preserve a reputation capable of attracting consumers and retaining their loyalty: ibid. [62].

244 Dinwoodie and Gangjee, above n.240, 344–5.

The interest that consumers have in not being deceived features in the determination of the scope of owners' rights because the legal protection of trade marks is justified as an essential element in a system of undistorted competition.[245] That the interest of consumers features so significantly in arguments concerning the recognition and scope of trade mark rights matters because, in terms of the tension between individualism and altruism, the interests of consumers overlap but do not align precisely with the interests of trade mark owners. At the same time, the interest that consumers have in the legal recognition and scope of trade mark rights, overlaps with but does not precisely align with the interest of the public in the free use of trade marks in public discourse.[246] The key point is that any relationship between form and substance, in the sense of the rule form being associated with securing claims and strengthening the position of right holders and the standard form being associated with limiting scope and facilitating public access, is at least partly obscured in trade mark law by the fact that owners' rights to exclude on the one hand, and the limits on scope on the other, are viewed through the filter of consumer interest which itself embodies a simultaneous commitment to individualism and altruism.

To understand why this is so, we can start with the general observation that modern information systems and networking, whilst augmenting human powers of organization and integration, also work to subvert the idea of a separate, independent subject.[247] The modern world is thus one

---

245 On the links between the notion of the average informed consumer, trade mark law and free market principles, see Davis, J, 'Locating the Average Consumer: His Judicial Origins, Intellectual Influences and Current Role in European Trade Mark Law' (2005) IPQ 183, 196–7. See also Davis, J, 'Revisiting the Average Consumer: An Uncertain Presence in European Trade Mark Law' (2015) IPQ 15, 21–2.

246 The uncertain relationship between the interests of consumers and mark owners is a reflection of the absence of a clear normative grounding of European trade mark law. As observed by Graeme Dinwoodie and Dev Gangjee,

> the roots of the average consumer concept in trade mark law … lie in the jurisprudence of the CJEU on misleading advertising, which became easy to transfer to the context of trade mark law when the CJEU first tackled case law under the Trade Mark Directive. But this apparently reflexive adoption of the 'average consumer' from EU advertising law occurred without much (if any) consideration of whether EU trade mark law possessed a different normative basis than consumer protection or advertising law.

Dinwoodie and Gangjee, above n.240, 364.

247 Castells, M, *The Rise of the Network Society*, 2nd edition (Wiley & Sons, 2010), 23 citing Raymond Barglow. Castells earlier observes that 'in a world of

in which individuals have to work to acquire an identity.[248] Identities can be constructed from a number of materials.[249] Which materials, how these are processed and the meaning ascribed to them are determined socially and thus linked to particular times and places.[250] In developed Western societies, modern patterns of production and consumption have created opportunities for an individual's identity to be at least partially constructed through their patterns of consumption:

> The vast variety of alternative possibilities of consumption in affluent post-Fordist markets provides a mechanism that allows people to conceive of an act of purchase – concluding, as it often does, a lengthy period of introspective exploration of one's very personal preferences – as an act of self-identification and self-presentation, one that sets the individual apart from some social groups while uniting him or her with others.[251]

The idea that the consumer's simultaneous desire for emulation and differentiation is an intrinsic feature of the human character[252] parallels Duncan Kennedy's view that the ambivalence between individualism and altruism are reflective of a 'fundamental contradiction' between the desires to fuse with others yet remain separate from them: to assert one's existential independence and authenticity while recognizing that one is socially formed and framed.[253] Thus, consumers qua consumers typically display a commitment to both individualism and altruism in their

---

global flows of wealth, power, and images, the search for identity, collective or individual, ascribed or constructed, becomes the fundamental source of social meaning': ibid., 3.

[248] Castells defines 'identity', as it refers to social actors as, 'the process of construction of meaning on the basis of a cultural attribute, or related set of cultural attributes, that is/are given priority over other sources of meaning': Castells, M, *The Power of Identity* (Blackwell, 1997), 6.

[249] Manuel Castells, for instance, suggests materials can be drawn from history, from geography, from biology, from productive and reproductive institutions, from collective memory and from personal fantasies, from power apparatuses and religious revelations: ibid., 7.

[250] Ibid.

[251] Streeck, W, 'Citizens as Customers. Considerations on the New Politics of Consumption' (2012) 76 New Left Review 27, 35. See also Holt, D, 'Why Do Brands Cause Trouble: A Dialectical Theory of Consumer Culture and Branding' (2002) 29 Journal of Consumer Research 70, 71; and Gerhardt, D R, 'Consumer Investment in Trade Marks' 88 (2009–10) North Carolina L Rev 427, 436 and 459–60.

[252] Described as such in Streeck, above n.251, 27.

[253] Kennedy, D, 'The Structure of Blackstone's Commentaries' (1979) 28 Buffalo L Rev 205, 211–13. See also Kelman, above n.33, 17.

simultaneous desire for emulation and differentiation. Trade marks are an essential component of the means by which consumers emulate and differentiate. Thus the social anthropologist James Leach draws a distinction between what he calls the consumable element in a transaction involving trade marks (the good itself) and the enduring or non-consumable element. He argues that consumers draw upon tropes both of interpersonal and of autonomous value creation and that, '[t]hey are in pseudo-personal relationships to the kinds of person that a trade mark appears to delineate, but are able to consider themselves autonomous from those other persons for the purpose of making their own identity through the consumption of trade marked goods'.[254] More fully, he explains thus:

> transactions governed by trade marks … have a dual aspect for the consumer. A pseudo-interpersonal relationship is established with the trader as if they were a person with whom the consumer could have an ongoing and identity-defining relationship. Yet at the same time, a sense of autonomy from relationships and thus a sense of self-determination and individual character emerges through a relation to an object, defined by the transaction as alienated from other people and thus available, as it were, to be wholly incorporated into the consumer subject. This fosters the constitution of their identity *apparently* without reference to other persons.[255]

Thus, the choice of what good to purchase allows an individual to differentiate themselves from others who make different purchase choices.[256] The social significance of this choice is given enhanced content by the so-called modern function of marks as symbols which evoke a broad set of associations and meanings going beyond mere trade origin.[257] Marks associated with 'luxury goods' can thus become

---

[254] Leach, J, 'An Anthropological Approach to Transactions Involving Names and Marks, Drawing on Melanesia' in Bently, L, Davis, J and Ginsburg, J (eds) *Trade Marks and Brands: An Interdisciplinary Critique* (Cambridge University Press, 2008), 322.

[255] Ibid., 324.

[256] Ibid., 340 (n.51 and n.52 respectively).

[257] Labelling the function of marks to act as symbols as 'modern' fits neatly with the view of some commentators that expressing personal identity through trade mark choice is a modern phenomenon: Gerhardt, above n.251, 459.

'emblems of prestige'[258] but marks can also be emblematic of characteristics or qualities other than raw purchasing power.[259]

The individualism that motivates an attempt at self-definition through purchasing goods of a certain brand will only work to do so if others have also made the same *informed* choice such that all understand that they share a common set of values that mark them out as a distinct group within a broader society. In this way a trade mark can become a 'connective force' linking individuals with shared values into distinct communities.[260] No doubt, through advertising, trade mark owners work hard to signal to consumers the particular social significance attached to membership of any particular community. Each informed act of purchase works to reinforce the symbolic content of the trade mark and in this way consumers participate in the creation of brands.[261]

The important thing to appreciate is that the social significance of any act of purchase turns on the informational content of that act which is determined by the trade mark owner's advertising and other efforts at communication; actual patterns of consumption; and public discourse. Sometimes these will all act to reinforce one another to produce a single coherent message. At other times they may run counter to one another.[262] And the content and weight attached to this discourse may be different between those within a particular community centred around allegiance

---

[258] On trade marks functioning as 'emblems of prestige' see the opinion of AG Ruiz-Jabaro Colomer in C-206/01 *Arsenal Football Club Plc* v *Reed* [2003] RPC 144 [47]. See also Gangjee, D, 'Property in Brands: The Commodification of Conversation' in Howe, H R and Griffiths, J (eds) *Concepts of Property in Intellectual Property Law* (Cambridge University Press, 2013), 35.

[259] Such as 'frugality' and a commitment to green politics on which see the account of reasons given for their choice by purchasers of the Toyota Prius in Gerhardt, above n.251, 448. See also and more generally Bently and Sherman, above n.1, 810–11.

[260] Holt, above n.251, 82; Gerhardt, above n.251, 465–6; Hollenbeck, C and Zinkham, G, 'Consumer Activism on the Internet: the Role of Anti-Brand Communities' (2006) 33 Advances in Consumer Research 479, 479.

[261] Gerhardt, above n.251, 453; Gangjee, above n.258, 36–7 and 50–54; and Wilf, S, 'Who Authors Trademarks?' (1999) 17 Cardozo Art and Entertainment LJ 1.

[262] See for instance the account of the consequences of increased advertising on the British fashion brand Burberry in: *The Daily Mail*, 'The Luxury Brand with a Chequered Past, Burberry's Shaken Off its Chav Image to Become the Fashionistas Favourite Once More', June 2008, accessed 24 January 2017 at http://www.dailymail.co.uk/femail/article-1023460/Burberrys-shaken-chav-image-fashionistas-favourite-more.html.

to a particular brand and those outside that community.[263] The internet has served to magnify these effects by facilitating communication but in ways that are harder for the owners of marks to control.[264]

The notion of consumer interest itself embodies a simultaneous commitment to individualism and altruism and whilst the legislation adopted the rule form in the case of identity on the assumption that this was a clear instance where trade mark owners' rights should be secure, the rule-like character of the legislative provisions has been compromised by the court precisely because these rights are secured by reference to consumer interest which requires a more nuanced balance to be struck between rights to exclude and the interests there are in sharing.

263 As observed by Deborah Gerhardt, 'consumers are especially influential when they organize into communities that critique or celebrate a brand. In evaluating a brand, consumers rely on information from a variety of sources in addition to the mark owner': Gerhardt, above n.251, 454.

264 Gerhardt observes that the social connections that influence brand perceptions are easier to maintain on the internet: Gerhardt, above n.251, 456–8. See also Gangjee, above n.258, 53–4. For an account of internet-based 'anti-brand' movements see Hollenbeck and Zinkham, above n.260.

6. Form and justifications

Merely exposing the conflict between rules and standards raises some difficult questions about the credibility of the dominant contemporary economic justifications for recognizing and enforcing intellectual property rights. The most widely accepted instrumental justifications for according rights in intellectual productions sit uncomfortably with the indeterminacy that inevitably comes with decision making according to other than clear and well-defined rules. For instance, the historical development of patent rights demonstrates that patents developed as a tool of economic development[1] and the most frequently voiced argument in favour of the patent system relies on the 'monopoly-profit-incentive' thesis. This asserts that without the intervention provided by the patent system, a market will tend to undersupply inventions because of the failure caused by free-riding.[2] In an unregulated market, potential producers of useful inventions will be deterred from making necessary investments in arriving at and developing their ideas for fear that they will not be able to appropriate the value of this investment because competitors will free-ride by taking the benefit of successful ideas without compensating the originator for the costs sunk in producing them. By granting innovators exclusive rights in their innovations, the patent system aims to remedy this market failure.

---

1 Schaafsma, P, 'An Economic Overview of Patents' (1997) 79 Journal of the Patent and Trade Mark Office Society 241, 242.

2 See for instance the reviews of the contemporary and historical justifications of intellectual property in Machlup, F, *An Economic Review of the Patent System. Study No. 15 of the United States Subcommittee on Patent, Trade marks and Copyrights* (US Government Printing Office, 1958), 77–8 and from which the term 'monopoly-profit-incentive' is taken. Useful outline reviews can also be found in: Schaafsma, above n.1; Landes, W and Posner, R, *The Economic Structure of Intellectual Property Law* (Belknap, 2003), 20–21; Posner, R, *Economic Analysis of Law*, 7th edition (Wolters Kluwer Law & Business, 2007), 38; and Guellec, D and van Pottelsberghe de la Potterie, B, *The Economics of the European Patent System – IP Policy for Innovation and Competition* (Oxford University Press, 2007), 4.

Under this view, the positive social and economic impacts that flow from the patent system depend on its effectiveness in encouraging individuals to invest in R&D. For an individual, investing in the generation of useful information, for example by funding an R&D programme, is one investment choice amongst many.[3] Any investment requires planning, foresight and organization in the employment of resources. The returns on any investment are to some extent uncertain, but in the competition to attract investment funds, R&D is on the face of it particularly unattractive for two reasons. First, it is extremely difficult to calculate the probability of success of any particular R&D project, success depending on 'inextricable tangle of objective uncertainties'.[4] Of course firms will try to evaluate the cost effectiveness of any proposed R&D project[5] but at the point where early investment decisions are made nearly all the variables that feed into a decision to invest in a particular research project will be uncertain. The costs that will be necessary to arrive at a desirable outcome cannot be known with certainty until they are actually incurred and these will be borne long before any revenue is realized. At that stage, the likelihood that a particular research project will be successful in the sense of producing something useful also cannot be known with certainty. And assuming that the project is successful, the revenue-generating value of any product coming out of the project will only become clear once that product is commercialized.[6] In short, substantial uncertainty surrounds the entire process and output can never be predicted with much accuracy from the inputs.[7] Secondly, investment in R&D tends to be irreversible in that the costs of a research project cannot be recouped if a project fails and the assets utilized tend to be

---

[3] There is evidence that invention is largely an economic activity pursued for gain rather than being driven merely by technological opportunity: Kamien, M and Schwartz, N, 'Market Structure and Innovation: A Survey' (1975) 13 Journal of Economic Literature 1, 7.

[4] Arrow, K, 'Economic Welfare and the Allocation of Resources for Invention' in *The Rate and Direction of Inventive Activity: Economic and Social Factors. A Report of the National Bureau of Economic Research* (Princeton University Press, 1962), 613.

[5] Mansfield, E and Wagner, S, 'Organisational and Strategic Factors Associated with Probabilities of Success in Industrial R&D' (1975) 48 J Bus 179, 190.

[6] Kamien and Schwartz, above n.3, 2; and Blair, R and Cotter, T, *Intellectual Property. Economics and Legal Dimensions of Rights and Remedies* (Cambridge University Press, 2005), 42–4.

[7] Arrow, above n.4, 616.

'idiosyncratic'[8] in that they cannot be redeployed without sacrifice of productive value.[9] Thus investment in R&D is not only uncertain but brings with it the likelihood that the resources deployed will be depleted if not entirely exhausted.[10] It is generally the case that uncertainty deters investment in idiosyncratic capital.[11]

The limited empirical data that is available indicates that the general state of affairs is that investment in R&D is made unattractive by uncertainty about market returns which leads to a reduction in firm-level R&D investment.[12] This is not necessarily a bad thing for the individual firm nor indeed the overall public good. The bias means that a firm might divert resources into different channels, for example to upgrade plant and

---

8 On the significance of asset specificity in transaction cost economics and the use of the term 'idiosyncratic' to describe transaction specific investments, see Williamson, O, *The Economic Institutions of Capitalism. Firms, Markets, Relational Contracting* (The Free Press, 1985), 52–6.

9 This is because a large proportion of R&D supports the salaries of research personnel: Czarnitzki, D and Toole, A, 'Patent Protection, Market Uncertainty, and R&D Investment' (2006) ZEW – Centre for European Economic Research Discussion Paper No. 06-056, accessed 24 January 2017 at http://ssrn.com/abstract=925621, 1. See also Goel, R and Ram, R, 'Irreversibility of R&D Investment and the Adverse Effect of Uncertainty: Evidence from the OECD Countries' (2001) 71(2) Economic Letters 287, 288. It has been suggested that the obviousness standard encourages firms to invest in proprietary knowledge prior to the commencement of an R&D project: Merges, R, 'Uncertainty and the Standard of Patentability' (1992) 7 High Technology LJ 1, 37.

10 In a pioneering and hugely influential study, Frank Knight famously drew a distinction between risk and uncertainty. Risk he understood to describe situations in which the probabilities of outcomes can be assigned, and uncertainty situations where this is not possible: Knight, F, *Risk, Uncertainty and Profit* (University of Chicago Press, 1971 (originally published in 1921 by Houghton Mifflin Co.)), 19–20 and 233. See also Langlois, R and Cosgel, M, 'Frank Knight on Risk, Uncertainty, and the Firm: A New Interpretation' (1993) 31(3) Economic Inquiry 456, 457 (noting that this understanding of the distinction remains dominant but then questioning this reading of Knight's work). Knight viewed decisions regarding invention to be fundamentally and irretrievably uncertain; however, empirical studies suggest that the probabilities of success of R&D are not completely beyond calculation: see in particular Mansfield and Wagner, above n.5.

11 Pindyck, R, 'Irreversibility, Uncertainty, and Investment' (1991) 29(3) Journal of Economic Literature 1110; and Goel and Ram, above n.9, 1.

12 A study of the German manufacturing sector showed that the median firm reduced R&D investment by 26 per cent in response to a 10 per cent increase in uncertainty on average: Czarnitzki and Toole, above n.9, 18–19. See also Goel and Ram, above n.9.

machinery or to enhance skills training for its workforce, which might of themselves produce greater efficiency gains than an equivalent investment in R&D.[13] But that said, at national and regional level innovation is undoubtedly an essential engine of economic growth[14] and, given that uncertainty can create a significant and general bias against investment in R&D, the state has an important role to play in creating conditions that work to overcome that bias. One thing the state can do to encourage investment in innovation is to offer the prospect of a prize in return for accepting the uncertainties associated with R&D.[15] The state, in providing a patent system, can be seen then as acting as a bookmaker: it offers the prospect of greater returns if greater risks are taken.[16] Just as a bookmaker induces gamblers to bet on horses which have a slim chance of winning a race by offering the prospect of huge winnings in the unlikely event that they do win, so too the state can encourage entrepreneurs to invest in R&D despite the long odds of success by the prospect of the prize of monopoly profits secured by the grant of a patent.[17] To be attractive, the prospect that this prize can be won has to

---

[13] In particular industries continued innovation can actually be harmful: Burk, D and Lemley, M, 'Policy Levers in Patent Law' (2003) 89 Virginia L Rev 1575, 1588.

[14] See e.g. Kamien and Schwartz, above n.3, 11 and Mowery, D and Rosenberg, N, *Paths of Innovation. Technological Change in 20th-Century America* (Cambridge University Press, 1998), 4. Also notable is the importance that the European Commission attaches to 'innovation' in its strategy for growth: *EUROPE 2020 A strategy for smart, sustainable and inclusive growth*, COM (2010) 2020, 9–12.

[15] Of course the intellectual property system is not the only way in which a government can act to stimulate innovation but the system has the huge advantage over other mechanisms of minimizing the government's information requirements because, '[t]he government doesn't need to estimate the cost or value of innovation. Instead, the government allows the patentee to capture a rough and limited proxy of consumer value and then lets the potential innovator decide whether the benefits of innovation justify the costs': Ayres, I and Klemperer, P, 'Limiting Patentees' Market Power Without Reducing Innovation Incentives: The Perverse Benefits of Uncertainty and Non-Injunctive Remedies' (1999) 97 Michigan L Rev 986, 1008.

[16] For a rather more sophisticated and detailed development of this analogy see Scherer, F, 'The Innovation Lottery' in Dreyfuss, R, Zimmerman, D and First, H (eds) *Expanding the Boundaries of Intellectual Property. Innovation Policy for the Knowledge Society* (Oxford University Press, 2001), 1516 and 18.

[17] And one thing to note here is that, on the face of it, the rewards do have to be great if the system is to work in this way: 'the possible gains must be in the nature of a first prize in a lottery, of a jackpot in a game of chance': Machlup,

be credible. The expectations secured by clear and ascertainable rules provide the degree of security necessary to make what would otherwise be unattractive investments, seem worth pursuing.[18]

Copyright law, too, is often justified as providing a necessary incentive aimed at encouraging authors, composers, artists, as well as publishers, record companies and film studios to invest in the production of new creations.[19] And as with investment in R&D, so too it is assumed (not unreasonably) that investment in the generation and publication of literary, dramatic, musical and artistic works is made unattractive by uncertainty about market returns.[20]

The monopoly profit incentive theory probably still holds the centre ground but arguably there is evidence of a shift from an 'incentives'-based paradigm to a 'proprietary' justification of intellectual property rights.[21] Founded on Harold Demsetz's 'progressive model' of the development of property rights,[22] one such justification looks to the

---

above n.2, 24. Based on the empirical evidence that a small minority of investors in innovation gain large rewards whilst the majority of innovative efforts confer only modest rewards Scherer concludes that a large reward is a crucial feature of the incentive system: Scherer, above n.16, 20.

18 For a fuller development of this argument see Booton, D, 'The Management of Uncertainty and the Patent Incentive' (2011) 24 IPJ 79.

19 See e.g. Breyer, S, 'The Uneasy Case for Copyright: A Study of Copyright in Books, Photocopies, and Computer Programs' (1970) 84 Harvard L Rev 281, 293–4; Landes, W and Posner, R, 'An Economic Analysis of Copyright' (1989) 18(2) Journal of Legal Studies 325, 326; Gordon, W, 'An Inquiry into the Merits of Copyright: The Challenges of Consistency, Consent, and Encouragement Theory' (1989) 41 Stanford L Rev 1343, 1348 and 1422; Towse, R, 'The Quest for Evidence on the Economic Effects of Copyright Law' (2013) 37(5) Cambridge Journal of Economics 1187, 1188; Towse, R, 'What We Know, What We Don't Know, and What Policy-Makers Would Like Us to Know about the Economics of Copyright' (2011) 8(2) Review of Economic Research on Copyright Issues 101, 104; and Towse, R, Handke, C and Stepan, P, 'The Economics of Copyright Law: A Stocktake of the Literature' (2008) 5 Review of Economic Research on Copyright Issues 1, 3, 5, 11.

20 Landes and Posner, above n.19, 328–9; and Carter, S, 'Does it Matter Whether Intellectual Property is Property?' (1993) 68 Chicago-Kent L Rev 715, 719.

21 Salzberger, E, 'The Law and Economics Analysis of Intellectual Property: Paradigmatic Shift from Incentives to Traditional Property' (2010), accessed 24 January 2017 at http://ssrn.com/abstract=1574994.

22 The classic article on the economic case for awarding property rights over exhaustible resources is Demsetz, H, 'Towards a Theory of Property Rights' (1967) 57 American Economic Review, 347, in which he argues that a primary function of property rights is that of guiding incentives to achieve a greater

social benefits that derive from the efficient management of valuable, scarce and exhaustible resources.[23] However, this way of thinking has been criticized as inappropriate in the case of intellectual property rights since it fails to take account of the fact that there is no rivalry in the consumption of information and that its use does not deplete or degrade it as a resource.[24] An alternative proprietary justification, advanced by Robert Merges, draws on transaction cost economics.[25] Merges notes that Demsetz's approach to property focuses attention on the initial definition and grant of property rights but pays little attention to transactions involving property rights.[26] Merges argues that from the point of view of transaction cost economics, intellectual property shares with other forms of property a role in facilitating bargaining by reducing transaction costs. Property rights, including intellectual property rights, reduce the costs of planning through giving one party a wide and unspecified measure of control and in this way the default rights that accompany property ownership provide a peerless form of transactional safeguard.[27] But again, to operate in this way, there must be relative certainty as to the scope of rights, who owns them, and how liable claims are to be revoked or otherwise not recognized.

Under the most frequently advanced economic justification for according rights in trade marks, rights are also understood to be important in managing uncertainty and reducing transaction costs. But the uncertainty addressed is that facing the consumer confronted with the choices that characterize a competitive market rather than the uncertainty faced by the trader operating in such a market. Understood as signs indicating the

---

internalization of externalities. Demsetz's arguments provide the foundation for the so-called 'tragedy of the commons', which is often advanced as an argument in support of the private ownership of property: Hardin, G, 'The Tragedy of the Commons' (1968) 162 Science, 1243.

23 Notable is Landes, W and Posner, R, 'Indefinitely Renewable Copyright' (2003) 70 University of Chicago L Rev 471, 475.

24 See for instance Lemley, M, 'Ex Ante versus Ex Post Justifications for Intellectual Property' (2004) 71 University of Chicago L Rev 129, 143; and, for a wider ranging criticism, Salzberger, above n.21, 35–7.

25 Merges, R, 'A Transactional View of Property Rights' (2005) 20 Berkeley Technology LJ 1477.

26 Ibid., 1482.

27 Ibid., 1486. In respect of the transaction cost advantages of property over contract see also Merges, R, *Justifying Intellectual Property* (Harvard University Press, 2011), 263. It could be argued that this justification begs the question. In a world devoid of intellectual property rights where individuals were free to copy the ideas of others, transaction costs would be zero: Breyer, above n.19, 316.

source of origin of products, trade marks have a role in promoting competition by facilitating the exercise of consumer preferences.[28] A particular mark attached to a good, it is supposed, provides potential consumers with coded but reliable information as to the characteristics of that product. Typically marks themselves are relatively simple and can be fully appreciated in a moment. Equally typically, the information that marks convey to the consumer concerning the quality and other desirable features of the good to which they are attached is relatively rich.[29] Trade marks then reduce consumers' search costs and have greater effect the more it is that differences in the quality and characteristics of competing goods are unobservable to the consumer at the point of sale.[30] For a producer, securing a trade mark is a necessary though insufficient condition for maintaining or enhancing its position in a competitive market. It is necessary because otherwise the non-observable qualities of its goods would not increase consumer demand. It is insufficient because consumer demand is driven by the quality and price of the substitutable goods available in the market. The relationship has been recognized by the European Court of Justice which has repeatedly stated that trade mark

---

[28] See for instance, Dinwoodie, G and Gangjee, D, 'The Image of the Consumer in EU Trade Mark Law' in Leczykiewicz, D and Weatherill, S (eds) *The Images of the Consumer in EU Law. Legislation, Free Movement and Competition Law* (Hart Publishing, 2016), 344 ('the protection of the consumer is a universal justification for trade mark law as a whole'). As well as facilitating competition, Andrew Griffiths has argued that trade marks have a further economic role as 'structuring devices in the organisation of production and distribution': Chapter 4 'Trade Marks and the Organization' in Griffiths, A, *An Economic Perspective on Trade Mark Law* (Edward Elgar Publishing, 2011). In this role trade marks still function primarily to convey and acquire information about the marked products and facilitate the efficient modularization of a stream of production through providing a reliable basis for communication concerning products that move down the stream: ibid., 184.

[29] That information may be derived from the consumers own experience of goods bearing that mark; advertising; and other sources such as reviews, advice from friends and other social interactions.

[30] Economides, N, 'The Economics of Trade Marks' (1988) 78 Trade Mark Reporter 523, 525–6; Griffiths, A, 'The Law and Economics of Trade Marks' in Bently, L, Davis, J and Ginsburg, J, *Trade Marks and Brands: An Interdisciplinary Critique* (Cambridge University Press, 2008), 246–8; and Landes, W and Posner, R, 'Trademark Law: An Economic Perspective' (1987) 30 Journal of Law and Economics 265, 268–70. See also Dogan, S and Lemley, M, 'Trade Marks and Consumer Search Costs on the Internet' (2004) 41 Houston L Rev 777, 786–8 and who also provide a critique of other economic justifications: ibid., 799–801.

rights are an essential element in the system of undistorted competition in which, 'undertakings must be able to attract and retain customers by the quality of their products or services, which is possible only thanks to the existence of distinctive signs allowing them to be identified'.[31] The upshot is that trade mark law allows producers to increase the range of features that contribute to a product's demand in a competitive market (especially unobservable features) whilst encouraging them to invest in maintaining the consistency of these features.[32]

Thus both producers and consumers have shared an interest in marks being capable of distinguishing the goods or services of one undertaking from those of other undertakings. But, as noted in the previous chapter, the trade mark owner's right to prevent a third party use of a sign is limited to circumstances where, because of the characteristics of the sign itself, and/or the goods to which it is attached, and/or the way it is used, the interests of consumers are compromised. In a highly effective simile, Jeremy Philips has likened the consumer's role in trade mark law to that of the canary which miners used to take underground with them to detect the presence of poisonous gases:

> When the canary falls off its perch, dead, the miner carrying the cage knows that it's time to act for his own good. So too, when the consumer falls off his perch, as it were, by being confused, the trade mark owner knows that it's time to act for his own good. In practical terms, neither the canary nor the consumer has much joy in terms of recovery.[33]

Less colourfully but to the same effect, Kitchen LJ has characterized the consumer in trade mark law as, 'a person who has been created to strike the right balance between various competing interests including, on the one hand, the need to protect consumers, and, on the other hand, the promotion of free trade in an openly competitive market'.[34]

---

[31] C-427/93 *Bristol Myers Squibb* v *Paranova* [1996] ETMR 1 [43]. See also C-10/89 *Cnl-Sucal* v *Hag* [1990] 3 CMLR 571 [13]; and C-349/95 *Loendersloot* v *George Ballantine* [1998] ETMR 10 [22].

[32] Economides, above n.30, 526–7; and Griffiths, above n.30, 248–9. See also Landes and Posner who also note that trade mark law encourages producers to engage in advertising with a view to establishing, in the minds of consumers, an association between the mark and the qualities of the good to which it is attached: Landes and Posner, above n.30, 270.

[33] Wilkof, N and Philips, J, 'The Consumer Protection Function of Trade Marks. Just So?' IPKat Blog of 21 November 2014, accessed 24 January 2017 at http://ipkitten.blogspot.co.uk/2014/11/the-consumer-protection-function-of.html.

[34] *Interflora Inc* v *Marks & Spencer plc* [2014] EWCA Civ 1403 [113].

In economic terms, to give right owners more extensive protection than is necessary to protect the interests of consumers would impose costs (if only the cost involved in the third party changing its sign) without any offsetting benefits.[35] It follows from all of this that the certainty required under trade mark law is that consumers are not confused as to the trade origin of marked products.

One way or another then, all the mainstream economic justifications see intellectual property rights, whether patent, copyright or trade mark, as providing some security of expectation so providing the beneficiaries[36] of the right with a means of managing some of the uncertainties associated with a competitive free market. Reducing uncertainty is not an end in itself though it is the means by which intellectual property rights achieve their end. As to that, the relatively simple picture painted by the economic theories outlined above is that rights operate to reduce some of the uncertainties associated with investment in innovation; investment in the generation and publication of artistic works; and/or transacting in the marketplace (whether as participant in a stream of production or as consumer). It follows that so far as rights are other than clear and their scope predictable, the behaviours that the rights are intended to spur will receive less encouragement. One consequence is that advocates for the system (or at least those who believe it is justified in economic terms) will emphasize the need for clarity and certainty in the law.[37] The BioIndustry Association (BIA) in its submissions to the Supreme Court in *Human Genome Sciences Inc* v *Eli Lilly & Co*[38] did just this. The context of the following passage from the judgement would suggest that that this is the opinion of the BIA but it is phrased in a way that makes it hard to distinguish from the opinion of the court:

> [F]unding for research and development on the potential therapeutic value of a newly discovered and characterised protein or its antibodies is dependent on the funders being reasonably confident that the patent (or patent application) concerned will be reasonably safe from attack (or likely to be granted). It is

---

[35] Landes and Posner, above n.30, 300.

[36] I use the term 'beneficiaries' here to embrace both right owners and consumers.

[37] See for instance David Vaver's criticisms of intellectual property law in Vaver, D, 'Reforming Intellectual Property Law: An Obvious and Not-so-Obvious Agenda. The Stephen Stewart Lecture for 2008' (2009) IPQ 143, 145–51.

[38] [2011] UKSC 51.

> also relevant that bioscience companies attract investment by reference to their patent portfolios, which gives rise to the same need for certainty.[39]

As the preceding chapters have set out to illustrate, intellectual property law remains stubbornly uncertain at its core and it is no challenge to find instances of central and important interests being determined by reference to incurably vague standards. This observation does not fatally undermine those justificatory theories that see intellectual property rights as enhancing security of expectation. Within the scope of their operation it is enough that the rights reduce uncertainty rather than remove it entirely. But as the BIA's intervention in in *Human Genome Sciences Inc* v *Eli Lilly & Co* illustrates, the argument that the expectations of right owners should be (more) certain will be able to draw some strength by reference to the economic justifications advanced in support of the intellectual property system.[40] As the preceding chapters have also illustrated, where the law is uncertain because of the operation of standards rather than rules, this is often for good reason and usually because some flexibility in the way a legal direction is understood and applied is desirable.

What follows is an explanation of what I think the rare rules within the system are doing and why they are positioned as they are. In the case of patents, copyright and trade mark, I set out to show that the rules that there are essential components in ensuring that the law has a social utility in that the rules within the system encourage individuals to labour diligently and invest freely in the well-founded expectation that they will be able to secure a legal right over the subject matter they have worked to produce. The system is designed in a way that encourages investment in creative activities and encourages participation in the system which itself brings social benefits. The second part of the analysis considers how

---

39 Ibid. [98].

40 On the requirement that a claimed invention has an inventive step, Cornish et al. observe that, 'the issue creates uncertainty about the validity of many patents and is one significant cause in lowering the practical value of the system as an incentive to invention and innovation' and that,

> the evaluative issue that the inventive step requirement introduces is the largest single cause of uncertainty about the validity of patents and hence a frequent inflator of the scale and length of patent disputes. … firm rules (such as define the factual comparison called for in determining novelty) are replaced by a vaguer, qualitative yardstick.

Cornish, W, Llewelyn, D and Aplin, T, *Intellectual Property: Patents, Copyrights, Trademarks & Allied Rights*, 8th edition (Sweet & Maxwell, 2013), 148 and 205 respectively.

form relates to the non-economic justifications that are sometimes advanced in support of intellectual property rights. The key conclusion here is that because the testing ground for claims of right is the realm of duties, it is hard to sustain the claim that intellectual property rights are somehow owed to creative individuals irrespective of whether that duty is seen as reward for individuals' creative efforts or whether because it is seen necessary somehow to protect their embodied personality.

As a first step in my exploration of the relationship between form and theory, I should reiterate the key observation that the certainty of a rule depends on the context over which it exercises control.[41] Justificatory theories such as the monopoly-profit-incentive thesis take systems as whole rather than elements within them as their context. Thus it is the patent *system*, if it is to have social and economic benefit, which must act to encourage individuals to invest in R&D. From here it is easy to get to the assertion that all components of the system should be tailored to further this end. There was, for instance, no attempt by the Supreme Court in *Human Genome Sciences Inc* v *Eli Lilly & Co* to distinguish between the tests for novelty, inventiveness or industrial applicability, nor indeed any of the other conditions that determine the validity of a patent, when it suggested that the funders of biomedical research had to be reasonably confident that a patent (or patent application) would be reasonably safe from attack (or likely to be granted). That said, the court's multiple use of the word 'reasonably' suggests, in a very non-specific way, that there is an understanding that certainty of expectation cannot be the sole consideration for all the elements that contribute to the question of whether a patent (or patent application) is valid. As has been said by Hart, Dworkin and others in relation to other branches of the law, it is wrong to assume that any particular law has a set of goals that are overriding in the sense that every feature of the law must be tailored to those goals. The aim of intellectual property law may well be to reduce uncertainty but this aim must be pursued subject to principles that may limit its efficiency.[42]

The idea that I want to explore further here is that examining those rather rare instances where there are rules within the system and the contexts over which these rules exercise control tells us something interesting about how the system might work in terms of the behaviours it stimulates. My initial focus in the case of the patent system is on the

---

41 Schlag, P, 'Rules and Standards' (1985) 33 UCLA L Rev 379, 407.

42 See for instance Ronald Dworkin's reflections on Hart's consideration of the goals of the criminal law in Dworkin, R, *Taking Rights Seriously* (Harvard University Press, 1977), 8.

condition that a claimed invention is to be new if it is to be patentable. As has been shown above, this condition is determined according to a rule which itself is supported by a complex but nevertheless rule-based scheme for determining priority. In the case of copyright law the focus will be on the condition that a work, to qualify for protection, must be 'original'. Again, as has already been shown, for most of the history of UK copyright law this condition has been determined by way of a rule, though that seems to be changing. I shall have something to say about trade mark law later.

What these two rules have in common is that they relate to the securing of the right concerned. Where they differ is in the fact that, in this, the originality condition operates alone in determining whether a work enjoys the protection of copyright whereas the novelty condition is partnered by the condition that a claimed invention must also involve an inventive step in the determination of validity.

That these rules relate to the securing of rights is hardly a surprise given that the difficulties and costs of promulgating detailed rules are worthwhile if the rule is to be frequently applied. Indeed, the greater the frequency with which a legal command will apply, the more desirable rules tend to be relative to standards, 'because promulgation costs are borne only once, whereas efforts to comply with and action to enforce the law may occur rarely or often. Rules cost more to promulgate; standards cost more to enforce'.[43]

Efficiency in the sense of minimizing promulgation and enforcement costs means that frequency of application is an important consideration in deciding whether an area is best regulated by way of rules or standards. One might therefore expect rules to operate in the securing of rights. By contrast, it will be relatively rare for a right holder to exercise that right by bringing an infringement action. Of itself, the relative infrequency of infringement actions does not lead inevitably to the conclusion that decisions should be decided by way of a standard. But, if there are good reasons for this to be so, then the pursuit of efficiency presents no bar for a standards-based regime being adopted. And the greater the relative infrequency of application, so the less impact a standards-based infringement test will have on the security of expectation provided by the rules operating in the securing of the right.

---

[43] Kaplow, L, 'Rules versus Standards: An Economic Analysis' (1992) 42 Duke LJ 557, 577. The costs of promulgation tend to be greater if the rule is a statutory one (which is typical): Ehrlich, I and Posner, R, 'An Economic Analysis of Legal Rulemaking' (1974) 3 J Legal Stud 257, 267.

That explanation works well enough so far as copyright is concerned. The subsistence or otherwise of copyright turns on the rule-like test of whether a work is original. Whether it is infringed turns on the standard-like test of whether what has been taken amounts to a substantial part of the work. In the case of patents however, the frequency of application of the novelty rule is matched by the frequency of application of the more standard-like condition that a claimed invention must also involve an inventive step. As all patents that proceed to grant are examined, the costs of administering a test for obviousness at the examinations stage could be considerable. The UK patent system manages this in two ways. In the first place, and as noted in the previous chapter, the obviousness test is different pre- and post-grant. At the examination stage the question is whether the invention *clearly* does not involve an inventive step. Post-grant, courts allow themselves a greater margin of uncertainty. At the same time, the range of evidence that examiners take into account in their decision making is relatively narrow compared to the range of evidence considered by courts in revocation proceedings. The process of examination, to this extent, is imperfect but because it reduces the complexity, time and cost of examination it is efficient for it to be so. This is essentially the same observation made by Mark Lemley in relation to the US patent system:

> Because so few patents are ever asserted against a competitor, it is much cheaper for society to make detailed validity determinations in those few cases than to invest additional resources examining patents that will never be heard from again. In short, the PTO doesn't do a very detailed job of examining patents, but we probably don't want it to.[44]

---

[44] Lemley, M, 'Rational Ignorance at the Patent Office' (2001) 95 North Western University L Rev 1495, 1497. The US Supreme Court went some way to acknowledge this in *Graham* v *John Deere Co.* Observing that there was a 'notorious difference' between the obviousness standard as applied by the Patent Office and by the courts, the Court noted that the primary responsibility for sifting out unpatentable material was in the Patent Office and that, in this, the Patent Office was confronted with a most difficult task given that almost 100 000 applications for patents were filed each year. This, the court said, provided a compelling reason for the Commissioner to strictly adhere to the statutory wording contained in the 1952 Act: *Graham* v *John Deere Co* 383 US 1 (1966), 18. For commentary see Rich, G, 'The Proposed Patent Legislation: Some Comments' (1967) 35 George Washington L Rev 641, 643 ('the legal standard was the same but the evidence was different').

The social benefits of a more cursory and more rule-like examination system are twofold.[45] First, to the extent that general taxes are used to subsidize the system by contributing a proportion of costs of each examination, there is a direct benefit to the public purse arising from the costs of examination being reduced. Secondly, to the extent that an individual applicant bears the cost of examination, reducing the costs of examination makes use of the system to protect an invention more attractive to an inventor vis-à-vis less socially beneficial alternatives, such as keeping the invention secret.

Patents are rights in which the conditions for securing the rights are subject to formal examination and that these conditions are rule-like promotes efficiency in decision making given the frequency of their application. Clearly the same cannot be true of copyright's originality condition. This too is a rule, but here, where the influence of promoting efficiency in examination does not obscure the significance of form, it is easier to see how the form of the condition has a role in supporting the economic functions of copyright. The question of whether a work is 'original' in the sense of being not copied is one which the author of the work is able to answer unequivocally both because the test is a simple rule which does not require the exercise of any judgement and because the author alone knows with absolute certainty the steps involved in the creation of a particular work. The author can thus arrange their affairs on the basis of an expectation that if they invest in the production of a work of a kind in which copyright can subsist, then they will enjoy exclusive rights in it.

A significant disadvantage of this scheme arises because of the information asymmetry as between the author and third parties in respect of the history of production of a work. Because the history of production of a work determines its author and typically then its first owner, this information asymmetry can lead to false claims to the ownership of a work being made by dishonest claimants. This observation allows me to explain a significant difference between copyright and patent law that I have drawn attention to at several points earlier in this book. Patent law, I have observed, has a communication function that is not shared with copyright law. A patentee must disclose her invention to guard against the possibility of her exploiting the invention without disclosing it. But such

45 I am not suggesting that the investigation of the inventive step, even at the examination stage, is an absolute rule. I doubt that it could ever be so. Rather, I would say that at the examination stage it is more rule-like than the same inquiry made post-grant. There is, if you like, less room for disagreement between reasonable persons at the examination stage compared to the position post-grant.

a public disclosure can act to deter potential competitors. A robust examination prevents the patent owner from benefiting from their disclosure in this way without actually having devised a patentable invention. It was precisely the impact of false claims that led to the introduction of a system for the examination of patent applications in the early twentieth century.[46] Although in the UK, patent applications had been subject to examination from 1883, this was mainly for formal defects and sufficiency of description.[47] Change was prompted by the 1901 report of the Fry Committee. Set up to inquire into the workings of the patent system, the Committee reported that 40 per cent or more of the patents registered were for inventions that had already been described in previous patents.[48] In 1905 the UK Patent Office began to search British patent specifications with a view to ascertaining whether what was claimed was novel.[49]

The nature of copyright works means that it would be infeasible to subject works to search and examination as a condition of grant.[50] But in the case of patent applications a substantive examination is possible because typically an invention can be described accurately and concisely and it is possible to categorize inventions in way that allows searches to be limited to relatively closely related prior art.[51] It is precisely the same characteristics which allow patent law to adopt objective measures of validity. Doing so is attractive in terms of furthering the public interest in that it guarantees that legal protection is only given to those inventions which add to the sum of human technical knowledge.[52] On the other hand, such objective conditions risk reducing the incentive to engage in inventive activity. That an individual inventor has laboured diligently and invested freely is neither necessary nor sufficient in securing a patent for

---

46 As Cornish et al. colourfully put it, easier patenting 'left the swashbuckler plenty of room to brandish dubious patents hoping that competitors would find it simpler to treat shadow as if it were substance': Cornish et al., above n.40, 125.

47 Ibid., 126.

48 Report of the Committee Appointed by the Board of Trade to Inquire into the Working of the Patents Act on Certain Specified Questions (Cd.506) (1901) 23 PP59, 602. See also Cornish et al., above n.40, 126.

49 Cornish et al., above n.40, 126

50 Which would be impracticable since such an examination would be extremely costly and in any event futile given that it would require searching a vast collection of published and unpublished material to find instances of duplication: Landes and Posner, above n.19, 345.

51 Ibid., 345.

52 c.f. copyright where that which is dross and that which is excellent receive equal protection.

her invention. That is so even if she laboured in the honest but mistaken belief that the outcome was new and inventive. Put another way, by the time an applicant arrives at the Patent Office seeking legal protection, the costs of invention are sunk. A wise inventor will accordingly undertake their own search of the relevant prior art before making a costly investment.[53] Such a search would be pointless if the inventor were not then able to use the results to predict reliably the outcome of a substantive examination undertaken by the Patent Office. At stake is not only the patent but also the option of keeping the invention secret since any application will be published whether or not a patent is subsequently granted. The rule-like character of the tests for novelty and (pre-grant) obviousness make the inventor's prediction more likely to accord with the Patent Office's conclusion. The form of the tests thereby encourages investment in inventive activities,[54] and more, in activities directed to producing inventions which are not already known and are not obvious developments of what is known. At the very least, the public derive a benefit from this encouragement by way of the forced disclosure of the resulting inventions in patent applications.

The well-informed inventor will nevertheless understand that a patent once granted risks being revoked, very commonly for lack of an inventive step.[55] That knowledge may deter risk averse individuals from making even an initial investment in invention.[56] But awareness of the precarious validity of granted patents is unlikely to have a significant overall effect because the great majority of patent owners can disregard the uncertain status of the great majority of their patents. This is because granted patents, whilst being typically of uncertain status cannot be known to be

---

[53] The position may be otherwise in the US not least because of the fear of accusations of 'wilful infringement': Lemley, above n.44, 1510.

[54] It also encourages rent seeking in the form of encouraging those inventive activities which are likely to result in a patent.

[55] On one measure the risks might be quite great. In the US for example it has been found that roughly half of all litigated patents are found to be invalid: Lemley, M and Shapiro, C, 'Probabilistic Patents' (2005) 19(2) Journal of Economic Perspectives 75, 76 and 80.

[56] So for instance Robert Merges has observed that, 'if there is a pervasive understanding that property rights can be adjusted after the fact … this understanding will naturally be incorporated into the settled expectations of all property holders': Merges, above n.27, 183. However, this effect might be limited by 'self-serving' bias ('the phenomenon that individuals are likely to interpret ambiguous information in ways that resound to their benefit') on which see Korobkin, R, 'Behavioral Analysis and Legal Form: Rules vs. Standards Revisited' (2000) 79 Oregon L Rev 23, 46.

unequivocally good, but nor can they be known to be unequivocally bad. If one subscribes to the view that a claimed invention is, at its priority date, either new and inventive or known and/or obvious, then the conclusion is that a significant (and perhaps large) proportion of the patents issued by the Patent Office are 'bad' in that they would have been rejected if more time and resources had been devoted to the examination.[57] This view is mistaken because it fails to take account of the nature of the test for obviousness and the differences in how it is understood and applied at the examination stage and post-grant. Of course there will be instances where an examiner will make a decision in ignorance of a particular piece of prior art. If validity turned only on the question of whether a claimed invention was new then in such circumstances it would be possible to say that the examiner's decision was wrong and advance clear reasons why it was wrong. But even with perfect information, an examiner's conclusion on the question of obviousness might differ from that of a court because answering that question involves the exercise of judgement: reasonable people can disagree. The likelihood of a difference is made all the greater because, for good reason and as explained above, examiners are more constrained than courts in the exercise of that judgement. For this reason I am reluctant to use the term 'bad' to describe any patents that issue from the Patent Office. But nor can all issued patents be described as 'good'. If an issued patent is found by a court to be invalid, for instance for want of an inventive step, the court is saying that *at the priority date* what has been claimed would have been obvious to the person skilled in the relevant art. Issued patents are both good and bad: they are like the health of Schrödinger's cat.[58]

Above I observed that granted patents were at risk of revocation if challenged. The 'if challenged' condition corresponds to the opening of the metaphorical box imprisoning (or entombing) the cat. It is a relatively

---

[57] So for instance Mark Lemley commenting on the US Patent system says,

> that the PTO issues many patents that would have been rejected had the examiner possessed perfect knowledge. This is particularly true since much of the most relevant prior art isn't easy to find – it consists of sales or uses by third parties that don't show up in any searchable database and will not be found by examiners in a hurry.

Lemley, above n.44, 1500.

[58] One consequence is that I doubt the usefulness of the distinction drawn by Ayres and Klemperer between Type I uncertainty (that valid patents will be unenforced) and Type II uncertainty (that invalid patents will be enforced): Ayres and Klemperer, above, n.15, 1019.

rare event. The significant costs of patent litigation mean that considerable resolve is required to challenge a granted patent in court. The inertia is all the greater given that not only the individual challenger (who bears the cost of litigation) will benefit from the revocation of a competitor's patent, but all other competing firms in the relevant industry. The challenger will thus gain only a portion of the benefit if they are successful and the patent is revoked.[59] This, coupled with the fact that most issued patents are of little or no commercial value, means that very few issued patents are ever litigated[60] and those that are the ones which are important enough commercially to justify the considerable costs of litigation.[61] The great majority of patent owners can thus disregard the uncertain status of the great majority of their patents. This is all the more true given that patents are used by their owners in a variety of ways other than as a weapon to restrain the activities of competitors. For many of these uses, a degree of insecurity about the validity of a granted patent does not matter very much if at all.[62]

That most issued patents are of questionable validity does, however, contribute to the social costs of the patent system, though these need to be set in the balance against the social benefits flowing from an improved efficiency in examination and an enhanced stimulus to investment in inventive activities.[63] Mark Lemley has identified a number of potential social costs associated with 'bad' patents issuing from the Patent Office.[64] The first, most obvious and most significant is what he calls the '*in terrorem* effect' of bad patents. By this he means that bad patents can act to deter potential competitors from entering a field. This effect he believes to be small given that, faced with a patent that potentially interferes with a business plan, a firm will either seek a licence from the

---

59 Lemley and Shapiro, above n.55, 85.

60 In the United States for instance, it has been found that only 1.5 per cent of issued patents are litigated and only 0.1 per cent are litigated to trial: ibid., 75 and 79.

61 Ibid., 79.

62 Ibid., 81; and Lemley, above n.44, 1514.

63 Ayres and Klemperer have convincingly argued that there is a further social benefit arising from uncertainty insofar as uncertainty and delay induce limited amounts of interim infringement so constraining the patent owners' market power, effecting pricing decisions and so offsetting some of the social cost of the patent system without having a significant impact on the incentive provided by the system: Ayres and Klemperer, above n.15. See also Johnston, J, 'Bargaining under Rules versus Standards' (1995) 11 Journal of Law, Economics and Organization 256.

64 See generally Lemley, above n.44.

patent owner if it believes the patent is valid and its planned activities will infringe, or it will seek to challenge the patent if it believes the patent is not valid. It will be a rare instance, he says, where a firm will change its plans without even entering into a licence negotiation with the patent owner.[65] Of course this is only a social cost if the patent is objectively 'bad' such that the competitor should lawfully be able to operate free of any concern that they might thereby infringe the patent. If the patent is objectively 'good' then it is working as it should. As I have already argued, it is, however, not very helpful to think in such black and white terms of patents issued by the Patent Office.

Lemley observes that a further problem is that the owners of bad patents can game the system by demanding royalty payments small enough that competitors take a licence rather than challenge the patent in court.[66] Although he accepts this is a cost he observes that it is small compared to the costs of instituting a more robust examination process.[67] The idea that patent owners might game the system in this way assumes they know their patents are objectively bad. I would argue that, given the way obviousness is approached by courts, this will happen only very rarely. Rather, a patent owner might have legitimate concerns that their patent might be invalidated for obviousness if it were challenged in court, which might then lead her to adopt strategies aimed at avoiding such challenges. The likely upshot is a greater willingness to grant licences and to do so on terms more favourable to licensees. Whilst this may be seen as taking unfair advantage of the system if done knowing with certainty that the licensed patent is invalid, it seems to me much less exploitative of the system if done under uncertainty and as a way of guarding against the risk of costly litigation and losing the patent.[68]

To my mind the most significant social cost associated with the uncertain status of issued patents is the potential to discourage any investment necessary to bring a product incorporating a patented invention to the market. Typically, a necessary step in the development of any technology is that which turns an invention into an innovation by taking

---

65 Ibid., 1516–17. That might well be true but it is likely that there will be some instances in which the existence of the patent means that follow-on inventors simply don't bother. Without data, however, this is mere speculation.

66 Ibid., 1517.

67 Ibid., 1518–19.

68 Giles Rich observes that, '[a] patentee can get into a lot of expensive trouble by suing on an invalid or too "weak" patent and if that becomes a social evil, it is easy enough to cure by increasing his risks': Rich, above n.44, 644. See also Ayres and Klemperer, above n.15, 1014.

a good idea and making of it something useful and valuable (whether socially or privately). In any particular case the distance between these two stages may be temporal or conceptual and likely both.[69] Importantly, the cost of innovation may be significant and high relative to the cost of arriving at the invention and the risks involved 'too great to be undertaken except under the shelter of a monopoly grant'.[70] Many see the patent system's role in providing necessary incentives to bring projects to completion as more important than its role in providing incentives to invent. Under this view it is accepted that good ideas would often arise without patents, but these ideas would never become practically useful to the public without patents to provide the incentive to commercialize the idea.[71] No doubt that is sometimes the case but typically the greater risk to investments is at the earlier stages of a research project.[72] As noted above, when early investment decisions are made, nearly all the variables that feed into a decision to invest in a particular research project will be uncertain. However, as a research project advances towards something marketable, so costs and benefits can be more reliably predicted.[73] Thus

---

[69] So for instance an 18-year 'incubation period' is typical of biomedical therapeutics: Bar-Shalom, A and Cook-Deegan, R, 'Patents and Innovation in Cancer Therapeutics: Lessons from Cellpro' (2002) 80 The Milbank Quarterly 637, 657. See also the comments of Lord Neuberger in *Human Genome Sciences Inc* v *Eli Lilly & Co* [2011] UKSC 51 [143].

[70] Machlup, above n.2, 36-7. At least in part, the importance of not producing a chilling effect on investment in bioscience led the UK Supreme Court to overturn the Court of Appeal in *Human Genome Sciences Inc* v *Eli Lilly & Co* [2011] UKSC 51 (in which respect see in particular the speeches of Lord Hope [141] and Lord Walker [171]).

[71] Note e.g. Giles Rich's example of Herbert Spencer's 'invalid chair' as a good idea never made available because Spencer chose not to patent it because he wanted to give it to the world without recompense to himself: Rich, G, 'The Relation Between Patent Practices and Anti-Monopoly Laws' (1942) 24 Journal of the Patent Office Society 85, 179.

[72] See e.g. in relation to pharmaceutical research, Gambardella, A, *Science and Innovation: the US Pharmaceutical Industry during the 1980s* (Cambridge University Press, 1995), 20–21. Ken Arrow has observed that, 'the outcome of any research project is necessarily uncertain and the most important results are likely to come from projects whose degree of uncertainty to begin with was greatest': Arrow, K, *Essays in the Theory of Risk-Bearing* (North-Holland Publishing Co., 1974), 138.

[73] The greater the temporal and/or conceptual distance between any stage in the research and a final marketable product so the greater the uncertainty as to the net worth of the project. This is why, in industries with long development times, the majority of projects started never reach fruition. A stark example is

the uncertain status of any patent, and with this the extent to which its owner believes she can rely on the market power that the patent confers, will generally be offset by the increased certainty of costs and benefits as a research project progresses towards a commercial application.

Nevertheless, one cannot deny that at least in some cases there is a risk that the uncertain status of issued patents will discourage necessary investment in the commercialization of an invention. I would argue, however, that if this is an effect, it arises because the patent system is at root not intended to stimulate that kind of investment (though this can be a socially useful effect nevertheless). The patent system cannot encourage someone to invest resources in commercializing an idea if that idea cannot be the subject matter of a patent (for instance because it is not new, or it is obvious or is otherwise unpatentable subject matter). If the system is to provide you with the shelter of a monopoly grant, you must have a patentable invention to start with. A patent holder's perception of the severity of the risk that their patent will be revoked will correlate positively with their knowledge of the prior art and their perception of the extent of the difference between the patented invention and the prior art. Certainly there will be little encouragement to invest significant resources in circumstances where a patent owner believes the issued patent is objectively bad, but that just puts them in the same position as anyone who aims to invest in the commercialization of subject matter that is not patentable and who goes ahead expecting to shoulder the risks associated with that.

So far as managing the uncertainty in more marginal cases is concerned, the patentee is caught on the horns of a well-known dilemma. Nearly fifty years ago, the highly influential US judge Giles Rich, criticizing a Report of the President's Commission to Study the Patent System which included a proposal to raise the standard of patentability in the Patent Office to equal that applied by the courts, posed and answered a riddle:

> All the talk about the strength and weakness of patents per se borders on gobbledygook until we learn to comprehend the riddle that: The stronger a

provided by the pharmaceutical industry. The development of new drugs, from applied research to commercialization, takes on average eight to nine years and only 1 out of 5000 compounds synthesized during applied research eventually reaches the market: Gambardella, above n.72, 20. Only 21 per cent of drugs that begin human testing are finally approved: Barton, J and Emanuel, E, 'The Patents-Based Pharmaceutical Development Process Rationale, Problems and Potential Reforms' (2005) 294 JAMA 2075, 2076.

> patent the weaker it is and the weaker a patent the stronger it is. To explain, a patent that is strong in that it contains broad claims which adequately protect the invention so they are hard to design around is weak in that it may be easier to invalidate and is therefore less likely to stand up in court because the claims are more likely to read on prior art or be broader than the disclosed invention … On the other hand, the patent with narrow claims of the kind the Patent Office readily allows quickly without a contest is weak as protection and as incentive to invest but strong in that a court will not likely invalidate it.[74]

It seems then that there is no option for patentees but to embrace uncertainty. An inventor can choose to draft claims of narrow scope and in so doing decrease the possibility of the granted patent subsequently being found invalid, but such a strategy comes at the cost of increased uncertainty as to whether the claims will embrace variants of the invention devised by the patentee's competitors. And of course adopting the reverse strategy means that an inventor is likely to be more confident that her competitors will not be able to work around the claims but her uncertainty as to the validity of the issued patent will be increased. Uncertainty then, as to validity, is positively correlated to the impact that a granted patent has on the activities of third parties. The key point then is that the uncertainty arises because, in patent law as much as in copyright, the realm of duties is the testing ground for claims of right. Thus it is the case, as Giles Rich observes, that, 'when the validity of a patent is contested in court, the results depend heavily on what impact the patented invention has had on the technology – the "art"'.[75] As noted above, there are very good reasons why claims of right should be so tested[76] and it is this that provides the most convincing reason why issued patents should be of uncertain validity when set against the claim that this uncertainty undermines whatever incentives are provided by the system.

A similar pattern occurs in trade mark law so far as the test for assessing whether a sign which is the subject matter of a trade mark application is confusingly similar to an already registered trade mark is more rule-like than the corresponding test for whether a sign used in the course of trade is confusingly similar to a registered trade mark. The consequence is that:

---

74 Rich, above n.44, 644.

75 Ibid., 649.

76 See above at p. 215.

> The protection afforded to a registered trade mark cannot be calculated by what sign appears on the Trade Mark Register, nor by what goods or services it is registered against. The protection afforded by registration is defined only at points of overlap, either with the public domain or with third parties' use of the registered trade mark.[77]

At root the trade mark system is not about creating an incentive for individuals to invest in the creation of marks and so it cannot be said that this differential is explicable as a useful feature of this function. It might be more convincingly argued that, as with the patent system, the differential evidences efficiency in the sense of reducing examination costs, so reducing the costs to the public of administering the system as well as acting as an incentive for individuals to use the system in preference to alternatives.[78] On the face of it, registering a trade mark will bring little social benefit where a trader, because they have built up sufficient goodwill in a registrable sign, could rely on passing off rather than trade mark law. In contrast to patents and trade secret protection, trade marks and passing off are complementary and cumulative and their underlying rationale is the same. It follows that in terms of social utility, on the face of it there is little to choose between the tort of passing off and the law relating to registered trade marks in that both reduce consumer search costs and facilitate rational choice. Many applicants for a trade mark have built up insufficient goodwill to have the option of relying on passing off.[79] For these applicants the choice is between either

---

77 Davis, J, 'Between a Sign and a Brand: Mapping the Boundaries of a Registered Trade Mark in European Union Trade Mark Law' in Bently, L, Davis, J and Ginsburg, J (eds) *Trade Marks and Brands: An Interdisciplinary Critique* (Cambridge University Press, 2008), 89.

78 In fact the argument does not hold water so far as reducing the burden on the public purse is concerned. Despite reducing its fees, OHIM (now EUIPO) has during the years of its operation accumulated a significant surplus (according to the most recent published annual accounts, the accumulated budgetary surplus as at December 2015 amounted to €320 million, accessed 24 January 2017 at https://euipo.europa.eu/tunnel-web/secure/webdav/guest/document_library/contentPdfs/about_euipo/the_office/annual_accounts/annual_accounts_2015_en.pdf). What to do with that surplus has provoked considerable debate: see for instance 'Stand off over OHIM Fees and Surplus Continues', 19 February 2014, *World Trademark Review* (Blog), accessed 24 January 2017 at http://www.worldtrademarkreview.com/Blog/detail.aspx?g=bd4cefdc-cff5-4711-bdd1-e1ed1cb3983b.

79 Except of course in the case of marks that lack inherent distinctiveness which can only be registered if they have acquired distinctiveness through use. If a mark has acquired distinctiveness then in all likelihood there would be sufficient goodwill in the sign to support an action of passing off. There may

securing a trade mark or entering the market using a sign for which there will be no legal protection in the immediate and short term. Of course during this period there is a risk that consumers will make ill-informed decisions but that hardly seems justification enough for encouraging traders' use of the trade mark system. Rather more convincing is the argument that, assuming the trader wants legal protection, in such circumstances, the costs of registration will be set in balance against the costs involved in the generation of goodwill and the perceived risks of harm to the business. The more costly registration is, so the likelihood that a trader will make a socially wasteful overinvestment in advertising in an attempt to accelerate the accrual of goodwill is increased.[80]

For all that, I suspect the greatest social utility in the trade mark system, in which it scores not only over the alternative of no legal protection but also over reliance on the action of passing off, is in its network effects. Registered rights are very visible; far more so than common law rights which only really become visible when exercised. The trade mark register gives anyone who cares to inspect it a good deal of information about what kinds of signs are being adopted as marks, how these are being used and by whom. The more that traders use the system, so shared understandings amongst traders as to use of trade marks develop and are constantly reinforced. Most obviously this reduces the frequency and costs of litigation but there is also a benefit to consumers. Of course consumers cannot be expected to develop an understanding of the significance of trade marks by way of a direct examination of the register but there is an indirect effect arising from the ubiquitous use by traders of signs as indicators of origin and quality of goods and services. In this way, any encouragement to use the system of registered trade marks can be seen as furthering the goal of reducing consumer search costs. Not only this, but encouragement to use the system, so far as this then helps to consolidate a common understanding, makes it easier to 'deal' with rights in signs in corporate transactions and arrangements so reducing transaction costs between traders.

---

exceptionally also be instances where a sign could not be registered as a trade mark, for instance because it is a prohibited shape or otherwise does not fall within the definition of a sign, but where there is sufficient goodwill to support an action of passing off: see e.g. *Reckitt & Colman Products Ltd* v *Borden Inc* [1990] RPC 341 (lemon juice marketed in a lemon shaped container); and *Cadbury-Schweppes Pty Ltd* v *The Pub Squash Co Ltd* [1981] RPC 429 (advertising themes and slogans) respectively.

80 It is also possible, though unlikely, that if registration of a preferred sign were not possible then the trader would not enter the market at all.

The overall conclusion is that investors, whilst not exactly being duped by the intellectual property system, are certainly being manipulated in a way that both encourages investment in creative activities and, in the case of registered rights, encourages participation in the system which itself brings social benefits. The positioning of rules and of standards within any system of law can influence behaviour so far as rules, within the scope of their application, provide clear and predictable outcomes whereas standards, precisely because they admit some flexibility into the way in which the law is interpreted and applied, contribute some uncertainty as to the scope of rights and correlative duties. The rule-like character of those conditions that must be satisfied if a right is to be claimed is directed at influencing the behaviour of investors as prospective right owners. Although the rights once obtained are uncertain in scope and precarious, they are so rarely put to the test that it is unlikely to significantly deter investors from seeing intellectual property rights as important aids in their efforts to gain returns on their investment. At the same time, the network effects arising from encouraging traders entering the system serves to further the social benefits attending reduced transaction costs.

In reflecting on the relationship between form and the theoretical justifications underpinning intellectual property rights I weaken my analysis by considering only the economic justifications.[81] More or less convincing challenges have been made to the dominant economic thesis that the prospect of monopoly profits secured by intellectual property rights provides an essential incentive to invest in innovation and creativity.[82] Critics of the 'monopoly-profit-incentive' thesis argue that, spurred by competition in the market and/or curiosity, innovation would occur without the incentives provided by the patent system[83] and even without the effect of these drivers the profits linked to being first to market and the natural lagging behind of imitators would encourage investment in innovation.[84] The idea that copyright provides a necessary incentive has also been questioned, most notably in relation to the book trade by

[81] Aldred, J, 'The Law and Economics of Trade Marks' in Bently, L, Davis, J and Ginsburg, J (eds) *Trade Marks and Brands: An Interdisciplinary Critique* (Cambridge University Press, 2008), 281.

[82] Machlup, above n.2, 24.

[83] Arrow, above n.4, 619–22; Fisher, M, 'Classical Economics and the Philosophy of the Patent System' (2005) IPQ 1, 19.

[84] Burk and Lemley, above n.13, 1585–6. For all that, there is empirical data that points to the fact that in the pharmaceutical industry the incentive theory is almost certainly holds true: Merges, above n.27, 282.

Stephen Breyer, who has argued that the advantages of being first to market and aggressive pricing strategies would in the majority of cases protect initial publishers from competition by copyists.[85]

The dominant economic thinking regarding trade marks, too, has not escaped assault. The idea that trade mark law can be justified as reducing consumer search costs has been questioned and it has been pointed out that the only real guarantee provided to the consumer is that the owner of a trade mark will take a share of the profits generated by the sale of the good to which it is attached.[86]

The empirical evidence as to the effects of the intellectual property system on social utility is inconclusive and paints a complex picture.[87]

---

[85] Breyer, above n.19, 299–302. The widespread availability of publishing platforms which allow ordinary users access to a global audience has further undermined the idea that copyright provides a necessary incentive. Vast quantities of copyright material is produced and made public on social networking sites and elsewhere, but without thought for economic gain on the part of the creators of this material: Towse (2013), above n.19, 1189; and Towse (2011), above n.19, 106.

[86] Aldred, above n.81, 269. Furthermore, a trade mark is not a reliable indicator of quality since it can mask changes in the owner's marketing strategies which may shift between investments which are made with a view to yielding returns over the relatively long term and short term boosts in profit that come from a reduction in costs. This will only be the case if the decision maker in the firm is concerned with future profits which may not be the case with a manager seeking to further his own interests rather than that of shareholders: ibid., 270–71. Andrew Griffiths observes that the identity that a trade mark provides can mask organizational details and that the fact that a trade mark identifies and distinguishes products as being those of one undertaking covers a wide range of organizational possibilities: Griffiths, above n.28, 166.

[87] For a recent review of the relevant literature see Boldrin, M and Levine, D, 'The Case against Patents' (2013) 27 Journal of Economic Perspectives 3. They assert that, 'there is no empirical evidence that they serve to increase innovation and productivity, unless productivity is identified with the number of patents awarded – which, as evidence shows, has no correlation with measured productivity': ibid., 3. Cohen, Nelson and Walsh in their seminal exploration of the motives for patenting across US manufacturing industries observed that in the majority of industries patents are rarely regarded as an effective means of appropriating returns on innovation: Cohen, W, Nelson, R and Walsh, J, *Protecting Their Intellectual Assets: Appropriability Conditions and Why US Manufacturing Firms Patent (or Not)*, NBER Working Paper No. 7552 (National Bureau for Economic Research, 2002), 5. In only two industries, pharmaceuticals and specialist chemicals, are patents viewed as essential for the development or introduction of a significant proportion of innovations: Mansfield, E, 'Patents and Innovation: An Empirical Study' (1986) 32(2) Management Science 173, 174;

The absence of verifiable data clearly showing that people are better off with intellectual property law than they would be without it has led Robert Merges to question whether maximizing utility is what intellectual property is about.[88] Merges argues that the 'first order' foundational principles justifying intellectual property rights are to be found in 'Lockean appropriation', 'Kantian (liberal) individualism' and 'Rawlsian attention to the distributive effects of property'.[89] It is perhaps a little unfair to single out Merges' analysis given that the invocation of Locke, Kant and Rawls in critical analyses of intellectual property law is far from original.[90] In part I do so only as a matter of convenience but mainly I have chosen Merges' work to critique because the particular way in which he frames his argument allows me to relate his argument to themes and ideas developed in this book.

Merges' understanding of John Locke's theory of appropriation is conventional enough in that he sees the axiomatic ownership of labour (stemming from the ownership of one's own body) as legitimizing appropriation.[91] It is the annexing or mixing of one's labour with resources held in common that gives rise to property rights.[92] In part, Merges understands that this is demanded because it encourages human flourishing by way of the transformation and adaptation, by human agency, that which is found in the state of nature.[93] So far as claims to intellectual property are concerned, Merges argues that the addition of intellectual labour to intellectual content in the public domain transforms

---

and Taylor, C and Silberston, Z, *The Economic Impact of the Patent System – A Study of the British Experience* (Cambridge University Press, 1973), 332. So far as copyright is concerned, there is no direct evidence of the incentive effect on authors or publishers: Towse (2011), above n.19, 110. Furthermore, data indicates that industries rather than individual creators benefit from copyright protection: Towse (2013), above n.19, 1196.

88 Merges, above n.27, 3, 6, 145 and 152–3.

89 Ibid., 13.

90 See e.g. Fisher, W, 'Theories of Intellectual Property' in Munzer, S (ed.) *New Essays in the Legal and Political Theory of Property* (Cambridge University Press, 2001), 170–72.

91 As observed by Peter Drahos, generally speaking people who use Locke's theory tend to concentrate on labour: Drahos, P, *A Philosophy of Intellectual Property* (Ashgate, 1996), 48. Drahos also gives his own account of how Locke's approach to property can be applied to the justification of ideas: ibid., 41–69. See also Hughes, J, 'The Philosophy of Intellectual Property' (1988) 77 Georgetown LJ 287, 297–330.

92 Merges, above n.27, 35.

93 Ibid., 40.

these materials into unique creative products. According property rights in the products so generated both honours the effort involved and calls forth more, and so, in this way promotes human flourishing.[94] Leaving aside general criticisms of Locke's theory of property and the modern incarnations of it,[95] Merges seems to fall into the error common when the tests for securing a legal right invite a focus on the efforts of the author or inventor as a condition and, as I explained in Chapter 5, such a focus risks confusing the distinct concepts of reward and incentive. From here it is easy to get to the mistaken conclusion that rights are given as a reward for those efforts. At various points in my account I have shown why this is wrong.

However, for Merges, Locke's appropriation theory is no more than a start to understanding intellectual property rights. His precise reasons for finding it insufficient of itself are slightly obscure, but it would seem that Locke's theory, without more, does not sufficiently acknowledge that many creative works include a 'personal dimension'.[96] This dimension he claims to find in the property theory of Immanuel Kant. Merges understands Kant to argue that individuals must have secure rights over things if they are to use things to set and pursue their personal ends:

> To make full use of things, to impose their will on things and thereby do the sorts of projects they need to do, people must be free to use all sorts of objects in all sorts of ways. Implicit in this is that people will often have objects under their authority or control for a considerable period of time. To be free, people must be able to set all sorts of goals or ends for themselves. And to pursue the ends that they set for themselves, people need stable durable claims over objects.[97]

Merges sees the Kantian property theory as equally applicable to intellectual property as much as any other. Stable possession is required

---

94 Ibid., 36, 38, 40 and 46.

95 Of which the most compelling is Harris who dismisses all versions of this natural property right theory as involving a 'spectacular non sequitur', in that, '[f]rom the fact that nobody owns me if I am not a slave it simply does not follow that I must own myself. Nobody at all owns me, not even me': Harris, J, *Property and Justice* (Oxford University Press, 2002), 196. For criticisms of Locke's theory specifically as it might be applied to intellectual property see Fisher, above n.90, 184–9.

96 Merges, above n.27, 67. In this Merges shares the conclusion of Justin Hughes, though Hughes adds support to Locke with the 'personality theory' of Hegel rather than Kant: Hughes, above n.91, 329.

97 Merges, above n.27, 70, 71, 72 and 74.

for a creator to fully work her will on a found object whether those objects are tangible or intangible.[98]

Leaving aside general criticisms of personality-based theories of intellectual property laws,[99] it is fair to say that, in this respect, Merges' is an idiosyncratic reading of Kant which does not accord with more detailed and rigorous explorations of Kant's writings as they relate to intellectual property law. Anne Barron, for instance, has observed that Kant saw speech as an exercise of an author's will and as such an aspect of the author's person. This was so even where an author's speech was materialized in writing.[100] It was for this reason that Kant saw any unauthorized publication of an author's work as wrongful. In effect, such a publication compelled the author to speak against his will.[101] But only superficially can Kant's reasons for condemning unauthorized publication be seen as providing a justification for the law according property rights in authorial works. As Barron convincingly argues, such a conclusion would be to profoundly misunderstand Kant's conception of human personhood. For Kant, things (the objects of property) were objects of the will and so different from persons. Writing, however, could not be objectified as a thing external to the self. Authors he saw as having inalienable personal rights over their communications with the public (whether these were in writing or otherwise) as aspects of their person but these rights were not to be understood as the same as property rights in things.[102] For Barron, and in direct contradiction to Merges, adopting a Kantian perspective on property requires making a clear distinction between rights in the physical manuscript and rights in the communications contained within it:

---

98 Ibid., 76.

99 On which see Fisher, above n.90, 189–92.

100 Barron offers a highly credible interpretation of Immanuel Kant's work, 'On the Wrongfulness of Unauthorised Publication of Books': Barron, A, 'Copyright Law and the Claims of Art' (2002) IPQ 368, 399. Another, briefer account, of Kant's philosophy as it applies to copyright and related rights is to be found in Drahos, above n.91, 80–81.

101 Barron, above n.100, 399–400.

102 Ibid. Note here that the inalienable right only applies to writing. In the work of visual art the idea or intellectual element cannot be separated from the material object, and for this reason Kant excludes paintings and sculptures from the category of works protected by a personal right to prevent the distribution of copies. For Kant, a work of visual art is merely a thing: ibid. See also Barron, A, 'Kant, Copyright and Communicative Freedom' (2012) 31 Law and Philosophy 1, 7 and 33.

> Kant's premise is that a book considered as a material object must be distinguished from a book considered as the vehicle for an activity of authorial speech. On the one hand, an author's manuscript, and every printed copy of it, is an ordinary object of property attracting an ordinary right of property vested in whomever is legitimately in possession of the object. This right would include the right to use the object, to sell the object and indeed to copy the object. On the other hand, a published book (considered as the vehicle of its author's speech) is also a communication from publisher to public in the name of the author. Hence it is also an action, and as such it has its existence in a person – the person of the author. For Kant, it follows that unauthorized publication of copies of the author's text – though not unauthorized reproduction as such – is wrongful. By selling copies of an author's text to the public, the unauthorized publisher is not just dealing with commodities – printed books – in his own name, but is disseminating an author's speech, thus compelling the author to speak against his will, to acknowledge the book as his own and be responsible for it.[103]

A more fundamental complaint, and one that Barron levels directly at Merges' work, is that Merges misrepresents Kant as an originator of liberal individualism. Certainly, Merges describes Kant's theory as evidencing: 'a radically individualistic and autonomous view of humans'.[104] Barron contests this representation as 'inconsistent with both the letter of Kant's texts and the spirit animating his philosophical system'.[105] There is no value in repeating the details of her assault here[106] and it is enough to note that a central concern is in Merges' representation of Kant's work. Thus she observes that Merges' justification of intellectual property rights depends on a reconstruction of Kant's theory of property 'that bears scant resemblance to anything in the *Rechtslehre*, where Kant's theory is set out'.[107]

Merges' argument is, however, interesting from our perspective because, as I shall demonstrate, in his defence of his particular version of

---

103 Barron (2012), above n.102, 6 and 34.

104 Merges, above n.27, 76. This notwithstanding his understanding that Kant's theory calls for the recognition of competing interests. Arguably there is no inconsistency here however. As Duncan Kennedy observed, individualism is distinct from pure egotism so far as, 'the notion of self-reliance has a strong affirmative moral content in the demand for respect for the rights of others': Kennedy, D, 'Form and Substance in Private Law Adjudication' (1976) 89 Harvard L Rev 1685, 1714–5.

105 Barron (2012), above n.102, 9.

106 The bulk of which is to be found in ibid., 41 (footnote 37).

107 Ibid., 41. Merges' attempts to link a theory of intellectual property to Locke and Kant is probably aimed at providing 'ideological legitimacy': on which note Drahos, above n.91, 48.

'Kantian individualism' as justification of intellectual property rights, Merges advances an argument that draws strength from seeing a correspondence between form and substance and, as such, it is an argument that finds a strong parallel with that advanced by Duncan Kennedy several decades earlier.

Merges sees the theories of Locke and Kant as related in sharing the notion of labour as a deeply personal activity.[108] Merges does, however, see an important distinction in that, under Locke's theory, individual rights arise in the state of nature. The emergence of a civil society is a later development that is voluntarily instituted by individuals as an effective means of protecting their rights.[109] In contrast, Merges understands that Kant was of the view that rights are only possible under an established legal order and thus, under his theory, the state (or civil society) necessarily precedes the development of the institution of property.[110] Merges explains the difference thus:

> Under conventional natural law theory, natural rights precede the establishment of the state. The state's job is to enforce these rights to the best of its ability. But there is no place for such prepolitical rights in Kant's thinking. The existence of rights and the establishment of the state go hand in hand. Rights are the expression of the general will, or a properly constituted legislature. They are not something to be confirmed or ratified by the state but rather are purely a creature of the state. Rights are in an important sense codetermined by the state: the state is the vehicle that carries them into being. They are not really conceivable without a state, so they cannot in any sense precede the state, at least not in their final, mature form.[111]

For Merges, this makes the Kantian approach to property more appealing as a justification for intellectual property law in particular because of its dependence on a robust central state for effective enforcement and hence viability.[112] For current purposes, what matters more is that it allows Merges to argue that the way that the law is understood, shaped and coloured by courts provides evidence that 'Kantian individualism' is foundational to intellectual property law. Again his precise argument is obscure but at root it is founded on the understanding that autonomy in the Kantian sense follows from conceiving of intellectual property as a

---

[108] For Locke this flows from the possession of our persons: labour then is the most personal of 'possessions': Merges, above n.27, 40.

[109] Ibid., 93. See also Drahos, above n.91, 53.

[110] Merges, above n.27, 93.

[111] Ibid., 95.

[112] Ibid., 93.

right and he observes that although often having recourse to utilitarian arguments, courts often talk about intellectual property rights as 'rights'.[113]

To argue that intellectual property rights are 'rights' is to give them 'an entrenched and fundamental status'.[114] For Merges, the hallmark of a 'right' is that social utility alone is not reason enough to override it.[115] In this respect, individual rights should be distinguished from third party 'interests'.[116] Merges' argument, although not expressed in such terms, draws on the correspondence between the rule form and what he understands of the Kantian conception of individualism. Merges's 'right' (as a guarantee which cannot be overridden by conflicting interests such as those directed to the maximization of social utility) is essentially a description of what Duncan Kennedy labelled as a 'rule'. What Merges is in effect doing then is pointing out a correspondence between the structures of arguments in the formal dimension in favour of rules and those in the moral dimension in favour of individualism. If there is a difference between Kennedy's account and that of Merges, it is in the fact that the latter derives its moral code from Immanuel Kant. That difference is, however, illusory because, as has already been noted, although invoking Kant, when Merges refers to 'autonomy' he has in mind the personal autonomy around which contemporary liberal individualism is organized.[117]

---

113 Ibid., 3. This view of intellectual property is not consistent with its origins. As Drahos observes, 'intellectual property rights … are continually referred to by the aggregated term of rights. Through that process of reference they have become deeply entrenched in the discourse of private property rights. Their relocation in the language of private property has obscured their origins in public privilege': Drahos, above n.91, 213.

114 Drahos, above n.91, 200.

115 Merges, above n.27, 3. In this he is broadly in accord with Ronald Dworkin's definition of individual rights as, 'political trumps held by individuals. Individuals have rights when, for some reason, a collective goal is not a sufficient justification for denying them what they wish, as individuals, to have or to do, or not a sufficient justification for imposing some loss or injury upon them': Dworkin, above n.42, xi. However, Dworkin did not thereby understand rights to be absolute and acknowledged that, 'one principle might have to yield to another, or even to an urgent policy with which it competes on individual facts': ibid., 92.

116 Merges, above n.27, 17.

117 Barron (2012), above n.102, 41. Duncan Kennedy seems to have anticipated arguments such as that advanced by Merges. Kennedy, in talking about common justifications for individualism says that,

It follows that I think the best that can be said of Merges' argument is that 'Kantian individualism' as he conceived it might go some way to explain intellectual property law at the theoretical level but only if we see this as primarily an 'aesthetic' argument. Saying that this justification is not one that can be verified empirically at least avoids the kind of attack made against the economic justifications advanced in support of intellectual property. But even so qualified, as a justification for intellectual property it simply will not do. As shown in the previous chapter, social utility is a constant and fundamental feature of the way in which courts approach intellectual property so far as the decisions that courts take – at least the ones that matter – tend to be shaped by concerns centring on imposed duties rather than on corresponding rights.

The observation that in intellectual property law the testing ground for claims of right is the realm of duties creates something of a difficulty for those who seek to justify intellectual property law as necessary to give effect to certain ethical obligations that society owes to those of its members who have created something, whether as reward for their efforts or because they have invested something of their personality in their creation. A right holder's position is neither strengthened nor weakened according to the degree of effort expended or the extent to which the work in issue embodies the creator's personality. And no amount of effort or investment of personality guarantees exclusive rights over that created. What few rules there are, and the guarantees they provide, are engineered to deceive. The way in which rules and standards operated in intellectual property law serve to encourage individuals to behave in socially useful ways whilst believing they are acting in their own self-interest. Perhaps most importantly, the existence and scope of an owner's interest is made concrete and secure only once tested against the conflicting interests of duty bearers.

So far as intellectual property law is concerned, the positioning of rules and standards within the system suggests an economic basis to the rights

---

> [a] third view is that there is a viable distinction to be made between the 'right' (law) and the 'good' (morals). Since the criterion for the legitimacy of state intervention is radically different from that for moral judgment, one can favor an individualist legal system while remaining opposed to the behavior that such a system permits or even encourages. This view is often associated with the claim that individuals have inalienable rights whose content can be derived from fundamental concepts like freedom or human personality. The individual can set these up in his defense when the state claims the power to make him act in the interests of others.

Kennedy, above n.104, 1716.

in issue. Thus rules are positioned in a way that gives at least the impression of a security of expectation that can be seen as encouraging socially useful patterns of behaviour. What security right holders enjoy is somewhat illusory in that standards dominate when the law is called upon to set their interests against those of duty bearers. The law then is structured in a way that acknowledges something of the costs and social harms associated with the grant of monopoly rights and, not unreasonably, is built on the assumption that it is in the realm of duties where the majority of problems will occur. But giving effect to the interests of duty bearers is not done by way of a set of narrowly drawn defences begrudgingly grafted onto a scheme that otherwise looks only to the interests of right holders. Rather, the inclusion of standards into the very core of the system means that the interests of duty bearers are reflected in the structure of the system as much as those of right holders themselves.[118] The intellectual property system is not one which allows an individual right owner to pursue their self-interests with indifference to the effect that this has on others in society. For this reason the term 'privilege' rather than 'property' seems so much more apt to describe intellectual property rights.[119] The privileges given to right holders are justified only so far that these procure the economic benefits claimed of the system. Whether the system is effective in its economic objects is altogether another matter. If the weight of evidence comes to suggest that the intellectual property system does not produce the economic effects that are claimed of it then it is without justification. The positioning of rules and standards within the system not only support an economic justification but undermine any claim that the rights have some kind of deontological foundation. Intellectual property rights owners cannot respond to challenges founded on economic arguments with desert-based arguments, however these are secured. Nor can they trump such challenges by declaring 'this is (my) property'. In short, if there is an argument to be had, it is economics which must set the scope of that argument.

---

118 A conclusion shared by Abraham Drassinower in respect of copyright law but by way of a different argument to that advanced in this book: Drassinower, A, 'Authorship as Public Address: On the Specificity of Copyright vis-à-vis Patent and Trade-Mark' (2008) 1 Michigan State L Rev, 199.

119 For accounts of the origins of modern intellectual property in a system of monopoly privileges see Palmer, T, 'Intellectual Property: A Non-Posnerian Law and Economics Approach' (1989) 12 Hamline L Rev 261, 265–70. See also Drahos, above n.91, 213.

Understanding intellectual property rights to be mere privileges has I think another implication. Famously Fritz Machlup concluded his 1958 economic review of the patent system with the observation that if:

> one does not know whether a system 'as a whole' (in contrast to certain features of it) is good or bad, the safest 'policy conclusion' is to 'muddle through'—either with it, if one has long lived with it, or without it, if one has lived without it. If we did not have a patent system, it would be irresponsible, on the basis of our present knowledge of its economic consequences, to recommend instituting one. But since we have had a patent system for a long time, it would be irresponsible, on the basis of our present knowledge, to recommend abolishing it.[120]

It is easy to be captivated by the rationality of this call for responsible policy making. But it is also a call for inertia. As I have already noted, half a century of further study and data gathering has not produced a clearer picture, and the empirical evidence as to the effects of the intellectual property system on social utility remains inconclusive.[121] Over the same period, a range of factors linked to globalization and developments in communication and information technology has made the intellectual property system look increasingly anachronistic. As observed by Tom Palmer:

> The relationship between intellectual property rights and technology poses a very important question: If laws are dependent for their emergence and validation upon technological innovations, might not succeeding innovations require that those very laws pass back out of, existence? Today this question should be considered in the context of drastically lowered costs of reproduction and transmission, increased costs of enforcement, problems arising from indeterminate or collective authorship due to new applications of computer technology, and similar issues. One need not conclude from such considerations that copyright did not emerge legitimately in a world of typography, but one should at least be led to question whether it fulfils a legitimate role in a world of electronics.[122]

In recent times scepticism towards intellectual property rights has increased and with this enhanced political influence. No doubt those industries for whom intellectual property rights are a central part of their business models feel under considerable pressure to justify their business practices and quite rightly fear that there may be significant reforms to

---

120 Machlup, above n.2, 80.
121 See for instance the account of Boldrin and Levine, above n.87.
122 Palmer, above n.119, 273.

the system on which their businesses are built. A willingness to embrace reform whilst at the same time demanding that any change be based on empirical evidence gives a false impression that these firms are open to change. Because empirical data is unlikely to be forthcoming, this manifestly 'reasonable' standpoint is in effect a call to maintain the status quo. Understanding intellectual property rights to be a privilege rather than property goes a small way to counter this tendency towards inertia so far as it requires that the burden of providing evidence should lie more heavily on those who benefit from the existing scheme of rights than on those who seek its reform in light of social, economic and technological change. Put another way, it is the duty bearers whose voice should be heard loudest in the debates about the future direction of the intellectual property system.

Index

adjudication, legal
see also decision making, judicial; discretion, judicial
binding precedents see binding precedents
coexistence of rule-like and standard-based solutions 26
context 28–9
creation of law by courts 30
deductive reasoning by courts 31
earlier binding precedents 25–6
equity, role of 26, 72
establishment of facts 31
and form 25–88
inductive reasoning of courts 26, 64–5, 67, 107
injunctive relief see injunctions
judicial discretion 25, 35
legal directions, wording of 32, 40
obviousness test, inventions 25, 34
passing off, tort of 25
prior art 34, 35, 37, 55, 56, 60
rules see rule-bound decisions
standards see standard-bound decisions
statutory provisions, effects 31–2
Aldous, Sir William 56, 57, 79, 80, 81, 113, 114, 129, 135, 140, 173, 225
altruism
commitment to 181
and individualism 16–17, 180, 182, 185, 189–92, 203, 204, 213, 217, 232, 249, 252–4, 256
standard-bound decisions 13, 203
America Invents Act (AIA) 91
pre-AIA US priority system 98, 99
anachronism 47, 48, 51, 291
appellate courts
copying of work, in copyright law 42–3
law-making an acknowledged role of 107
lower court's decision based on error of principle 42, 43
Apple Computer 236–7
appropriation theory 284
arbitrary decisions 109, 111, 118
architecture 213
Arrow, K 258
Atkinson, John (Baron) 194–5
Ayres, I 260, 273–5
balance of convenience test 84, 85
balance of probabilities test 2, 31

Barron, Anne 285
Bently, L 100, 118, 120, 149, 160, 161–2, 178, 213
bias, decision making 6–7
see also prejudices
arbitrary decisions 109, 111, 118
avoiding perceptions of 91, 105–24
coherence requirement 114–15
hypothetical and extreme examples 115–16
instances of 109
morality issues 111–24
'ordre public', contrary to 117, 119, 120, 121
risk 6, 91–2, 111
binding precedents
see also adjudication, legal; decision making, judicial; discretion, judicial
classical trinity (principles of law binding present and future courts) 49, 53

classification decisions 64
decision making, judicial 59
earlier 25–6
ex ante versus *ex post* decision making 93
flexibility of standards 47
guidance of future decisions 48
BioIndustry Association, case law 108, 265, 266
Bochnovic, John 152–6, 158, 159
'bright line' test 3, 4, 151, 221
Brimelow, Alison (EPO President) 144
Burrell, R 28

Castells, Manuel 253
cDNA fragments, case law 119
celebrity endorsement 52, 53
celebrity merchandising 53
Christie, Andrew 33
classical trinity (principles of law binding present and future courts) 49, 53
coherence requirement, judicial decision making 44, 45
morality issues, and bias 114–15
Colomer, Ruiz-Jarabo 115
colour, registration as a trade mark 27–8
compensation, entitlement of employee inventors to 38–9, 41
compilations 10, 162–4, 193, 195, 196, 198
computer programs 7, 164, 165
confidentiality, breach of 76
confusion, likelihood of in trade mark cases 6, 101, 102, 103
consequential reasoning 106
constructive trusts 74
context, importance in legal adjudication 28–9
Convention on the Grant of European Patents *see* European Patent Convention (EPC)
copying of work 10, 18, 42–3, 167, 195
see also copyright; skill, labour and judgement
electronic 180, 183
and infringement 148, 212, 219
music 193, 194, 200, 204
negligence 43
and originality 163, 198, 199–200
paintings 201, 202–3
part of a work 148, 167, 218
photographs 201–2
proof of 213
protection against 216
significant characteristics 236
skill, labour and judgement 193, 194, 198, 201
subconscious 20
unaltered 211
wholesale 216
work which is itself copied 10, 148
copyright 9–10, 12–13, 14, 19–21, 192–223
artistic work 201, 202–3, 210
classification of works, proposal for abolition 33
compilations 10, 162–4, 193, 195, 196, 198
copying of work *see* copying of work
denial of 195–6
established characters 44–5
'Europeanization' of UK copyright law 217
examination 271–2
ideas versus expression 190, 208, 212–14
Information Society Directive 165, 168, 191, 205, 217, 220, 221, 222
infringement claims 41, 54, 148, 167, 193, 204–17, 219
and internet 182–3
literary, dramatic, musical and artistic works: originality requirement 160
morality issues, and bias 111–13
originality condition *see* originality condition, copyright
partial taking 10, 14, 37, 59, 72, 93, 165, 167, 168, 217, 219
piracy 183
protectable subject matter, defining boundaries of 27, 147–8, 160–70, 176

reproduction right 217
risk 215, 216, 221
rule-bound decisions 148, 219, 222–3, 248
skill, labour and judgement, originality 161–3, 166, 193, 194, 196–9
statutory defences based on 'fair dealing' 39
subsistence and infringement 27, 169, 269
substantial taking 13, 72, 169, 190, 206, 211, 213, 221
traditional UK law 160
UK approach to categorization 167
Cornish, W 74, 82, 84, 153, 155, 161, 223, 230, 266, 271
Court of Justice of the European Union (CJEU) 14, 33, 93, 175, 217, 263–4
European integration, harmonization and form 143, 144
ex ante versus *ex post* decision making 100, 101, 103
trade marks 235, 240, 241, 244, 248
courts
creation of law by 30, 107
disagreements between EPC and UK courts 130
inductive reasoning of 26, 64–5, 67, 107
whether EPO decisions binding on UK courts 130
Creative Commons organization 184
critical legal studies movement 40–41

damages, entitlement of owners to claim 75, 83
decision making, judicial
see also adjudication, legal; bias, decision making; discretion, judicial; rule-bound decisions; standard-bound decisions
arbitrary decisions 109, 111, 118
assessment and weighing of relevant factors 37, 39
attempts by EPO to disguise 137
binding precedents 59
containing rulings in points of law versus propositions of good sense 63
deductive reasoning by courts 31
distribution pattern 29
ex ante versus *ex post* 92–105, 224
facts *see* facts, judicial decision-making
faith in decision making of experts 118
flexibility in 27, 32
founding of decision on an error of principle 42, 43
guidance of future decisions 48
inductive reasoning by courts 26, 64–5, 67, 107
prejudices, perceptions of 91
principled decisions 55, 59
rules or standards 26–7
deductive reasoning by courts 31
Demsetz, Harold 261–2
digitization 7, 183
Dinwoodie, Graeme 251
Diplock, William John Kenneth (Baron) 15, 48, 49, 50, 59–61, 84, 92, 223, 225, 226
discoveries, exclusion from patentable subject matter 70
discretion, judicial 25
concepts/definitions 41–2
explanative 48
findings of primary fact 42
of future decision makers 48
infringement of copyright 54
purpose of legal provision, clarity of 36
rules versus standards debate 36, 37
strong versus weak sense 35
Diver, Colin 31
Drahos, Peter 54, 149, 177, 178, 206, 215, 229, 283, 285, 288
Drassinower, Abraham 290
duties, creation of scheme 29
Dworkin, Ronald 30–31, 35, 38, 40, 41, 267

electronic communications 182
employee inventors, entitlement to compensation 38–9, 41
Endicott, T 46, 54
EPC *see* European Patent Convention (EPC)
EPO Boards 124, 127
  see also European Patent Office (EPO)
  Boards of Appeal 8, 128, 129, 138, 145
    Enlarged Board of Appeal 96, 139, 144, 145
    Technical Board of Appeal (TBA) 68–9, 120, 140
equity
  duality between law, and 74, 86
  as instrument of justice 84
  recourse to 5
  role in legal adjudication 26, 72
European Commission, Green Paper (1997) 142
European Court of Justice *see* Court of Justice of the European Union (CJEU)
European Patent Convention (EPC) 7, 8
  core purpose 127, 138
  disagreements with UK courts 130
  and European Union 127
  harmonization attempts 135
  invention to have been made available to the public 173
  inventions and moral issues 117
  member states 125, 130
  patentable subject matter under 29, 67–8
European Patent Office (EPO) 7, 29, 272, 273
  see also inventions; patents
  Administrative Council 141
  'any hardware approach' 132, 133–4
  attempts to disguise decision making 137
  Boards *see* EPO Boards
  decisions of, whether binding at national level 130
  Examining Division 68
  law-making power 67
  morality issues, and bias 117
  Opposition Division 119–20, 122–3
  primary responsibility 140
  problem and solution approach 152
  Technical Board of Appeal (TBA) 131, 132
European Union (EU) 14
  first-to-file approach 91, 98
  harmonization mechanisms 127
  impact of UK's probable exit from 29, 221
  institutions 142
  integration and harmonization 91, 125–46
  member states 160
  originality condition, copyright 220, 221
  patent system 29, 137–8
ex ante versus *ex post* decision making 91, 92–105, 224
  trade marks 99–105
experimentation, inventions 59, 60, 62

facts, judicial decision making
  assessment of 35–6
  discovery of 36
  establishment of 31
  finding of specific fact versus inference from facts specifically found 36
  findings of primary fact 42
  hearing of appeals, errors of principle 42, 43
  inventions 34
  person skilled in the relevant art 56
fairness
  adoption of relevant factors 41
  application by judges 6, 71
  copyright statutory defences based on 'fair dealing' 39
  employee inventors' entitlement to compensation 38–9, 41
  fair dealing, publication of private memoranda 45
  and obviousness 44
  principles laying beyond legal provision 43–4

trade marks 247–8
ubiquity of term, in English law 44
filtration processes, case law 60
final injunctions 78–9, 80, 81–2
flexibility
injunctions 4–5
judicial discretion and legal standards 27, 32, 45, 47
passing off, tort of 48–9
value in 3
flocculating agents, case law 60, 61
Fox, H 154–5
Fry Committee 271

Gangjee, Dev 251
Gerhardt, Deborah 256
glutamine synthetase inhibitors, plant cells resistant to 123
goodwill 50, 53, 65, 66
Gratwick, S 153, 154
Griffiths, Andrew 158, 263, 264
Griffiths, Jonathan 206–7

H2-preprorelaxin, case law 119
Handler, M 28
Hargreaves Review (2011) 182, 214
harmonization and integration, European 125–46
adoption of rules and standards at supra-national level 7, 125–6
Biotechnology Directive example 127
codification 125–6
harmonization goal as overriding objective 138
originality test 165
and UK Court of Appeal 128
Hepatitis C virus (HCV), case law 80
Heydon, J D 44
Hoffmann, Leonard Hubert (Baron) 15, 34, 37, 38, 42, 43, 54–5, 63, 128, 130, 150, 152, 156, 159, 168, 172, 173, 205–7, 211, 216, 217, 220, 248
Hohfeld, Wesley 29–30, 105, 215
Holmes, Oliver Wendell 203
Hughes, Justin 197, 207, 231, 283, 284

ideas versus expression 190, 208, 212–14
identity 11, 17, 192, 206, 253
defined 253
double 239, 241, 246
individual 123, 253
trade marks 10, 149, 175, 191, 239, 240, 241, 244, 248, 251, 254, 256, 282
individualism 12, 181
and altruism 16–17, 180, 182, 185, 189–92, 203, 204, 213, 217, 232, 249, 252–4, 256
economic 186, 187
Kantian 287–9
liberal 23, 283, 286, 288
and patents 191
political 188
and rules 188, 189, 203
and trade marks 191
inductive reasoning of courts 26, 64–5, 67, 107
inflexibility
see also flexibility
non-express trusts 72
and requirement regarding harm 72
of rules 46–7, 71
infringement claims 27
copyright 41, 54, 148, 167, 193, 204–17, 219
counter-claims 170
declarations of non-infringement of copyright 169
national courts, decisions of 29
partial taking 167
relative infrequency of actions 268
termination of infringement 84
tests determining 28
trade marks 101–3, 238–9
injunctions 4–5, 26
final 78–9, 80, 81–2
interim 5, 84, 85–6, 87
post-expiry 77, 82
reasonableness 77
springboard 75–8
transaction costs 83
UK compared to US 80–81
intellectual property (IP) law

see also copyright; inventions; patents; trade marks
creation of scheme of duties as opposed to rights 29
damages, entitlement of owners to claim 75, 83
description of colour by reference to (trade marks) 27–8
economic justifications underpinning 46
enforcement 74–5
intangible abstract objects of IPRs 54
no rivalry in the consumption of intellectual goods 179
public power of intellectual property 11
rights and remedies of owners 74
rules, infrequently encountered 19
shareability of information 180
terminology 27
Intellectual Property Office, UK, Trade Marks Manual 115
interim injunctions 5, 84, 85–6, 87
internet 182–3
interpersonal/social dimension 178–256
and rivalry 179
inventions
see also patents; priority dates, patents/inventions
compensation, entitlement of employee to 38–9, 41
concept of invention 135, 151
degree of novelty or difference from the prior art 159
exclusions 135
experimentation, product of 59, 60, 62
fair share of benefit, employee inventions 38–9
industrially applicable condition 151
inventive step requirement 34, 59–60, 97, 151, 153, 159, 160, 166
morality issues, and bias 117
novelty requirement 34, 35
obviousness test see obviousness test, inventions
prior art see prior art
requirement of inventiveness 153
simple facts 34
software-implemented, patentability 130, 132
and state of the art 33
technical character 131, 135, 136–7, 139
tests 153
whether patentable under the terms of the EPC 29

Jacob, Sir Robert Raphael Hayim 'Robin' 32, 56, 61–3, 70, 103, 128, 129, 133, 138, 139, 145, 161, 195, 199, 212, 219, 223, 245
judicial activism, limits 187–8
judicial discretion see discretion, judicial
justifications underpinning intellectual property law 257–92
economic 18, 46
research and development (R&D), investment in 21, 258–61
theories 267
trade marks 262–3

Kamien, M 258
Kant, Immanuel 23, 190, 284–9
individualism 287–9
Kelman, Mark 188–9
Kennedy, Duncan 12, 35–6, 40, 180–82, 185–9, 253, 286–8
Kitchen, Sir David James 264
Klemperer, P 260, 273–5
Knight, Frank 259
Kozinski, Alex 233–4

Laddie, Sir Hugh Ian Lang 53, 62
laissez-faire theory 186
Lalande, Michel-Richard de 162, 193, 194, 199
Landes, W 82, 201, 206–7, 211, 229, 230, 257, 261–5, 271
legal directions
content and scope 47
extraction for an earlier decision 47
morality conditions 111

personal convictions, figuring in decision making process 91
standards, framed as 93
wording of 32, 40
legislation
bias, avoiding perceptions of in decision making 91, 105–24
creation of law by courts 30, 107
defined 32
European integration and harmonization 91, 125–46
ex ante versus *ex post* decision making 91, 92–105
legislative power and harmonization 89–146
limits on law-making powers 89
past decisions, unavailability of 107–8
patent law 58–9
Lemley, Mark 269, 272, 273, 274, 275
Lewison, Kim Martin Jordan 102–3
licences, compulsory 80–81
likelihood of confusion, trade marks 6, 101, 102, 103
literary works, originality 193, 200, 207
Llewellyn, Karl 125–6
Locke, John 283, 284
luxury goods 254–5

MacCormick, Neil 31, 32, 48, 63–4
Machlup, Fritz 291
MacMillan, Hugh (Baron) 196
Mansfield, E 258
Mansfield, William Murray (eighteenth-century judge) 228
Medicines Patent Pool (MPP) 184
Merges, Robert 262, 272, 283, 284–9
Justifying Intellectual Property 23
misrepresentation 49–51
see also passing off, tort of
deceptive 51, 52
material 50
reappraisal of notion 52
reliance upon 50
monopoly-profit-incentive thesis 267, 281
morality issues, and bias 111–24
copyright 111–13
impartiality of judge 114
patents 117–18
surveys and opinion polls 121–2
trade marks 114–15
Munich Diplomatic Conference (2000) 69, 137, 141, 143
music, copying of 193, 194, 200, 204

Neuberger, David Edmond (Baron) 28, 65, 67, 78–80, 90, 108, 125, 129–30
novelty requirement, inventions 34, 35
protectable subject matter, defining boundaries of 151, 159
tests 151

obiter dicta 47
obviousness test, inventions 25, 34, 42, 63, 223, 224, 227
see also inventions
ex ante versus *ex post* decision making 94
and fairness 44
harmonization and integration, European 140
'obvious to try' test 60, 61, 62, 64
protectable subject matter, defining boundaries of 152–3, 154–5
requirement of non-obviousness 157
Office for Harmonisation in the Internal Market (OHIM) 279
Boards of Appeal 116, 117
Guidelines 115
Oliver, Peter Raymond (Baron) 36, 49, 50, 53, 65, 157, 159, 163, 198–201
open access movement 183
opinion polls 121–2
'ordre public', patents contrary to 117, 119, 120, 121
originality condition, copyright 148, 160–68, 190, 192, 270
see also copyright
computer programs 164, 165
and copying 163, 198, 199–200
creativity 195
databases 165

dispensing with 168
European law 220, 221
Information Society Directive 165
literary works 193, 200, 207
meaning 205
photographs 164, 165
'rule-like' nature 169
skill, labour and judgement 161–3, 166, 193, 194, 196–9, 201
UK test 165

Palmer, Tom 291
Parker, Hubert Lister (Baron) 35, 50
partial taking, copyright 10, 14, 37, 59, 72, 93, 165, 167, 168, 217, 219
passing off, tort of 25
see also misrepresentation
Australian law 66
celebrity endorsement 52, 53
classical trinity 49, 53
common law nature 48–9
goodwill 50, 53
'Jif Lemon' case 49, 53
misrepresentation 49–51
name choices and packaging, similarities in 51
own-brand products 51, 52
proof of relevant commercial activity 66
public perception 51
trade mark registration system 100
Patent Office *see* European Patent Office (EPO)
patents 14–16, 223–32
see also European Patent Convention (EPC); European Patent Office (EPO); inventions; novelty requirement, inventions; prior art; priority dates, patents/ inventions
competitiveness of particular firm 58
concept of patentability 117
established characters 44–5
European system 29, 137–8
examination of applications in the UK 153
exclusion of discoveries from patentable subject matter 70
first-to-file approach 91, 98
goal of stimulating innovative activity 57
grant of letters patent 155
impact of UK's probable exit from the EU 29
and individualism 191
insular nature of law 118
in terrorem effect of bad patents 274
interpretation problems versus classification 64
inventive concept 55
legislation 58–9
morality issues, and bias 117–18
'obvious to try' test 60, 61, 62, 64
'ordre public', contrary to 117, 119, 120, 121
person skilled in the relevant art 55, 56, 57, 59
post-grant matters, unitary patents 29
prejudices 56, 57
priority in patent claims 91
protectable subject matter, defining boundaries of 27, 147, 150–60, 170–74, 176
as registered rights 150–51
royalty payments 275
rule-based nature of substantive examination, in Europe 136–7
rule-bound decisions 136, 270
software-implemented inventions, patentability 130
statutory provisions 55
substantive examination, European 136, 137
unitary 29
US system 80–81, 269
validity 174
Patents Convention *see* European Patent Convention (EPC)
Penner, James 231
Philips, Jeremy 264
pipe corrosion, case law 60–61
piracy 183
plant biotechnology, case law 122, 124

policies
justification of judicial decisions 45
principles compared 40
weight dimension 40–41
Posner, R 82, 201, 206–7, 211, 229, 230, 257, 261–5, 271
post-expiry injunctions 77, 82
Pound, Roscoe 46
precedent doctrine *see* binding precedents
prejudices
see also bias, decision making
absence of rules 91
patent law 56, 57
Prescott, Peter (QC) 68, 69, 133, 134, 136
principles
errors of principle, judicial decision-making 42, 43
justification of judicial decisions 45
policies compared 40
principled decisions 55
weight dimension 40–41
prior art 20–22, 126, 132, 153, 158, 170–72, 271–3, 277, 278
see also inventions; novelty requirement; patents
devices 152
documents 60
ex ante versus *ex post* decision making 97
legal adjudication 34, 35, 37, 55, 56, 60
and novelty 151, 159
priority dates, patents/inventions 36, 56, 157, 173, 174, 273
see also inventions; patents
date of filing of application 95
default position 95
earlier relevant applications 95, 96
establishing priority 97
ex ante versus *ex post* decision making 94, 95, 97
interpersonal/social dimension 224–6, 229
and Paris Convention 96
'poisonous priority' 96
rule-based determination 97, 268
and TRIPS Agreement 96
in United States 98
progressive model of property rights 261–2
promotional goodwill 53
protectable subject matter, defining boundaries of 147–77
copyright 27, 147–8, 160–70, 176
formal examinations 150
obscurity 136
patents 27, 147, 150–60, 170–74, 176
registration systems 150
tangible property 149
trade marks 27, 148–9, 174–6
public interest test, compulsory licences 80–81
Pumfrey, Nicholas Richard 68, 70, 130, 156, 209, 212, 213

reasonableness, injunctive relief 77
research and development (R&D) 21, 258–61
uncertainty 258, 259
Rich, Giles 276, 277, 278
rights
allocation at work 72–3
creation of scheme of duties as opposed to 29
ownership, law relating to 72–3
tests determining claims to 28
risk 18, 21, 22, 28, 59, 62, 67, 106, 121, 143, 145–6, 232
bias 6, 91–2, 111
copyright law 215, 216, 221
deliberate taking of 85–6
justifications underpinning intellectual property law 260, 271, 273, 275–7, 280, 284
risk adverse individuals 58, 149, 272
versus uncertainty 259
rule-bound decisions 25
see also adjudication, legal; legislation; standard-bound decisions

absolute precision in drafting, impossibility of 33
adoption of general rules at supra-national level 7, 125–6
and arbitrary decisions 109
bias, avoiding perceptions of 106–7
choice between rules and no rules 89, 91
clarity and predictability characteristics 26–7, 36, 45, 136
and codification 125–6
coexistence of rules with standards 26
comparison of rules with principles and policies 40
comparison of rules with standards 2, 26–7, 35–6, 37, 45, 92
concepts 30–31
copyright 148, 219, 222–3, 248
deliberate taking of risk 85–6
ex ante versus *ex post* decision making 94
formulation of the rule as a rule 32
ideal rules 30, 90, 136
impossibility of perfect rules 90
individualism 188, 189, 203
inflexibility of 46–7, 71
infrequent occurrence of rules in intellectual property law 19
interim injunctions 84, 85–6, 87
inventions 151
legislative provisions formulated as rules 32–3
limits on law-making powers 89
originality condition, copyright 148
over- or under-inclusiveness as to purpose 46
patents 136, 270
prejudice, in absence of rules 91
priority dates 96, 97, 268
recognition of rule as binding by courts 32
rules versus standards debate 1, 26, 30–31, 35–6, 46, 91, 185
source of binding rules 32
trade marks 248
undesirable outcomes 47

Schlag, Pierre 26
Schwartz, N 258
Senftleben, M 241
Shapiro, C 272
Sherman, B 100, 118, 120, 149, 160, 161–2, 178, 213
similarity test
  copyright 167
  trade marks 6, 11, 101–3, 175, 176, 244
skill, labour and judgement 161–3, 166, 196–9
  copying of work 193, 194, 198, 201
  copyright infringement 206–7
Social Darwinism 187
social psychology studies 182
software-implemented inventions, patentability 130, 132
Spence, M 46, 54
Spencer, Herbert 276
springboard injunctions 75–8
standard-bound decisions
  see also adjudication, legal; bias, decision making; rules
  administration costs, increasing 46
  adoption of standard at supra-national level 7, 125
  altruism 13, 203
  assessment of confusion, in trade mark cases 101
  assessment of facts 35–6
  and codification 125
  coexistence of standards with rules 26
  coherence requirement 44, 45
  comparison of standards with factors 38
  comparison of standards with rules 2, 27, 35–6, 37, 45, 92
  discretion, exercise of 36
  economic efficiency 93
  efficiency considerations 46
  errors of principle, appealing of decisions 42, 43
  ex ante versus *ex post* decision making 93, 94
  flexibility and dynamism requirements 27, 45, 47
  and foresight 5–6

foresight requirement 105
interim injunctions 84, 85–6, 87
legal directions framed as 93
limits on law-making powers 89
negligence 42
principles 40
priority in patent claims 91
reference by appellate courts to standards 42
rules versus standards debate 1, 26, 30–31, 35–6, 46, 84, 91, 185
uncertainty up to point when decision made 150
standards of conduct 72
state of the art, inventions 33, 34
statutory provisions
effect on legal adjudication 31–2
imprecise language 32–3
substantial taking, copyright 13, 72, 169, 190, 206, 211, 213, 221
Sunstein, Cass 1, 30, 32, 33, 35, 37–41, 46, 47, 71, 86, 89, 92, 106, 125, 182
Supreme Court, UK 65, 108
surveys 121–2

technical character, patents/inventions 131, 135, 136–7, 139
territory, right of property owners to exclude others from 29–30
Trade Mark Register 279, 280
trade marks 10–11, 17–18, 22, 232–56
brand extension 237–8
colour, registration as a trade mark 27–8
Commission reform proposals 246
double identity 239
established characters 44–5
ex ante versus *ex post* decision making 99–105
exclusive rights provided to owners 17
fair competition 247–8
form and substance, correspondence between 191
functions 244–5, 250–51
graphic representation requirement 28
grounds for refusing registration 27, 100, 101, 104–5, 175
identity 10, 149, 175, 191, 239, 240, 241, 244, 248, 251, 254, 256, 282
and individualism 191
information systems and networking 252–3
informed choice 255
infringement claims 101–3, 238–9
keywords 242
likelihood of confusion 6, 101, 102, 103
luxury goods 254–5
morality issues, and bias 114–15
network effects 280
owners' rights versus claimed rights to free use 235–6
protectable subject matter, defining boundaries of 27, 148–9, 174–6
public policy, contrary to 116
registration system 27, 100–101
rule-bound decisions 248
similarity test 6, 11, 101–3, 103, 175, 176, 244
Soviet Union, representation of the coat of arms 116
sports clubs and associations 236–7, 240
statutory defences to infringement claims 238–9
ubiquitous nature of 233
trusts, non-express 72

uncertainty 46, 54, 67, 82, 84, 150, 259–62, 269, 274–8
patents or inventions 152, 153, 273, 278
reducing 19, 21, 22, 265, 266, 267
research and development (R&D) 258, 259
and rights 262
versus risk 259
validity 266, 273, 278
unconscionability 4, 72, 74

United States
America Invents Act (AIA) 91, 98
compared to United Kingdom 80–81
first-to-invent scheme, priorty determination 91
patents 80–81, 269
priority dates, patents/inventions 98

Vaver, David 80, 265

Wagner, S 258
Waldron, Jeremy 197, 215
Wendell Holmes, Oliver 203
White, Alan 223

Younger, Judge 111–13